THE MEDIATION SYSTEM OF CHINA FROM AN INTERDISCIPLINARY PERSPECTIVE

Delivering a much-needed in-depth, interdisciplinary exploration of mediation practices in China, this study removes the common misconception that mediation is merely a mechanical application of norms. It provides a comprehensive understanding of China's mediation practices by blending cultural, social and legal analyses with detailed case descriptions from fieldwork. Readers will gain insights into the interactive dynamics between legal norms and the social environment at the grassroots level in China. This book helps readers understand mediation and Chinese law within their broader cultural, social and political contexts, offering insights beyond the purely legal dimension. The book is an invaluable resource for scholars, students and practitioners in the fields of Chinese law, dispute resolution and sociolegal studies. It offers a unique perspective that contextualises mediation within the sociopolitical landscape, providing readers with a richer, more nuanced understanding of Chinese legal culture.

HAO XIONG is an associate professor and assistant dean at Fudan University Law School and a Fulbright scholar at Harvard Law School.

THE MEDIATION SYSTEM OF CHINA FROM AN INTERDISCIPLINARY PERSPECTIVE

HAO XIONG
Fudan University, Shanghai

CAMBRIDGE
UNIVERSITY PRESS

CAMBRIDGE
UNIVERSITY PRESS

Shaftesbury Road, Cambridge CB2 8EA, United Kingdom

One Liberty Plaza, 20th Floor, New York, NY 10006, USA

477 Williamstown Road, Port Melbourne, VIC 3207, Australia

314–321, 3rd Floor, Plot 3, Splendor Forum, Jasola District Centre, New Delhi – 110025, India

103 Penang Road, #05–06/07, Visioncrest Commercial, Singapore 238467

Cambridge University Press is part of Cambridge University Press & Assessment, a department of the University of Cambridge.

We share the University's mission to contribute to society through the pursuit of education, learning and research at the highest international levels of excellence.

www.cambridge.org
Information on this title: www.cambridge.org/9781009581219

DOI: 10.1017/9781009581196

When citing this work, please include a reference to the DOI 10.1017/9781009581196

First published 2025

Cover image: Top View of Traditional Residential Buildings in Suzhou / AerialPerspective Images / Moment / Getty Images

A catalogue record for this publication is available from the British Library

Library of Congress Cataloging-in-Publication Data
Names: Xiong, Hao, author.
Title: The mediation system of China from an interdisciplinary perspective / Hao Xiong, Fudan University, Shanghai.
Description: Cambridge, United Kingdom ; New York, NY : Cambridge University Press, 2025. | Includes bibliographical references and index.
Identifiers: LCCN 2025018121 (print) | LCCN 2025018122 (ebook) | ISBN 9781009581219 (hardback) | ISBN 9781009581172 (paperback) | ISBN 9781009581196 (epub)
Subjects: LCSH: Mediation–China. | Compromise (Law)–China. | Dispute resolution (Law)–China.
Classification: LCC KNQ1758.S47 X56 2025 (print) | LCC KNQ1758.S47 (ebook) | DDC 347.51/09–dc23/eng/20250616
LC record available at https://lccn.loc.gov/2025018121
LC record available at https://lccn.loc.gov/2025018122

ISBN 978-1-009-58121-9 Hardback

To my beloved parents

CONTENTS

List of Figures xi
List of Tables xii
Acknowledgements xiii
List of Abbreviations xiv

PART I **Introduction**

1 **Why an Interdisciplinary Perspective? Why Chinese Law? And How to Study?** 3
1.1 Why an Interdisciplinary Perspective? 3
1.1.1 Interdisciplinary Legal Studies 3
1.1.2 The Value of Interdisciplinary Legal Studies in China 5
1.2 Why Chinese Law? 10
1.2.1 Personal Reason 10
1.2.2 Practical Value 12
1.2.3 Theoretical Value 15
1.3 How to Study the Chinese Mediation System and Understand Its Complexity 19
1.3.1 The Development of Alternative Dispute Resolution Paradigms 19
1.3.1.1 Interest-Based Paradigm 19
1.3.1.2 Person-Based Paradigm 22
1.3.1.3 Chinese Holism Way of Dispute Resolution 24
1.3.2 The Starting Point of Studying Alternative Dispute Resolution in China 28
1.3.2.1 Thinking Like a Local Lawyer 28
1.3.2.2 Recommendations for the Choice of Methods: Emphasising Empirical Research 35

PART II **Foundation**

2 **Context: Culture, Society and Politics** 43
2.1 Chinese Culture and People's Mindset 43
2.1.1 Confucianism as a Mindset 43
2.1.2 Culture and the Characteristics of the Chinese Mindset 44

2.2 The Social Context and Chinese Mindset 49
2.3 Political Context and Chinese Mindset 51
2.4 Stability in Chinese Context 56
2.5 The Tension between Mediation with Chinese Characteristics and Legal Rationalism 62

3 **History: Development of the Chinese Modern Dispute Resolution System** 66
3.1 A Brief Introduction to the History Before the Reform and Opening Up 66
3.2 From the Early 1980s to 1990 69
3.3 From the Early 1990s to 2002 71
3.4 From 2003 to 2013 75
3.5 New Developments in Xi Jinping Era 80
3.6 Theoretical Analysis 85

PART III **Legal Framework of Mediation in China**

4 **Style, Category and Legal Framework of Mediation** 93
4.1 Style and Category of Mediation in China 93
4.1.1 Styles of Mediation 93
4.1.2 Mediation Styles in China 96
4.2 Categories of Mediation in China 99
4.3 Legal Framework of Mediation in China 108
4.3.1 Provisions in the Civil Procedure Law That Directly Regulate Mediation 108
4.3.2 People's Mediation Law 113
4.3.3 Relevant Judicial Interpretations 116

PART IV **Chinese Mediation in Action**

5 **Global and China's ADR Movement** 141
5.1 Global ADR Movement 141
5.2 China's ADR Movement 145
5.3 Fengqiao Experience in Action at the Local Level 152

6 **Case Study One: The Feasibility of Mediation in the Grassroots Society of China** 164
6.1 Empirical Study on Mediation in China 164
6.1.1 Meaning of Empirical Study 164
6.1.2 Irreplaceable Value of Empirical Method in Chinese Mediation Studies 165
6.1.3 The Difficulty of Conducting Empirical Study in China 169
6.2 Fieldwork Place 171

6.3 Case Study: An Adjacency Rights Dispute in a Rural Village 174
6.3.1 Basic Facts of the Dispute 174
6.3.2 Dispute Resolution Process and Preliminary Analysis 176
6.4 Why Mediation Is Feasible for Southwest Grassroots China 184
6.4.1 Why Mediation Is Feasible for the Disputants 184
6.4.1.1 Preserving Face and Repairing Interpersonal Relationships 184
6.4.1.2 Technical Difficulties in Taking the Litigation Track 187
6.4.1.3 A Humane Legal Product 188
6.4.2 Why Mediation Is Feasible for the Judge 192
6.4.2.1 The Necessary Thresholds for Judges: Legal Education and Entrance Exam 192
6.4.2.2 Mismatch: Uniform Legal Profession Exam and the Grassroots Judge's Quality 195
6.4.2.3 Mismatch: Law School Education and Grassroots Legal Needs 198
6.4.2.4 Match: Experience-Oriented Knowledge and Mediation 202
6.4.2.5 Match: Judges Are Deeply Embedded in the Local Social Context 204
6.5 Conclusion 206

7 **Case Study Two: Two Sides of Mediation in the Grassroots Society of China 209**
7.1 Introduction 209
7.2 Context: Having Lunch Together 211
7.2.1 More than Eating 211
7.2.2 Lunch, *Guanxi* and Independent Trial 214
7.3 Case One: A Succession Dispute and the Implementation of Mediation in Solving Hard Cases 220
7.3.1 Basic Facts of the Dispute 220
7.3.2 Dispute Resolution Process and Preliminary Analysis 221
7.4 Case Two: A Housing Demolition and Relocation Dispute and the Function of Mediation in Solving Sensitive Cases 224
7.4.1 Basic Facts of the Dispute 224
7.4.2 Dispute Resolution Process and Preliminary Analysis 225
7.5 Two Sides of Mediation 227
7.5.1 The Bright Side 227
7.5.1.1 Expand the Capacity and Range of Case Acceptance 227
7.5.1.2 Earn More Direct Support from the Government 229
7.5.1.3 Be Good at Solving Complex Problems 230

7.5.2 The Dark Side 234
7.5.2.1 Impairing Justice and Individual Rights 234
7.5.2.2 Confusing the Role of Judges 237
7.6 Conclusion 239

Appendix I: Glossary of Chinese Terms 241
References 248
Index 278

FIGURES

2.1 A comparison of Hofstede's cultural dimensions in Brazil, China, Germany and the United States. 58
3.1 Number of articles in *People's Daily* including the keywords mediation (*tiaojie*, 调解)', 'ruling the state according to the law (rule of law, *yifa zhiguo*, 依法治国)' and 'harmonious society (*hexie shehui*, 和谐社会)' (1999–2008). 78
3.2 Number of mainland newspaper articles including the keywords mediation (*tiaojie*, 调解)', 'ruling the state according to the law (rule of law, *yifa zhiguo*, 依法治国)' and 'harmonious society (*hexie shehui*, 和谐社会)' (1999–2010). 79
3.3 Solved cases in court of first instance through court mediation and litigation. 81
6.1 Mediation agreement template. 170
6.2 The place where the dispute happened. 175
6.3 A fragment of the plaintiff's original claims. 184
6.4 The living conditions of the village. 185

TABLES

2.1 Conflict-handling styles of respondents 60
2.2 Rate of conflict-handling styles among all responses 61
4.1 Provisions relating to mediation in the civil procedure law 109
5.1 Rewards and punishments standard at the grassroots court 158

ACKNOWLEDGEMENTS

The journey of writing *The Mediation System of China from an Interdisciplinary Perspective* has been an immensely rewarding experience, and I am deeply grateful to those who have supported and inspired me along the way.

First and foremost, I would like to express my sincere gratitude to Professor Allen Snyder from the University of San Diego. It was under his guidance that I first ventured into the field of alternative dispute resolution, and his passion for the subject has continuously inspired me throughout my career. Without his early influence, this book would not have been possible.

I am also profoundly thankful to my supervisor, Professor Zhao Yun from the University of Hong Kong. His unwavering support and insightful advice have been a constant source of encouragement throughout my academic journey. Professor Zhao has not only shaped my thinking but has also provided me with the guidance needed to develop and grow as a scholar. For that, I am forever grateful.

This book would not have come to fruition without the dedicated work of Mr Joe Ng, my editor. His professionalism, meticulous attention to detail and thoughtful approach have been invaluable in turning this manuscript into a published reality. I am deeply appreciative of his expertise and commitment to excellence.

Lastly, my deepest thanks go to my parents. Their endless love and support have been my foundation. For their belief in me and their encouragement through every challenge, I am eternally grateful.

To all those mentioned above, and to everyone else who has contributed to the completion of this work, thank you.

ABBREVIATIONS

ACR	Association for Conflict Resolution
ADR	alternative dispute resolution
BACMC	Beijing Arbitration Commission Mediation Center
CJR	Civil Justice Reform
CPC	Communist Party of China
HDRD	housing demolition and relocation disputes
MBA	Master of Business Administration
MSFMCP	2010 Model Standards for Mediation Certification Programs
PLC	Political and Legal Committee
PRC	People's Republic of China
SCMC	Shanghai Commercial Mediation Center
SPC	Supreme People's Court

PART I

Introduction

1

Why an Interdisciplinary Perspective? Why Chinese Law? And How to Study?

1.1 Why an Interdisciplinary Perspective?

1.1.1 Interdisciplinary Legal Studies

In legal academic tradition, the black-letter approach[1] occupied the central position, especially since Thomas Hobbes and Jean Bodin unprecedentedly enhanced the state normative aspect of the law.[2] However,

[1] Black-letter approach 'focuses heavily, if not exclusively, upon the law itself as an internal self-sustaining set of principles which can be accessed through reading court judgments and statutes with little or no reference to the world outside the law'. See Mike McCoville and Wing Hong Chui, 'Introduction and overview' in Mike McCoville and Wing Hong Chui (eds.), *Research Methods for Law* (Edinburgh: Edinburgh University Press, 2007), p. 1. Gary Slapper and David Kelly also argued that

> Black-Letter approach is posited on the existence of a discrete legal universe as the object of study. Such an approach is clearly manifested in the phrase 'the law is the law'. . .Black letter law and legal formalism assume and claim to operate a form of mechanistic jurisprudence in which legal decisions are reached by means of marshalling and applying the appropriate legal rules. . .To simplify, the operation of legal formalism depends upon the application of legal rules by impartial experts to particular facts in order to derive inescapable and hence unquestionable outcomes, those outcomes being merely the result of the logical application of the rules.

See Gary Slapper and David Kelly, *The English Legal System* (New York: Routledge, 2016), p. 20. Due to the dominance of the civil law (continental law) tradition in the mainstream legal academia in China, the focus of legal studies was on legal texts and statutes, which is called legal dogmatic – '*fa jiaoyixue* (法教义学)'. However, this situation began to change in the 1990s. The field of legal studies expanded to encompass broader topics such as comparative law, legal reform, the relationship between law and society, legal ethics and human rights. In the Chinese legal academic circle, juristiche dogmatic and the interdisciplinary studies of law (such as legal anthropology, legal sociology and legal economics) have been debated in the academic field regarding the effectiveness of different methods of studying Chinese law, and now they are developing in parallel. See Meng Hou, 'The social science research of law in China: an examination of its academic history' (2020) 3 *Social Science* 12–14 [侯猛："法的社会科学研究在中国：一个学术史的考察"，载《社会科学》2020年第3期].

[2] W. Michael Reisman, *Law in Brief Encounters* (New Haven: Yale University Press, 1999), pp. 8–10.

mainstream legal scholarship gradually realised that law is a 'multidimensional net'[3] that is deeply rooted in cultural and social beliefs and is affected by human activities. To quote Eugen Ehrlich, 'all law is social law'.[4] The social context, in many cases, can invalidate the working of the law in books.[5] As Gerhard Dannemann further noted,

> Most legal rules and institutions operate in a context made up of other rules, institutions, and areas of law; substantive rules interact with the rule of procedure, etc. Therefore, areas of law which initially fall outside the scope of a particular inquiry become relevant to the understanding of those rules which are within the scope. . .There appears to be a broad consensus within the modern debate that it is important to look beyond the law for the context in which a rule, institution, or entire legal system operates, which may include economic, social, cultural, political, but also religious or geographical issues.[6]

Indeed, 'law is an indissoluble amalgam of historical, social, economic, political, cultural and psychological data; a compound, a hybrid, a "monster", an outrageous and "heterogeneous collage"'.[7] Without an interdisciplinary understanding, legal studies would become problematic and superficial. Therefore, the existing legal scholarship is increasingly showing an inclination to use more diverse, open-minded, contextual and socio-legal-oriented paradigms and methodologies to analyse legal issues. Fiona Cownie spotted this tendency:

> Whatever they call themselves, the majority of academic lawyers occupy the middle ground between the two extremes of pure doctrinal analysis and a highly theoretical approach to the study of law. Arguably, the law is a discipline in transition, with a culture where a small group still clings to a purely doctrinal approach, but a very large group (whether they describe themselves as socio-legal or not) are mixing traditional methods of analysis with analysis drawn from a range of other disciplines among the social sciences and humanities.[8]

[3] Peter Sack and Jonathan Alck (eds.), *Law and Anthropology* (Aldershot: Dartmouth, 1992), p. xxvi.

[4] Eugen Ehrlich, *Fundamental Principles of the Sociology of Law* (New York: Arno Press, 1975), p. 42.

[5] Poh-Ling Tan, *Asian Legal Systems: Law, Society and Pluralism in East Asia* (Sydney: Butterworths, 1997), p. 394.

[6] Gerhard Dannemann, 'Comparative law: study of similarities or differences?' in Mathias Reimann and Reinhard Zimmermann (eds.), *The Oxford Handbook of Comparative Law* (New York: Cambridge University Press, 2006), p. 414.

[7] Pierre Legrand, 'How to compare now' (1996) 16(2) *Legal Studies* 233, 236.

[8] Fiona Cownie, *Legal Academics: Culture and Identities* (Oxford: Hart, 2004), p. 58.

1.1.2 *The Value of Interdisciplinary Legal Studies in China*

In the Chinese legal studies context, interdisciplinary legal studies, including social–legal and empirical studies, are even more significant because of at least two reasons. Firstly, the defects of the traditional black letter approach are even more apparent because of a wide gap between the adoption of Westernised legal principles since the late 1970s and the reality of China.[9] The process of legal construction in modern China has been accompanied by various stages of learning from and adopting foreign legal systems. Following the reform and opening-up period, China's legal development underwent a new phase of extensive learning from Western countries. This process was necessary and constituted an essential part of China's reintegration into the global framework. However, the unique Chinese realities, which differ fundamentally from their Western counterparts, have often been overlooked within this framework. Due to China's rich cultural heritage and the inherent complexity and heterogeneity within this vast country, solely adopting Western legal systems has increasingly proven insufficient to address the social realities in China. The Western-oriented legal construction may simplify or even efface the complexity and reality of Chinese society from the analytical and institutional framework in the process of unilateral Western-style academic research. Consequently, the adopted legal system and its concomitant scholarship have, to some extent, failed to cater to the real social needs and were not able to respond to the actual intellectual challenges, eventually becoming subservient to the adopted norms.[10]

[9] Albert H. Y. Chen, *An Introduction to the Legal System of the People's Republic of China* (Hong Kong: Lexis/Nexis, 5th ed., 2018), p. 1; Limin Wang, 'Transformation and modernization of the Chinese science of law in the early 20th century' (2006) 4 *US-China Law Review* 1. The particularities of China include but are not limited to the following aspects: China emphasises the need to combine legal reasoning with consideration of social consequences in the judicial process. The significant social and economic differences between the eastern and western regions create challenges for the uniform application of the law. A large portion of the agricultural population still resides in a society characterised by limited social mobility and legal requirements within familiar social circles. The higher education population is limited, secular and pragmatic ideologies operate within the legal realm and traditional culture significantly influences modern legal structures. Politically, China maintains a hybrid legal system with distinctive features of socialism with Chinese characteristics.

[10] For example, in the area of dispute resolution, is it just and humane to push people living in rural China, who cannot afford a lawyer, to go to court and require them to debate in a language, procedure and manner with which they are totally unfamiliar? Can we simply

Not only the normative legal system but also the knowledge system of legal studies lacked sufficient Chinese subjectivity in the process of Western learning spreading to the East since the reform and opening-up period. Speaking of this, Deng Zhenglai points out that due to multiple ruptures in China's academic tradition during the modern revolutions, the life of China's own academic heritage has been suppressed or interrupted. The continuity of China's modern academic tradition began with the Reform and Opening-up policy, marking the second phase of 'learning from the West and applying it to the East' (*xixue dongjian*, 西学东渐) in China. Thus, the social scientists in China have two identities. First, they have been the constructivists of the modern Chinese social sciences since the late 1970s. Secondly, their/our identity is constructed on the foundation of Western social sciences,[11] which has made China's social sciences system, including the legal scholarship, deeply embedded in the Western academic structure. In Deng's words, this is a kind of 'path dependence'.[12] China's legal scholarship has attached itself to Western legal scholarship under the false assumption that the set of circumstances are the same in China as in the West. The questions, methodologies and even answers for Chinese legal scholarship have been provided by Western legal scholarship. This has resulted in the entirety of China's contributions in the field of legal studies being grouped simply as a subheading or footnote of Western legal scholarship under the title 'China'. Thus, Chinese legal scholars have been fiercely criticised for their ignorance of China's legal reality, the real needs of the Chinese people[13] and their failure to provide China's

call this a great progress in China's legal development regardless of the experiences and feelings of those deeply involved in the realistic Chinese legal system? This is one of the real intellectual challenges to which China's legal scholarship needs to respond rather than merely introducing Western concepts and discussing the adversarial system versus the inquisitorial procedure at a textbook level.

[11] Zhenglai Deng, *The Thoughts on the Social Sciences of China* (Shanghai: Sanlian, 2000), pp. 45–49 [邓正来：《关于中国社会科学的思考》，上海：三联出版社2000年版].

[12] Zhenglai, *The Thoughts on the Social Sciences of China*, pp. 46–47 [邓正来：《关于中国社会科学的思考》，上海：三联出版社2000年版]. The original Chinese text goes as follows:

> 归根到底，对社会科学建构过程与知识间关系的这种认识，具有着这样一种底蕴，即我们不仅是中国社会科学的建构者，而且是这种社会科学的被建构者：建构者与被建构者在我们身上的这种同一性，在某种程度上规定了我们生产与再生产社会知识的'路径依赖'品格。

[13] See Su Li, *Sending Law to the Rural China: A Study on Chinese Legal Institution at the Grassroots Level* (Beijing: China University of Politics and Law Press, 2000) [苏力：《送法下乡：中国基层司法制度研究》，北京：中国政法大学出版社2000年版].

own ideal image for legal development.[14] As to this, Li Su also made a similar argument by following Hayek's concept of spontaneous order:

> It is impossible that a Chinese legal system is just a group of regulations, norms and strictly-designed judicatory regimes copied from the West. In fact, it closely links with the values, ideology, attitudes, and behavior of hundreds of millions of Chinese. From this perspective, the development of the Chinese legal system must depend on the practice of Chinese people rather than some experts who are familiar with the legal theory and foreign laws or the legislative institutions.[15]

Secondly, China is in the midst of a dramatic social transformation, which may invalidate the formalistic and stable rules existing at the abstract level. When analysing the limits of the black letter approach, Li Su said that the 'Black Letter approach . . . just puts the legal regulations in an unquestionable position and pushes the social life to obey it. However, as a part of the social system, the law has to inter-coordinate with the other parts of the society, located in an era of transformation'.[16] If we only focus on the statutes, codes and legislation, there is a possibility that these static rules may, to a certain extent, mask the dynamic social and legal reality. Due to this, Li Su suggested that research on the legal system should go beyond – not abandon – the black letter approach.[17] Therefore, when researching China's legal issues, the social,

[14] See Zhenglai Deng, *Where Does Chinese Legal Study Go: An Outline for Building the Ideal Image of Chinese Law* (Beijing: Commercial Press Ltd, 2006) [邓正来：《中国法学向何处去：构建"中国法律理想图景"时代的论纲》，北京：商务印书馆2006年版].

[15] Su Li, *Rule of Law and Local Resource* (Beijing: The University of Politics and Law Press, 1996), pp. 19–20 [苏力：《法治与本土资源》，北京中国政法大学出版社1996年版]. The original Chinese text goes as follows:

> 中国现代法治不可能只是一套细密的文字法规加一套严格的司法体系，而是与亿万中国人的价值、观念、心态以及行为方式相联系的。要建立法治，在一个维度上看就是要重新建立人们在社会中对他人行为的预期。正是从这个意义上，中国法治之路必须依靠中国人民的实践，而不仅仅是几位熟悉法律理论或外国法律的学者专家的设计和规划，或全国人大常委会的立法规划。

[16] Su Li, *It May Be Happening* (Beijing: Law Press, 2004), p. 234 [苏力：《也许正在发生》，北京：法律出版社2004年版]. The original Chinese text goes as following:

> 法条主义就是把法条作为不可置疑的权威，要求社会生活服从法条；而当代中国处于变革时期，作为社会生活系统组成部分之一的法治必须同社会生活的其他部分相互协调。因此，对法律制度的研究必须在一定程度上超越——而不是抛弃——法条主义。

[17] Su Li, *It May Be Happening*, p. 234 [苏力：《也许正在发生》，北京：法律出版社2004年版].

cultural, economic and political reality as a part of interdisciplinary legal studies should also be taken into account; the focus should not only remain on the legislation and normative system.

The research focus of this book – China's mediation system – is a field full of transformations and changes. For example, in Shanghai, the central government has granted greater legislative autonomy to the Pudong New District, encouraging it to experiment with legal system reforms.[18] Therefore, Article 13 of the Provisions of Promotion of Commercial Mediation in Pudong New District, enacted in 2022, stipulates that:

> Pudong New District supports various mediation organizations in establishing and improving pre-authorized mediation, unilateral commitment mediation, and other mechanisms for the swift resolution of small-scale commercial disputes, under the guidance of the district's judicial administrative department. This aims to achieve more efficient, cost-effective, and convenient dispute resolution. Pudong New District encourages various commercial industry associations to guide their member units in pre-authorizing mediation organizations based on a voluntary principle for the swift resolution of small-scale commercial disputes.[19]

Pre-authorising mediation is an institutional innovation that signifies a shift from the traditional mediation model. This innovation is based on the experience and data collected by Pudong New District in the realm of financial mediation. In the field of financial disputes, the widespread use of electronic banking means that the evidence chain in disputes between consumers and financial institutions (such as banks) is relatively complete and clear. Therefore, in small financial disputes, mediation centres introduce relevant laws, similar case precedents and basic evidence to the parties and conduct a preliminary evaluation of the case. If after receiving

[18] See Opinions of the CPC Central Committee and The State Council on Supporting High-level Reform and Opening Up in Pudong New Area to Build a Leading Area for Socialist Modernization [中共中央、国务院关于支持浦东新区高水平改革开放打造社会主义现代化建设引领区的意见], www.gov.cn/zhengce/2021-07/15/content_5625279.htm?ivk_sa=1024320u (last accessed 24 September 2023). In this Opinion, institutional pilot trials in China (Shanghai) Pilot Free Trade Zone of Pudong New District are required. One of the specific requirements is in Pudong, institutional opening-up pilot programmes should be initiated to explore experiences that can be applied nationwide to promote institutional opening up. Efforts are being made to align areas, such as commercial disputes with international norms and practices.

[19] Provisions of Promotion of Commercial Mediation in Pudong New District [浦东新区促进商事调解若干规定], www.shanghai.gov.cn/ysjjjf3/20230529/78f97e5fc68449aaa7107d01340c0fc7.html (last accessed 24 September 2023).

this information, the parties agree to grant the mediator a 'general authorisation', allowing the mediator to decide the case within the legal framework, the mediator can quickly handle the case. The parties sign the expedited mediation result based on thorough initial communication, evaluation and authorisation. In this process, the parties have very limited involvement in the subsequent dispute resolution procedure, which greatly improves the efficiency of handling small financial disputes. To a certain extent, this innovative dispute resolution mechanism challenges the conventional notions of mediation, as it combines elements of mediation, neutral evaluation and adjudication. Scholars and legal practitioners may need to re-evaluate the principle of 'voluntariness' in alternative dispute resolution (ADR) from a new perspective, especially regarding its relationship with national institutions and the efficiency of dispute resolution. Drawing on the experience of Shanghai's Pudong New District, local authorities have found this new mediation approach to be effective and successful in resolving small financial disputes. Consequently, the insights and experience gained through this institutional innovation transcend traditional mediation literature, representing invaluable knowledge that is absent from Chinese legal scholarship.

Whether responding to real issues in China or paying attention to continuous changes in practice, we must adopt a methodology that goes beyond the written law rather than merely focusing on normative texts. This, therefore, stresses the importance of interdisciplinary approaches in legal studies. It should be noted that the improvement of China's comprehensive national strength and the expansion of its international influence have led the Chinese academic community to pay more attention to domestic issues and become more confident in studying Chinese laws. From the perspective of social psychology, this confidence in returning to Chinese subjectivity when studying Chinese laws largely stems from international comparisons, whether in academia or by ordinary people. Increased international exchanges have made Chinese people more aware of the hardships of modernization and significant achievements China has made, particularly in economic development. Correspondingly, researchers should also take the experiences and developments of China's legal system in managing the rule of law in such a vast and complex country seriously. This shift is also reflected in national policies. In 2023, the General Offices of the Central Committee of the Communist Party of China and the State Council issued the 'Opinions on Strengthening Legal Education and Legal Theory Research in the New

Era', requiring all regions and departments to earnestly implement it in light of actual conditions. The Opinions provide that:

> [We should] closely implement of the principle of comprehensively governing the country according to law in the new era, earnestly strengthen the legal theoretical research rooted in Chinese culture, [develop the legal theory] based on China's national conditions, and solve China's problems, summarize and refine the concepts, viewpoints and theories of socialist rule of law with Chinese characteristics that are with subjectivity awareness, original and distinctive, and write the paper on the land of the motherland, not to be a 'porter' of Western theories. To construct China's independent legal knowledge system.[20]

1.2 Why Chinese Law?

1.2.1 Personal Reason

For a researcher or anyone who wants to get engaged with Chinese legal studies, the very first question concerns the necessity of studying Chinese law. The question is straightforward and clear: Why do you choose to study Chinese law, not Japanese law, not US law, not UK law? Decades ago, the question was also faced by a scholar who wanted to launch into Chinese legal studies. When recalling this experience, William Afford, the US leading expert in Chinese legal history, confessed the similar question he faced when he began his Chinese legal studies:

> [T]he first substantive question posed to me as I commenced my graduate work in Chinese studies during the autumn of 1972 was by the late Arthur Wright, who asked why I, a young man of seeming intelligence, was intent on wasting my time on the study of Chinese legal history.[21]

If an individual desires to delve deeper into Chinese law, personal interest alone can serve as a potent driving force. This intrinsic motivation holds profound significance for academic scholars as well. Numerous researchers underscore the pivotal role played by internal interest, personal

[20] General Office of the CPC Central Committee and General Office of the State Council issued the Opinions on Strengthening Legal Education and Legal Theory Research in the New Era [中办国办印发《关于加强新时代法学教育和法学理论研究的意见》], www.moe.gov.cn/s78/A01/s4561/jgfwzx_zcwj/202303/t20230307_1049619.html (last accessed 5 July 2023).

[21] William P. Alford, 'Law, law, what law? Why Western scholars of China have not had more to say about its law' in Karen G. Turner et al. (eds.), *The Limits of the Rule of Law in China* (Seattle: University of Washington Press, 2000), p. 45.

passion and a sense of academic impulse. Dr Robert Morris, a professor at the University of Hong Kong Faculty of Law, has meticulously compiled a comprehensive list of diverse reasons that inspire various scholars to embark on research endeavours. Notably, the items on this list appeal to the inner feelings of researchers rather than being driven by pure rationality and abstraction. They aim to showcase the emotional forces that give rise to academic curiosity and scholarly passion. This list serves as a valuable tool for assessing whether a researcher genuinely possesses a deep and abiding interest in a specific research subject.

- An issue or problem makes you angry – offends morality, decency and justice.[22]
- An issue or problem excites you.[23]
- There is something new you want to teach the world.[24]
- You wish to reveal a secret.
- You wish to effect change.[25]
- An issue or problem is on the cutting edge of your subject.[26]
- You want to enter a dispute with a new argument.[27]
- The discussion which you wish existed about your subject does not exist.
- Your research is 'something that will surprise the world'.[28]
- There is a developing area of law, and that is important.[29]

[22] See Christine Loh and Civic Exchange (eds.), *Functional Constituencies: A Unique Feature of the Hong Kong Legislative Council* (Hong Kong: Hong Kong University Press, 2006).

[23] See Robert J. Morris, 'Configuring the bo(u)nds of marriage: the implications of Hawaiian culture and values for the debate about homogamy' (1996) 8(2) *Yale Journal of Law & the Humanities* 105.

[24] See Karen Man Yee Lee, *Equality, Dignity, and Same-Sex Marriage: A Rights Disagreement in Democratic Societies* (Leiden: Martinus Nijhoff Publishers, 2010).

[25] See Ron Suskind, *The Way of the World: A Story of Truth and Hope in an Age of Extremism* (New York: Simon & Schuster, 2008).

[26] See Colin Tudge, *The Link: Uncovering Our Earliest Ancestor* (New York: Little, Brown & Co., 2009).

[27] See Bill Moyers, *Moyers on Democracy* (New York: Doubleday, 2008).

[28] John Adams, *Diary and Autobiography of John Adams*, L. H. Butterfield, Leonard C. Faber and Wendell D. Garrett (eds.) (Cambridge, MA: Belknap Press of Harvard University Press, 1961), vol. 4, I:78, 95; quoted from Susan Dunn (ed.), *Something That Will Surprise the World: The Essential Writings of the Founding Fathers* (New York: Basic Books, 2006), pp. 3–4.

[29] See Norman Polythress and John P. Petrila, 'PCL-R psychopathy: threats to sue, peer review, and potential implications for science and law. A commentary' (2010) 9(1) *International Journal of Forensic Mental Health* 3.

The reasons that drive a scholar's entry into a particular research field listed above are often not utilitarian but are driven by curiosity, passion and genuine interest. This aspect is sometimes overlooked in the academic world because when completing academic research, personal interest is generally not encouraged to be expressed – at least not in the writing of academic papers. Instead, we are expected to discuss aspects that legitimise our research as more 'useful'. However, a researcher's sincere personal commitment and genuine engagement in their work are indispensable, especially in producing high-quality research.[30] Therefore, when discussing why one should study Chinese law or China's dispute resolution system, it is particularly important to emphasise the dimension of intrinsic interest. As a reader, you might pause your reading and ask yourself: Why are you reading this book about Chinese law? Do you have an intrinsic interest in it, and if so, what exactly is it?

1.2.2 Practical Value

As per Morris' recommendation, high-quality academic research should stem from the personal inclinations of researchers. It hinges on the extent to which an academic question can evoke learners' doubts, curiosity and emotional engagement. However, personal interest alone is insufficient. Scholars, in their pursuit of expertise in a specific field, must aspire to fulfil universal or other related purposes. Their objective extends beyond satiating personal curiosity and research interests; it encompasses the creation of new knowledge, not solely for their benefit but for the advancement of scholarly pursuits as a whole.

> What, then, in university terms, is knowledge about Law? This question is wholly different from the question, what is knowledge about the law? The university law department should work within certain confines, and search for a particular kind of knowledge...Knowledge here is equated with theory and distinguished from facts...In this case, theoretical work indicates the attempt to understand processes and structures; to go beyond the immediate; to do that which might enable us to say, 'Now we know more.' The accumulation of facts, in contrast, implies a concern with that which is immediate and of the surface. It implies a concern with that which, if successful, [might] lead us to say, 'Now we know

[30] Hao Xiong, *Guide to Thesis Writing: From Initial Ideas to Research Completion* (Shanghai: Fudan University Press, 2019), pp. 38–40 [熊浩：《论文写作指南：从观点初现到研究完成》，上海：复旦大学出版社2019年版].

> differently.' It is not the subject of the pursuit which is the point of concern; it is the form of that pursuit.[31]

The primary objective of academic research is the generation of new knowledge. Consequently, within the academic community, it is uncommon for researchers to justify their engagement in a specific research project solely based on personal interest. Such a rationale is generally considered insufficient.[32] Researchers are tasked with establishing the legitimacy of their research by elucidating why it holds significance for the literature in the field and even for society as a whole. In doing so, researchers must demonstrate that their work has practical implications and provides theoretical value.

The practical significance of studying Chinese law encompasses two key aspects. Firstly, it relates to the economic importance of China. Given the rapid growth of China's economy, both the International Monetary Fund (IMF) and the World Bank now consider China the world's largest economy in terms of purchasing power parity (PPP). This measurement adjusts countries' GDPs to account for price differences. It is expected that China's economy will soon surpass that of the United States by other metrics as well. According to the latest estimate, this transition is predicted to occur by 2035.[33] As China's economy continues to expand and its interactions with other countries increase, various legal issues with global ramifications emerge, including matters related to investments in China and Chinese investments abroad, international trade and collaborations with China to resolve various bilateral or multilateral issues on the global stage. Consequently, understanding Chinese law, especially China's mindset, methods, preferences and rules for dispute resolution, has become increasingly relevant and valuable for the outside world.

The second aspect regarding the importance of the study of Chinese law is related to its political importance. China's institutional development and legal structure can provide inspiration and reference to the world as they are different from the Western paradigm. African scholar

[31] A. G. D. Bradney, 'University legal education in the twenty-first century' in John P. Grant, R. Jagtenberg and K. J. Nijkerk (eds.), *Legal Education 2000* (Aldershot: Avebury, 1988), pp. 271–272.

[32] Gary King, Robert Keohane and Sidney Berba, *Designing Social Inquiry: Scientific Inference in Qualitative Research* (Princeton, NJ: Princeton University Press, 1994), p. 15.

[33] GT Staff Reporters, 'China likely to be No.1 economy by 2035 with continuous momentum: international think tank', *Global Times*, 5 May 2024, www.globaltimes.cn/page/202403/1309857.shtml (last accessed 28 May 2025).

Dambisa Moyo's speech on TED 'Is China the New Idol for Emerging Economies' can be seen as one of the typical examples in this regard. According to Moyo,

> The fact of the matter is that this has become a very poignant question because there is for the first time in a long time a real challenge to the Western ideological systems of politics and economics, and this is a system that is embodied by China. Moreover, rather than have private capitalism, they have state capitalism. Instead of liberal democracy, they have de-prioritized the democratic system. Moreover, they have also decided to prioritize economic rights over political rights. I put it to you today that it is this system that is embodied by China that is gathering momentum amongst people in the emerging markets as the system to follow because they believe increasingly that it is the system that will promise the best and fastest improvements in living standards in the shortest period of time.
>
> First of all, it's China's economic performance over the past 30 years. She's been able to produce record economic growth and meaningfully move many people out of poverty, specifically putting a meaningful dent in poverty by moving over 300 million people out of indigence. It's not just in economics, but it's also in terms of living standards. We see that in China, 28 percent of people had secondary school access. Today, it's closer to 82 percent. . .Second, China has been able to meaningfully improve its income inequality without changing the political construct. Today, the United States and China are the two leading economies in the world. They have vastly different political systems and different economic systems, one with private capitalism, and another one broadly with state capitalism. However, these two countries have identical GINI Coefficient, which is a measure of income equality. Perhaps what is more disturbing is that China's income equality has been improving in recent times, whereas that of the United States has been declining. . .Thirdly, people in the emerging markets look at China's amazing and legendary infrastructure rollout. This is not just about China building roads and ports and railways in her own country – she's been able to build 85,000 kilometers of road network in China and surpass that of the United States – but even if you look to places like Africa, China has been able to help tar the distance of Cape Town to Cairo, which is 9,000 miles, or three times the distance of New York to California. Now, this is something that people can see and point to. Perhaps it's no surprise that in a 2007 Pew survey, when surveyed, Africans in 10 countries said they thought that the Chinese were doing amazing things to improve their livelihoods by wide margins, by as much as 98 percent. . .Finally, China is also providing innovative solutions to age-old social problems that the world faces. If you travel to Mogadishu, Mexico City, or Mumbai, you find that dilapidated infrastructure and logistics continue to be a stumbling block to the delivery of medicine and healthcare in the rural areas. However, through a network

> of state-owned enterprises, the Chinese have been able to go into these rural areas, using their companies to help deliver these healthcare solutions.
>
> ……
>
> The question that is left for us in general is, what then should the West be doing? And I suggest that they have two options. The West can either compete or cooperate. If the West chooses to compete with the Chinese model, and in effect go around the world and continue to try and push an agenda of private capitalism and liberal democracy, this is basically going against headwinds, but it also would be a natural stance for the West to take because in many ways it is the antithesis of the Chinese model of de-prioritizing democracy and state capitalism. Now the fact of the matter is, if the West decides to compete, it will create a wider schism. The other option is for the West to cooperate, and by cooperating I mean giving the emerging market countries the flexibility to figure out in an organic way what political and economic system works best for them.[34]

As some scholars argued, 'at the end of the Cold War, scholars were pondering how far Western ideas would spread in an international environment defined by "the end of history". China's rapid and continuous growth in the past three decades alters this backdrop'.[35] In this case, the China's model, which is a state-led development model focusing on development as the top priority and enhancing good governance in all aspects by initiating gradual and pragmatic reform,[36] may arouse the interest and curiosity of the world.[37]

1.2.3 *Theoretical Value*

Hence, both the economic and political significance bestow Chinese law, including its dispute resolution system, a domain with substantial research value. Nevertheless, going beyond the practical aspect, the

[34] Dambisa Moyo, 'Is China the new idol for emerging economies?', *TED Talk*, June 2013, www.ted.com/talks/dambisa_moyo_is_china_the_new_idol_for_emerging_economies/transcript#t-649013 (last accessed 20 January 2022).

[35] Li He, 'The Chinese model of development and its implications' (2015) 2(2) *World Journal of Social Science Research* 128.

[36] He, 'The Chinese model of development', 130–132.

[37] Chinese academic circles have always maintained sensitive observations and critical reflection on the development experience of the West. See Qinjun Liu and Wenliang Guo, 'From "Beijing Consensus" to "China Model": an overview of overseas scholars' research on "China path" since China's reform and opening up' (2019) 2 *Socialism Studies* 156 [刘庆军、郭文亮：《从"北京共识"到"中国模式"——改革开放以来海外学者对"中国道路"的研究进展》，《社会主义研究》2019年第2期].

theoretical dimension is equally meaningful. Theory is not confined to specific or situational knowledge. Situational knowledge offers specific answers to particular phenomena, while theory encompasses generalised knowledge. A theory constitutes a logically sound narrative elucidating the underlying mechanisms of a category of social phenomena, and its explanatory power extends to a wide array of social realities.

For instance, when John had a disagreement with his parents and felt unhappy, he sought advice from a dispute resolution expert. The guidance provided was tailored to that specific case, representing personalised consultation aimed at resolving a particular issue within a specific context. In other words, it amounted to situational knowledge, addressing problem-solving within a distinct scenario. Simultaneously, the dispute resolution expert equipped John with a document listing fundamental tips for cross-generational communication or the foundational structure of principled negotiation theory. These insights could enhance the quality of intergenerational communication and go beyond the confines of John's specific case, offering valuable guidance that could be applied to a number of similar family conflict situations. In this context, the listed points hold theoretical significance. To reiterate, if knowledge is formulated solely for addressing specific issues, it remains limited to case-by-case resolution or consultation. However, if the knowledge is generally (if not universally) applicable and relevant across multiple situations, it qualifies as a theory.

Coming back to Chinese legal studies, it means more than just mastering the laws of a particular country. It also provides researchers with an opportunity to understand the complexity of a vast system, enrich their thoughts, inspire creativity and ultimately help to expand our imaginations of the future world. Speaking of the theoretical value of Chinese legal studies, Albert Chen said:

> If one adopts the classification of the legal systems in the contemporary world into three major categories – the common law family, the civil law family, and the family of socialist laws – then all these families have their origin in the Western European states which appeared towards the end of the Middle Ages. . .The case of China provides, therefore, an example of the transplant of law and legal institutions from one part of the world to another, and their interaction with local culture and traditions deserves study.[38]

[38] Chen, *An Introduction to the Legal System*, pp. 1–2.

Based on this, some important theoretical questions can be raised that make Chinese legal studies attractive and meaningful for readers in other jurisdictions:

(1) To what extent are we prisoners of our past? Can China grow out of its traditional legal culture?
(2) What is the significance of the concept of families of legal systems in comparative law? Does contemporary Chinese law belong to the civil law family?
(3) Does ideology matter to legal development? Can the legal history of the People's Republic of China (PRC) so far be accounted for in terms of shifts in official ideology?
(4) What is the relationship between legal and economic development? Is the marketisation of the economy the most important force behind legal change in contemporary China?
(5) What is the significance of globalisation and China's entry to the World Trade Organization in 2001 for Chinese legal development?
(6) What is the relationship between legal and political reforms in China? To what extent does the lack of political reform hinder legal progress?
(7) Is there an autonomous logic of legal, institutional growth, particularly the development of legislative and judicial institutions, the legal profession and legal discourse? Will the legal reforms engineered by the ruling party unleash unintended consequences that challenge the party's monopoly of power?
(8) Is there a universal trajectory of legal evolution, so that the contemporary Chinese legal system may be regarded as a developing one, less advanced than its Western counterparts but in the process of catching up and maturing?
(9) Will there be an ultimate convergence of the legal systems and laws of humankind, so that as Kant envisaged in his conception of universal history, all political communities in the world will eventually evolve into peace-loving liberal constitutional states that practice the rule of law and respect human rights?[39]

The most fundamental theoretical meaning of studying Chinese law, in this case, is to make international lawyers or researchers be equipped with the ability to understand the complex legal system or rule of law in a

[39] Chen, *An Introduction to the Legal System*, pp. 1–2.

big country. As Sebastian Heilmann and Elizabeth J. Perry pointed out, China is a complicated issue for scholarship, not just law:

> Due to its idiosyncratic developmental pathway over the past thirty years, contemporary China presents an enigma not only to the field of Chinese politics, which did not predict the surprising resilience of the Communist system under reform and has yet to provide a convincing explanation for it. It also poses a major puzzle to the field of comparative politics, where prevailing theories of modernization, democratization, and regime transition to date offer little illumination for the case of post-Mao China. China stands as a 'Black Swan' challenge to the social sciences.[40]

Yes, considering China's uninterrupted civilisation spanning thousands of years, its unique culture and the highly diverse internal ethnic composition, understanding and discussing the rule of law in China presents a particularly challenging arena. The varying stages of socioeconomic development across different regions, the vast geographic area and the complexity of dispute resolution require us to place legal processes within a more intricate, dynamic and heterogeneous environment. Understanding the rule of law and dispute resolution in such a large and extraordinarily complex country undoubtedly enriches our imagination of the world and the functioning of dispute resolution systems. Exploring how a super-complex nation like China manages its legal processes and resolves disputes offers invaluable insights that can enhance our comprehension of legal operations on a global scale. Enhancing this understanding is very important for both the Chinese and the rest of the world. According to Martin Jacques,

> And yet we still insist, by and large, in thinking that we can understand China by simply drawing on Western experience, looking at it through Western eyes, using Western concepts. If you want to know why we unerringly seem to get China wrong – our predictions about what is going to happen to China are incorrect – this is the reason. Unfortunately, I think, I have to say that I think the attitude towards China is that of a kind of little Westerner mentality. It is kind of arrogant. It is arrogant in the sense that we think that we are the best, and therefore we have the universal measure. Secondly, it is ignorant. We refuse to address the issue of difference. You know, there is a very interesting passage in a book by Paul Cohen, the American historian. Moreover,

[40] Sebastian Heilmann and Elizabeth J. Perry, 'Embracing uncertainty: guerrilla policy and adaptive governance in China' in Sebastian Heilmann and Elizabeth J. Perry (eds.), *Mao's Invisible Hand: The Political Foundations of Adaptive Governance in China* (Cambridge, MA: Harvard University Press, 2011), p. 4.

> Paul Cohen argues that the West thinks of itself as probably the most cosmopolitan of all cultures. But it is not. In many ways, it is the most parochial, because, for 200 years, the West has been so dominant in the world that it is not really needed to understand other cultures, and other civilizations. Because it could, if necessary by force, get its own way. Whereas those cultures – virtually the rest of the world, in fact, which have been in a far weaker position, vis-a-vis the West – have been thereby forced to understand the West, because of the West's presence in those societies. And therefore, they are, as a result, more cosmopolitan in many ways than the West.[41]

1.3 How to Study the Chinese Mediation System and Understand Its Complexity

1.3.1 The Development of Alternative Dispute Resolution Paradigms

1.3.1.1 Interest-Based Paradigm

Alternative dispute resolution studies will indeed involve different knowledge and methods. In dispute resolution studies, a singular and simplified methodological and theoretical framework stemming from one particular discipline, like the norm-based approach or black letter approach, is far from enough.

> ...[T]he search for a single theory that would provide definitive guidance in all cases is quixotic, not only because of the existence of irreducible difference and contingency across contexts and situations but also because it misconstrues what actually happens when universal principles are applied in the real world.[42]

As a result of the interdisciplinary legal studies in the 1970s, the law school and the business law school cooperated and developed ADR theories.[43] A landmark paradigm regarding ADR, namely principled negotiation theory, was created in the 1970s by the Harvard Negotiation Project. Unlike traditional adversarial negotiation, principled negotiation theory

41 Martin Jacques, 'Understanding the rise of China', *TED Talk*, October 2010, www.ted.com/talks/martin_jacques_understanding_the_rise_of_china (last accessed 20 May 2024).

42 Jane K. Cowan, Marie-Bénédicte Dembour and Richard A. Wilson (eds.), *Culture and Rights: Anthropological Perspective* (Cambridge: Cambridge University Press, 2001), p. 21.

43 See Roger Fisher et al., *Getting to Yes: Negotiating Agreement Without Giving In* (New York: Penguin Books, 2011).

focuses on cooperation and mutual benefit rather than competition and individual gain. Unlike positional bargaining, which centres on parties' fixed positions and often leads to compromise, principled negotiation emphasises understanding underlying interests, separating people from the problem, generating multiple options and using objective criteria to evaluate solutions. This approach aims to create win–win outcomes, fostering more creative and sustainable agreements.

According to the principled negotiation theory, the ability to distinguish between 'position' and 'interest' is its primary principle. The positional mindset focuses on a particular demand, which assumes that the amount of money, time, material goods, respect, status or honour is limited; therefore, the parties should strengthen their position and strive to win as much as they can, rather than enlarge collaborative opportunities.[44] This mindset may eventually strain and shatter the relationship between the parties and construct an antagonistic setting.[45] Therefore, the principled negotiation theory argues the focus of dispute resolution should be on interest instead of position. Interest-based approach believes that the position is superficial and changeable because the interests, which cover the party's basic needs, wants and motivations, are the fundamental drivers of the party's behaviour.[46] The interest-based approach provides a wide range of possibilities, from substantive goals such as money to emotional desires such as recognition or even seeing another person happy, for the parties to negotiate.[47] If interests are satisfied, the antagonistic position can be adjusted.

Therefore, the perception that opposing relationships are immutable is misleading. As Morton Deutsch, the founder of the win–win theory argued, in most situations, people have a mixture of interests so it is common for some of their goals to be initially positive while some are negatively interdependent.[48]

[44] Christopher W. Moore and Peter J. Woodrow, *Handbook of Global and Multicultural Negotiation* (San Francisco, CA: Jossey-Bass, 2010), p. 82.

[45] Moore and Woodrow, *Handbook of Global and Multicultural Negotiation*, p. 82.

[46] Bruce Patton, 'Negotiation' in Michael L. Moffitt and Robert C. Bordone (eds.), *The Handbook of Dispute Resolution* (San Francisco, CA: Jossey-Bass, 2005), p. 280.

[47] Patton, 'Negotiation', p. 280.

[48] Morton Deutsch, 'Cooperation and competition' in Morton Deutsch and Peter T. Coleman (eds.), *The Handbook of Conflict Resolution: Theory and Practice* (San Francisco, CA: Jossey-Bass Publishers, 2000), p. 24.

> Disputants hold multiple interests, it is reasonable to expect that sometimes they will have some interest that is opposed (You want to pay less, but I want to receive more from you.) Disputants may have other interests that are differing, but not opposing. (I care about a change in policy and you care about confidentiality.) Finally, it is reasonable to assume some of the disputants' interests are shared. (You and I both want the project to be completed on time. You would prefer a cleaner environment. And so would I. Both divorcing parents want their children to receive a quality education.) Share interests present the opportunity for crafting an arrangement that makes both sides better off in a non-competitive way.[49]

Facing this situation of a mixture of interests, the 'effective actions' will improve the actor's chances of obtaining a goal, whereas the 'bungling actions' may worsen the actor's chances of obtaining the goal.[50] Whether conflict and tension can be well managed depends, to a large extent, on whether the parties can recognise the existence of non-conflicting interests, including both the common and different ones, and adopt effective actions. In some highly complex social life, such as an analytical framework, the interest-based approach also has strong explanatory power. In the real regime-and-religion interaction situations, for example, Koesel has noted that the Communist Party of China and religion have traditionally been seen as fundamentally opposed due to ideological reasons. According to classical Marxist and Leninist theory, religion is expected to eventually disappear, and Communist Party members are prohibited from believing in any religion. However, in practical life, Koesel found that Chinese local governments often engage in cooperative interactions with religious institutions. For instance, local governments help Buddhist abbots waive their fees for MBA degrees in exchange for greater support from the temple in attracting tourists; similarly, religious groups assist local governments in building roads in exchange for official acceptance.[51] This type of cooperative interaction is very common in China. According to the principled negotiation theory, viewing the secular state and religion as a static opposition is a form of 'positional' thinking. Koesel's observation demonstrates the dynamism of real life, where different actors have different interests. In non-conflict areas, these

[49] Michael L. Moffitt, 'Disputes as opportunities to create value' in Michael L. Moffitt and Robert C. Bordone (eds.), *The Handbook of Dispute Resolution* (San Francisco, CA: Jossey-Bass, 2005), p. 176.

[50] Moffitt, 'Disputes as opportunities', p. 176.

[51] Karrie J. Koesel, 'Religion and the regime: cooperation and conflict in contemporary Russia and China' (2017) 69(4) *World Politics*, 676, 692–693.

interests can be exchanged, allowing for cooperation through mutual benefit.

Therefore, a pronounced theoretical divergence between the paradigms of litigation and mediation becomes apparent. Litigation tends to transmute the genuine, experiential and tangible conflict or dispute process into legal abstractions through legal analysis and rationale, subjecting it to the rigidity of specific statutory laws. In contrast, when viewed through the lens of ADR theory, the litigation approach is perceived as inherently flawed. This is primarily due to its failure to adequately account for the individual interests and needs of the parties involved, instead constraining them within the confines of a conceptual battleground. Within this framework, certain scholars posit that the litigation mindset can be characterised as 'fragmented'. It dissects the entire dispute into discrete factual fragments (evidence), often excluding many pertinent aspects that may lack direct legal relevance but possess a substantial bearing on the parties, such as their personal histories and emotional states. The outcome of winning and losing, along with logic based on legal rights, tends to fix parties in inflexible opposing positions.

> Specifically, litigation is the process of extracting the civil rights and obligations in dispute between the parties from the overall social facts involved in the dispute and their associated social relationships. It seeks to resolve disputes within established normative frameworks. In contrast, modern mediation employs a comprehensive approach, consolidating legal relationships from multiple related disputes for consideration. Comprehensive thinking, in the process of resolving conflicts and disputes, primarily involves examining the nature of the dispute, its causes, the degree of contradiction, and other factors within the broader context of economics, law, ethics, customs, psychology, and society. It emphasizes a multidimensional perspective in thinking, diversity in choosing solutions, flexibility in employing methods, and comprehensive adjustment of interests to achieve a genuine resolution of the matter at hand.[52]

1.3.1.2 Person-Based Paradigm

Although the theory of ADR has the characteristics of interdisciplinarity, the human being as an element has not been paid enough attention. According to *Getting to Yes*, to separate the people from the problem is

[52] Yongan Liao et al., *The Idea Innovation and Mechanism Reconstruction of Mediation in China* (Beijing: China Renmin University Press, 2019), pp. 32–33 [廖永安等：《中国调解的理念创新与机制重塑》，北京：人民大学出版社2019年版].

considered as one of the fundamental principles of dispute resolution. 'A more effective way for the parties to think of themselves is as partners in a hard-headed, side-by-side search for a fair agreement advantageous to each.'[53] In this case, human subjectivity was not taken seriously by the original negotiation theory. The development of mediation in the later period then gradually changed this situation. In 1994, Robert A. Baruch[54] and Joseph P. Folger[55] published their landmark book *The Promise of Mediation: Responding to Conflict Through Empowerment and Recognition* on the basis of interdisciplinary studies. This book systematically criticises the traditional dispute resolution model and clearly states that the real centre of mediation must be a person; in this case, mediation is not only a problem-solving process but an opportunity for the disputing parties to achieve moral and educational growth.[56] Following their transformative mediation theory,

> while fully harmonizing with transformative mediation, humanistic mediation emphasizes a greater departure from skill-based techniques and gives less attention to problem-solving. By highlighting the humanizing capacities of mediators, parties, and communication processes. The humanistic approach deepens a dialogue process as it fosters good mediator presence and the uninterrupted flow of 'heart language' between parties.[57]

This transformation, compared with the interests-based paradigm, is considered the second generation of dispute resolution theory in Western scholarship.

> In cases of parties who share the group level experience of identity and perceive these group identities as clashing, second-generation models of conflict engagement (which extend beyond the needs and interest-based formulas of the first generation) may be more useful in order to first affirm and then complexify the group identity – to question it, deconstruct it and make it available in a transitional moment for more nuanced

[53] Fisher et al., *Getting to Yes*, p. 40.

[54] Robert A. Baruch is the Harry H. Rains Distinguished Professor of Alternative Dispute Resolution (ADR) Law at Hofstra University School of Law.

[55] Joseph Folger is a Professor of Adult and Organizational Development at Temple University.

[56] Robert A. Baruch Bush and Joseph P. Folger, *The Promise of Mediation: Responding to Conflict Through Empowerment and Recognition* (San Francisco, CA: Jossey-Bass, 1994), p. 81.

[57] Ted Lewis and Mark Umbreit, 'A humanistic approach to mediation and dialogue: an evolving transformative practice' (2015) 33(1) *Conflict Resolution Quarterly* 3.

> and interactive mode with other groups and their identities. This mode of intervention assumes a more humanistic and moral approach to mediation and is compatible with Buberian notions of I-Thou dialogue and with the Levinasic philosophy of infinite love while encountering the face of the other.[58]

In transformative mediation, conflicts are not seen as mere problems and should not be oversimplified as such. Conflict should instead be regarded as an opportunity, evolving the transformation from a state where one cannot engage in dialogue with the other party, cannot understand them and cannot see them as equal human beings with the same subjectivity value but an incomprehensible monster, to the new stage where the parties can face the counterpart directly, understand them and, if not accepting them, seeing them as an equal individual with joys and sorrows in life. This change naturally presents an opportunity for one's further personal growth and moral development. Therefore, in the ontology of transformative mediation, there is a fundamental belief in the social connection and moral impulses of human beings. The potential for moral and social growth is suppressed by adversarial litigation, which turns people into alienated adversaries. Transformative mediation thus aims to restore this sense of humanity, reestablish social connections and revive moral impulses within individuals. This is achieved by challenging their intrinsic passivity and enhancing their capacity for understanding, ultimately helping them resolve disputes in a more positive manner through in-depth interpersonal dialogue.[59]

1.3.1.3 Chinese Holism Way of Dispute Resolution

Compared with the Western dispute resolution theory, the Chinese dispute resolution theory does not focus on the analysis of structural elements of dispute (like the ICON model, including interests, criteria, options and non-agreement alternatives, according to the principled negotiation theory) but emphasises a holistic nature of dispute resolution process. This holistic view makes the theory and practice of mediation in China maintain the basic characteristics of interdisciplinarity. In both

[58] Jay Rothman and Michal Alberstein, 'Individuals, groups and intergroups: theorizing about the role of identity in conflict and its creative engagement' (2013) 28(3) *Ohio State Journal on Dispute Resolution* 631, 654.

[59] Hao Xiong, 'The changes of foreign mediation typologies and the ideological roots: from the perspective of legal anthropology' (2023) 3 *World Social Sciences* 189, 198 [熊浩："域外调解的类型范式及其变迁的思想之根：基于法律人类学的视角"，载《世界社会科学》2023年第3期].

traditional and contemporary Chinese society, dispute resolution is not limited to a single discipline or the black letter's level. Beyond the law, *qingli* (情理) is always taken into consideration in the dispute resolution context. In other words, people's feelings (*qing*) and socially accepted common norms (*li*), alongside the law, are all fundamental elements that the dispute resolver should comprehensively balance when mediating a dispute. In other words, the dispute resolution process in China tends to holistically address multiple facets of conflict resolution. Beyond the logical analysis and application of laws, it is crucial to guide and satisfy the parties' needs (including psychological needs) and restore and rebuild social relationships. This approach aims to substantively resolve conflicts rather than merely issuing judgments that leave underlying tensions or grievances unresolved. In a more fundamental dimension, conflict is not just a legal case but a human problem.[60] In the conception of dispute resolution in China, it is crucial to recognise that non-legal or interdisciplinary elements, known as '*qingli*' or otherwise, play a significant role in the process of handling conflicts and their resolution or transformation. The holistic approach to dispute resolution in specific cases emphasises capturing and utilising these non-legal elements, thereby transcending mere legal formalism.

The 'Fengqiao experience' (枫桥经验) in modern times can vividly exemplify this Chinese holistic way of mediation. The Fengqiao experience advocates resolving disputes in a highly situational way. For example, Fengqiao experience will resolve the dispute in a way closer to the masses, paying special attention to 'persuade people with reason, and not to overwhelm people with power; keep patience, do not force rough; investigate and study the fact and situation, do not make subjective assumptions; be honest'.[61] In the famous Lao Yang Mediation Studio in Fengqiao, its mediation method emphasises situational design; that is, 'using the method of discipline for children, using the method of counselling for young people, and using the mediation of marital disputes by inviting the matchmaker and the couple's relatives who know the law to join the dispute resolution process'.[62] Therefore, in addition to facts and

[60] Carrie Menkel-Meadow, 'From legal disputes to conflict resolution and human problem solving: legal dispute resolution in a multidisciplinary context' (2004) 54 *Journal of Legal Education* 4, 10–11.

[61] Yuhe Yu and Tianju Pan, 'On the function of resolving disputes in "Fengqiao Experience"' (2014) 5 *Journal of Hunan Police College* 14, 15 [于语和、潘天驹："'枫桥经验'的解纷功能简论"，《湖南警察学院学报》2014年第5期].

[62] Shirong Wang and Chenge Chu, '*The Fengqiao Experience*': *An Empirical Study on the Modernization of Grassroots Social Governance System and Capacity* (Beijing: Law Press,

rules, Fengqiao experience will pay special attention to personal feelings and social relations, and use social relations as a resource for substantive dispute resolution. Such a mediation model provides us with important interdisciplinary materials to further develop the dispute resolution paradigm.

In addition to emphasising the normative, subjective and social dimensions of conflict resolution at the micro level, holism has also become the value foundation of China's macro dispute resolution policy. For instance, in China's litigation system, a clear tendency towards holism is evident. This means that the goals of litigation in China extend beyond accurately applying the law to encompass various other aspects. For example, the tasks, scope of application and basic principles of the Civil Procedure Law (CPL) are stipulated in Chapter 1. Article 2 of the CPL provides that:

> The tasks of the Civil Procedural Law of the People's Republic of China are the protection of the rights of litigants for the exercise of litigation rights, ensuring ascertainment of facts and distinguishing between right and wrong by People's Courts, correct application of laws, the prompt trial of civil cases, confirmation of civil rights and obligations, the sanction of civil offenses, protection of legitimate rights and interests of litigants, educating citizens to comply with the law voluntarily, safeguarding social order and economic order, safeguarding smooth establishment of socialism.

This holistic tendency is also clearly reflected in the judicial policy of the Supreme People's Court (SPC). In *Several Opinions on Cultivating and Practicing Socialist Core Values in the Work of People's Courts* issued by SPC in 2015, it emphasised that the courts should pursue

> the organic unity of political effect, legal effect and social effect. The courts should make the judgment based on the development of the Times, national conditions, culture, comprehensive consideration, rational, emotional and other factors, strengthen the guiding role of socialist core values, and improve the legal identity of judicial judges, social identity and reasonable recognition of the law.[63]

2018), p. 364 [汪世荣、褚宸舸：《"枫桥经验"：基层社会治理体系与能力现代化实证研究》，法律出版社2018年].

63 'Make justice more warm – Promoting the integration of socialist core values into the requirements of The Times and the way to develop the interpretation and reasoning of judgment documents' [让司法更有温度 – 推进社会主义核心价值观融入裁判文书释法说理的时代要求和养成之道], www.court.gov.cn/jianshe-xiangqing-364101.html (last accessed 5 July 2023).

The emphasis on the subjectivity and social nature of dispute resolution, aiming for a comprehensive and thorough resolution of conflicts, is deeply influenced by Chinese culture and philosophy's negative perception of conflict. In traditional Chinese society, engaging in a dispute is not viewed favourably as it implies a deviation from customary rituals. Individuals with decency and education would refrain from litigation, demonstrating a civilised approach. Therefore, the process of dispute resolution in China encompasses not only legal judgments but also ethical education and moral development of the disputing parties linked to societal aspects.[64] This cultural and philosophical understanding manifests at the micro level as a holistic and diverse approach to dispute resolution methods. At the macro policy design level, it translates into the state integrating various dispute resolution mechanisms to form a pluralistic dispute resolution mechanism ('多元化纠纷解决机制, *duoyuanhua jiufen jiejue jizhi*') system. The fundamental value orientation of China's pluralist dispute resolution differs from the basic concept of modern Western ADR, which emphasises the release of social autonomy and self-empowerment. Instead, it attempts to construct an integrated system through the state. This system comprises mechanisms that allow all kinds of dispute resolution methods, such as mediation, conciliation, arbitration, notary public dispute resolution and administrative rulings, reconsideration and litigation, to operate in a coordinated manner. These methods are not competitors or mere alternatives; they are mutually supportive components with equal legal effect, transitioning from one to another along clearly defined pathways. This approach effectively manages social conflicts and disputes, achieving the political governance goal of social stability.[65]

To sum up, regardless of the fundamental paradigms in alternative dispute resolution in both the Western and Chinese contexts, it should be recognised that the legal norm is just one element and likely not the most

[64] If comparing with the relevant provisions of China's Civil Procedure Law with the Rules of Civil Procedure for the United State District Court, this difference is even more obvious. The Rule 1 of Rules of Civil Procedure for the United State District Court provides that 'these rules govern the procedure in all civil actions and proceedings in the United States district courts, except as stated in Rule 81. They should be construed, administered, and employed by the court and the parties to secure the just, speedy, and inexpensive determination of every action and proceeding'.

[65] Zhiqiang June Wang and Jianfu Chen, 'From alternative dispute resolution to pluralist dispute resolution: towards an integrated dispute-resolution mechanism in China' (2020) 16 *International Journal of Law in Context* 165, 177.

crucial in the theoretical framework of mediation. Whether centred around interests, human factors or adopting a holistic perspective to accommodate more elements, numerous non-legal factors genuinely influence the process and outcomes of dispute resolution. Therefore, in studying the process of mediation, going beyond the black letter approach and adopting an interdisciplinary perspective becomes crucial. Researchers should pay particular attention to the non-legal factors manifested during the mediation context and process. Otherwise, the theoretical explanations and institutional designs for mediation will be narrow or ineffective.

1.3.2 The Starting Point of Studying Alternative Dispute Resolution in China

1.3.2.1 Thinking Like a Local Lawyer

The initial step for foreigners seeking to understand Chinese law is to recognise and appreciate the cultural and societal distinctions that set China apart from Western nations. Under a unified, domestic-law-based and standardised legal training, however, lawyers' mindset would inevitably be institutionalised by their own domestic legal institutions. 'When the French, or the Spanish, or the Italians, or the Dutch, or the Germans adopt a legislative text, they do something typically French, typically Spanish, typically Italian, typically Dutch, and typical German.'[66] Each legal tradition makes a specific and nonreplicable contribution to the legal system as it purports to formulate an original worldview.[67] All lawyers are initially trained as national/local lawyers in the legal education, training, qualification exam and accessing system. There is no exception for academic lawyers. Therefore, when they study or draw lessons from foreign law, they are inevitably equipped with the very local and national mindset; they thus inevitably compare the foreign legal issues with their domestic situation even just describing.[68] Following this concept, people have to 'think like a local lawyer' most of the time (Pierre Legrand); in other words, Chinese law, methodologically speaking, needs

[66] Legrand, 'How to compare now', 233, 236.

[67] Legrand, 'How to compare now', 233, 240.

[68] Jingwen Zhu, *A General Introduction of Comparative Law* (Beijing: Renming University Press, 2nd ed., 2008), p. 6 [朱景文著：《比较法总论（第二版）》，北京：中国人民大学出版社2008年].

to be defined as local knowledge first. Legal universalism is questionable at the methodological level.

The language itself, for instance, embodies the characteristics of Chinese law, which is difficult to understand for foreign lawyers. The term 'state' is a good example. If someone looks it up in a dictionary, he/she may find its Chinese translation of the English term 'state' as '国家 (*guojia*)'. If people learn this term from the dictionary perspective, they may think that the word 'state' has the same meaning as the term '国家' (state) in the Chinese context. However, when carefully checking the definitions of 'state' and '国家', respectively, it can be found that they have different meanings. The word 'state' means 'a politically organized body of people usually occupying a definite territory' according to the Merriam-Webster Dictionary, whereas '国家' not only includes the political territory meaning but contains the moral elements of a family which cannot be found in the definition of 'state' from the perspective of English. In Chinese, '国家' contains a meaning that a country or state is constructed together as one family unit. '国家' can be translated, in the literal sense, as 'a nation of families' or 'the nation as a family' or even 'a nation ruled by a family'.[69] In the Chinese tradition, the leaders of the country are just like the patriarchs of a family.

In contemporary Chinese society, particularly among the younger generation, it is not uncommon for the elderly to ask rather personal questions, some of which may encroach upon the youth's privacy. These inquiries often include questions like 'Do you have a boyfriend or girlfriend?' or 'Why are you currently single?', and may even extend to topics such as 'What is your current salary?' In cases where a romantic relationship exists, elders might inquire about marriage plans with questions like 'When do you intend to get married?' or 'When will you be starting a family?' This phenomenon contributes, to some extent, to the stress experienced by the younger generation in China due to interactions with elders. The reason for this social phenomenon is that the concept of family tends to blur the boundaries between individuals. The family is often perceived as a moral collective where members provide mutual assistance and support to one another. This perspective contrasts with a model where individuals form contractual relationships through legal means. Within the familial context, the ties of blood create a situation where individual rights become intertwined, resulting in a distinctive

[69] See Pao-Min Chang, 'Chinese perspectives on nation, state and the world' (2001) 5(1) *World Affairs: The Journal of International Issues* 102, 102–122.

Chinese family dynamic. This dynamic, in turn, has an impact on the Chinese people's perspective on their nation.

This 'one family' cultural conception regarding nation and state makes it easier for the Chinese populace to generate support for national policies. This can partly explain why various international survey organisations often report high levels of public approval for the Chinese government and why the government receives more understanding from the public when intervening in citizens' personal lives. Utilising these examples, it becomes evident that without a comprehensive understanding of Chinese culture, international lawyers and policymakers may overlook valuable insights and arrive at misleading conclusions. This underscores the importance of encouraging foreign students to learn the Chinese language. Chinese should not be perceived merely as a means of communication; rather, it should be regarded as a system of symbolic representation through which the profound meanings of Chinese culture can, to some extent, be deciphered.

Another example illustrating the uniqueness of the relationship between the state and society is the field of consumption studies. This area of study serves as an exemplar highlighting the limitations of the Western analytical paradigm when explaining Chinese social phenomena. In the analysis regarding daily consumption in Chinese society, Ning Wang discovered that in the theoretical framework of Western sociology, 'state' as a variable is not paid enough attention to and is even absent. That is because the influence of the state on people's daily consumption is not so obvious in Western countries. Consumption in Western countries is a personal choice that mainly happens at the individual level and is driven by the market. Whereas, when Wang analyses daily consumption in China, the 'state' is perhaps the most important variable which constructs people's consumption choices and restricts consumption desire, especially in Mao's era – the ideological promotion of the 'hard work and struggle' ethos, along with the national recognition of frugal moral exemplars, has successfully restrained the common people's desire for daily consumption. With the advent of economic reforms and opening-up, China's macroeconomic policies rapidly shifted towards a market-oriented economy. This change in official ideology and policy ushered in the arrival of contemporary consumerist society in China.[70]

[70] See Ning Wang, *From the Ascetic Society to the Consumer Society: Transformations of the Institutions of Consumption, Incentive to Labor and the Structures of Subjectivity in Urban China* (Beijing: Social Sciences Literature Press, 2009) [王宁：《从苦行者社会到消费者

In this case, the limitations of simply copying Western theory to explain China's reality emerged. That does not necessarily mean the Western theory is wrong but means its explanatory power is limited due to the change in the social context. This can also partly explain the limitations of Western theories in dealing with China:

> The conventional political science has complained that this explanatory framework [of the conventional political science] has not proven particularly useful in understanding the complex dynamics of an innovative, competitive, and powerful China, however. In light of the country's unusual development record, it has become increasingly problematic to try to shoe-horn China into the shop-worn categories of Cold War regime types, even by adding numerous attributes to the original categories.[71]

The third case illustrating the limitations of prevailing theories comes from the author's research on the political and religious relationships in grassroots communities in southwest China.[72] In different historical periods in China, religion as a kind of group with mystical forces has been a worry for the secular state, as it may play a significant role in toppling weak authorities.[73] When it comes to Chinese modern times, political control over religions has not been relaxed. Under this climate, the so-called state–religion antagonism paradigm was gradually developed, which emphasises the incompatible tension between the state and religions.[74] This paradigm was reasonable considering the atheist stance of the Communist Party of China[75] and the extreme hostile tension between state and religion in the history of China.[76] However,

社会：中国城市消费制度、劳动激励与主体结构转型》，北京：社会科学文选出版社2009版].

71 Heilmann and Perry, 'Embracing uncertainty', p. 4.

72 See Hao Xiong, 'Party branch established in the wat: social cooperation between local authorities and religion in the Theravada Buddhist community of southwest China' (2023) 21(1) *China: An International Journal* 45.

73 Lawrence Cox, 'Freedom of Religion in China: religious, economic and social disenfranchisement for China's Internal Migrant Workers' (2007) 8 *Asian-Pacific Law & Policy Journal* 370, 375.

74 See Daniel Bays, 'American public discourse on church in China' (2009) 2 *The China Review* 1, 1–16. For some empirical analysis in this regard, see Carsten T. Vala, 'Protestant reactions to the nationalism agenda in contemporary China' in Francis Khek Gee Lim (ed.), *Christianity in Contemporary China: Social-Cultural Perspectives* (New York: Routledge, 2013), p. 64.

75 Xuezeng Gong, 'Survey of Marxist perspectives on religion in new China' in Lü Daji and Xuezeng Gong (eds.), Chi Zhen (trans.), *Marxism and Religion* (Leiden: Brill, 2014), p. 295.

76 Chan Kim-Kwong, 'Religion in China in the twenty-first century: some scenarios' (2005) 33 *Religion, State & Society* 87, 87–88.

in southwest China in the Dai community on the southern border, it is now very common that the grassroots organisations of the Communist Party of China (CPC) also exist in the wats[77] by establishing their units in the name of a party's room, a party member activity centre, a party cadre centre and so on. This is not an accidental phenomenon, as the CPC's substantial presence prevails in almost every village wat in Dehong. It is a significant signal revealing the CPC's social existence in the religion-affiliated ethnic minority community. But surprisingly, the state–religious antagonism relationship was not found in the Theravada Buddhism community. On the other hand, religion and local government maintain harmonious interaction in the wat. The most significant reason behind this phenomenon is that religion and the grassroots government found non-ideological and non-conflicting types of interests, that is, social service cooperation in the wats. If the research paradigm is transferred from the state–religion antagonism paradigm to the interests-based approach, it is not hard to understand that both the CPC and religion have multifunctional characteristics and common pragmatic interests. Religion needs the CPC to support its development, and the CPC needs religion to expand its influence in the Dai community. This mutual need makes non-ideological social services an area where both sides can cooperate. By sharing the public service provision, the social functions of state and religion are not only compatible but also mutually beneficial. Perhaps in the ideological field, their interests are conflicting, but in the social service field, their interests are overlapping or at least exchangeable. Collaboration then becomes an effective strategy for both the subnational government and religion to seek stability, influence and legitimacy.[78] If the non-conflicting interests are identified, religious activities, collective events, village service, social reunions and the party's

[77] In Dehong, the temple is called wat (*Zhuang*, 奘). The Theravada Wat and Han Temple in the Dai community are called *Zhuangfang* and *Zhuangxie*, respectively. Most Theravada wats were destroyed in the Cultural Revolution period and were rebuilt in the 1980s. Nowadays, the participants of religious activities are not necessarily affiliated with Buddhism but with a demonstration of their collective identity as Dai. In today's Dai village, the people who strictly follow the religious rules and attend the religious rituals are mainly of the older generation. It was found in the interview that the younger generations, although they also participate in important religious events like the Water Sprinkling Dai Festival and the Open-Door Festival, will, in general, be less passionate about the religion than the older generation. See Liu Jiang, *Guanchun: A Village of Headmen and Their Families in Change* (Kunming: Yunnan University Press, 2008), pp. 44–140 [刘江：《官纯：变迁中的土司属官寨》，昆明：云南大学出版社2008年版].

[78] Koesel, 'Religion and the regime', 676, 704.

publicity become shared goals and a common responsibility for both the CPC and religion. In other words, if the purely ideological differences and conflicting interests can be well managed at the local level, religion and the party can cooperate and become harmonious. Such an empirical discovery challenges previous analytical paradigms, showcasing the real interaction methods and logic of state–religion relations in China. The dispute resolution theory provides a completely different theoretical framework for explaining China's political and religious relationships.[79]

From the examples and case studies mentioned above, it is not difficult to observe that China has its own unique characteristics in terms of language, social structure and the interaction patterns of social entities. Admittedly, China has much in common with other countries. However, the so-called Beijing Consensus also highlighted China's idiosyncratic modernisation process, including its unique process of legal modernisation.[80] While not everyone may agree with the conclusion presented by the Beijing Consensus, it still can remind us, as Yang Gan suggested, of the difficulty and super complexity of understanding China.[81] Therefore, if the researchers have no awareness of the nuanced difference of the law and the limitations of the analytical framework derived from their own legal tradition, the Chinese legal studies may just be seen as the self-reflection of their own legal system in the so-called comparative studies. As Teemu Ruskola has pointed out,

> But just what does it mean to claim that China suffers from a (relative or absolute) lack of – law?... How the West has constructed its cultural identity against China in terms of the law. Why, despite vigorous efforts to debunk it, does the view of China's lawlessness continue to prevail – not only in popular opinion and among policy-makers, but even among legal scholars who do not specialize in China as well as China scholars who do not specialize in law? Chinese civil law, for example, has been discovered and re-discovered periodically in the West. What

[79] See Xiong, 'Party branch established in the wat', 45.

[80] 'Beijing Consensus', http://fpc.org.uk/fsblob/244.pdf (last accessed 16 May 2011).

[81] Yang Gan, *Three Traditions* (Beijing: Sanlian Press, 2007), pp. 8–9 [甘阳：《通三统》，北京：三联出版社，2007年版]. The original Chinese text goes as follows:

> 理解中国是非常困难的，不能按照各种流行的看法来理解中国。从西方的角度来说，21世纪最大的问题是中国。中国对西方是一个问题，因为西方统治全世界已经数百年，以西方为主形成的这个世界有一套他们的规范和程序，现在中国似乎像一个突然闯进来的人，导致整体体系都在摇荡。

> preconceptions make it possible for it to be discovered and forgotten again so quickly, leaving it to wait for yet another round of – discovery?[82]

That is to say, China has become 'the other' – a distorted reflection of Western law. Consequently, this perspective can hinder the comparative study between Chinese law and other jurisdictions because what is often presented as findings on Chinese law may, in fact, be mere projections of the researchers' own biases and preconceptions. This distorted view fails to capture the true nature and nuances of Chinese legal practices, leading to a superficial understanding that lacks depth and accuracy. As a result, meaningful and objective comparisons are challenging, if not impossible, because they are based on a fundamentally flawed premise. Therefore, it is crucial for researchers to move beyond these ingrained stereotypes and approach Chinese law with a fresh perspective, acknowledging its unique characteristics and contributions to the global legal landscape. Only then can we achieve a more accurate and fruitful comparative legal study. For the same reason, William Alford also reminded researchers that:

> Rather, what concerns me is that our efforts at engaging in broad theoretical work may unwittingly lead us to believe that we are considering foreign legal cultures in universal or value-free terms when, in fact, we are examining them through conceptual frameworks that are products of our values and traditions, and that are often applied merely to see what foreign societies have to tell us about ourselves.[83]

While overexaggeration of the differences between the West and the East is not recommended, and researchers of Chinese law should not dismiss Western theories as invalid or irrelevant when encountering China's realities, it is necessary to acknowledge that all knowledge production is inevitably situated within a specific context – defined by a particular country, culture, political – legal system, ideology and power relations. In this regard, all knowledge can be labelled with a local stamp. If 'local' is used here to indicate the inherent limits of the knowledge producers, it underscores that, even if the knowledge producer subjectively believes their theory to be universal or general, it is still context-bound. For example, the common law, which originally evolved from custom and a 'case-by-case' approach, was a form of 'local practice' in early English history.

[82] Teemu Ruskola, 'Legal orientalism' (2002) 101 *Michigan Law Review* 179, 184.

[83] William P. Alford, 'On the limits of "grand theory" in comparative law' (1986) 61 *Washington Law Review* 945, 946.

This is not to argue for absolute relativism. Instead, the aim is to emphasise that while universality as a value judgement or human project can be embraced in different social and cultural contexts through dialogue and combined efforts, assuming universality as a methodological premise is problematic. Believing that local knowledge can be naturally and uncritically transformed into a universal theory is misleading and naive; such a belief equates to an Ultimate Truth rather than knowledge, making it more akin to religion than to social or legal studies. Again, these examples do not deny the validity of Western theory as a whole but highlight the contextual differences and nuanced limitations of such knowledge. When conducting Chinese legal research, especially in the field of dispute resolution, it is crucial to remember that there may simply be no analogs of those categories in another culture, and, even if there are, their sociological significance in that context may be quite different.[84] Any analytical framework in different contexts may contain different variables, and there is always the possibility that the same variables may play different roles in different contexts.

1.3.2.2 Recommendations for the Choice of Methods: Emphasising Empirical Research

In the field of alternative dispute resolution, several reasons underscore the irreplaceable role of socio-legal or interdisciplinary methods. Firstly, the interdisciplinary approach is essential in mediation studies. Mediation, in essence, is a cultural practice. In her review of *Dispute Resolution* by Stephen B. Goldberg et al., Sally Engle Merry criticised the standardised theory for ignoring the cultural context:

> Because the book offers a tool kit of techniques along with rules about when each tool should be employed, the complexity of actual situations and the surrounding social fabric fades into the background. Exercises in bargaining for law students have the same abstract unreality. At best, this simplification gives students a false sense of easily being able to get to the bottom of issues and settle cases; at worst, it fosters the kind of quick typification and routine treatment of cases that, ironically, ADR advocates often cite as the central problem with conventional adjudication.[85]

Similarly, John L. Comaroff and Simon Roberts have argued that any dispute resolution procedure can only be understood within the 'total

[84] John L. Comaroff and Simon Roberts, *Rules and Processes: The Cultural Logic of Dispute in an African Context* (Chicago, IL: The University of Chicago Press, 1981), p. 8.

[85] Sally Engle Merry, 'Book review: dispute without culture' (1987) 100 *Harvard Law Review* 2057, 2060.

fabric of the sociocultural system'.[86] They assert that the dispute resolution process is 'inevitably informed by fundamental social values and even social identity'.[87] This means that dispute resolution studies are highly sensitive to cultural context; 'the sociological meaning of such conflict is revealed only by a methodology that analyses it in the context of extended social processes'.[88] To achieve this, it is necessary to design an approach that accounts for both the overall logic of dispute processes and their systematic contextualisation.[89]

The most important step to understanding and respecting China's mediation reality, in this case, is through empirical studies. It is interesting to note that empirical data, which needs to be based on fieldwork and participatory observation or data collection, is crucial but scant for studying Chinese dispute resolution. As Donald C. Clarke noted:

> . . .information about China's judicial system, even in the form of reliable and representative statistics, is not always what it seems. In other words, without a deeper understanding of the functioning of China's courts and other legal institutions, it is very easy to look for the wrong type of information and to misinterpret the information we have. Like the drunk in the joke who looked for his lost car keys under the streetlamp because the light was better here, we may be tempted to overvalue those elements of China's judicial system for which we have data simply because the data is available. Thus, a priority in an empirical research agenda at this stage of our understanding should be further study of the actual functioning of China's various legal institutions so that we have a better idea of what questions to ask.[90]

To address the tension between theory and Chinese realities, prioritising empirical research becomes essential. This approach requires researchers to understand that law is not the determining factor but is itself determined by various factors. Consequently, research should broaden its focus beyond mere textual analysis of the law, often referred to as the black letter approach. Instead, it should consider the social context, ideological aspects and economic factors, viewing the law as an integrated

[86] Comaroff and Roberts, *Rules and Processes*, p. 216.

[87] Simon Roberts and Michael Palmer, *Dispute Processes: ADR and the Primary Forms of Decision-Making* (Cambridge: Cambridge University Press, 3rd ed., 2020), p. 2.

[88] Comaroff and Roberts, *Rules and Processes*, p. 13.

[89] Comaroff and Roberts, *Rules and Processes*, p. 246 (emphasis added).

[90] Donald C. Clarke, 'Empirical research into the Chinese judicial system' in Erik G. Jensen and Thomas C. Heller (eds.), *Beyond Common Knowledge: Empirical Approaches to the Rule of Law* (Stanford, CA: Stanford University Press, 2003), p. 181.

part of these elements. In mediation study more specifically, because mediation places greater emphasis on interaction, context and the parties involved compared to litigation, dispute resolution is achieved not merely by applying rules but by uncovering the interests and needs of the parties. This means that mediation reflects more of the emotional, dynamic cultural characteristics rather than the rational, static normative features. Therefore, research methodologies must move beyond a norm-centric path and emphasise empirical research and interdisciplinary approaches.

To truly understand the Chinese mediation system, researchers should immerse themselves in the environment and establish an analytical framework from an insider's perspective. Engaging in empirical research transforms an external observer (etic perspective) into an internal participant (emic perspective), providing unique opportunities to discern the genuine distinctions between Chinese law and Western law in comparative research. The concepts of emic and etic perspectives, coined by anthropologist Kenneth Pike in 1956, emphasise the importance of adapting to the local context, as reflected in the saying, 'When in Rome, do as the Romans do'. This immersive approach will enable a deeper and more accurate understanding of the unique characteristics and practical workings of Chinese mediation. In this case, the following suggestions may facilitate foreign researchers in gaining a better understanding of Chinese law.

- A China-centred perspective of Chinese law
- Localise and immerse yourself in the local context
- Understand law as local knowledge/living wisdom
- Project-oriented approach, interacting with people, mastering the language

In summary, the emphasis and tendency on the contextual dimension of law in interdisciplinary legal studics, the particularities of China and Chinese legal research, the theoretical advancements in dispute resolution beyond normative legal studies and the differences between mediation and litigation all lead to special methodological requirements when studying dispute resolution in China. Based on this foundational understanding, each chapter of this book will attempt not only to focus on rules but also to demonstrate the processes, contexts and deeper mechanisms of how mediation operates in China.

This book is divided into seven chapters. Chapter 1 lays the groundwork for the book by emphasising the importance of an interdisciplinary perspective for studying Chinese law. It highlights the value of integrating cultural, social and legal dimensions, particularly within the Chinese context, to gain unique insights and practical applications in understanding mediation. The chapter explains why Chinese law is a valuable study area, presenting personal motivations and broader practical and theoretical values. It also explores methodologies for studying Chinese mediation, examining the development of alternative dispute resolution paradigms, including interest-based, person-based and Chinese holistic approaches. It emphasises the importance of thinking like a local lawyer. It recommends empirical research methods to capture the complexity and nuances of Chinese mediation practices, setting the stage for a comprehensive analysis.

Chapter 2 establishes the foundational context of dispute resolution in China by delving into the cultural, social and political factors that shape Chinese mediation practices. The chapter highlights the significant influence of Confucianism on the Chinese mindset, emphasising harmonious, integrative and compromising approaches to conflict resolution. It discusses how Chinese people's dispute resolution strategies are deeply rooted in social relationships (*guanxi*) and local governance structures, particularly in rural areas. Additionally, it addresses the interaction between state law and local customs, illustrating the unique dynamics within China's diverse and transitional society. The chapter concludes by emphasising the importance of empirical research and interdisciplinary methods to understand the complexities of Chinese mediation deeply.

Chapter 3 explores the historical development of the Chinese mediation system in modern China, employing a diachronic approach that integrates both quantitative and qualitative data. This chapter traces the evolution and patterns of dispute resolution systems and policies from the late Qing dynasty to contemporary China, illustrating the impact of historical events on current practices. It aims to deduce the theoretical characteristics of the Chinese mediation system, specifically 'politically correct pragmatism', by analysing the interplay between political ideology and practical adaptations over different historical periods in the area of Chinese mediation.

Chapter 4 provides a systematic overview of the legal framework governing mediation in China. It categorises mediation into different styles and types and discusses how these are applied within the Chinese legal context. The chapter explores the regulatory systems underpinning mediation, including the judicial interpretations provided by the Supreme People's Court and local legislative efforts. A significant portion of the chapter is dedicated to analysing the latest developments and challenges in the legislation of commercial mediation in light of the Singapore Mediation Convention. The concept of 'politically correct pragmatism' is also highlighted, showcasing how political correctness and pragmatic flexibility dynamically interact within mediation legal rules. This comprehensive review of mediation regulations provides readers with a detailed understanding of the Chinese ADR system, emphasising its unique characteristics and the interplay between state law and local practices.

Chapter 5 delves into the ADR movement both globally and in China. Through an interdisciplinary methodology and fieldwork, it details how the policy of 'persisting and developing the Fengqiao experience' is transmitted from the central government to the grassroots level. The chapter provides an in-depth analysis of how grassroots communities and judicial organisations in China implement central policies, innovate based on practical conditions and adapt pragmatically. It highlights the local characteristics of dispute resolution and the challenges faced by macro-level policies in addressing significant regional socioeconomic disparities in China.

Chapter 6 provides a detailed empirical case study on the feasibility of mediation in grassroots societies in China. This chapter employs qualitative methods, including participant observation and thick description, to illustrate the entire process of court mediation in a rural village in Yunnan Province. It highlights the unique micro skills and techniques used by grassroots judges to facilitate dispute resolution, emphasising the importance of mediation in preserving face and repairing interpersonal relationships. The chapter argues that mediation is particularly suitable for the rural context due to the social, cultural and economic characteristics of the region. It also discusses the challenges faced by grassroots judges, including their educational background and the mismatch between formal legal training and local needs. The findings suggest that mediation is a more effective and humane approach to dispute resolution in underdeveloped areas, offering a practical alternative to litigation. It is worth mentioning that legal research in China largely presents an urban-centric characteristic, with scholars often criticising the field for neglecting legal practices outside major cities like Beijing and Shanghai. From this perspective, the anthropological study of the mediation process in a village in an underdeveloped region of China is significant. It helps readers fill a frequently overlooked piece of the puzzle regarding dispute resolution practices in China.

Chapter 7 explores the dual facets of mediation in the grassroots society of China, particularly within the context of a developed city.

Through fieldwork in the T District Court in southwest China, this chapter illustrates how mediators leverage their skills and local wisdom to navigate complex cases while interacting with government officials. The chapter provides an in-depth analysis of the judicial ecology in grassroots society, highlighting the role of social connections (*guanxi*) and the everyday interactions between judges and local authorities. It further discusses two detailed case studies, emphasising both the advantages and drawbacks of mediation. These insights contribute to understanding the nuanced application of mediation in a modern urban context, reflecting on its effectiveness, challenges and the interplay between formal legal structures and local customs.

As a Chinese scholar studying mediation through empirical research methods, the author believes that truth is not fully encapsulated in numbers. Numbers, devoid of warmth, often obscure or diminish the inherent human aspects of the real world. Instead, truth is found in stories. The author refers to stories that arise from deep immersion in local society and repeated, in-depth exchanges with those who possess genuine local knowledge. These stories provide an insightful understanding and a sympathetic comprehension of the investigated society and its people. Therefore, the author hopes to provide you with such stories. This book aims to offer more than just numbers, legal provisions or concepts. It seeks to provide images, feelings and stories. As a reader interested and curious about Chinese law or Chinese mediation (an intrinsic motivation that is crucial for you), the book aims to help you not only understand but also feel the real functioning of Chinese mediation. This will give you a more vivid and concrete reading experience. By the end of the book, the author hopes you will have gained this understanding and experience.

PART II

Foundation

2

Context

Culture, Society and Politics

Every legal system is situated within a specific cultural, social and political context. In the case of the Chinese mediation system, it is essential to provide a description of the local context. Knowing the local context will enhance readers' understanding of the practice of dispute resolution in China.

2.1 Chinese Culture and People's Mindset

2.1.1 Confucianism as a Mindset

In general, it is commonly understood that 'the Chinese emphasise harmonious interdependent social existence . . . would prefer integrative, compromising and even avoiding and try to minimize the use of dominating'.[1] Culture is always considered an important factor that determines Chinese people's inclination towards dispute resolution. According to the *Confucius Analects*, 'The Master said "In hearing litigations, I am like any other body. What is necessary, however, is to cause the people to have no litigations."'[2] Disputes or conflicts, according to Confucius, upset the natural peaceful order and should be handled via reasonable compromise instead of fighting for rights. Even today, influenced by the traditional Chinese values, norms, and philosophies, Chinese managers in joint ventures tend to adopt contingent, long-term, contextual and holistic approaches to conflict resolution.[3] Following this framework, scholars further break down the concept of culture into smaller elements of

[1] Irene Hau-siu Chow and Daniel Z. Q. Ding, 'Moral judgement and conflict handling styles among Chinese in Hong Kong and PRC' (2002) 21(9) *Journal of Management Development* 666, 667.

[2] Confucius, *Confucian Analects, Great Learning and the Doctrine of the Mean*, James Legge (trans.) (New York: Cosimo Inc, 2009), p. 257.

[3] Daniel Z. Ding, 'Exploring Chinese conflict management styles in joint ventures in the People's Republic of China' (1996) 19(9) *Management Research News* 43.

behaviour, including face, *guanxi* (interpersonal relationships) and seniority, to explain Chinese people's conflict-handling style.[4]

However, contemporary China has undergone profound transformation compared to its traditional societal structure. Consequently, it is overly simplistic to attribute Chinese people's dispute resolution strategies solely to the teachings of the *Confucian Analects* from centuries past. Viewing the cultural context merely through the lens of dogma found in classical texts fails to adequately explain the behaviours exhibited by Chinese individuals in modern society. In this regard, culture should not be confined to textual interpretations but rather understood as a cognitive structure or collective subconscious, shaping individuals' enduring and stable mindsets. Viewed from this perspective, Confucianism transcends mere classical texts; on the other hand,

> Confucianism may be defined as the state of mind in which the concept of the indeterminate intuited manifold moves into the background of thought and the concrete differentiation in their relativistic, humanistic, transitory comings and goings from the content of philosophy.[5]

2.1.2 Culture and the Characteristics of the Chinese Mindset

From the perspective of mindset, the Chinese understand things in concrete ways. The typical example comes from the understanding of Chinese characters '仁(*ren*)', which is the most frequently mentioned concept in Confucian philosophy. Firstly, from the perspective of the text, '仁(*ren*)' has multiple definitions in different parts of the *Confucius Analects*. For example,

> Filial piety and fraternal submission! – are they not the root of all *benevolent actions (仁)*.
>
> The Master said, 'Fine words and an insinuating appearance are seldom associated with *true virtue (仁')*.'
>
> Fan Ch'ih asked about *benevolence (仁)*. The Master said, 'It is to love all men.'

[4] See Kwang-Kuo Hwang, 'Guanxi and Mientze: conflict resolution in Chinese society' (1997) VII(1) *Intercultural Communication Studies* 17; Guo-Ming Chen and William J. Starosta, 'Chinese conflict management and resolution: overview and implications' (1997–1998) 7 *Intercultural Communication Studies* 1.

[5] Filmer S. C. Northrop, 'The complementary emphases of Eastern intuition philosophy and Western scientific philosophy' in Charles A. Moore (ed.), *Philosophy: East and West* (Princeton, NJ: Princeton University Press, 1946), p. 187, quoted from Yulan Fung, *A Short History of Chinese Philosophy* (New York: The Macmillan Company, 1948), p. 24.

> Chung-Kung asked about *perfect virtue (仁)*. The Master said, 'It is, when you go abroad, to behave to everyone as if you were receiving a great guest; to employ the people as if you were assisting at a great sacrifice; not to do to others as you would not wish done to yourself.'
>
> The Master said, 'the man of *virtue (仁)* makes the difficulty to be overcome his first business, and success only a subsequent consideration – this may be called *perfect virtue (仁)*'.[6]

In this case, when a reader looks up the meaning of '仁 (*ren*)' in a dictionary, they can find many different answers, such as benevolence, kernel, humanity, sensitivity and so on. In other words, the meaning of the most fundamental concept in traditional Chinese culture is diverse, has multiple interpretations and even uncertainty. According to Zongsan Mou, one of the most important representatives of modern neo-Confucianism, the different definitions of '仁 (*ren*)' actually reflect Chinese people's mindset and its distinctions compared to Western thought. Zongsan Mou noted:

> Since Socrates, Western thinkers have consistently approached virtue from a conceptual standpoint, seeking to define it in clear terms. While this approach may differ from the methods employed in disciplines like biology and physics, it shares a common conceptual thinking process in the pursuit of understanding. However, this approach to knowledge is not universally embraced and is viewed unfavorably within Chinese culture. If one were to pose the question 'what is justice' to Confucius, he would not employ the Socratic method of providing a definitive definition or textual analysis. Instead, he demonstrates and instills the essence of virtue through everyday experiences, prompting individuals to reflect on whether they feel inner peace. This approach to understanding virtue lacks the analytical rigor typically associated with Western philosophical inquiry, yet it resonates with its audience due to its practical, compassionate, and truthful nature. For instance, when Zai Yu questioned the rationale behind the traditional three-year mourning period for the death of parents, expressing doubt over its duration and suggesting a shorter timeframe, Confucius did not offer scientific evidence or logical arguments in response. Rather, he addressed the matter of conscience and inner peace, emphasizing the importance of feeling at ease with one's decisions.[7]

[6] Confucius, *The Analects of Confucius*, https://ctext.org/analects (last accessed 18 May 2024).

[7] Zongsan Mou, *Nineteen Lectures on Chinese Philosophy* (Shanghai: Shanghai Ancient Books Publishing House, 1997), p. 46 [牟宗三：《中国哲学十九讲》（上海：上海古籍出版社1997年版）]. The original Chinese text is as follows:

> 西方从苏格拉底以来一向是以这种态度来了解德性，也就是从概念思考的态度来给它一个定义。这种了解虽然好像和我们了解生物学、

Chinese people comprehend the meaning and value of beings by setting aside the view of reality obtained from theorising and focusing on the way things show up in concrete, flowing and sensible context. In Chinese traditional culture, the balance between 'emotion' and 'rationality' is the best example. Evidence can be found in a frequently used Chinese idiom called '心安理得 (*xi'an lide,* peace of heart and a clear conscience)'. In this daily used phrase, the first character is the heart (心). It represents emotional feelings, which are concrete, individualised and contextual. The second part, '理得', is reason or rational judgement, which means something makes sense from a rational point of view. In other words, Chinese culture always advocates a balance between emotional and rational judgement, between special and general evaluation. It is thought that if the abstract rules are strictly applied rationally to a particular case, individual justice may not be achieved perfectly. At the same time, it is also believed that if the judgement is too emotional, personal randomness and uncertainty can become a stumbling block to justice as well. In this case, the synthesis of rationality and sensibility in specific situations will constitute the content of justice. 'For a Westerner, it is usually sufficient for a proposition to be logically sound. For a Chinese,' as Yutang Lin observed, 'it is not sufficient that a proposition is logically correct, but it must be "in accord with human nature", to be *chinch'ing*, is a greater consideration than to be logical.'[8] 'Being in accordance with human nature' constitutes a contextual and tangible criterion in the application of justice, necessitating comprehensive evaluations that encompass not only logic but also emotional and individual circumstances.

To gain a deeper insight into the mindset of Chinese individuals, Western philosophical concepts can offer valuable insights, even though

了解物理学不很相同，但是从概念思考这个地方讲，是相同的。这还是知识的态度。这个态度是中国文化里面所不取的，以这种态度来了解道德是不恰当的。假如你拿什么是公道这个问题来问孔子，他不会用苏格拉底这种态度来答复你。比如说问仁，孔子并不把仁当作一个概念来下定义，也不是从文字上来训诂，他是从你的生活来指点，当下从心之安不安来指点仁。这就不是用知识的态度来讲仁。所以孔子的话大家很容易了解，他的话具体、亲切、真切。比如说宰予说父母死了为什么要三年丧呢？三年的时间太久了，短一点行不行呢？一年行不行呢？这个行不行没有科学根据呀，也没有逻辑的证明的。这是良心的问题，你良心有没有感觉的问题。

[8] Yutang Lin, *My Country and My People* (London: Heinemann Education Books Ltd., 1977), p. 86. The *qingli* (情理) is also a context through which justice for the Chinese can be established.

their meanings may not align perfectly. Existentialism, which stands in contrast to essentialism,[9] bears some resemblance to the Chinese mode of thought. In light of the definition of existentialism,

> (1) Existence is always particular and individual – always my existence, your existence, and his existence; (2) Existence is primarily the problem of existence (i.e., of its mode of being); it is, therefore, also the investigation of the meaning of being; (3) This investigation is continually faced with diverse possibilities, from among which the existent (i.e., the human individual) must make a selection, to which he must then commit himself; and (4) Because these possibilities are constituted by the individual's relationships with things and with other humans, existence is always a being-in-the-world – i.e., in a concrete and historically determinate situation that limits or conditions choice. Humans are therefore called Dasein ('being there') because they are defined by the fact that they exist, or are in the world and inhabit it.[10]

In Chinese society, a prevailing mindset akin to existentialism can be observed. Conversely, essentialism, more in line with the thought patterns of continental legal traditions, particularly in European continental law, seeks to define the intrinsic nature of law and establish a uniform framework. Under this paradigm, law is applied through abstract logical reasoning. Understanding these distinctions helps contextualise the praise bestowed upon 'a judge, an artist who combines emotions, common sense with law' in the *People's Court Daily*, the official newspaper of the Supreme People's Court of China.[11] In this narrative, an adjudicator who can intertwine emotions and common sense with legal proceedings emerges as an exemplar for Chinese judges, signalling a departure from the Western judicial ethos where adherence to the letter of the law holds greater significance. As Yutang Lin summarised in this regard:

> Chinese logic is highly personal, like women's logic. A woman would not introduce to a professor of an operation for appendicitis in New York by that

[9] 'The essentialist perspective advocates that individuals in categories such as class, ethnicity, gender or sex share an intrinsic quality that is verifiable through empirical methods (whether currently known or unknown). Furthermore, essentialism focuses on what individuals are, not who they are, and individuals are viewed as inherently a certain way and not developing through dynamic social processes. Essentialism is contrasted to social constructionism. Essentialism contends agency is limited'. See Essentialism, https://sociologydictionary.org/essentialism/ (last accessed 28 February 2022).

[10] 'Existentialism', *Stanford Encyclopedia of Philosophy*, https://plato.stanford.edu/entries/existentialism (last accessed 18 March 2020).

[11] Rong Shen, 'Wei Changping: an artist who combines emotions, ethics with law', *The News of People's Court* (13 May 2010) [沈荣："巍长鹏：情理法相容的'执行艺术家'"，载《人民法院报》2010年5月13日].

> lovable old Doctor Cabot you should look ichthyology as a professor of ichthyology but as the brother-in-law of Colonel Harrison who died in India while she was undergoing this handsome forehead. In the same way, a Chinese judge cannot think of law as an abstract entity, but as a flexible quantity as it should be personally applied to Colonel Huang or Major Li. Accordingly, any law which is not personal enough to respond to the personality of Colonel Huang or Major Li is inhuman and therefore no law at all.[12]

In Chinese culture, the inclination and customary approach towards understanding phenomena in a concrete, contextual and pragmatic manner, as opposed to in an abstract, logical and conceptual way, are not confined to philosophical discourse but extend to everyday life. Elizabeth Perry's analysis of grassroots social protests and riots illustrates this point. She observed that for the Chinese people, the concept of rights is not merely an abstract notion derived from discourses on natural entitlements shielding individuals from state encroachment. Instead, it is intricately linked to tangible, real-world demands. Perry quoted the protesting activists' words saying, 'We're seeking wages and welfare, not power (quan) or politics'.[13] Perry noted that

> There is no doubt that the terms 'rights' (quanli) and 'citizen' (gongmin) suffuse both official and popular discourse in contemporary China. But workers who demand that as 'citizens' they have a 'right' to eat would seem to be following more in the moral economy footsteps of Mencius and Mao than in the liberal tradition of Locke or Jefferson.[14]

Therefore, when Chinese people encounter disputes, they are

> . . .oriented towards mediation and compromise, towards recognizing the extent to which another person's emotions and dignity are involved in his or her claim (rather than towards the abstract question of the justice of his or her claims) is likely to avoid any clear, uncompromising to depersonalize claims in order to emphasize the question at issue. Confucian tradition personalizes all claims, seeing them in the context of social human relationships. It thus rejects the notion that a sharp legal distinction, or a formal legal pronouncement, can alone resolve a dispute between parties by reestablishing harmony and mutual respect. Confucian tradition treats justice above all as a form of fireside equity.[15]

[12] Lin, *My Country and My People*, pp. 76–77.

[13] Elizabeth J. Perry, 'Chinese conceptions of "rights": from Mencius to Mao – and now' (2008) 6 *Perspectives on Politics* 37, 47.

[14] Perry, 'Chinese conceptions of "rights"', 37, 45.

[15] Poh-Ling Tan, *Asian Legal Systems: Law, Society and Pluralism in East Asia* (Sydney: Butterworths, 1997), p. 16.

2.2 The Social Context and Chinese Mindset

In real-life situations, *guanxi* serves as a quintessential representation of the Chinese way of thinking, embodying existentialist characteristics. It provides Chinese individuals a framework that facilitates the integration of emotions, rationality (common sense) and legal considerations in making decisions. This tendency is evident even in modernised cities like Shanghai where the instinctive reaction of most Chinese when encountering a problem is to leverage *guanxi* – seeking assistance from someone they know – rather than strictly adhering to rules or relying on institutional mechanisms.

The conscious cultivation of interpersonal relationships characteristic of *guanxi* can find its roots in the living conditions of traditional Chinese agricultural society. Originating from an agricultural civilisation, China historically operated around small village units, wherein intimate and continuous interactions among villagers were essential for both daily life and production. Proximity in living spaces fostered deep familiarity among villagers, and their collaboration was indispensable for a successful production outcomes. This situation still exists today. During the author's fieldwork in a county court in southwest grassroots China, a judge lamented the difficulty of adjudicating certain cases due to personal acquaintance with both the plaintiff and the defendant. This challenge stemmed not from intentional procedural violations by the judge[16] but rather from the prevalent lack of social mobility in small county towns where close social connections and strong networks are the norm. Such structural constraints pose formidable challenges for judges and are difficult to entirely overcome.[17] Similarly, in urban contexts, a 2018 report

[16] According to Article 47 of the Civil Procedural Law (1991, amended in 2023): 'Under any of the following circumstances, a judge shall voluntarily disqualify himself or herself, and a party shall be entitled to request disqualification of such a judge verbally or in writing: (1) The judge is a party to a case or is a close relative of a party to a case or a litigation representative thereof. (2) The judge is an interested party to a case. (3) The judge has any other relationship with a party to a case or a litigation representative thereof, which may affect the impartial trial of the case. Where a judge accepts any treat or gift from a party to a case or a litigation representative thereof or meets with a party to a case in violation of legal provisions, a party shall be entitled to require disqualification of such a judge. A judge who commits any conduct in the preceding paragraph shall be subject to legal liability in accordance with law. The provisions of the preceding three paragraphs shall also apply to court clerks, interpreters, identification or evaluation experts, and surveyors'.

[17] Hao Xiong, 'The feasibility of court mediation in the grassroots society of southwest China: a case study from Yunnan' (2014) 44 *Hong Kong Law Journal* 277, 298–299.

from China Europe International Business School revealed that 71 per cent of senior managers acknowledged the importance of maintaining favourable relationships with the Chinese government. Additionally, 53 per cent of foreign companies admitted to allocating more resources to nurturing *guanxi* in China than in their home countries.[18]

Such a social environment also shapes the Chinese preference for mediation. In this context, Xiaotong Fei explained how the social context and structure in the Chinese traditional society, which consists of familiar things and acquaintances, influence people's mindsets. Fei noted:

> Knowledge acquired from familiarity is specific and is not deduced from abstract general principles. People who grow up in a familiar environment do not need such principles. They only need to know the specific relationship between means and ends within the scope of their activities. They do not seek universal truths. When I read the Analects, I noticed that Confucius gave different definitions of filial piety (xiao) to different people. I realized then the special character of rural society. What is filial piety? Confucius did not give an abstract explanation but gave different answers to different students by describing concrete behavioral examples. Finally, he concluded that filial piety is simply a peaceful mind. Sons and daughters should become thoroughly familiar with their parent's personalities in the course of daily contact, and they should try to please them in order to achieve peace of mind. The basic methods of human interaction in rural society rest on familiarity and on maintaining a peaceful mind.[19]

Similarly, Kwang-Kuo Hwang also believes the social environment and lifestyle of traditional village constructed Chinese people's reference to harmony and dependence on *guanxi*:

> such a value system was gradually formed and sustained by the agricultural ecology of traditional Chinese society which was characterized by a high population density with relatively low social mobility. Bound to their residing area, the agricultural way of production enabled most Chinese families to obtain limited resources. In order to distribute resources among members of a group, it was necessary to emphasize the value of harmony.[20]

Both the familiar *guanxi* and the value of harmony are not abstract philosophical concepts; they are very vivid and concrete processes and

[18] Report from China Europe International Business School (2018), www.ceibs.edu/pdf/survey/CEIBS_Doing_Business_in_China_Survey_2018_en.pdf (last accessed 21 February 2020).

[19] Xiaotong Fei, *From the Soil: The Foundations of Chinese Society*, Gary G. Hamilton and Zheng Wang (eds.) (Berkeley, CA: University of California Press, 1992), pp. 43–44.

[20] Kwang-Kuo Hwang, 'Guanxi and Mientze', 17, 22.

arise out of interpersonal interactions. This social mindset is useful for understanding the popularity of mediation in China. As opposed to litigation, mediation leads to no clear winner or loser, and the process of dispute resolution does not rely on abstract rules. Instead, it is realised through real and concrete interactions between people. In the context of litigation, the prevailing notion is that the 'winner' of a lawsuit embodies righteousness and justice. However, the triumph of one party often comes at the expense of another, resulting in strained interpersonal relations and diminished social harmony. This highlights the reality that

> the processing of the dispute by the court is unlikely to result in a genuine resolution of it; that is, a solution acceptable to both parties. The dichotomous right/wrong judicial solution is likely to appear as an imposed two-against-one solution which may make continuing relations between the disputants difficult or impossible.[21]

2.3 Political Context and Chinese Mindset

The third aspect of Chinese people's preference for mediation is related to the political structure of its traditional society: The Emperor's authority does not extend to the county level, in Chinese '皇权不下县, *huangquan buxiaxian*'. This expression illustrates the historical administrative setup of China, highlighting the central imperial government's restricted direct sway over local counties. In Chinese traditional society, 'the governance of an emperor historically was a politically cultural one, or to some extent, symbolic. . .pre-modern China was ruled by power-sharing between the king and the gentry class.'[22] In traditional China, the nation was divided into provinces, prefectures and counties, each with its own cadre of officials tasked with governance. At the county level, local magistrates and officials wielded substantial power and autonomy, often making independent decisions in accordance with local circumstances and requirements. Although the emperor and the government at the capital maintained ultimate authority over the entire empire, their direct influence and presence were generally not deeply felt at the grassroots county level. As a result, the governance at the basic level was highly

[21] Roger Cotterrell, *The Sociology of Law: An Introduction* (London: Butterworths, 2nd ed., 1992), p. 211.

[22] Suli Zhu, '"Federalism" in contemporary China – a reflection on the allocation of power between central and local government' (2003) 7 *Singapore Journal of International & Comparative Law* 1, 3.

localised. The dispute resolution process would cater to the parties' specific needs and situational conditions. Therefore, in the local society, as a Western missionary noted in 1899:

> the management of the village is in the hands of the people themselves . . . Every Chinese village is a little principality by itself . . . the government of China, while in theory more or less despotic, places no practical restrictions upon the right of free assemblage by the people for the consideration of their affairs.[23]

At that time, due to the inability of central control to directly reach the grassroots at the local level, the resources of local governance stemmed not only from the law (*fa*, 法) but also from moral order, ritual (*li*, 礼) and folk customs (*su*, 俗). Chinese folk customs are highly localised and quite diverse as a result of the huge size of the country. As the old Chinese proverb said, 'Ten miles have different customs, and a hundred miles have different habits' (*shili butongfeng, baili butongsu*, 十里不同风，百里不同俗). This expression underscores the significant variation in customs and habits across short distances in China. As a vast nation with a deep history and diverse geography, China encompasses numerous ethnic groups, languages, dialects and regional cultures. Consequently, customs, traditions and habits can exhibit substantial differences when comparing one region to another. The combination of legal and extra-legal elements when governing the local society makes the operation of a unified legal system difficult. In this case, the pragmatic and localised mediation system can release the tension between the application of uniform law enacted by the central government and the concrete local situations. However, it also led to diverse models of local governance across regions.

Following the establishment of the People's Republic of China, the Communist Party significantly expanded its influence across all facets of society by establishing grassroots Party organisations in every community and village throughout the country. This effective state-building endeavour enabled the extension of social control and service provision into rural areas through the establishment of administrative structures and infrastructure at the grassroots level. This gradual realisation of the rule by law at a tangible level paved the way for what Su Li termed as 'sending the law to the countryside' (in Chinese, '送法下乡, *songfa*

[23] Arthur H. Smith, *Village Life in China* (Boston: Little, Brown, 1970, reprint with Myron Cohen's Introduction), pp. 170–172.

xiaxiang'), ensuring the dissemination of Party and government policies to even the most remote corners of the nation.[24] These strategies aimed to deepen the state's control over rural areas by delivering public goods and expanding Beijing's political influence. Operating from a top-down approach, this strategy facilitated the penetration of state power from urban centres into the countryside.[25]

Although the unification of the legal system in contemporary China has dramatically improved, it is still a challenge to ensure the uniform application of the law, on the one hand, and accommodate the quite diverse social conditions, on the other, in such a geographically large country with multiple ethnic groups and unbalanced regional development levels. Even in contemporary China, Deng Xiaoping's pragmatism-oriented reform in the 1980s and 1990s further carried Chinese regional divergence but did not eliminate it. As the result of Deng's policy regarding 'let some people get rich first',

> Income disparity in terms of per capita GDP between China's coastal and interior provinces has been on the rise since the early 1980s when China's urban and industrial reform started and has accelerated since the early 1990s when larger scale and more intensive reforms began to take place after Deng Xiaoping's southern China tour in 1992.[26]

Although political unity has been strengthened, the level of social and economic development is still not uniform. Therefore, political control and expansion cannot completely eliminate the diversity of governance models at the various local levels. It's a mutually reinforcing cycle: China's social reality gives rise to its model of governance, and this model solidifies the regional differences as a response. To achieve effective local legal governance in such a huge country as China, there exists a system: 'in fact, most of China's regional development policies are based on three zones: east, central and west. A regional dimension has been a crucial component of China's development policies'.[27] This model avoids directly violating the established state laws, on the one hand, and permits

[24] Su Li, *Sending Law to the Countryside: A Study of Chinese Grassroots Judicial System* (Beijing: China University of Political Science and Law Press, 2000), p. 53 [苏力：《送法下乡：中国基层司法制度研究》（北京：中国政法大学出版社2000年版）].

[25] Su Li, *Sending Law to the Countryside*, p. 53 [苏力：《送法下乡：中国基层司法制度研究》（北京：中国政法大学出版社2000年版）].

[26] Su Li, *Sending Law to the Countryside*, p. 53 [苏力：《送法下乡：中国基层司法制度研究》（北京：中国政法大学出版社2000年版）].

[27] Minjia Chen and Yongnian Zheng, 'China's regional disparity and its policy response' (2008) 16(4) *China & World Economy* 16, 17.

a variation in practice, on the other hand. To quote Yongnian Zheng's term, China's governance model now is following 'de facto federalism'. It means that China adopted an institutionalised pattern in which:

> The activities of government are divided between the provinces and the center in such a way that each kind of government has some activities on which it makes final decisions; it is increasingly becoming difficult, if not impossible, for the national government to unilaterally impose its discretion on the provinces and alter the distribution of authority between governments; and the provinces have primary responsibility for the economy and, to some extent, politics within their jurisdictions.[28]

In this case, the mindset of 'putting a thing into a concrete context when analysing it' is the result of a series of political and structural factors. In a vast country with huge internal variations, governance that relies on highly abstract uniform rules is not easy. 'China is a very complex land where multiple realities are operating beneath a facade of a unitary nation-state...Variation across the province and even within the province is enormous.'[29] In this case, mediation, as a flexible and localised mechanism for dispute resolution, can strike a balance between national standardised regulations and varying regional social conditions by prioritising practicality over legality and emphasising the integration of reason and emotion. Thus, within the practical political structure of China, it becomes a more feasible institutional arrangement for resolving disputes.

Under the administration of Xi Jinping, such a tradition continues. Xi places special emphasis on developing Fengqiao experience (*fengqiao jingyan*, 枫桥经验) in social governance and dispute resolution area. Fengqiao experience is a grassroots social governance model created by the cadres and people of Fengqiao Town, Zhuji City, Zhejiang Province, in the early 1960s.[30] Fengqiao experience would emphasise the localisation of dispute resolution. It follows the principle of starting and relying on the masses, sticking to not letting the contradictions remain and resolving them on the spot, and realising the solution with less arrest

[28] Yongnian Zheng, 'Explaining the source of de facto federalism in reform China: intergovernmental decentralization, globalization, and central-local relations' (2006) 7 *Japanese Journal of Political Science* 101, 107.

[29] Tony Saich, *Governance and Politics of China* (New York: Palgrave Macmillan, 3rd ed, 2011), p. 9.

[30] Daoshun Ge, 'Society: justice, inclusiveness, safety and harmony' in Yingqiu Liu et al. (eds.), *The Chinese Dream and Zhejiang's Practice – General Report Volume* (Singapore: Springer, 2019), p. 166.

and good public security,[31] and it requires that 'small matters are handled within villages, large matters are handled within the town, contradictions are not escalated to higher authorities and are resolved at the local level.'[32] Different from the judicial adjudication process, Fengqiao experience pays more attention to the contextual characteristics of dispute resolution and is guided by people's emotions. As Xi Jinping pointed out, 'it was necessary to foster a new outlook on stability and stressed that safeguarding social harmony and stability was also the achievement of the officials and that being peaceful and harmonious was essential to scientific development.'[33]

The strategy of localising dispute resolution has also been implemented within the judicial sphere. Chinese local courts have been explicitly or implicitly granted authority to devise specific schemes for handling disputes and have even been permitted to experiment with new rules and procedures ahead of national law or Supreme People's Court's (SPC) interpretation in some cases.[34] In other words, employing different local judicial practices, which are not just limited to a certain area, is an ongoing custom as a strategy to achieve better governance in such a large and diverse country.[35] Consequently, the model of 'adaptation to local conditions', wherein different governance schemes are permissible in various regions, becomes both feasible and legitimised within the court system.

The design of the dispute resolution system, particularly within the ADR domain, is deeply influenced by this model. Considering the economic disparities, cultural variations and contextual nuances inherent in dispute resolution, diverse institutional designs will persist under reforms, experimentation or adjustments tailored to local conditions. This pragmatic, flexible and context-sensitive institutional arrangement concerning dispute resolution offers parties a more adaptable and

[31] Liqun Wei (ed.), *General Theory of Social Governance in China* (Singapore: Springer, 2019), p. 312.

[32] Ge, 'Society: justice, inclusiveness', p. 166.

[33] Youxing Lang, 'Primary-level local governance' in Guangjin Chen and Yang Jianhua (eds.), *Chinese Dream of Practice in Zhejiang – Society* (Singapore: Springer, 2019), p. 166.

[34] Benjamin L. Liebman, 'A return to populist legality? Historical legacies and legal reform' in Sebastian Heilmann and Elizabeth J. Perry (eds.), *Mao's Invisible Hand: The Political Foundations of Adaptive Governance in China* (Cambridge, MA: Harvard University Press, 2011), p. 174. This book will provide more details in later chapters in this regard.

[35] As mentioned by the author in Chapter 1, the reforms and innovations in Shanghai's commercial mediation system serve as an embodiment of these localised institutional experiments.

localised dispute resolution service, while also reinforcing the Chinese people's inclination towards contextually resolving disputes. This governance model is a natural consequence of the significant differences within the country. While this model enhances contextual flexibility in dispute resolution, it does pose a challenge to the unity of the rule of law. Nevertheless, the local and contextual characteristics of the Chinese dispute resolution system, particularly in the realm of ADR, will continue to evolve as the underlying reasons for this phenomenon are structural rather than personal or temporary.

2.4 Stability in Chinese Context

These contextual factors, encompassing cultural, social and political perspectives, aid in understanding the popularity and widespread use of mediation in China. However, with the progress of urbanisation in China, the influence of acquaintance society is indeed waning. Consequently, the number of disputes resolved through litigation, a confrontational method of dispute resolution, is increasing annually in Chinese society. In essence, times are changing and evolving, underscoring the importance of staying abreast of developments and, through the use of more specific data rather than abstract concepts, comprehending the cultural, social and political context inherent in China's mediation practices.

When quantitatively describing, comparing and measuring the cultures of different countries, the Dutch psychologist Geert Hofstede has made important contributions by proposing cultural dimensions theory. According to Hofstede, culture refers to 'the common mental process of people in an environment. Culture is not an individual characteristic, but includes the characteristics of a group of people created by the same education and life experience'.[36] Hofstede and his collaborators divided six dimensions to quantitatively analyse the cultures of different countries, providing cultural studies a contemporary dimension and scientific significance. These six dimensions are: (a) power distance (refers to the

[36] Geert Hofstede, 'Motivation, leadership, and organization: do American theories apply abroad?' in Steve Mortensen (ed.), *Cross-Cultural Communication: An Eastern Perspective*, Guan Shijie and Hu Xing (trans.) (Beijing: China Social Sciences Press, 1999), p. 2 [[荷]海尔特·霍夫斯泰德："美国的动机、 领导和组织的管理理论适用于国外吗？"，载[美]史蒂夫·莫滕森编，《跨文化传播学：东方的视角》，关世杰、胡兴译，北京：中国社会科学出版社1999年版].

degree of acceptance of hierarchy; lower scores represent higher acceptance of hierarchy and stronger recognition of the role of social hierarchy playing in social management and power operation); (b) individualism and collectivism; (c) masculinity and femininity (not referring to the biological sex; masculinity represents tenacity, self-confidence and the pursuit of achievement, while femininity represents humility, gentleness, care for life and pursuit of happiness); (d) attitude towards uncertainty; (e) long-term orientation; and (f) indulgence.[37] Through these six important dimensions, Hofstede turned the abstract and intangible culture into mindsets and behavioural preferences, making 'human' the real characteristic of culture.

As regards Hofstede's dimension of power distance, Chinese people accept the hierarchical order of bureaucracy and individuals are more easily influenced by authority; in the dimension of individualism and collectivism, China is a country with a very strong collectivism, and Chinese people are more willing to establish a sense of belonging and a cognitive framework from the perspective of 'us', that is, the perspective of group; in the dimension of masculinity, Chinese people pursue the sense of accomplishment more than happiness and comfort, working relentlessly in exchange for more income rather than more leisure; in the dimension of avoiding uncertainty, Chinese people believe that rules can be flexible and believe in pragmatism in life; in the dimension of long-term orientation, Chinese people believe that the truth depends on the certain historical background and needs to be discussed accordingly, and they are willing to make plans and even sacrifice for the future in order to better achieve the goal; and in the dimension of indulgence, China's society restrains desires, and individual behaviour is subject to evident social discipline.[38] If we look at the above dimensions on an international scale, then the contextual characteristics of Chinese culture will be more evident. From the data in Figure 2.1, it is easy to find that compared with Brazil, Germany and the United States, China has obvious differences in five dimensions, which means Chinese people have the highest acceptance of authority, the strongest collectivism, flexibility and inclination to long-term value. Furthermore, Chinese people are most easily influenced by social discipline and thus are self-restrained.

[37] See Jean-Pierre Cohen and Marc Jacobs, *Negotiate Like a Local*, Wang Kaihua (trans.) (Shanghai: Fudan University Press, 2019), p. 122 [[比]让-皮埃尔·科恩、[比]马克·雅各布斯：《跨国谈判本土化战略》，王凯华译，上海：复旦大学出版社2019年版].

[38] See 'China, Hofstede Insights', www.hofstede-insights.com/country/china/ (last accessed 8 November 2021).

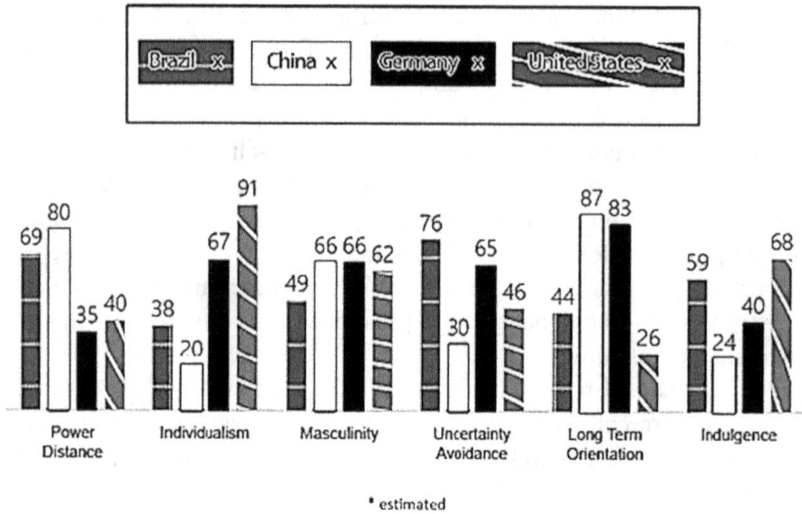

Figure 2.1 A comparison of Hofstede's cultural dimensions in Brazil, China, Germany and the United States.[39]

As culture is divided into six dimensions within Hofstede's theoretical framework, a single definition does not encompass the full contextual characteristics of contemporary Chinese culture. However, based on the above analysis, we can conclude that the social and cultural context of contemporary China has a clear collectivistic preference for 'trust in authority' and 'dependence on society'.

Admittedly, there might be one critical question on the above conclusion: As the value of human independence and individualism have grown significantly in China since the reform and opening-up, will the 'trust in authority' and 'dependence on society' be undermined? The author believes that it does not mean China's fundamental cultural structure has undergone an essential change towards individualism despite China witnessing a growing individual value and independence, which, in turn, enriches Chinese culture. On one side, based on Hofstede's data analysis, culture, as an ultra-stable structure, evolves and changes very slowly and will maintain a high stability for quite a long period of time. On the other side, the social surveys in China over the recent years have further

[39] 'Country Comparison, Hofstede Insights', www.hofstede-insights.com/country-comparison/brazil, China, Germany, the usa/ (last accessed 21 June 2021). The original picture is a colour version.

confirmed the judgement on cultural stability. For example, in the 'Interpersonal Values' section of the Survey on Contemporary Chinese Social Values launched by the Chinese Academy of Social Sciences in 2013, 42 per cent of interviewees believed that 'the relationship between people is interdependent, and other people are essential to my own success', which is the response by the largest proportion of participants when answering the question 'how is the relationship between people in society'.[40] Even if we focus on the younger generation in contemporary China, the interviewees born in the 1980s or 1990s recognise the overall, long-term and community-based core values (such as social stability and national prosperity) significantly more than the core values of individualism and independence (such as participation in decision making, freedom of speech). Thus, there is an argument that the younger Chinese people hold a very different worldview than the young in Western countries. The influence of tradition on the Chinese mindset does not disappear against the backdrop of growing individualism. The country has not seen a large-scale postmodern contempt or denial of tradition and authority that once appeared in the West but has preserved cultural stability.[41]

Another, more direct study by the author also confirms the stability of the Chinese context in the area of dispute resolution. Based on the data analysis of 1,668 samples randomly selected from 37,908 middle-class respondents with diverse social characteristics, the author explores the conflict-handling styles of the Chinese middle class and the influencing factors by using the Thomas–Kilmann Instrument[42] and Statistic

40 Weiping Sun (ed.), *Research Report on Social Values in Contemporary China* (Beijing: China Social Sciences Press, 2013), pp. 190–191 [孙伟平主编：《当代中国社会价值观调研报告》，北京：中国社会科学出版社2013年版].

41 See Leiping Bao, et al., *Deep Modernization: Value Conflict and Identity of 'Post-80s' and 'Post-90s' Groups* (Shanghai: Shanghai Academy of Social Sciences Press, 2020), p. 9 [包蕾萍、程福财等：《深度现代化："80后""90后"群体的价值冲突与认同》，上海：上海社会科学学院出版社2020年版].

42 The Thomas-Kilmann Instrument (TKI) is a widely used assessment tool and framework designed to measure an individual's preferred conflict-handling style. Developed by Kenneth W. Thomas and Ralph H. Kilmann in the early 1970s, this instrument was commonly used in different areas as a tool for conflict management and assessment to help people measure conflicting behaviour models and tendencies when engaged in conflict. According to TKI, the five conflict-handling approaches are classified by two underlying dimensions, namely, assertiveness and cooperativeness. High concerns for self and others are linked to competing, collaborating, compromising, avoiding and accommodating conflict-handling styles. In 1977, Thomas collaborated with Kilmann in the completion of a more valid and effective instrument with the objective of assessing conflict-handling styles. See Ralph H. Kilmann and Kenneth W. Thomas, 'Developing a

Table 2.1 *Conflict-handling styles of respondents*

	Styles	Numbers	Percentage (%)	Ranking
Conflict-handling styles	A. Competing	289	17.326	4
	B. Collaborating	315	18.885	3
	C. Compromising	452	27.098	2
	D. Avoiding	455	27.278	1
	E. Accommodating	157	9.412	5
Total		1,668	100.0	

Package for Social Science. The TKI survey was adopted from Shell's influential book entitled *Bargaining for Advantage: Negotiations, Strategy for Reasonable People.*[43] The results reveal that the mainstream conflict-handling styles of the Chinese middle class remain on the lines of Confucianism and collectivism culture. At 27.28 per cent, the results showed that the avoiding tendency was the most preferred conflict-handling style. If compromising (27.10 per cent) and accommodating (9.41 per cent) were also included, the relatively harmonious or low-profiled conflict-handling styles together would account for a majority of 63.79 per cent. Table 2.1 presents the results of the TKI survey.

The Shells' calculation method of the TKI only uses the highest number to represent the conflict-handling style of respondents, excluding all other numbers for other selections.[44] In order to verify the accuracy of the results and control accidental mistakes of respondents, the author uses another method to collect statistical data. The author recounted the

forced-choice measure of conflict-handling behavior: the "Mode" instrument"' (1977) 37 (2) *Educational and Psychological Measurement* 309, 309–325; Kenneth W. Thomas, 'Conflict and conflict management: reflections and update' (1992) 13(3) *Journal of Organizational Behavior* 265, 265–274.

43 Richard G. Shell, *Bargaining for Advantage: Negotiation Strategies for Reasonable People* (New York: Penguin Books, 2nd ed., 2006), pp. 238–240.

44 Shell's survey comprised 30 double-choice questions. The respondents were instructed to select one option that they felt comparatively acceptable. For example, respondents were presented with two choices, namely 'E. I work to preserve the relationship with my counterpart' and 'B. I tried to identify the underlying issues' (Shell, *Bargaining for Advantage*). One of the two scenarios (E or B) corresponds to one of the five conflict styles (A: competing; B: collaborating; C: compromising; D: avoiding; and E: accommodating). After completing the 30 questions, Shell's calculation method would sum the number of different conflict styles, where the highest number(s) indicated the tendencies of the conflict styles of the respondents.

Table 2.2 *Rate of conflict-handling styles among all responses*

Conflict-handling styles	Cumulative number of choices	Percentage (%)	Ranking
A. Competing	8,050	16.087	5
B. Collaborating	10,038	20.060	3
C. Compromising	11,669	23.319	1
D. Avoiding	11,142	22.266	2
E. Accommodating	9,141	18.267	4

different options for conflict style in all the questions. The result indicated that, in this case, the compromising and the avoiding styles remained at the first and second ranks, whereas the competing style ranked last. Table 2.2 displays the result. Therefore, the study concluded that the avoiding and compromising styles were the mainstream conflict-handling styles using different statistical methods.

This finding aligns with the existing studies indicating that Chinese individuals typically employ noncompetitive methods in response to conflict.[45] Through various statistical methods, the author confirmed that avoidance and compromise are the primary conflict-resolution approaches among middle-class samples. Thus, Chinese culture continues to exert a stable influence on people's conflict-handling styles. The collective nature of Chinese culture fosters a strong identification with larger social groups beyond immediate family units.[46] Consequently, 'the sense of communitarism takes precedence over the sense of individual interests. As a consequence, such values as relationships and harmony are particularly highly valued.'[47] This preference for avoidance and compromise resonates with the principles of Confucianism and collectivism.

The cultural, social and political context can continuously influence the institutional design of Chinese mediation. In the practice of mediation, the disputing parties in China are often regarded as embedded in a network of social relations rather than highly isolated and atomised individuals. From this perspective, resolving disputes is not only simply

45 See Kwok Leung, 'Some determinants of conflict avoidance' (1988) 10(1) *Journal of Cross-Cultural Psychology* 125, 125–133.

46 Huang Youqin, 'Collectivism, political control and gating in Chinese cities' (2006) 27(6) *Urban Geography* 507, 507–525.

47 John H. Dunning and Changsu Kim, 'The cultural roots of guanxi: an exploratory study' (2007) 30(2) *World Economy* 329, 329–341.

negotiating at the table but also involving a broader community that connects with the parties.[48] Based on such philosophy, unlike the Western counterpart which cultivates professional mediators, China's mediation still relies on local authority figures, such as officials of CPC or the Communist Youth League, police, bureaucrats and labour union activists, rather than professionals.[49] These authority figures' engagement in the mediation embodies the trust in authority in China's dispute resolution and consequently brings the criticising-and-educating nature into the mediation process. Some more detailed empirical studies on the mediation process have further confirmed the stability and persistence of this social and cultural influence at the micro level of ADR. According to James A. Wall Jr and Michael Blum, in contemporary China, 'educating' is the most common strategy adopted by people's mediators, 0.55 times average per case. In contrast, 'mediator assist' is used only 0.21 times per case.[50] The mediators will teach the parties what to do and what they should do, and their work has the meaning of social education in spite of the personal settlement of disputes. The mediator's authoritative intervention in the dispute resolution preserves the trust in authority, a contextual feature of contemporary China's dispute resolution, in each specific and individual dispute resolution. In the cultural, social and political context of contemporary China, mediation transcends being merely a personal choice of behaviour or a tool for consensus building. Rather, it emerges as a process necessitating the mediator's intervention and education to preserve interpersonal relationships and clarify behavioural significance. This elevates mediation to a social role beyond its conventional function of simply 'smoothing differences between individuals'.

2.5 The Tension between Mediation with Chinese Characteristics and Legal Rationalism

If it is the case that in China, mediation would not only consider the law and logic but also the non-legal aspect of the case in the concrete context,

48 Catherine H. Tinsley, 'Culture and conflict: enlarging our dispute resolution framework' in Michele J. Gelfand and Jeanne M. Brett (eds.), *The Handbook of Negotiation and Culture* (Stanford, CA: Stanford University Press, 2004), pp. 199–200.

49 Xin Xu (ed.), *Mediation: China and the World* (Beijing: China University of Political Science and Law Press, 2013), pp. 4–5 [徐昕主编：《调解：中国与世界》，北京：中国政法大学出版社2013年版].

50 James A. Wall, Jr. and Michael Blum, 'Community mediation in the People's Republic of China' (1991) 35(1) *Journal of Conflict Resolution* 3, 14.

this mindset will generate tensions between Chinese mediation ways and the legal rationalism or rule of law. Although China has a long history of its own legal tradition and conception of law, the European continental law and the adjudication system began to be adopted in the late nineteenth century.[51] As is well known, the modern Western civil law tradition and system are established on the basis of Western ontological foundation, which shapes Western people's values, ideas and modes of thinking. Law, in this regard, has strong generalising and centralising tendencies.[52] In other words, 'if you examine the literature on jurisprudence you will find that legal institutions are studied for the most part in more or less complete abstraction from the rest of the social system of which they are a part.'[53] The tendency to think at a high level of generalisation and abstraction is even more obvious and dominant in legal scholarship, especially in the civil law tradition.[54] For example, in the civil law jurisdictions,

> The student starts his study with codes and textbooks. He learns about the Justinian codifications and their influence on his present-day legal system. He is taught general principles and how to think in abstractions. It becomes part of his being to appreciate classification and co-ordination of subject matter, and to take for granted a comprehensiveness of the law as systematic and a whole.[55]

Based on the civil law tradition, norms and logic can form a self-consistent system that is separate from the concrete context. As Max Weber argued,

> Present-day legal science, at least in those forms which have achieved the highest measure of methodological and logical rationality, i.e., those

[51] Jianfu Chen, *From Administrative Authorization to Private Law: A Comparative Perspective of the Developing Civil Law in the People's Republic of China* (Netherlands: Martinus Nijhoff Publishers, 1995), p. 1. See also Zhong Xin Fan and Feng Ye, 'The legal modernization of China and the influence from civil law system' (2003) 1 *Journal of Henan Administrative Institution of Politics and Law* 39 [范忠信，叶峰："中国法律近现代化与大陆法系的影响"，《河南省政法管理干部学院学报》，2003年第1期].

[52] Peter H. Schuck, *Diversity in America: Keeping Government at a Safe Distance* (Cambridge, MA: The Belknap Press of Harvard University Press, 2003), p. 35.

[53] A. R. Radcliffe Brown, 'On social structure' in Henrietta L. Moore and Todd Sanders (eds.), *Anthropology in Theory: Issues in Epistemology* (Malden, MA: Blackwell, 2006), p. 126.

[54] Peter de Cruz, *Comparative Law in a Changing World* (London: Cavendish, 2nd ed., 1999), p. 38.

[55] Joseph Dainow, 'The civil law and common law: some points of comparison' (1966–1967) 15 *American Journal of Comparative Law* 419, 429.

> which have been produced through the legal science of the Pandectists' Civil Law, proceeds from the following five postulates: viz, first, that every concrete legal decision by the *'application' of an abstract legal proposition* to a concrete 'fact situation'; second, that it must be possible in every concrete case to derive the decision *from abstract legal propositions by means of legal logic*; third, that the law must actually or virtually constitute a *'gapless' system*; fourth, that whatever cannot be 'construed' *rationally* in legal terms is also legally irrelevant; and fifth, that every social action of human beings must always be visualized as either an 'application' or 'execution' of legal propositions, or as an 'infringement' thereof, since the 'gaplessness' of the legal system must result in a gapless 'legal ordering' of all social conduct.[56]

According to Weber, 'the rational structure of law and administration has undoubtedly been among the most central elements of this social order',[57] which means the ideal type, modern law should be formal, value free and impersonal; it is abstract and general at least in the civil law context.[58] As a transplanted civil law country, China inherited the legal system from the continent of Europe, which is centred on legislation, codification and doctrine, on a very high level of abstraction.[59] It inevitably leads Chinese legal scholars and ordinary people to follow the civil law model, to think from general principle to general principle.[60] It is then believed that law is a self-content system in the pure reasoning domain, which can be generally applied to every corner of the jurisdiction with no need to concern about the local and situational differences and particularities.[61]

[56] Max Weber, *Economy and Society: An Outline of Interpretative Sociology*, Guenther Roth and Claus Wittich (eds.), Ephraim Fischoff et al. (trans.) (New York: Bedminster Press, 1968), pp. 657–658 (emphasis added).

[57] Max Weber, *The Protestant Ethic and the Spirit of Capitalism*, Stephen Kalberg (trans.) (London: Taylor & Francis, 2001), p. 159.

[58] Richard M. Coughlin, *Morality, Rationality and Efficiency: New Perspective on Socio-Economics* (Armonk, NY: M. E. Sharpe, 1991), p. 159.

[59] Joseph Dainow, 'The civil law and common law', 419, 428.

[60] Peter de Cruz, *Comparative Law in a Changing World*, p. 38.

[61] That is why anthropology can provide legal studies with significant inspiration and complement. Anthropology refused to think at the generalised, centralised and abstract lever. On the contrary, it has 'coped with the difference between stated norms and observed practice by absorbing both into ideal-real or multiple-norm models'; and is 'concerned with law as a reflection of a particular social order.' By using case study, anthropology can 'bring the minutiae of social interaction into focus and thereby reveal certain general processes in detail'. See Sally Falk Moore, "Law and anthropology" (1969) 6 *Biennial Review of Anthropology* 252, 283, 294.

In some respects, the civil law tradition runs counter to the principles of Confucianism and the Chinese way of thinking. Differentiated from the abstraction of legal theory, however, many disputants and even the judges, especially in rural areas, need to establish their cognitive judicial competence from a sensible and intuitive scenario rather than from one general principle to another. Chinese justice is more like art which concerns the concrete situation of the interaction between judges and parties, not a science mainly depending on normative reasoning.[62] Mediation in this case plays a very constructive role by transferring the abstract legal framework into a very concrete, situational, conversational mechanism. The disputing parties can express their emotions[63] and maximise the particularities in practice. For many Chinese legal practitioners, mediation is the embodiment of Chinese justice, which can be seen and intuited rather than indoctrinated.

[62] Lin, *My Country and My People*, pp. 76–77. Theoretically speaking, this is related to the discussion around cultural legitimacy. The cultural legitimacy theory argues that 'within a given cultural tradition, a certain human value or need is believed to be fundamental and is accorded or guaranteed to every human being, then that value has cultural legitimacy'. In this regard, 'The prime feature underlying cultural legitimacy is the authority and reverence derived from internal validity. A culturally legitimate norm or value is respected and observed by the members of the particular culture, presumably because it is assumed to bring satisfaction to those members' (see Abdullahi Ahmed An-Na'im, 'Problems of universal cultural legitimacy for human rights' in Abdullahi Ahmed An-Na'im and Francis M. Deng (eds.), *Human Rights in Africa: Cross-Cultural Perspectives* (Washington, D.C.: The Brookings Institution, 1990), pp. 333, 336. According to the cross-country research on mediation, it shows that 'mediators rely on techniques that traditionally have been employed and accepted in their society. Likewise, they rely on the power and prestige granted to them by their society'. (James A. Wall, Jr. and Ann Lynn, 'Mediation: a current review' (1993) 37(1) *The Journal of Conflict Resolution*, 169) Therefore, we can say that mediation works because it enjoys this kind of cultural legitimacy in China's context.

[63] Kimberlee K. Kovach, *Mediation in A Nutshell* (St. Paul, MN: Thomson/West, 2010), pp. 41–42.

3

History

Development of the Chinese Modern Dispute Resolution System

3.1 A Brief Introduction to the History Before the Reform and Opening-Up

The modernisation of China's dispute resolution system began in the late Qing dynasty at the start of the twentieth century. In traditional imperial China, the legal system emphasised substantive law over procedural law. On 11 March 1902, the Qing government issued a decree to revise laws and then further decrees for the establishment of a law revision institution, the appointment of a Minister for the Revision of Laws and other related matters. This series of decrees marked the commencement of legal revision activities. Shen Jiaben (沈家本) and Wu Tingfang (伍廷芳), two prominent Chinese legal scholars and reformers in the late nineteenth and early twentieth centuries, made efforts to separately enact criminal procedural and civil procedural laws. In their report to the emperor, they emphasised, after comparing with foreign legal systems, that according to the general trend of nations, there were two urgent areas in China that needed reform. Firstly, the introduction of a jury system, and secondly, the establishment of a legal profession. Thus, an initial attempt to draft procedural law blending Western criminal and civil procedure elements was started, including concepts like jury trials and lawyers from common law systems.[1] In addition to procedural law, the late Qing dynasty also introduced the Articles of Association for Trial Offices at all Levels (*geshenpantin shiban zhangcheng*, 《各级审判厅试办章程》) in 1907. This draft modernised the Chinese dispute resolution system by incorporating Western elements, such as the separation of civil and criminal

[1] Xiaoxin Ye, *Chinese Legal History* (Shanghai: Fudan University Press, 2015), p. 350 [叶孝信：《中国法制史（第二版）》，上海：复旦大学出版社2015年版].

procedures and the prosecutor system. These reforms significantly influenced the trial system in modern times.[2] These new laws were considered to incorporate Western legal institutions, deviating from China's traditional legal culture.[3] However, these laws could not be enforced due to the 1911 Revolution and the collapse of the Qing dynasty.

Since 1912, the Kuomintang administration incorporated legal institutions from countries following civil law traditions, collectively known as the 'Six Laws'. The term 'Six Laws' was derived from Japan, which had modelled its legal system on French law after the Meiji Reform. These laws included the constitution, civil law, civil procedural law, criminal law, criminal procedural law and administrative law. Notably, commercial code was considered an integral part of civil code due to the Kuomintang administration's 'civil and commercial integration' policy.

In 1935, a new civil procedural law was enacted, featuring two key aspects. Firstly, it introduced exclusive jurisdiction clauses for certain cases, such as real estate and bills. Secondly, it established a mediation system where the mediator could continue as the judge if mediation efforts failed.[4] This law also introduced a summary procedure to enhance dispute resolution efficiency and improved the preserving procedure, allowing parties to seek temporary execution (*jia zhixing*, 假执行), temporary disposition (*jia chufen*, 假处分) and temporary restraint (*jia gouya*, 假扣押). In this period, Kuomintang administration attempted to replicate the court system of Germany and Japan. It implemented a three-level and three-trial system, comprising local courts, provincial courts and the supreme court. Each court was further divided into segments to handle civil and criminal cases separately. However, due to financial constraints and policy fluctuations, this court system was not fully implemented. Before the end of the Anti-Japanese War, only a quarter of counties had established local courts, with many still following the tradition of county offices handling judicial authority.

The Communist Party of China (CPC) was founded in 1921 in Shanghai, with the goal of addressing social and political issues in a rapidly changing China. Inspired by Marxist and Leninist ideologies, the CPC aimed to

[2] Ye, *Chinese Legal History*, p. 350 [叶孝信：《中国法制史（第二版）》，上海：复旦大学出版社2015年版].

[3] Ye, *Chinese Legal History*, p. 350 [叶孝信：《中国法制史（第二版）》，上海：复旦大学出版社2015年版].

[4] Ye, *Chinese Legal History*, p. 391 [叶孝信：《中国法制史（第二版）》，上海：复旦大学出版社2015年版].

champion workers' rights and challenge imperialism. During the Chinese Civil War (1927–1949), the CPC established its own governance and legal systems, implementing land reforms and promoting social equality within the Liberated Areas (*jiefangqu*, 解放区), often in rural and remote parts of the country. The CPC believed that the Kuomintang law was only the protection of the landlord class, the bourgeoisie's tool, a weapon to suppress the people and a law that did not conform to the interests of the masses.[5] Therefore, the CPC abolished the Six Laws system and declared the abolition of all Kuomintang laws in these areas.[6] Instead, they based judicial work on new laws enacted by the people's government. Given the incomplete state of these laws, the judiciary relied on laws, orders, regulations and policies to guide legal procedures. Mediation thus played a significant role. As Jerome Alan Cohen noted, mediation was used to be a strategy creatively developed by the Communists in liberated areas to solve disputes and realise social mobilisation for political ends.[7] In the 1940s, the CPC in the Shan-Gan-Ning Border Region developed an innovative method for dispute resolution known as 'Ma Xiwu's adjudicating style' (*maxiwu shenpan fangshi*, 马锡武审判方式). This dispute-resolution style is named after Ma Xiwu, a renowned Chinese judge known for his commitment to fairness and justice in the legal system. This kind of style was centred on the people and carried out circuit trials to make it more accessible for the masses. Ma Xiwu went deep into the countryside to investigate and relied on the masses to correct mistakes and solve difficult cases. He respected the opinions of the masses during the trial, and at the same time, he also led the masses to receive education through trial activities.[8] Such style was an effective mechanism to resolve the disputes happening in the liberated area compared to the establishment of formal and institutionalised dispute resolution procedures. Ma Xiwu's adjudicating style is different from judicial professionalism. According to Cong Xiaoping, it represented an effort by the revolutionary government to connect indigenous culture with the contemporary legal

[5] Yanlong Han and Zhaoru Chang, *Selection of Legal Documents in the Base Areas During the Period of China's New-Democratic Revolution* (Beijing: China Social Sciences Press, 1984), pp. 85–87 [韩延龙，常兆儒：《中国新民主主义革命时期根据地法制文献选编》，北京：中国社会科学出版社1984年版].

[6] Han and Chang, *Selection of Legal Documents*, pp. 85–87 [韩延龙，常兆儒：《中国新民主主义革命时期根据地法制文献选编》，北京：中国社会科学出版社1984年版].

[7] Jerome Alan Cohen, 'Chinese mediation on the eve of modernization' (1966) 54(3) *California Law Review* 1201, 1204–1205.

[8] Ye, *Chinese Legal History*, p. 437 [叶孝信：《中国法制史（第二版）》，上海：复旦大学出版社2015年版].

framework in order to avoid conflicts arising from rigid legal formalities. Ma's way established methods for involving the masses in shaping a modern judiciary and redefined the evolving relationship between the state and society.[9] Therefore, it has exerted a profound influence on China's dispute resolution policy in the future and even become a symbol of China's judicial mass line.

The People's Republic of China was founded in 1949. China became a socialist country. Because law, according to classical Marxist theory, is a tool for the ruling class to suppress the working class, the Six Laws of the Kuomintang were abolished, and a new legal system with socialist characteristics was established in 1951. The polity regime shifted to 'people's democratic dictatorship'. Unique trial institutions like ad hoc People's Tribunals and Revolutionary Courts were established, with legal advisers instead of lawyers. Mass trials were frequently used to resolve disputes, emphasising democratic methods over coercive ones.[10]

In the second stage from New Democracy to Socialism (1953–1956), China learned from the Soviets and transplanted the Soviet legal system broadly. In 1954, the first Constitution in China was enacted. And after that, the National People's Congress started to codify the laws systematically. Chinese legal system developed quickly during this period. Law schools were set up, lawyers began to practice and the Supreme People's Court (SPC) also drafted civil procedural law in 1957. It seemed that China was gradually stepping into the road to the rule of law. However, the modernisation process of China's dispute resolution system was subsequently and regrettably interrupted by a series of political movements that disrupted not only the legal framework but also the broader sociopolitical landscape.

3.2 From the Early 1980s to 1990

After the Cultural Revolution, China restarted its legal construction in the late 1970s.[11] Deng Xiaoping spoke highly of the rule of law, stating that,

> To safeguard people's democracy, the legal system must be strengthened. Democracy must be institutionalized and written into law in such a way

[9] Cong Xiaoping, '"Ma Xiwu's way of judging": villages, the masses and legal construction in revolutionary China in the 1940s' (2014) 72(1) *The China Journal* 29.

[10] Daniel Druckman and Paul F. Diehl, *Conflict Resolution* (London: SAGE, 2006), p. 72.

[11] Chenguang Wang, 'Introduction: an emerging legal system' in Chenguang Wang and Xianchu Zhang (eds.), *Introduction to Chinese Law* (Hong Kong: Sweet & Maxwell, 1997), p. 12.

> as to ensure such institutions and laws do not change with the change of leaders, and do not change with the change of their views and attention. The problem now is that the laws are very incomplete, and many laws have not yet been enacted. The words of leaders are often regarded as 'law', and disagreeing with the words of leaders is called 'illegal'. When the words of leaders change, the 'law' will also change. Therefore, we should concentrate our efforts on enacting the Criminal Law, the Civil Law, the procedural law and other necessary laws, such as the Factory Law, the people's commune Law, the Forest Law, Grassland Law, Environmental Protection Law, Labor Law, Foreign Investment Law, etc., which should be discussed and adopted through certain democratic procedures, and strengthen the procuratorial and judicial organs to ensure that there are laws to be followed, laws to be enforced strictly, and violations to be prosecuted. The relations between the state and enterprises, enterprises and enterprises, enterprises and individuals, etc., must also be determined in the form of law. Many of the contradictions between them have to be solved by law. At present, the workload of legislation is very large, and manpower is very insufficient, so the legal provisions can be rougher at the beginning and gradually improved. Some local laws and regulations can be tried out first, and then, after summarizing and improving, they can formulate laws for general use throughout the country. . .In short, something is better than nothing, and fast is better than slow.[12]

At the same time, Deng took a big step forward in reforming and reconstructing the legal institutions. He eliminated the impact of the Cultural Revolution and focused on economic development rather than class struggle. After the Cultural Revolution ended, the Ministry of Justice itself was reestablished in 1979, emphasising that mediation was to be the primary avenue for resolving civil disputes.[13] In this context, the Procedural Provisions on People's Court Adjudicating Civil Case (1979, expired) provided that 'give priority to mediation when handling civil disputes. In those disputes which can be solved by mediation, the adjudication shall be avoided; if adjudication is necessary, the mediation shall be applied first in general.'[14]

[12] 'Improve the Socialist Legal System' [健全社会主义法制], Official website of the National People's Congress of PRC, www.npc.gov.cn/zgrdw/npc/xinwen/2003-07/03/content_316490.htm (last accessed 6 September 2023).

[13] Stanley B. Lubman, 'Dispute resolution in China after Deng Xiaoping: "Mao and mediation" revisited' (1997) 11 *Columbia Journal of Asian Law* 229, 274.

[14] *Provision on Civil Trial of People's Court (Tentative 1979, Expired)* [人民法院审判民事案件程序流程的规定（试行，已废止）], www.lawyee.net/act/act_display.asp?rid=24748 (last accessed 12 May 2017).

It is not surprising that mediation has become a distinctive character in Chinese civil procedural law for a long time. However, the significance of adjudication was gradually recognised by the regime since Deng's period. In 1982, the *Civil Procedural Law* (tentative 1982, expired) further adjusted the 'mediation first' preference to some degree. According to Article 6 of the Civil Procedural Law (tentative, 1982, expired), 'the People's Court should mediate disputes when hearing civil cases; if the mediation is invalid, adjudication shall be conducted timely'. It is true that 'Despite the emphasis on mediation in the 1982 Law of Civil Procedure the radical slogan for court work that "mediation is primary and adjudication is secondary" is no longer stressed in the legal literature'.[15]

In 1991, the preference for mediation was amended at the legislative level. The Civil Procedural Law (1991) confirmed voluntariness and lawfulness as the principles of court mediation in the civil justice realm by providing that 'when adjudicating civil cases, the people's courts may mediate the disputes according to the principles of voluntariness and lawfulness; if a mediation agreement cannot be reached, the courts shall render judgments without delay'. In this new *CPL* (1991), an independent chapter was set up to specifically regulate court mediation. In Chapter 8, the law provides the general regulations regarding the principle (Article 93), format (Article 94), assistant mediation (Article 95), mediation agreement (Article 96), written mediation document (Article 97 and 98) and the failure of mediation (Article 99). Since then, court mediation has become one of the options for both the parties and the judges to choose when coping with disputes.

3.3 From the early 1990s to 2002

During this period, Xiao Yang, the president of the SPC had established a series of reforms to promote the development of the trial system. The reform of the civil trial method during the Xiao Yang period adjusted the distribution of power and rights between the judge and the parties, changed the civil litigation model, established an adversarial litigation structure, set up a legal proof model, emphasised the attestation of the court, improved the avoidance system and decreased the use of mediation to achieve procedural justice. What's more, Xiao Yang endeavoured to professionalise the judge system. During the Xiao Yang period, the

15 *Provision on Civil Trial of People's Court* [人民法院审判民事案件程序流程的规定（试行，已废止）].

reform of the judge system achieved the professionalisation of judges by reforming the judge selection system, promoting the classification of court personnel, strengthening the professional training of judges and strengthening the judicial responsibilities of judges to pursue the professionalisation of judges.[16]

Furthermore, to accommodate the social interests, enhance international recognition and maintain legitimacy, the rule of law ('to rule the country according to the law', *yifazhiguo*, 依法治国) was formally adopted as a constitutional principle in China's legal regime in 1999. Considering the special relationship between the Party's governance model and the state,[17] the rule of law inevitably turned into a top-to-bottom ideological propaganda movement through the Party's 'unifying our thinking' (*tongyi sixiang*, 统一思想) mechanism before and after 1999. Following this Party's new ideology, almost all levels of Chinese governments in different hierarchies and many social institutions borrowed this saying and rewrote it as 'to rule the province according to law', 'to rule the city according to law', 'to rule the county according to law', 'to rule the village according to law', 'to rule the factory according to law', 'to rule the university according to law' so on and so forth.[18] The rule of law then became a national ideological movement.

Under the social movement in the 1990s called 'rule of law', the media hyped the 'rights awareness' and encouraged people to go to court even for a 2-yuan dispute.[19] After hearing about 2-yuan litigation, Xiao Yang commented that 'it is a delightful phenomenon that people will more frequently use the law to solve conflicts.'[20] At that time, there is no exaggeration to say that:

> through newspapers, television, and movies, community legal propaganda work, legal education classes, etc. people paid more attention to the law

[16] Feiyun Luo, 'Civil justice reform under the administration of Xiao Yang', PhD Dissertation, Nanjing University of Science and Technology (2015) [罗飞云：《肖扬时期民事司法改革研究》，京理工大学，2015].

[17] Albert H. Y. Chen, *An Introduction to the Legal System of the People's Republic of China* (Hong Kong: Lexis/Nexis, 5th ed., 2018), pp. 108–111.

[18] Hao Xiong, 'Litigation of Si family: a legal and anthropological observation on a civil compensation dispute happened in ethnic minority grassroots community' (2010) 5 *Academy* 25, 26–28 [熊浩："思家诉讼：一个中国少数民族基层社区民事赔偿案件的法学与人类学观察"，《学园》2010年第5期].

[19] Dong Zhang (ed.), *Starting from Two Yuan Litigation* (Beijing: Law Press, 1999), p. 9 [张栋：《从"两元钱官司"开始》北京：法律出版社1999年版].

[20] Zhang, *Starting from Two Yuan*, p. 359 [张栋：《从"两元钱官司"开始》北京：法律出版社1999年版].

> and became more aware of their rights: in a 1997 survey of 1,500 Chinese 'about 60 percent of respondents said the most important thing in their social lives was respecting individual freedom and interests.' Scholar Fan Yu even argues that the former 'disgust for lawsuits' has been transformed into a belief in the 'omnipotent power' and 'worship' of the litigation process.[21]

All of these social phenomena, though not totally wrong, were constructed by political mobilisation and were a component of the ideological movement named the 'rule of law', motivated by the Party to a remarkable degree. It is also quite clear that politics reconstructed people's cognition of court mediation in the 1990s. Influenced by this ideological movement, the amount of litigation in China grew drastically. According to the statistics, the rate of solving disputes by litigation and mediation was 39.4:100 in 1990, but the ratio of litigation increased rapidly to 63.8:100 in 1998 compared with the cases solved by mediation.[22] There was an obvious trend that the amount of litigation (including civil, criminal and administrative cases) grew while mediation declined from 1994 to 2001.[23] It was also reported that this trend continued after 2002. For example, in 2004 and 2008, only 26.7 per cent of the civil and commercial cases were disposed of through court mediation.[24] It should be admitted that the reasons for this phenomenon are complicated. The economic development,[25] social transformation,[26] the improvement of the legal and rights awareness of ordinary people[27] and other factors all may have led to the growth of litigation. Although it is a

21 Aaron Halegua, 'Reforming the People's mediation system in urban China' (2005) 35 *Hong Kong Law Journal* 715, 719.

22 Bo Han, 'People's mediation: return in post litigation era' (2002) 12 *Law Science* 45, 46 [韩波："人民调解——后诉讼时代的回归"，载《法学》2002年12期].

23 Benjamin L. Liebman, 'China's courts: restricted reform' (2007) 21 *Columbia Journal of Asian Law* 1, 6–7; Randall Peerenboom and Xin He, 'Dispute resolution in China: patterns, causes and prognosis' (2009) 4 *East Asia Law Review* 1, 9–14.

24 Jingang Fang, 'China's change from the improvement of mediation process' (Conference paper, 2009), quoted from Vicki Waye and Ping Xiong, 'The relationship between mediation and judicial proceedings in China' (2011) 6(1) *Asian Journal of Comparative Law*, Article 2, 5–6.

25 See Tiechuan Hao, *Order and Progress: Report on the Rule of Law in Primary Stage of Socialism of China* (Beijing: Law Press, 2004) [郝铁川：《秩序与渐进：中国社会主义初级阶段依法治国研究报告》，北京：法律出版社2004年版].

26 See Emile Durkheim, *The Division of Labour in Society* (London: Macmillan, 1984); see also David S. Clark, 'Civil litigation, access to justice, and social change: research issues in longitudinal court studies' (1988) 12 *Southern Illinois University Law Journal* 713.

27 Lubman, 'Dispute resolution in China after Deng Xiaoping', 297–298.

fact that there are more disputes in China,[28] it does not make sense that litigations grew so dramatically in this period, but the number of mediations dropped. However, as a nonexclusive explanation, the political ideology movement titled 'rule of law' and the encouragement of litigation for even a 2-yuan dispute can provide a reasonable explanation for both the growth of litigation and the drop in mediation in almost the same period. In other words, the simultaneous dramatic increase in litigation and a reduction in mediation also means some cases which can/should be settled by the nonlitigation approaches enter the litigation track eventually as the result of the politicisation of the rule of law.[29]

This argument was actually confirmed by the SPC. Jiachen Liu, the then vice president of the SPC, said that 'in today's society, there is a tendency that litigation rights have been abused. People, on every occasion, go to the court even for some small issues and no one is willing to compromise.'[30] According to Liu, this litigious culture cannot help the parties to solve the problem satisfactorily; more seriously, it may increase social conflicts and waste many judicial resources.[31] Indeed, under such a climate, people's preference to litigate to solve disputes is not because they have a clear understanding and rational assessment of different dispute resolution approaches; on the contrary, it is because they think China has entered a new era called 'rule of law' so they want to use litigation to show that they are modern citizens equipped with strong legal and rights awareness. Rule of law, as one of the overwhelming ideologies at that time, actually affected people's behaviour and provided a politically correct choice for the people when they encountered disputes. The ideologisation of the rule of law caused the absence of court mediation and restructured the people's preference for litigation at that time.

[28] See Lianhe Hu, Angang Hu and Lei Wang, 'An empirical study on the change and tendency factor of social instability' (2007) 6 *Exploration* 105 [胡联合、胡鞍钢、王磊："关于我国社会不稳定因素变化态势的实证分析"，载《探索》2007年第6期].

[29] It is worth mentioning that although the amount of mediation shrank significantly in the 1990s generally, it also kept its popularity in some Chinese basic-level rural courts. It also shows the diverse situations in China in terms of dispute resolution across regions. See Sida Liu, 'Beyond global convergence: conflicts of legitimacy in a Chinese lower court' (2006) 31 *Law and Society*, 75, 96–97.

[30] Jiachen Liu, 'Constrict the tendency of abusing litigation, guide the social dispute resolution' [刘家琛：遏制滥用诉讼手段倾向，引导解决社会矛盾合理分流], www.chinacourt.org/public/detail.php?id=6678 (last accessed 1 May 2017).

[31] Liu, 'Constrict the tendency of abusing litigation' [刘家琛：遏制滥用诉讼手段倾向，引导解决社会矛盾合理分流].

3.4 From 2003 to 2013

After experiencing many years of legal construction, China, as some scholars point out, is no longer a lawless country in terms of codification of laws and regulations. However, China is still far from the real rule of the law society to date.[32] To a certain extent, as Tony Saich further stated:

> It is clear that when Jiang, Hu, and their advisers use the phrase 'rule of law' they do not mean a system that gives primacy to the law above political considerations and Party policy. Instead, it is a way to manage power, regulate the economy, and discipline society in light of rapidly changing circumstances. In this sense, while it might provide greater predictability it is just another weapon in the arsenal of party control.[33]

As has been argued, in the past decades, the public has been ideologically motivated to use lawsuits to solve their disputes. However, the more people choose the judicial services the more they feel that it is far away from satisfaction for various reasons. The judicial system earned the wrath of the public during this period due to its poor performance in safeguarding social justice and individual rights. Serious problems existing in the justice system include the adaptation of the Western-oriented litigation system, especially for the disadvantaged people living in rural and poor areas,[34] judgment enforcement problems,[35] judicial corruption[36], mass disturbances caused by inappropriate dispute resolution,[37] the low quality of judicial officers,[38] sustained growth in the

[32] Jiefen Li, *Legal Reform Versus the Power of the Party and State in the People's Republic of China: Rule of Law or Rule by Law* (Lewiston, NY: Edwin Mellen Press, 2008), pp. 6–7.

[33] Tony Saich, *Governance and Politics of China* (London: Palgrave Macmillan, 3rd ed., 2011), p. 165.

[34] See Li Su, *Sending Law to the Rural China: A Study on Chinese Legal Institution at the Grassroots Level* (Beijing: China University of Politics and Law Press, 2000) [苏力：《送法下乡：中国基层司法制度研究》，北京：中国政法大学出版社2000年版].

[35] See Hanchao Jing and Zijuan Lu, 'Difficulty in enforcement and countermeasures' (2000) 5 *Chinese Journal of Law* 124 [景汉朝、卢子娟："执行难"及其对策，载《法学研究》2000年第5期].

[36] See Eric Chi-yeung Ip, 'Judicial corruption and its threats to national governance in China' (2008) 3(1) *Journal of Administration and Governance*, http://joaag.com/uploads/8_IpFinal.pdf (last accessed 7 March 2015).

[37] As Randall Peerenboom and He Xin said, 'Social-economic cases affect many parties. . .they also have a great potential to lead to social disturbance. Local officials, worried about social instability and its effect on their future career prospects, often pressure courts not to accept such cases.' See Peerenboom and He, *Dispute Resolution in China*, 1, 47.

[38] See Limin Wang, 'The quality of judges and judicial corruption' [王立民："法官素质与司法腐败"，载人民网], www.people.com.cn/GB/guandian/29/173/20011128/614378.html (last accessed 27 March 2017). Although it is a fact that the professional quality

number of petitions,[39] bureaucratism in the courts[40] and so on and so forth. It should be noted that these complaints cannot be simply categorised into different grievances as mentioned. To put it differently, these concerns are quite differentiated from each other, although in all instances, people are angry towards the court. However, it is clear that 'late-twentieth-century court reforms failed to create effective institutions for resolving citizens' grievances'.[41]

Facing such pressure and demands for reform, the authorities have to create a way to cope with the problems in the legal system and find a tool for legal institutions to promote their legitimacy and authority somehow. On different occasions, the Party regime explicitly expressed the view that the Western political and legal systems, including the separation of the three powers, are not suitable for China's situation,[42] as believed by China's right-wing intellectuals, the political liberalists of China, to be the correct way to solve various problems in the justice system. Instead of following the Western proposal, the authorities had to explore the resources from their own traditional experience that is politically correct. In late 2007, President Hu Jingtao introduced the new principles governing the Chinese legal regime at the meeting of the Communist Party of China's Central Political–Legal Committee. That is, the 'Three Supremes', including 'Supremacy of the business of the CPC (*dangde shiye zhishang*, 党的事业至上), Supremacy of the interests of the people (*renmin liyi zhishang*, 人民利益至上), and Supremacy of constitutional law and law (*xianfa falü zhishang*, 宪法法律至上)'.[43] Sounding politically correct, in the National High Court Presidents Conference held in June 2008, the newly appointed President of the Supreme People's Court Shengjun Wang stated that 'facing the new situation and new mission,

and performance of judges have been improved, it is still far away from the satisfaction and expectations of the public.

39 Peerenboom and He, *Dispute Resolution in China*, 1, 38–41.

40 Shengjun Wang, 'The bureaucratism still exists in People's Courts', [王胜俊："官僚主义、衙门作风现象仍然存在"], www.iyaxin.com/govlianghui/2009-03/10/content_773537.htm (last accessed 10 March 2016).

41 Carl F. Minzner, 'China's turn against law' (2011) 59 *American Journal of Comparative Law* 935, 941.

42 See Theory Department of Renming Daily, *Six Why – Answer to Some Important Questions*' (Beijing: Renming Daily Press, 2009) [人民日报理论部：《"六个为什么"：对若干重大问题的解答》，北京：人民日报出版社2009年版].

43 Jingtao Hu, 'Refresh the political–legal work in our country' [胡锦涛：扎扎实实开创我国政法工作新局面]， http://news.xinhuanet.com/newscenter/2007-12/25/content_7312439.htm (last accessed 30 March 2017).

the People's Court shall stand at the new historical starting point and keep pace with the times. The Court should hold the Three Supremes as the guiding ideology all along.'[44] This new policy is a significant change in the tone and content of judicial leadership compared with the administration of Yang Xiao, the ex-president of the SPC.[45] Jerome A. Cohen commented that Wang's direction is an 'apparent return to the past, to the use of law as an instrument of "proletarian dictatorship" implemented through the "mass line" in the guise of "democratization"'.[46] In a sense, some scholars said that the golden years of China's legal reform, initiated during Xiao's tenure, are over.[47]

Actually, the 'apparent return to the past' has already happened in the political regime from around 2003. If we analyse the discourse of the CPC carefully, it is clear that although the CPC leaders are still emphasising the value and importance of the rule of law (ruling state according to the law, *yifa zhiguo*, 依法治国) in their public speeches, meetings and official documents, but the degree and frequency of that emphasis are declining. As it has been pointed out by Palmer,

> While the importance of the rule of law continues to be stressed by the Chinese leadership, there is now also a strong emphasis on the need for the people and the state to enjoy a close and harmonious relationship. The construction of this 'harmonious society' is the responsibility of both the Communist Party and the Chinese state – whose interests are now seen as fused rather than in need of separation.[48]

These changes can be also observed in the *People's Daily*, which is the most important organ and mouthpiece of the Central Committee of the CPC and also a sensitive and effective indicator of China's political-social life.[49]

44 Shengjun Wang, '"Three supremes" are the guiding ideology of the court' [王胜俊："三个至上是法院始终坚持的指导思想"], http://news.xinhuanet.com/legal/2008-06/23/content_8420938.htm (last accessed 13 April 2016).

45 Jerome A. Cohen, 'On the three supremes', http://blogs.law.harvard.edu/guorui/2008/10/23/jerome-cohen-on-the-three-supremes/ (last accessed 30 March 2015).

46 Cohen, 'On the three supremes'.

47 Xianchu Zhang, 'Civil justice reform with political agenda' in Guanghua Yu (ed.), *Development of the Chinese Legal System: Change and Challenges* (London: Routledge, 2010), p. 255.

48 Michael Palmer, 'Compromising courts and harmonizing ideologies: mediation in the administrative chambers of the People's Courts in the People's Republic of China' in Andrew Harding and Penelope (Pip) Nicholson (eds.), *New Courts in Asia* (London: Routledge, 2010), p. 268.

49 For a general introduction about the importance of *People's Daily* in PRC's social and political life, please see Won Ho Chang, *Mass Media in China: The History and the Future* (Ames: Iowa State University Press, 1989), p. 92.

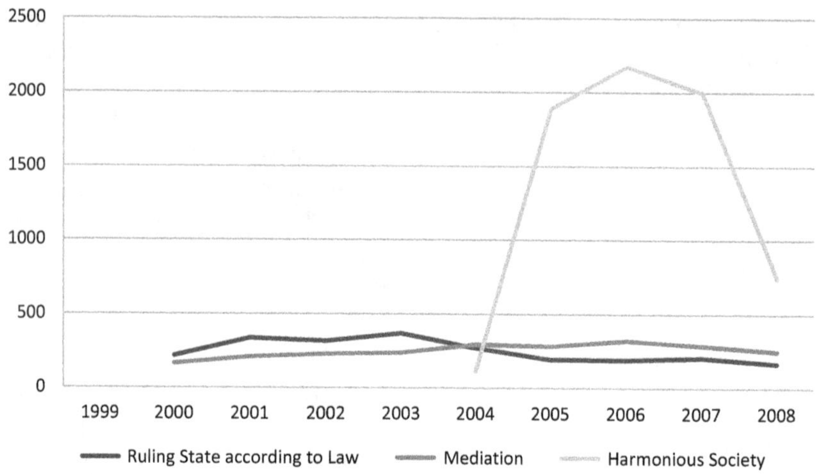

Figure 3.1 Number of articles in *People's Daily* including the keywords mediation (*tiaojie*, 调解)', 'ruling the state according to the law (rule of law, *yifa zhiguo*, 依法治国)' and 'harmonious society (*hexie shehui*, 和谐社会)' (1999–2008).[50]

Figure 3.1 shows the statistics about the frequency of the three keywords of 'mediation (*tiaojie*, 调解)', 'ruling the state according to the law (rule of law, *yifa zhiguo*, 依法治国)' and 'harmonious society (*hexie shehui*, 和谐社会)' appearing in the *People's Daily* from 1999 to 2008. Through a discourse analysis,[51] it is clear that from 1999 to 2008, the 'rule of law' is mentioned

[50] The data is collected and counted through WiseSearch. http://libwisesearch.wisers.net/ws5/index.do?srp_restore=discard&new-login=true (last accessed 8 April 2015). It is interesting to point out that if searching these three keywords in all the mainland newspapers existing in WiseSearch database from 1999 to 2010, the 'rule of law' is still the most frequent but also maintains a downwards tendency, whereas 'court mediation' and 'big mediation' keeps an upwards tendency in general. This reflects a number of factors. Firstly, the political leanings are differentiated in the media of today's China. Given the different positions of the media, the newspapers may set their own agendas which may be different from *People's Daily*'s when reporting the news and analysing social issues. Secondly, the 'ideological state apparatuses' are still highly influential. Although not totally the same, the media system of China shares the similar tendency of the frequency of the mentioned three words with *People's Daily*'s in general.

[51] In linguistics, discourse analysis is an important theoretical tool to understand how the social and political life of people is shaped and constructed. Regarding media language particularly, discourse analysis can show us the dominance and inequality, the projection of power, the ideological underpinning and discourse's affiliation with social change. Considering the irreplaceable role of *People's Daily* in the PRC, some scholars have used the discourse analysis method to examine the discourse of *People's Daily*. Some examples include Yufang Qian, *Discursive Constructions around Terrorism in the People's Daily*

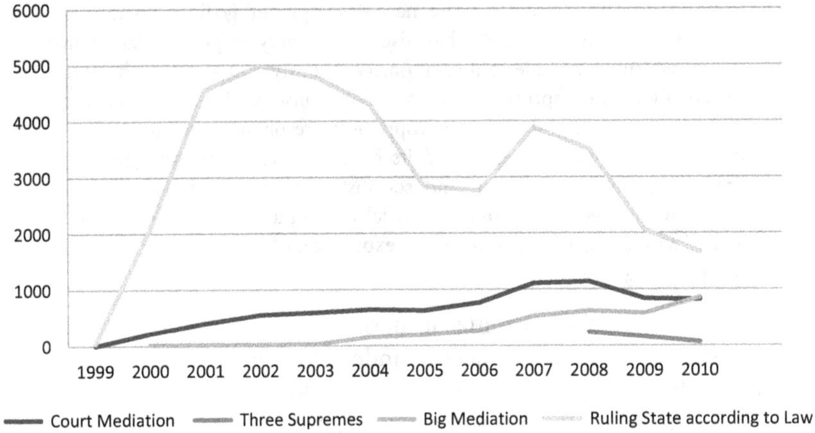

Figure 3.2 Number of the mainland newspaper articles including the keywords mediation (*tiaojie*, 调解)', 'ruling the state according to the law (rule of law, *yifa zhiguo*, 依法治国)' and 'harmonious society (*hexie shehui*, 和谐社会) (1999–2010).

less frequently in the *People's Daily* compared with the increasingly heated new mainstream ideology narrative: 'harmonious society'.

From Figure 3.1, it can be also observed that the growth of mediation in the propaganda and political narratives accompanies the emergence and increase of Hu Jingtao's new political discourse 'harmonious society' and has even overwhelmed the 'rule of law' from around 2004 in the *People's Daily*. It shows the fact that mediation is one of the isomorphic discourses of the harmonious society existing in the legal regime, but the rule of law is not from a propaganda point of view (Figure 3.2). According to my fieldwork in southwest China, when asked about which approach can safeguard social harmony better, 98.2 per cent of judicial staff and 99.2 per cent of lawyers chose mediation instead of litigation. This reflects that even the legal professions working at the grassroots level understand the substantial relationship between big mediation policy and harmonious society. This underlying connection shows that the driving force of the current mediation-oriented legal policy is political. Speaking of this, Palmer persuasively noted,

(China) and The Sun (UK) Before and After 9.11: A Corpus-Based Contrastive Critical Discourse Analysis (Lausanne: Peter Lang, 2010); Su Gao, 'Comparative discourse analysis between English and Chinese news tests: by using functional grammar to analyze the textile dispute report in People's Daily and New York Times' (2007) 3(4) *Canadian Social Science* 68.

> In the PRC, it is clear that the new development goal of creating a 'socialist harmonious society' has also been a very important factor in the transformed attitude to mediation. With Party and state much more closely aligned, compromise and ostensibly consensual decision-making are now considered especially appropriate for resolving unfortunate contradictions between the state and its citizens. The 'harmony ideology', drawing on both Confucian and socialist communitarian values, also carries within itself an impulse of social control and rights suppression, as well as serving as something of an expression of the Chinese collective self-pitted against the external world.[52]

Without a doubt, the meaning of 'harmonious society' is complicated, which reflects the Party's concerns under Hu Jintao's administration in terms of frequent social protests, the adoption of the mantle of Confucianism, the attempt to repair social divergence, the strategy to hammer political protests and the care for the interests of disadvantaged people like the farmers and the poor. Considering the connection between harmonious society and the big mediation policy, the policy can be reasonably considered a politics-driven shift in the justice system. Based on the Party's evaluation of the social situation and the concern about its legitimacy crisis in the judicial system, this policy was designed and promoted. In this political climate, court mediation grows significantly and becomes the most vital institutional arrangement in the area of dispute resolution (Figure 3.3).

3.5 New Developments in Xi Jinping Era

In Xi Jinping's era, more positive changes are taking place. Xi's administration issued the Decision on Several Important Issues Regarding the All-Around Promotion of Ruling the State According to Law (the 4th Decision) at the Communist Party of China's Fourth Plenum of the 18th Party Congress,[53] a comprehensive and ambitious plan with the aim of completely revamping the Chinese judicial system. Even though the Party's dominance in the legal system is reconfirmed,[54] many rule of

[52] Palmer, 'Compromising courts and harmonizing ideologies', p. 269.

[53] See 'Decision on several important issues regarding the all-around promotion of ruling the state according to law', *People's Daily* [中共中央关于全面推进依法治国若干重大问题的决定], http://cpc.people.com.cn/n/2014/1029/c64387-25927606.html (last accessed 15 April 2017).

[54] As some observers noticed that 'In the 4th Decision where the phrase "the leadership of the Party" appears 14 times, the answer to the relationship between the leadership of the

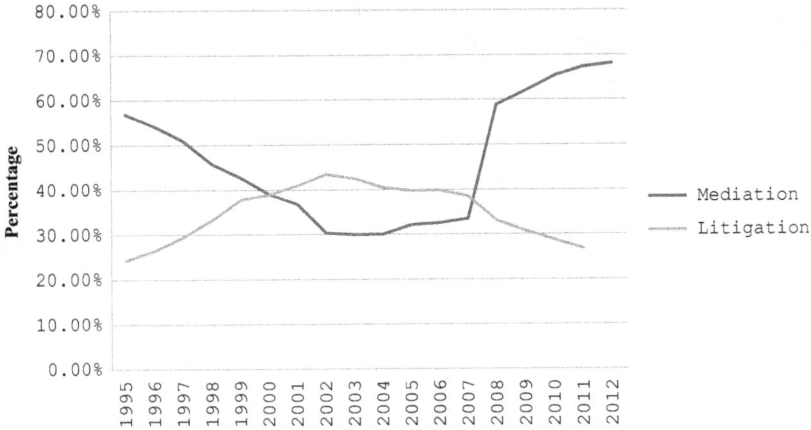

Figure 3.3 Solved cases in court of first instance through court mediation and litigation.[55]

law measures can be found. For instance, it is the first time that the CPC used the wording 'governing the country according to the Constitution' and 'administration according to the Constitution'.[56] To effectively promote reform, the Leading Group for Reform of the Social System (also known as the Central Leading Group for Reform of the Judicial System) was established at the central level in early 2014. This group is tasked with deepening reform by improving the classified management of judicial personnel, enhancing judicial accountability, securing the employment of judicial staff, advancing the centralised management of personnel, unifying the financial and material resources of local courts at the provincial level and implementing other measures related to the reform of the judicial system.[57] According to the principle that major reforms shall be first conducted on a pilot basis, China launched pilot reforms in respect of the aforesaid issues in some provinces, autonomous

Party and rule of law seems settled'. See Sanzhu Zhu, 'Socialist rule of law in the 21st century China' (2015) 7 *Hague Journal on the Rule of Law* 75, 78.

55 The data of litigation from 2008 to 2012 cannot be found in the national census. The ones which are listed in the above chart are estimated by the author according to the SPC's annual reports to the National People's Congress.

56 Zhu, 'Socialist rule of law', 75, 79.

57 See Supreme People's Court, 'Court reform in China (white papers)' [中国法院的司法改革（白皮书）], http://english.court.gov.cn/2017-03/14/content_28552928_3.htm (last accessed 30 March 2017).

regions and municipalities directly under the control of the central government in three batches to understand the impediments in the implementation of reform across the country. After the pilot programmes, the major reforms were implemented nationwide in an all-around way in July 2016.[58] It is thus believed that these initiatives are not window dressing – Beijing is aware of the need to 'improve governance, address widespread public grievances and respond to public opinion. They are also part of a long-term endeavour to build a system of rule of law since Deng Xiaoping's era'.[59]

In the area of alternative dispute resolution, some scholars have observed that Zhou Qiang, the then-president of the SPC, leveraged his strong legal education background to lead the court system back towards judicial professionalism. Consequently, in this round of court reform, judicial mediation no longer received the same level of priority as it had previously.[60] In practice, the dispute resolution policies of this period began to align with the social governance requirements of promoting the Fengqiao experience of the CPC. The SPC collaborated with various government and industry departments to establish diversified industry mediation. More specifically, the SPC has initiated joint efforts with various departments, including the Ministry of Public Security, the Ministry of Justice, the Ministry of Human Resources and Social Security, the Ministry of Civil Affairs, the National Development and Reform Commission, the China Securities Regulatory Commission, the China Insurance Regulatory Commission, the All-China Federation of Returned Overseas Chinese, the All-China Federation of Industry and Commerce, the All-China Women's Federation and others. They have jointly issued over 20 coordination documents in areas such as people's mediation, family disputes, securities and futures disputes, insurance disputes and notary participation in judicial assistance affairs in courts. They have established more than 3,000 coordination mechanisms to comprehensively promote the improvement and optimisation of the diversified dispute resolution system.[61] By integrating

[58] See Supreme People's Court, 'Court reform in China' [中国法院的司法改革（白皮书）].

[59] Yongnian Zheng and Wei Shan, 'Understanding Xi Jinping's "Rule of Law" Campaigning' (2015) 7 *East Asian Policy* 5, 6–7.

[60] See Hualing Fu and Michael Palmer, *Mediation in Contemporary China: Continuity and Change* (London: Wildy, Simmonds & Hill Publishing, 2017).

[61] Supreme People's Court (ed.), *Judicial Reform of Chinese Courts (2013–2018)*, (Beijing: People's Court Press, 2019), p. 30 [最高人民法院编：《中国法院司法改革（2013–2018）》，人民法院出版社2019年版].

public resources with those from non-governmental, commercial and other sectors, the SPC aims to enhance the overall capacity for dispute resolution.[62] The ongoing reform of diversified dispute resolution mechanisms is based on the premise of the strong social function of the judiciary. Through social work methods and legal means, these social functions of the court are extended to other organisations and institutions that can replace the judiciary in performing these functions, allowing the limited and valuable judicial resources to be used in the exercise of adjudication functions.[63] The court, in this case, has assumed the role of a 'multi-door courthouse', effectively channelling different cases to the appropriate dispute resolution avenues such as mediation centres, arbitration institutes, government departments and various social service organisations.

In addition to the aforementioned collaboration between courts, government agencies and social organisations in resolving social disputes, within the courts themselves, a mechanism for integrating mediation with litigation has also been progressively established. By 2020, courts at all levels had set up 3,835 specialised litigation–mediation connection centres and appointed 29,921 dedicated staff members. More than 3,000 grassroots courts nationwide instruct 800,000 people's mediation organisations and 4,000,000 people's mediators to carry out professional work, and people's mediation organisations resolve nearly 10,000,000 disputes every year.[64] Courts nationwide have officially staffed 12,648 full-time mediators in litigation service centres or litigation–mediation connection centres, and these full-time mediators have mediated 1,739,000 cases, including 1,480,000 successfully mediated ones, with a success rate of 85 per cent. The number of cases diverted to specially invited mediation accounts for approximately 40 per cent of the total number of civil and commercial cases in the first instance.[65]

There is no doubt that the new round of judicial reform has promoted the development of judicial professionalism. Moreover, in line with the CPC's policy direction on social governance and the Fengqiao experience, it has begun to experiment with the appropriate diversion of

62 Supreme People's Court of PRC, 'The reform of diversified dispute resolution mechanism of China's courts (2015–2020)', www.dffyw.com/sitedata/resource/files/202103/20210303192252mi1x.pdf (last accessed 30 April 2022).

63 Huiling Jiang, 'Ten years of reform and innovation, setting sail for new horizons', 13 April 2015, *People's Court Daily* [蒋惠岭：《十年改革创新路扬帆逐浪再起航》，《人民法院报》2015年4月13日第2版].

64 Supreme People's Court of PRC, 'The reform of diversified dispute resolution'.

65 Supreme People's Court of PRC, 'The reform of diversified dispute resolution'.

mediation and litigation, specifically returning the work of adjudication to the courts while channelling mediation tasks through the courts to various social mechanisms. However, it should be noted that unlike professionalism in a Western context where the legal profession is an autonomous community zealously pursuing 'spirit' and even challenging the state, professionalism in China has a more complex meaning. At the institutional level, for example, the provincial committees are set up to select judges. Although the committees would choose judges based on their professional performance, there would still be a political element because the committees would also include officials in charge of upholding the Party's discipline by vetting possible candidates based on their political quality, integrity, and self-discipline.[66] At the ideological level, the ideological guidance of the legal system has not been relaxed. When talking about the ideological or spiritual aspect of the legal profession and the construction of judicial credibility, CPC aims to strengthen legal professionals' political affiliation rather than professional autonomy. For instance, the Central Committee of CPC and the General Office of the State Council issued the Opinions on Deepening the Reform of the Lawyer System in 2016. These opinions were discussed by the Leading Group of Comprehensively Deepening Reform of CPC (*zhongyang quanmian shenhua gaige lingdao xiaozu*, 中央全面深化改革领导小组) led by President Xi and form the most important official document regarding the legal profession in recent years. In this document, it is stressed that:

> The ideological and political construction must be strengthened, and the ideological and political construction should be put in the first place. The basic requirement of the legal professions is to adhere to the leadership of the Communist Party of China and to uphold the socialist rule of law. The Lawyers' self-consciousness and firmness to follow the path of the socialist rule of law with Chinese characteristics should be enhanced.[67]

As a response to this requirement, the Ministry of Justice established the national lawyers' Party committee at the central level and then respective Party committees can be expected to be established at the local and law

[66] Weixia Gu, *Dispute Resolution in China: Litigation, Arbitration, Mediation and Their Interactions* (New York: Routledge, 2021), p. 39.

[67] See 'The Central Committee of CPC and the General Office of the State Council issued the Opinions on Deepening the Reform of the Lawyer System' [中共中央办公厅 国务院办公厅印发《关于深化律师制度改革的意见》], www.gov.cn/xinwen/2016-06/13/content_5081785.htm (last accessed 5 May 2018).

firm level. Xuanguo Xiong, the then deputy minister of the Ministry of Justice and the newly elected party secretary of the national lawyers, said that:

> Lawyers should adhere to the Party's leadership throughout lawyers' work processes and ensure the Party's theory and policy can be fully implemented into the lawyers' work. The lawyers should unswervingly adhere to the socialist path with Chinese characteristics and the socialist rule of law with Chinese characteristics.[68]

3.6 Theoretical Analysis

A brief overview of the modern history of China's dispute resolution system provides key insights. The nature of these policy changes can be analysed and interpreted through various theoretical paradigms, such as administrative absorption of society,[69] organisational involution[70] or adaptive governance

[68] See 'The Party committee of national lawyer system is established', People.com.cn [全国律师行业党委成立], http://dangjian.people.com.cn/n1/2017/1101/c117092-29620996.html (last accessed 5 May 2018).

[69] 'Administrative absorption of society' is a term used by Chinese political scientist Xiaoguang Kang, which means that 'the state enters into society by means of a "social approach"'. With regard to the mediation policy particularly, the state actually enriched and emphasised the social conflict resolution function of the court by absorbing court mediation and combining the people's mediation mechanism in and with the court. According to Kang, the social governing skills of the Chinese government are becoming rich and veteran, 'passive control strategy' and 'positive replacement strategy' are flexibly adapted according to the social conditions. He said:

> In the social sphere in Chinese mainland today, the strategy of 'functional replacement' includes in the main following measures: continuance, meaning continuing to make use of old organizations; development, meaning developing new organizational forms adapted to the totally new environment; incorporating, meaning accepting into the government administrative system those social organizations that have sprung up spontaneously; and laissez-faire, meaning giving free rein to organizations that don't really count either way.

See Xiaoguang Kang and Heng Han, 'Administrative absorption of society: a further probe into state-society relationship in Chinese mainland' (2007) 28(2) *Social Sciences in China: Special Issue: NGOs and Social Transition in China* 116, 117. See Hou Liwen, 'Administrative absorption of society: state penetration and neighborhood committee administration' (2019) 2 *Journal of Shenzhen University (Humanities and Social Sciences)* 112 [侯利文："行政吸纳社会：国家渗透与居委会行政化"，《深圳大学学报（人文社会科学版）》2019年第2期].

[70] 'Involution' is a concept firstly used by anthropologist Alexander Goldenweiser and then developed by Clifford Geertz to describe 'those culture patterns which, after having

and guerrilla policy style.[71] All these paradigms rest on some similar theoretical and realistic understandings. Firstly, the Party has no intention, at least in the foreseeable future, to effect fundamental administrative restructuring according to the blueprint provided by Western countries.[72] The bottom line, the 'Four Cardinal Principles', which were explicitly stated by Deng Xiaoping in 1979 to safeguard the one-party-dominated state system, is still very clear. In the new era, the concept of 'Four Confidences', coined by Xi Jinping, has become the dominant ideology.[73] Secondly, the Party

reached what would seem to be a definitive form, nonetheless fail either to stabilize or transform themselves into a new pattern but rather continue to develop by becoming internally more complicated'. According to Goldenweiser, 'the primary effect of pattern is. . .to check development, or at least to limit it. As soon as the pattern form is reached further change is inhibited by the tenacity of the pattern. . . But there are also instances where *pattern merely sets a limit, a frame. . .within which further change is permitted if not invited*'. See Alexander Goldenweiser, 'Loose ends of a theory on the individual pattern and involution in primitive society' in Robert H. Lowie (ed.), *Essays in Anthropology: Presented to A. L. Kroeber in Celebration of His Sixtieth Birthday, June 11, 1936* (Berkeley, CA: University of California Press, 1936), pp. 99–104 (emphasis added); see also Clifford Geertz, *Agricultural Involution: The Process of Ecological Change in Indonesia* (Berkeley, CA: University of California Press, 1963), pp. 79–82. This concept then is borrowed by China's political researchers to explain the political–legal reform in China. See Lusheng Wang, 'The risk of internal involution in China's judicial reform and its governance' (2022) 3 *Studies of Law and Business* 16 [王禄生："我国司法改革的内卷化风险及其治理"，《法商研究》2022年第3期].

71 'Adaptive governance' is summarised by political scholars according to Chinese history of politics. Some political theorists found that 'China's governance techniques are marked by a signature Maoist stamp that conceives of policy-making as a process of ceaseless change, tension management, continual experimentation and ad hoc adjustment'. Based on abundant empirical observations, they summarised that the governance of China highly depends on its 'capacity of actors in a system to further resilience through their actions and interactions, intentionally or unintentionally. The foundation of adaptability in this sense is response diversity: a variety of reactive, digestive, pre-emptive, and proactive operations and procedures that facilitate continual adjustment to and absorption of endogenous and exogenous challenges'. See Sebastian Heilmann and Elizabeth J. Perry, 'Embracing uncertainty: guerrilla policy and adaptive governance in China' in Sebastian Heilmann and Elizabeth J. Perry (eds.), *Mao's Invisible Hand: The Political Foundations of Adaptive Governance in China* (Cambridge, MA: Harvard University Press, 2011), p. 8. See also Xin Jingyi and Shui Yu, 'Multi-agents, intertwined power and rural adaptive governance' (2020) 2 *Truth Seeking* 90 [辛璄怡、于水："主体多元、权力交织与乡村适应性治理"，《求实》2020年第2期].

72 Elizabeth J. Perry and Merle Goldman, 'Introduction: historical reflections on grassroots political reform in China' in Elizabeth J. Perry and Merle Goldman (eds.), *Grassroots Political Reform in Contemporary China* (Cambridge, MA: Harvard University Press, 2007), p. 15.

73 The 'four confidences' were introduced by Xi Jinping during the celebration of the 95th anniversary of the founding of the Communist Party of China. These confidences include confidence in the path, theory, system and culture. Confidence in the path underscores

welcomes adaptive and constructive suggestions and institutional arrangements to improve its governing capacity and legitimacy.[74] In this context, the nature and mainspring of the Chinese judicial policy is 'politically correct pragmatism'. It means a pragmatically driven legal policymaking mechanism operating within the politically correct zone defined by the Party is the predominant principle of China's legal system. Therefore, reform in China is marked by experimental and piecemeal changes. The popular term in the post-Deng era among the CPC leaders is *yu shi ju jin* (与时俱进), meaning that the development of policies should adapt to the development of the time change and realistic social needs. The Party thus must be adaptable and flexible to the changing governance environment.[75]

It is true that pragmatism enjoyed a long history in China and pervades Chinese people's day-to-day lives. Although pragmatism can be defined differently in Chinese and Western contexts,[76] it shares some basic characteristics in common. Pragmatism emphasises the adaptability of human beings to the environment and believes that experience is the source of truth.[77] Examining Chinese modern legal history from the selective adoption of Soviet-style legal institutions to Mao's slogan 'seeking truth from fact' regarding the law as an instrument for class domination or as serving the goal of economic development, legal pragmatism

the appropriateness and leading role of the socialist path with Chinese characteristics. Confidence in the theory demonstrates a steadfast belief in the theoretical system of socialism with Chinese characteristics. Confidence in the system reflects trust in the institutional frameworks that ensure national stability and development. Confidence in the culture emphasises the intrinsic value of Chinese culture and its contributions to the world. Collectively, these four confidences constitute the ideological backbone of socialism with Chinese characteristics and act as a pivotal spiritual force driving China's ongoing development and progress.

74 See Yue Xie, 'Party adaption and the prospects for democratization in authoritarian China' (2008) 44(2) *Issues and Studies* 79.

75 Li He, 'The Chinese model of development and its implications' (2015) 2(2) *World Journal of Social Science Research* 128, 132–133.

76 According to Xingzhong Yu, 'In the United States, pragmatism exists within the context of an established, sophisticated legal system, built on constant and inviolable principles. It is a society founded on the rule of law. In China, the emphasis on the instrumental facets of law lacks a similar foundation'. See Xingzhong Yu, 'Legal pragmatism in the People's Republic of China' (1989) 3 *Journal of Chinese Law* 29, 49.

77 Fangtong Liu, Songjie Huang and George F. McLean (eds.), *Philosophy and Modernization in China* (Washington, D.C.: The Council for Research in Values and Philosophy, 1997), pp. 92–93; see also Youlan Feng, *Preface of Sangsongtang* (Zhengzhou: Henan People's Press, 2001), pp. 179–180 [冯友兰：《三松堂自序》，郑州：河南人民出版社2001年版].

is obviously prevailing in China's legal regime.[78] Not to mention Deng Xiaoping's famous and influential pragmatic comment, saying 'It doesn't matter whether a cat is black or white, so long as it catches mice.'[79] On one hand, pragmatism makes the Chinese legal policy more flexible and adaptive, which can rapidly cater to the newly emergent judicial and social needs. On the other hand, as Xingzhong Yu said,

> [influenced by pragmatism] Law [in China] is not understood in the context of relations between law and morality and rights and freedom as it is in many Western countries. The only source for the law is 'actuality' (shiji) as determined by the CPC. 'Actuality' is relied on, almost ritualistically, as a justification for all legislation. . .Actuality, moreover, is tied with the idea of 'objective' (keguan de) determination of 'actuality' and of the needs of development. . .'Actuality' produces law that 'adapt[s] to the objective needs of development'.[80]

Due to this pragmatism, the legal regime moved away from Xiao Yang's professionalism-oriented dispute resolution approach and adopted the mediation first and mass line strategy in early 2008, later transitioning smoothly to an integrated mode during Xi Jinping's era in the context of social governance policy. This shift allowed for a flexible dispute resolution mechanism within a rigid political–legal framework aimed at addressing social and political challenges faced by the state. This approach, termed 'politically correct pragmatism', enables the regime to increase the adoption of dispute resolution system and restore the Party's legitimacy through adaptive measures without fundamentally overhauling the political–legal system.

Although dispute resolution policies in China have varied across different historical periods, the underlying dynamics consistently oscillate between pragmatism and political correctness. At times, pragmatism dominates; at other times, the emphasis shifts towards reinforcing political correctness. This fluctuation between pragmatism and political correctness is central to understanding China's dispute resolution policy. This paradigm is crucial for explaining the judicial reforms across different historical periods in China, including the latest round of legal reforms under Xi Jinping's administration, where both political correctness and pragmatism are not only strengthened but also integrated. Because in Xi's

[78] Yu, 'Legal pragmatism in the People's Republic of China', 41.

[79] David S. G. Goodman, *Deng Xiaoping and the Chinese Revolution: A Political Biography* (London: Routledge, 1994), p. 3.

[80] Yu, 'Legal pragmatism in the People's Republic of China', 43.

reforms, the emphasis on political correctness has become more pronounced, solidifying the comprehensive leadership of the CPC, while the drive towards pragmatism in judicial professionalism has also become more evident. The underlying principle of politically correct pragmatism holds that if the foundational principles are protected, pragmatic reforms are feasible.

PART III

Legal Framework of Mediation in China

4

Style, Category and Legal Framework of Mediation

4.1 Style and Category of Mediation in China

4.1.1 Styles of Mediation

In 1996, according to the mediator's strategic characteristics and behaviour in the mediation process, Leonard L. Riskin proposed two modes of mediations: evaluative mediation and facilitative mediation. This classification has important typological significance and has a profound impact on mediation research. In an evaluative mediation, the mediator proactively intervenes as an expert in dispute resolution, using his own knowledge and experience to substantially influence the dispute resolution process and results. In a facilitative mediation, the mediator's role is to establish procedures and facilitate communication, and they will not intervene or exert substantial influence on the parties' judgement and decision making, which features a 'negatively effective' behaviour. Riskin pointed out that in an extreme evaluative mediation, the mediator will instruct and manipulate some or all of the conclusions and effects of mediation, while in an extreme assisting mediation, the mediator will simply request the parties to negotiate and understand each other.[1] Thus, it is easy to conclude that classifying mediation as evaluative and facilitative does not truly reflect the real mediation process but theoretically constructs a set of ideal mediation types that are mutually dialectical. In real mediation practice, the process of mediation is an intertwined evaluation and assistance to varying degrees; that is, evaluation and assistance are integrated in practice rather than opposed to each other.

Although in legal practice, evaluative mediation and facilitative mediation are differentiated by mediator's intervention, different legal systems do have different emphasis on these two mediation modes. For example, in a rather long history, facilitative mediation has been the mainstream

[1] See Leonard L. Riskin, 'Understanding mediators' orientations, strategies, and techniques: a grid for the perplexed' (1997) 1 *Harvard Negotiation Law Review* 7, 23–24.

paradigm of mediation in the Anglo-American world, and its basic concepts have had a profound impact on the construction of Western mediation rules and ethical norms.[2] Under the facilitative mediation model in these legal systems, mediators are required not to provide their own opinions to the parties. There are two reasons for this requirement. First, from the perspective of the parties, the core of mediation is the autonomy of the parties, which is unlike the authoritative judgment of the court. The mediator's evaluative intervention conflicts with such a requirement of autonomy. Second, from the mediator's perspective, mediators need to abide by strict neutrality, which gets violated when mediators make suggestions for the parties based on their own experience and knowledge.[3] Although the paradigm dominance of facilitative mediation encountered dual challenges from mediation practice and academic research in the 1980s and 1990s[4] and there was a tendency towards harmonicity, its basic value still affects the rhetorical description and behavioural regulation of mediation in the legislation of Western countries. For example, in the model law the Uniform Mediation Act of the United States issued in 2001, mediation is defined as 'a process in which a mediator facilitates communication and negotiation between parties to assist them in reaching a voluntary agreement regarding their dispute'.[5] In Practice Standards of the Australian National Mediation

[2] See Roger Seaman, *Explorative Mediation at Work: The Importance of Dialogue for Mediation Practice* (London: Palgrave Macmillan, 2016), p. 4; Heather Conway et al., *The Emotional Dynamics of Law and Legal Discourse* (Oxford, UK: Hart Publishing, 2016), p. 215; Katina Foster, 'A study in mediation styles: a comparative analysis of evaluative and transformative styles', www.mediate.com/articles/fosterk1.cfm (last accessed 10 December 2022).

[3] See Ellen A. Waldman, 'The evaluative–facilitative debate in mediation: applying the lens of therapeutic jurisprudence' (1998) 82(1) *Marquette Law Review* 155, 156–157.

[4] The critique of facilitated mediation is multidimensional. For example, in practice, since mediation is a complex process of interpersonal interaction, there is a transition spectrum from narrow evaluative mediation to narrow facilitative mediation, so it is impossible to just 'assist' in practice. After all, the boundary between 'suggestion' and 'control' is very blurred in real dispute resolution practices. Second, the setting of facilitative mediation constitutes a standard framework for mediation, while the insistence on a specific mediation model actually ignores the diversity of mediation cultures and practices in different jurisdictions. See Dorcas Quek Anderson, 'Facilitative versus evaluative mediation: is there necessarily a dichotomy?' (2013) *Asian Journal on Mediation* 66, 69.

[5] It is worth mentioning that the 'assistance' and 'facilitation' were further explained in the legislative description of the U.S. Uniform Mediation Act drafted by the National Uniform State Law Committee. By 'assistance', as distinguished from an arbitration process, it means the mediator shall not forcibly make a decision. For 'facilitation', the legislator stated that this is not a preference for a specific mediation style, and that the legislator

Standard, the restrictions on the conduct of mediators are more clearly expressed. The standard stipulates that

> mediators do not advise upon, evaluate or determine disputes. They assist in managing the process of dispute and conflict resolution whereby the participants agree upon the outcomes, when appropriate. Mediation is essentially a process that maximizes the self-determination of the participants. The principle of self-determination requires that mediation processes be non-directive as to content.[6]

In Hong Kong Special Administrative Region of PRC, the legislation on mediation strictly follows the path of facilitative mediation. Article 4 of the Mediation Ordinance in Hong Kong clearly stipulates the boundaries and specific content of the mediator's behaviour: mediation is a structured process comprising one or more sessions in which one or more impartial individuals, without adjudicating a dispute or any aspect of it, assist the parties to the dispute to do any or all of the following: (a) identify the issues in dispute; (b) explore and generate options; (c) communicate with one another; and (d) reach an agreement regarding the resolution of the whole, or part, of the dispute.[7] To complement the process, the Mediation Code in Hong Kong clearly stipulates the scope of the mediator's responsibilities and provides two-way guidance for the mediator's behaviour by making a 'positive list' and a 'negative list'.

> The Mediator will be neutral and impartial. The Mediator will assist the Parties to attempt to resolve the Dispute by helping them to: (a) systematically isolate the issues in dispute; (b) develop options for the resolution of these issues; and (c) explore the usefulness of these options to meet their interests and needs. The Mediator will not: (a) give legal or other professional advice to any Party; or (b) impose a result on any Party; or (c) make decisions for any Party.[8]

recognises the diversity of mediation methods. See www.uniformlaws.org/HigherLogic/System/Download-DocumentFile.ashx?DocumentFileKey=9b244b42-269c-769e-9f89-590ce048d0dd&forceDialog=0 (last accessed 11 November 2022). It should be noted that this interpretation makes the U.S. Uniform Mediation Act reflect the conciliation theory of the mediation model, but the typical behavior and legislative wording of 'evaluative mediation' have not been adopted in the definition of mediation in the legislative text.

6 Practice Standards of the Australian National Mediation Standard, www.fedcourt.gov.au/services/ADR/mediation/mediation_standards.pdf (last accessed 30 September 2023).

7 Mediation Ordinance in Hong Kong, China, www.elegislation.gov.hk/hk/cap620!sc?xpid=ID_1438403538324_001 (last accessed 20 June 2021). The emphasis marks are added by the author.

8 Hong Kong Mediation Code, www.hkmaal.org.hk/en/HongKongMediationCode.php (last accessed 19 July 2022).

4.1.2 Mediation Styles in China

In contrast to the above-mentioned mediation legislations, the People's Mediation Law of the People's Republic of China defines mediation as 'a people's mediation commission *persuades* the parties concerned in a dispute *to reach* a mediation agreement on the basis of equal negotiation and free will and thus *solves* the dispute between themselves' (emphasis added). Even though people's mediation is considered to have the attribute of citizen autonomy and citizen participation is out of their own will, in terms of the definition of 'mediation', the laws of Chinese mainland still use wording that has overt intervening connotation. In other words, the normative texts of Chinese mainland laws use more intrusive and proactive expressions, which enable mediators to obtain a substantive power to intervene in the dispute resolution process. Such a basic setting of 'assessment-based mediation' is also very obvious in the more recent local legislation in mainland China. For example, Article 24 of the Shanghai Municipal Regulations on Promoting Diversified Resolution of Conflicts and Disputes, which took effect since 2021, stipulates: 'People's mediation organizations shall, on the basis of equal consultation, mutual understanding and mutual accommodation, *propose* conflict resolution solutions to *help* parties voluntarily reach an agreement' (emphasis added). In other words, the legislation in Chinese mainland allows mediators, as an active subject, to substantively intervene in the process of dispute resolution by 'proposing a solution to conflicts and disputes'. Provisions of the Supreme People's Court about Several Issues Concerning the Civil Mediation Work of the People's Court (2004, amended in 2020) contain more direct provisions on this matter. Article 6 of the Provisions provides that 'the parties may propose mediation proposals themselves, and the mediators may also propose mediation proposals for the parties to consider during negotiations'.

The mediation in mainland China is more inclined towards the evaluative mediation mode, which widely affects various mediation forms such as people's mediation, administrative mediation, lawyer mediation, commercial mediation and judicial mediation. For administrative mediation and judicial mediation, since mediators in these mediations are the officials with authority, their influence on the process and outcome of the dispute resolution will be even more pronounced. In the court mediation context, it has been noted that the mediation sometimes may be transformed into quasi-adjudication. In Chinese judicial system, it is common that the court mediation and the trial are both hosted and completed by the same judge for the same case. In other words, if the parties are unable to settle the case at the mediation stage, and, in fact, they have wasted the judge's time, the noncooperative party may suffer from an unfavourable judgment in the later trial. The parties thus may be subject to some degree of coercion and come to understand that mediation in practice is not a totally consensual process.[9] Judges can exert evaluative pressure on the mediation process, which is to help themselves to save time or achieve the requirements of key performance indicator regarding the mediation rate. F. Peter Philips has recorded his vivid observation regarding the characteristics of Chinese evaluative mediation style. When Philips came to China for mediation training, one of the trainees, who was the judge from the Supreme People's Court (SPC), said:

> I have been a judge for thirty-five years. I have conciliated 10,000 cases. And you're trying to tell me how to do an opening statement? There is no need for an opening statement by the judge. Our civil procedure law provides that I am obligated to offer my services as a conciliator in any case before me. I always do. . .And what I do is to say, 'I'm going to now conciliate this case. Stop lying, all of you stop lying. Tell me what really happened.' And they tell me what really happened because I am a very respected judge. Then I go back to my office. I look up the law to find out what the right answer is. Then I come back and I say, 'According to the law, you owe him RMB 10,000. Now, you will either pay him the RMB 10,000 or we will go back to the trial. And if we go back to the trial, then in front of your children and in front of your mother and in front of your business partners I will point to you and say, 'You owe him RMB 10,000.'[10]

Such an expression may appear somewhat exaggerated, but it does reflect the evident 'evaluative' characteristic of mediation in China. In more recent fieldwork, it is also found that although the judge would not intervene in the mediation process arbitrarily, the judge would develop a sophisticated way to control the parties rather than just facilitating the communication between them. By using incomprehensible jargon in the

[9] Michael Palmer, 'Compromising courts and harmonising ideologies: mediation in administrative chambers of the People's Courts in the People's Republic of China' in Andrew Harding and Penelope (Pip) Nicholson (eds.), *New Courts in Asia* (New York: Routledge, 2010), p. 266.

[10] F. Peter Philips, 'Commercial mediation in China: the challenge of shifting paradigms', www.businessconflictmanagement.com/pdf/BCMarticle-china-paradigm.pdf (last accessed 29 October 2022).

adjudicative procedure, the judge suggests to the parties that adjudication might not be an ideal approach to handling this dispute between them and then naturally lead the parties to the mediation approach based on the so-called parties' voluntariness.[11] Therefore, when resolving the dispute, although the parties would be asked whether they are willing to mediate and the parties' voluntariness is guaranteed by the law, the dispute resolution process is still controlled and constructed by the mediators.

In the professionalised commercial mediation context, although the extent may vary, the mediation style is not limited to the facilitative scope either. According to the mediation code of the commercial mediation organisation, the voluntariness of the parties is the fundamental principle. However, the mediator code does not restrict the intervention of mediators but tries to create a subtle definition of mediation in order to integrate the facilitative and evaluative styles and expand the mediator's reasonable control and intervention in the dispute resolution process. For example, Article 5 of the Code for Mediators of Beijing Arbitration Commission Mediation Center (BACMC) states that 'a mediator shall pay full respect to the autonomy of the parties in the proceedings and conclusion of mediation', but it also requires the mediator shall 'actively guide the progress of mediation proceedings by his (her) creativity and experience, best satisfying the needs of the parties in light of the dispute'.[12] Similarly, the Mediators Code of Shanghai Commercial Mediation Center (SCMC) cautions that 'the mediator shall not force the parties to reach a settlement agreement', but at the same time, 'A mediator shall guide the parties concerned to gradually reduce their differences and reach a reconciliation agreement based on mutual understanding and mutual accommodation, adhering to the spirit of "talking business in business and valuing peace"'.[13] In both BACMC and SCMC rules, no prohibitive norms restrain the mediator's active and evaluative engagements in the mediation process. In practice, commercial mediation does not exist outside of China's dispute resolution culture; therefore, the mediator's evaluative interventions also exist.

[11] Hao Xiong, 'The feasibility of court mediation in the grassroots society of southwest China: a case study from Yunnan' (2014) 44 *Hong Kong Law Journal* 277, 282–284.

[12] Codes for Mediators, BACMC, www.bjac.org.cn/english/page/tj/guifan.html (last accessed 5 August 2021).

[13] Codes for Mediators, SCMC, www.scmc.org.cn/page67?article_id=83&menu_id=57 (last accessed 5 August 2021).

In some international commercial mediation cases, it has been noted that 'the mediator actively verified the authenticity of the goods delivered by the respondent on the spot through the internet, and contacted the freight forwarder to confirm the authenticity of the ocean bill of lading'.[14] Such proactive behaviour by mediators is described in another case, highlighting the mediator's hands-on approach in resolving dispute.

> After carefully understanding the explanations of both parties, conducting case investigations on the leased site, and consulting the local government, the mediation center concluded that the subject of the contract and the agreed lease price violated the law. . . Therefore, the mediation center pointed out it was illegal for the respondent to cut off water and power and restrict the applicant from purchasing raw materials from other enterprises. At the same time, it was also pointed out that the main body of the land and buildings leased by the applicant was not eligible.[15]

4.2 Categories of Mediation in China

In the Chinese legal system, mediation is developed under the supervision of the government. Chinese mediation system is generally classified according to the subject of the procedure, that is, the features of the mediator instead of the extent of the mediator's interference. Chinese mediation can be roughly divided into four main types: administrative mediation, people's mediation, judicial mediation[16] and the newly developed professionalised mediation represented by commercial mediation.[17]

[14] He Guicai, *Review and Analysis of Foreign-related Commercial Mediation Cases* (Beijing: Guangming Daily Press, 2013), p. 56 [何贵才：《涉外商事调解案例评析》，北京：光明日报出版社2013年版].

[15] Guicai, *Review and Analysis*, p. 66 [何贵才：《涉外商事调解案例评析》，北京：光明日报出版社2013年版].

[16] Fan Yu, *Textbook on Alternative Dispute Resolution* (Beijing: Renmin University Press, 2020), pp. 117–118 [范愉：《非诉讼程序（ADR）教程》，北京：人民大学出版社2020年版].

[17] Some researchers argue that mediation in China can be categorised into four distinct types: (1) people's mediation; (2) administrative mediation; (3) judicial mediation; and (4) institutional mediation, which encompasses mediation combined with arbitration (see Gabrielle Kaufmann-Kohler and Fan Kun, 'Integrating mediation into arbitration: why it works in China' (2008) 25 *Journal of International Arbitration* 479, 483.) However, the classification of Chinese mediation presented in this paper differs slightly from those perspectives. According to recent policy documents, at the end of 2023, Chen Wenqing, the Secretary of the Central Political and Legal Affairs Commission, emphasised the development directions for China's mediation system: 'Improve people's mediation,

Administrative mediation is the component of administrative procedure and will be conducted by administrative agencies like the policeman or other administrative enforcement officials as the mediator. Its principles, including 'free will and legality, without detriment to the national interest, public interest, or lawful rights and interests of others' are confirmed by Article 60 of the Administrative Litigation Law of the People's Republic of China (2017 Revision). Concerning the legal effect of administrative mediation agreement, Article 95 of the Administrative Litigation Law further explains that 'where a citizen, a legal person, or any other organization refuses to comply with a judgment, ruling, or administrative mediation agreement, the administrative agency or a third party may apply to the People's Court of first instance for enforcement, or the administrative agency may conduct enforcement according to the law'. That is to say, the administrative mediation agreement is not directly enforceable. Compared to people's mediation, 'since the administrative bodies are responsible for enforcing relevant laws and regulations, they have the legal and technical expertise necessary for a more efficient, timely, and proper settlement of disputes'.[18] Because different cases can be mediated by different administrative organs, the administrative mediation practice is governed and regulated by different laws. For example, Article 41 of the Environmental Protection Law of the People's Republic of China states that,

> a dispute over the liability to make compensation or the amount of compensation may, at the request of the parties, be settled by the competent department of environmental protection administration or another department invested by law with power to conduct environmental supervision and management.

solidify administrative mediation, strengthen judicial mediation, and refine industry-specific professional mediation (especially enhancing commercial mediation, particularly international commercial mediation, as well as lawyer mediation)'. From this policy statement, it is clear that mediation in China can be categorised into four types. See Chen Wenqing: 'Emphasizing the importance of adhering to and developing the "Fengqiao Experience" for the new era, with the aim of enhancing the legal resolution and prevention of conflicts and disputes' [陈文清：'坚持和发展新时代枫桥经验，提升矛盾纠纷预防化解法治化水平']，https://baijiahao.baidu.com/s?id=1785427778902199547&wfr=spider&for=pc (last accessed 13 May 2024). During my participation in the consultative meeting held by the Ministry of Justice on the legislation of commercial mediation, the official classification adopted aligned with the four types of mediation mentioned by Secretary Chen Wenqing.

18 Jeffrey K. L. Lee, 'Mediation in mainland China and Hong Kong: can they learn from each other?' (2014) 16(1) *Asian-Pacific Law & Policy Journal* 100, 105.

People's mediation is the second type. It is integrated into the Chinese grassroots government service system and is conducted by the people's mediators, who are grassroots civil servants and cadres of the government with certain authority but not legal professionals in most cases.[19] People's mediation is a quasi-official dispute resolution mechanism with support and supervision from the government. People's mediation is usually conducted in urban or rural communities to deal with disputes with moral characteristics, such as family or neighbourhood issues, and simple civil cases. In recent years, the specialisation and professional level of people's mediation have been improved in some developed cities. For example, in Shanghai, based on people's mediation mechanism, the doctor–patient mediation committee, the residential property dispute committee and the traffic dispute mediation committee are established respectively.[20] But they are all people's mediation, which is not run by the market mechanism. In other words, the mediation service is free for the disputants, and government funds will pay the remunerations of mediators. Due to the low degree of institutionalisation and professionalisation, the legal regulation of people's mediation is relatively rare. In the current legal system, there is only one law, the People's Mediation Law (2010), which is very simple and principled, guiding the people's mediation practice nationally. As the practice of people's mediation needs to follow the local knowledge and cater to local needs, the people's mediation processes are different in different places and are carried out with significant regional characteristics.

The third type of mediation is court mediation, which is also the most important and influential one. Court mediation is an institutionalised and standardised dispute resolution procedure existing in the judicial system. The court mediation provides the ideal models and institutional framework based on which other forms of mediations are constructed as the relatively simplified versions. At present, the relative statute does not

[19] Xin Xu, *Mediation: China and the World* (Beijing: China University of Political Science of Law Press, 2013), pp. 4–5 [徐昕主编：《调解：中国与世界》，北京：中国政法大学出版社2013年版].

[20] Article 18 of the Regulation of Shanghai Municipality on Promotion of Diversified Dispute Resolution (2021) provides that 'all districts in this Municipality have set up professional people's mediation committees for medical and patient disputes, consumption disputes, property disputes, traffic accidents disputes, intellectual property disputes, labor disputes and other disputes, to mediate contradictions and disputes in related fields under the guidance of the district judicial administrative department and the competent departments of relevant trades'.

provide a clear definition of court mediation. In general, court mediation can be defined as a form of court-connected ADR in which judicial staff and another invited facilitator play the role of the mediator to assist the disputing parties to achieve a mutually acceptable resolution in a written form.[21] Although the principles of court mediation are voluntariness and lawfulness provided by Article 9 of the Civil Procedural Law of the PRC, it is an evaluative mediation in which judges play a very influential and even an adjudicative role. Unlike the ordinary mediation agreement which is similar to a civil contract between equal parties, the court mediation agreement (*minshi tiaojieshu*, 民事调解书) is legally binding like an enforceable judgment. In Chinese, the meaning of court mediation (*fayuan tiaojie*, 法院调解) is equal to judicial mediation (*sifa tiaojie*, 司法调解).

The final one is professional mediation, exemplified by commercial mediation. Commercial disputes are the ones related to contract, trade, investment, finance, securities, intellectual property rights, technology transfer, real estate, project contracting, transportation, insurance and disputes in commercial and maritime, which cover very broad dispute types. At the domestic legal level, due to the adoption of a unified civil and commercial law system in China, there is no specific legislative definition of commercial disputes. However, at the level of other normative legal documents, when China acceded to the New York Convention, the SPC, in its 'Notice Regarding the Implementation of the Convention on the Recognition and Enforcement of Foreign Arbitral Awards by China', issued in 1987, provided a judicial interpretation of the term 'commercial' that is very broad in its scope. This definition provides a comprehensive and inclusive understanding of what constitutes a commercial dispute under Chinese law.

> According to China's reservation declaration upon acceding to the Convention, China applies the Convention only to disputes arising from economic rights and obligations governed by contract and non-contractual commercial legal relationships under Chinese law. The term 'contractual and non-contractual commercial legal relationships' specifically refers to economic rights and obligations arising from contracts, torts, or as stipulated by relevant laws, such as disputes related to the sale of goods, property leasing, engineering contracting, processing and contracting, technology transfer, joint ventures, cooperative operations, exploration and

[21] Hao Xiong, '"Is court mediation feasible?" Quantitative research on the attitudes of legal professionals in southwest grassroots society of China' (2015) 45 *Hong Kong Law Journal* 963, 964–965.

> development of natural resources, insurance, credit, labor services, agency, consulting services, maritime, civil aviation, railway, and road transportation of goods and passengers, as well as commercial dispute mediation practices and product liability, environmental pollution, maritime accidents, ownership disputes, and so on. However, it does not include disputes between foreign investors and the host country's government.

Although China has introduced the market economy since 1978 with the Reform and Opening-up Policy, commercial mediation as an independent form of mediation is a rather new phenomenon. The earliest modern commercial mediation institutions, including the Beijing Arbitration Commission Mediation Center (BACMC) and Shanghai Commercial Mediation Center (SCMC), were established around 10 years ago. BACMC was founded in 2011 in Beijing. According to BACMC's official introduction, it was established with the aim of providing 'high-end commercial mediation services, and endeavors to promote the use of mediation to settle commercial disputes and the harmonious industrial development'.[22] SCMC similarly was also founded in 2011. It is a third-party commercial mediation institution established with the approval of the Shanghai Municipal Commission of Commerce and the Shanghai Administration Bureau of Non-Governmental Organisations, aiming to provide 'independent, just, professional, efficient, economical and flexible services to settle commercial disputes, maintaining and promoting harmony and the commercial relationship'.[23] Because there are no national mediation rules and unified mediator ethical standards in China, both commercial mediation centres have made their own mediation rules, which follow the professional approach but are subtly different from the rules of their Western counterparts.

Recently, China has begun to further promote the construction of a commercial mediation system in line with the inflow of global capital to the Asian market.[24] For example, Articles 17 and 18 of the Regulation of Shanghai Municipality on Promoting the Pluralist Resolution of Conflicts and Disputes provide that market-oriented mediation organisations shall be encouraged under the guidance and supervision of the judicial administrative department. Moreover, the establishment of organisations specialising in both domestic and international mediation

[22] BACMC Introduction, www.bjac.org.cn/english/page/tj/mediation.html (last accessed 18 July 2021).

[23] Overview of the SCMC, www.scmc.org.cn/page67?article_id=196&_l=en&menu_id=86 (last accessed 18 July 2021).

[24] Matthew Erie, 'The new legal hubs: the emergent landscape of international commercial dispute resolution' (2020) 60(2) *Virginia Journal of International Law* 225, 227.

of commercial disputes in the fields of investment, finance, real estate, technology transfer, intellectual property and international trade shall be encouraged.[25] Although there is no uniform commercial mediation law in China at both the national and local levels, due to China's accession to the Singapore Mediation Convention, the positive value of the development of commercial mediation in optimising the business environment and promoting diverse dispute resolution as well as the limited impact of alternative dispute resolution systems on the country's basic political framework, the faster development of China's (international) commercial mediation rules in the future can be expected. There has been a concerted effort at both central and local levels to prepare and plan for the legislation of commercial mediation. The Ministry of Justice plans to finalise optimising the commercial mediation regulations in recent years and developed regions such as Shanghai and Guangdong are also drafting their own commercial mediation regulations.

However, as of late 2024, these relevant laws have not yet been finalised. This results in a lack of clear legal provisions regarding the definition of commercial mediation, its applicable legal scope, the ethical standards and qualification certification system for mediators and the handling of conflicts of interest and fraudulent mediation.[26] The lack of specific commercial mediation legislation in China has created significant obstacles to the effective functioning of commercial mediation, necessitating urgent legal reforms to establish clear guidelines and standards for the practice. For example, the ethical standards and qualification certification for mediators are not standardised, with guidelines varying across different mediation and arbitration institutions. Moreover, Chinese mediators often believe they have a broad discretion in conducting mediation, which raises issues of impartiality and independence, especially in judicial mediations where judges may take a dominant approach.[27] Therefore, the absence of comprehensive legislation has led to inconsistencies and inefficiencies in the practice of commercial mediation in China. Establishing unified laws and standards is crucial for ensuring the integrity and effectiveness of commercial mediation in the country.

In response, the central government adheres to the principle of politically correct pragmatism, encouraging local governments to take

[25] Regulation of Shanghai Municipality on Promoting the Pluralist Resolution of Conflicts and Disputes (2021) [上海市促进多元化解矛盾纠纷条例], www.lawinfochina.com/display.aspx?id=35124&lib=law (last accessed 6 February 2021).

[26] Meng Chen, 'Commercial mediation in Mainland China: pitfalls & opportunities' (2023) 23 *Pepperdine Dispute Resolution Law Journal* 167, 197–199.

[27] Chen, 'Commercial mediation in Mainland China', 198.

the lead in experimentation. However, several specific obstacles exist in local legislation. On one hand, China's dispute resolution culture significantly differs from that of the West (a point detailed in Chapter 5 on the ADR movement), which can lead to value conflicts in commercial mediation legislation, such as whether it should empower individuals or integrate society. These cultural challenges are reflected in the drafting of specific provisions, such as whether to mandate facilitative mediation, impose restrictions on mediator behaviour or establish 'mediation in accordance with the law' as a fundamental principle to control the negative externalities of dispute resolution. [28] Additionally, determining the extent to which voluntariness and confidentiality should be protected also presents foundational issues that extend beyond regulatory supply to the harmonisation, adaptation and transformation of the dispute resolution culture.

On the other hand, both the Ministry of Justice and local administrative departments face specific legal obstacles in the legislative process for commercial mediation. First, Article 15, Paragraph 2 of the Administrative Licensing Law states,

> Local regulations (地方性法规) and rules of the people's governments of provinces, autonomous regions, and municipalities directly under the central government (政府规章) shall not establish administrative licenses concerning the qualifications, certification, and registration of enterprises or other organizations that ought to be uniformly determined by the State.[29]

[28] Hao Xiong, 'The challenges of Singapore Convention to Chinese mediation system' (2022) 52(3) *Hong Kong Law Journal* 1057, 1063–1079.

[29] Because different translation systems or scholars will translate these words into different English expressions, it is important to memorise the Chinese pronunciation of different legal sources and the awareness of Chinese characters. For example, 地方性法规, 自治条例, 单行条例, 部门规章 and 地方政府规章 are also translated into local decree, autonomous decree, special decree, administrative regulation and departmental rules promulgated by agencies under the State Council and local rules, respectively.

It should be noted that since there is no official English translation of Chinese laws, only relying on the English translation is sometimes misleading. For example, Article 11 of the Civil Procedural Law (1991, amended in 2023; CPL) states that:

> Citizens of all nationalities shall have the right to use their native spoken and written languages in civil proceedings. Where minority nationalities live in aggregation in a community or where several nationalities live together in one area, the people's courts shall conduct hearings and issue legal documents in the spoken and written languages commonly used by the local nationalities. The people's courts shall provide translations for any participant in the proceedings who is not familiar with the spoken or written languages commonly used by the local nationalities.

Without modifications, this rule precludes local legislation from setting provisions for mediator qualifications and mediation organisation registration. Second, according to the Singapore Mediation Convention, if China seeks to explore 'individual mediation' – allowing qualified individual mediators to engage in international commercial mediation and recognise the enforceability of international commercial mediation agreements made by individual mediators – it must amend the Civil Procedure Law. Article 205 of the Civil Procedure Law states,

> To apply for judicial confirmation of a mediation agreement reached under the mediation of a legally established mediation organization in

This is one version of translation from the website of National People's Congress, which translates '民族' into nationality. See www.npc.gov.cn/zgrdw/englishnpc/Law/2007-12/12/content_1383880.htm (last accessed 9 May 2023). It is worth mentioning that there is no official English-translated version of Chinese law. Hence there are different translated versions from different channels. The Chinese expression '各民族公民都有用本民族语言、文字进行民事诉讼的权利' in this article is translated as 'citizens of all nationalities shall have the right to use their native spoken and written languages in civil proceedings' or 'citizens of all ethnicities shall be entitled to use their native spoken and written languages in civil procedures' in different English versions of CPL. The latter translation is provided by the authoritative website of the Chinese legal database – *Beida Fabao* (北大法宝), the biggest legal database in China. However, the problem here is *minzu* (民族) is translated differently in different ways. China is a unified multi-ethnic country. According to the English–Chinese dictionary, it is true that *minzu* can be translated into the English term 'nationality'. This translation whereas may cause misleading understanding because this translation seemly provides that English or other foreign languages can be used in the court proceeding in both the spoken and written ways. However, it is not the case. According to the CPL, in the regions inhabited by ethnic minorities or several ethnic groups, the CPL allows People's Courts to use the common language of the ethnic minority in the civil proceeding. This article is formulated in consideration of the situation of China's fifty-six ethnic groups and diverse local conditions. If the parties are ethnic minorities, they are not proficient in Mandarin and can only communicate in their native language; People's Courts in this case shall provide an interpreter for participants in proceedings. The relevant cost will be paid by the court. Therefore, the term '*minzu*' should only be translated into 'ethnic groups' or 'ethnicities' instead of 'nationality' in the CPL context. That is to say, Chinese, including the Chinese ethnic minority dialects, is the language that shall be used in court proceedings but not the languages of all nationalities (such as English, French, German, Japanese, Spanish and so on). In the cases where the litigation participant can only speak English or a foreign language, the court would support the language translation. However, unlike in the Chinese ethnic minority case, the cost of the translation of the foreign language will be paid by the party. This situation is stipulated in Article 273 of CPL, which states that

> People's Courts trying foreign-related civil lawsuits shall use language or text commonly used in the People's Republic of China. Where a litigant request for provision of translation, translation may be provided, and the expenses shall be borne by the litigant.

> accordance with the law, both parties to the mediation agreement shall, within 30 days from the date when the mediation agreement takes effect, jointly file an application with the following People's Court.

This provision implies that Chinese courts confer enforceability through judicial confirmation only on mediation organisations established by law, excluding individuals.[30] During official research meetings, the author was informed that when the National People's Congress revised the Civil Procedure Law in 2021, this issue was considered. However, relevant departments and experts argued that the scope of enforceability for court-confirmed mediation agreements should be strictly limited and that the conditions for granting enforceability to agreements signed by individual mediators were not yet mature. Therefore, any local legislation seeking to deviate from the Civil Procedure Law must proceed with extreme caution.

In conclusion, while there is a genuine need for the professionalisation of mediation, particularly commercial mediation, and a necessity to comply with international conventions, significant work remains in adjusting cultural norms, constructing institutional frameworks and harmonising legislation. The development of commercial mediation legislation in China will involve multiple dimensions of dispute resolution and the existing legal system, far beyond simply creating, supplementing or transplanting relevant provisions from another jurisdiction. Addressing these issues requires collaborative efforts from China's legal community, judicial institutions and mediation practitioners to ensure that Chinese commercial mediation legislation aligns with international standards, thereby promoting mediation as an effective tool for resolving both domestic and international disputes.

[30] Compared with Chinese Civil Procedural Law, Singapore Mediation Convention (2018) adopts the direct enforcement mechanism; and the mediation agreement according to the Singapore Convention is final. The convention has very simple requirements for mediation documents. According to Article 4 of the Singapore Mediation Convention, 'A party relying on a settlement agreement under this Convention shall supply to the competent authority of the Party to the Convention where relief is sought: (a) The settlement agreement signed by the parties; (b) Evidence that the settlement agreement resulted from mediation, such as: (i) The mediator's signature on the settlement agreement; (ii) A document signed by the mediator indicating that the mediation was carried out; (iii) An attestation by the institution that administered the mediation; or (iv) In the absence of (i), (ii) or (iii), any other evidence acceptable to the competent authority'. See Singapore Mediation Convention, https://uncitral.un.org/sites/uncitral.un.org/files/singapore_convention_eng.pdf (last accessed 1 October 2023).

4.3 Legal Framework of Mediation in China

4.3.1 Provisions in the Civil Procedure Law That Directly Regulate Mediation

While the Chinese Civil Procedure Law (1991, amended in 2023) primarily regulates civil litigation procedures, some of the sections of it still concern ADR.[31] This section will provide a brief overview of the relevant ADR-related provisions within this law (Table 4.1).

From the above provisions regarding mediation, some characteristics of mediation in Chinese courts can be observed. Firstly, there is an emphasis on mediation in accordance with the law. According to Article 9 of the CPL, People's Courts trying civil cases shall carry out mediation under the principles of voluntary participation and legitimacy. According to the mainstream theory of mediation, mediation does not emphasise the law and facts but the future.[32] Mediation is a dispute resolution mechanism that emphasises improving the future prospects and resolving issues between parties by shifting the focus away from the past and towards a better future. In mediation, the law serves as one of the negotiation aspects but is not the sole determinant. Litigation, on the other hand, primarily delves into the past when addressing disputes, concentrating on establishing what occurred in the past and the evidence that can be presented in court. According to Su Li,

> In order to promote the development of mediation, the restriction should be loosed in terms of the requirement of '[mediating] according to the law.' Firstly, even though mediation can be implemented according to the

[31] According to mainstream Chinese legal scholarship, Civil Procedure Law is defined as the basic law of the People's Republic of China. That is because, on one hand, from the perspective of the content, all fundamental stipulations on civil procedure that aim to guarantee the realisation of civil substantive rights are stipulated in CPL, while other specific regulations, such as the Law on People's Assessors, People's Mediation Law, Arbitration Law and so on, stipulate only a certain aspect of civil procedure. On the other hand, from the perspective of the hierarchy of law, the formulation and implementation of other regulations on civil procedure must not be contrary to the spirit of the Civil Procedure Law, otherwise, they would be invalid. Based on the above two points, it is generally stated in Chinese legal scholarship that the Civil Procedure Law is the basic law, whose influence is not restricted to the civil adjudication area. See Weiping Zhang (ed.), *Civil Procedure Law* (Beijing: Law Press, 2019), p. 13 [张卫平主编：《民事诉讼法学》，北京：法律出版社2019年版]; Liu Jiaxing and Pan Jianfeng (eds.), *Civil Procedure Law* (Beijing: University of Beijing Press 2017), p. 10 [刘家兴，潘剑锋主编：《民事诉讼法学教程》，北京：北京大学出版社2017年版].

[32] Thomas D. Barton, 'The modes and tenses of legal problem solving, and what to do about them in legal education' (2007) 43(2) *California Western Law Reviews* 389, 389–416.

Table 4.1 *Provisions Relating to Mediation in the Civil Procedure Law*

Article No.	Content
Article 9	Basic Principle of Court Mediation: When trying civil cases, the People's Courts shall conduct mediation under the principles of free will of the parties and legality; and if mediation fails, shall enter a judgment in a timely manner.
Article 97	On-the-Spot Mediation: When a People's Court conducts mediation, mediation may be conducted by one judge or by the collegial bench, and mediation shall be conducted on the spot as much as possible.
Article 98	Mediator Invited: When a People's Court conducts mediation, it may invite relevant entities and individuals to provide assistance. The invited entities and individuals shall assist the People's Court in mediation.
Article 99	Requirements of Mediation Agreement: A mediation agreement must be based on the free will of both sides, and the parties shall not be forced to reach a mediation agreement. The content of a mediation agreement shall not violate any legal provisions.
Article 100	Format and Effect of Mediation Agreement: When a mediation agreement is reached, the People's Court shall prepare a consent judgment. A consent judgment shall state the claims, facts of the case and results of mediation. The judges and court clerk shall affix their signatures and the People's Court shall affix its seal to a consent judgment, which shall be served on both sides. Once a consent judgment is signed by both sides, it shall become legally binding.
Article 101	The Situation Where a Mediation Agreement Document Is Not Needed: (1) divorce cases where both parties have reconciled through mediation; (2) adoption cases where an adoptive relationship has been maintained through mediation; (3) cases where performance on the spot is possible; (4) other cases where a consent judgment is not required. A mediation agreement that does not require a consent judgment shall be recorded in the transcripts and become legally binding immediately after both sides and the judges and court clerk affix their signatures or seals to the transcripts.
Article 102	To Judge in Time: Where no mediation agreement is reached or one party retracts before a mediation agreement is served on the party, the People's Court shall enter a judgment in a timely manner.

Table 4.1 (*cont.*)

Article No.	Content
Article 125	Mediation First Principle: Where mediation is appropriate for the civil dispute involved in an action instituted by a party in a People's Court, mediation shall be conducted first unless the parties refuse mediation.
Article 145 Article 179	The Applicable Stage of Mediation: Where mediation is possible before a judgment is entered, mediation may be conducted; and if mediation fails, a judgment shall be entered in a timely manner. When trying an appeal case, the People's Court of Second Instance may conduct mediation.
Article 205	Judicial Confirmation of Mediation Agreement: To apply for the judicial confirmation of a mediation agreement reached under the mediation of a legally established mediation organisation in accordance with the law, both parties to the mediation agreement shall, within 30 days from the date when the mediation agreement takes effect, jointly file an application with the following People's Court: (1) If a People's Court invites a mediation organisation to conduct preliminary mediation, the application shall be filed with the People's Court that makes the invitation. (2) If the mediation is conducted by the mediation organisation, the application shall be filed with the primary People's Court at the place where the party is domiciled or the subject matter or the mediation organisation is located. If the dispute involved in the mediation agreement shall be under the jurisdiction of an intermediate People's Court, the application shall be filed with the corresponding intermediate People's Court.
Article 206	The Legal Effect of Judicial Confirmation of Mediation Agreements: After accepting an application, if the application complies with legal provisions upon examination, the People's Court shall issue a ruling to affirm the validity of the mediation agreement, and if one party refuses to perform or fails to fully perform the mediation agreement, the opposing party may apply for enforcement to the People's Court; or if the application does not comply with legal provisions upon examination, the People's Court shall issue a ruling to dismiss the application, and the parties may, through mediation, modify the mediation agreement or reach a new mediation agreement and may also institute an action in a People's Court.

> law, the key point of mediation is to achieve a successful dispute settlement rather than to act by the law. Secondly, from the perspective of society, if the mediation is carried out regardless of the law, it will not necessarily produce an unjust outcome. On the contrary, it may deepen our understanding of law [in context] and may create new feasible regulations. Thirdly, no matter whether the judge is concerned with the law or not, legal regulation will become an inevitable counter in the bargaining process of mediation. Fourthly, it is only necessary to require the judge-mediator not to gain personal interests from mediation and not to prejudge any party. That will be fine if the outcome is just in general and is not too far away from the moral common sense or does not excessively accommodate the outdated social conventions and customs.[33]

Despite the aforementioned challenges, China has made 'mediation in accordance with the law' a fundamental principle in its legislation. This legal stipulation arose due to the historical absence of proficient mediators and alternative dispute resolution (ADR) services, placing the primary responsibility for mediation on the courts. On one hand, China lacks truly professional mediators and established professional standards for mediation. For instance, the scarcity of trained professionals in this field and the relatively recent commencement of ADR education in law schools contribute to this issue. Currently, only a handful of universities in China offer comprehensive ADR training for law students, resulting in a limited market for qualified ADR service providers. To prevent mediation from deviating excessively from legal standards and to ensure basic quality, mediation in accordance with the law has become an important consideration. This principle is intended to keep mediation aligned with the path of justice. On the other hand, due to the insufficient marketisation and professionalisation of social mediation services, a significant number of disputes, even those resolved through mediation, eventually reach the courts. As judicial institutions, courts

[33] Su Li, 'On Active Justice and Big Mediation' (2010) 1 *China Legal Science* 5, 13 [苏力：《关于能动司法与大调解》，载《中国法学》2010年第1期]. The original Chinese text goes as follows:

> 要想促进调解的发展，就必须适度摆脱法条的约束，放松对调解的'依法'要求。第一，调解可以依法，但着眼点不是依法，而是调解成功。第二，从社会角度来看，背离了法律的调解不一定就不公正，相反可能丰富对法律的理解，创造新的法律。第三，在不关注是否依法的调解中，法律仍然在起作用 - 现行法律规定始终会成为调解双方讨价还价的筹码。第四，调解中只要求作为调解者的法官不能从中谋利、有意偏袒一方，调解结果基本公道，距离中国社会的基本道德共识不能差距太大或过于迁就陈规陋习。

naturally emphasise that the resolution of disputes must conform to legal standards of justice. Therefore, the principle of mediation in accordance with the law also reflects the judicial inertia inherent in court mediation.

Secondly, as discussed in Chapter 2, mediation historically took precedence in China due to cultural, social and political factors. Consequently, in contemporary judicial practice, judges employ various methods to encourage parties to opt for mediation, aiming to achieve a high mediation success rate. The Civil Procedure Law provides institutional support for this kind of 'guidance' of judges. In China, if a judge proposes mediation and the parties are unwilling to cooperate and choose litigation instead, the same judge will continue to preside over the case, even if it eventually goes to trial. This means that if mediation ultimately fails, the judge will need to invest additional time and effort in adjudicating the same case, rendering the time spent on mediation seemingly futile. Such a scenario may lead judges to develop negative perceptions of uncooperative parties. Judges may also pressure parties to compromise or concede by alluding to potentially unfavourable judgment outcomes, which can disrupt the relationship between mediation and litigation and compromise the parties' voluntary participation. Therefore, in certain developed regions like Shanghai and Zhejiang, some courts have authorised qualified social mediation centres or organisations to conduct mediations when social and economic conditions permit. In cases where out-of-court mediation proves unsuccessful, the case is subsequently adjudicated by court judges.[34]

Thirdly, regardless of the type of mediation agreement, it must undergo judicial confirmation by the court to become legally binding. Courts play an important role in the enforcement of mediation agreement in China. All the mediation agreements made outside the court are treated as the same thing with the same legal validity. Thus, no mediation agreement can be directly enforced unless it is confirmed by the People's Court. Although Chinese judicial authority now is encouraging the development of a diversified dispute resolution system, the mediation agreement made by a commercial mediation organisation shall be of a nature of a civil contract after both parties affix their signatures or seals to it.[35] The SPC further requires that all the mediation agreements made by different organs and organisations should be confirmed by the court having jurisdiction for the validity of

[34] For more details, see Chapter 6.

[35] 'Several Opinions of the Supreme People's Court on Establishing a Sound Conflict and Dispute Resolution Mechanism that Connects Litigation and Non-litigation', Article 10, www.pkulaw.com/en_law/2b9298312f576756bdfb.html (last accessed 26 June 2021).

such an agreement after the mediation organisation and mediator affix their signatures or seals to it.[36] Moreover, not all mediation agreements can be confirmed by the People's Court. Article 3 of Notice by the Supreme People's Court of Issuing the Measures for the Implementation of the Pilot Program of the Reform of Separation between Complicated Cases and Simple Ones in Civil Procedure (2020) provides that 'where a civil mediation agreement is reached through mediation by a people's mediation committee, specially invited mediation organisation, or specially invited mediator, the parties may jointly move the People's Court for judicial confirmation within 30 days from the effective date of the mediation agreement'. In other words, the mediation agreement made before an independent mediation professional would not be confirmed by the court unless this mediator has been registered by the court as the specially-invited mediator. These provisions reflect the power of state control over the private dispute resolution process and limit the enforceability of individual mediation. The Civil Procedure Law amended in 2023 has further expanded the scope of judicial confirmation of mediation agreement reached under a legally established mediation organisation in accordance with the law. As previously discussed, the CPL indeed expands the scope of judicial confirmation of mediation agreements beyond the People's Mediation Committee to include other mediation institutions. However, the main entities involved in mediation remain legally established mediation organisations rather than individual professionals.

4.3.2 People's Mediation Law

The system of people's mediation is a constitutional institution in China. According to the Constitution of the People's Republic of China (1954, amended in 2018), Article 111 states that,

> residents' committees and villagers' committees shall establish people's mediation, public security, public health, and other subcommittees to handle public affairs and public services in the residential areas to which they belong, mediate civil disputes, and help maintain public order; they shall convey residents' opinions and demands and make proposals to the people's government.

This provision is located in the fifth section of the constitution, Local People's Congresses and Local People's Governments, highlighting that

[36] 'Several Opinions of the Supreme People's Court on Establishing', Article 20.

the people's mediation system is not only a form of alternative dispute resolution but also an extension of the Chinese government's reach and civil autonomy into grassroots society service provision.

The current People's Mediation Law in China, legislated in 2010, provides a foundational institutional framework for the practice of people's mediation. The People's Mediation Law consists of six chapters (including General Provisions and Supplementary Provisions) and primarily regulates People's Mediation Committees, People's Mediators, Mediation Procedures and Mediation Agreements. Overall, the law provides a flexible, pragmatic and low-barrier regulatory framework for mediation, with the overarching goal of achieving substantive dispute resolution. The People's Mediation Law stipulates that parties have the right to request that mediation be conducted publicly or privately and that mediators must not disclose personal privacy or business secrets. However, confidentiality is not established as a fundamental principle of mediation in the People's Mediation Law. On the contrary, to uphold community values and achieve more effective conflict resolution, the law allows people's mediators to invite relatives, neighbours, colleagues, individuals with specialised knowledge or experience and representatives from relevant social organisations to participate in the mediation process based on the needs for mediating a dispute and with the consent of the parties concerned (Article 20). It also states that 'People's mediation commissions encourage impartial, decent persons who are dedicated to mediation work and approved by the people to participate in mediation work' (Article 20).

In addition, the law requires people's mediators to take appropriate precautions if a dispute is likely to escalate during mediation and to promptly report to the local public security organ or other competent department if a dispute is likely to become a public security or criminal case (Article 25). These provisions signify a departure from the principles of strict confidentiality and voluntariness by the parties in mediation. It is evident that the law's fundamental objective is the effective resolution of societal disputes and the substantive resolution of conflicts rather than maximising the control of parties over disputes. Under the practical principle of achieving substantive dispute resolution, confidentiality or other principles are relatively secondary and should be upheld only if they contribute to problem resolution; otherwise, they can be adjusted.[37]

[37] Xiong, 'The challenges of Singapore Convention', 1073–1079.

The flexibility of the People's Mediation Law is closely related to its need to be applicable across the diverse regions of China. The dispute resolution needs addressed by the People's Mediation Law arise not only from modern metropolises, such as Beijing and Shanghai, but also encompass more extensive underdeveloped regions and grassroots villages. It is crucial to remember that communities in Shanghai, villages in Guizhou and frontiers in Xinjiang all constitute the grassroots of China. The People's Mediation Law needs to be applied in these highly heterogeneous areas. For example, when mediating grassroots disputes in underdeveloped areas of China, mediators often invite non-parties to participate in the dispute resolution process. This is because in close-knit communities, repairing relationships requires the collective effort of other community members. This is also an educative process as witnessing the dispute resolution process can help prevent similar conflicts and establish norms for handling disputes within the community. When the community witnesses the mediation process, it does not produce a clear winner and loser but rather a win–win resolution that incorporates the broadest consensus. This helps people understand the advantages of mediation in repairing social relationships and encourages them to use mediation to resolve conflicts. It should not be forgotten that China is a huge and diverse nation, and at the grassroots level, dispute resolution carries different functions and needs to address various issues. The cohesive nature of community relationships, the ties of familiarity in a society based on personal connections and the approachability of interactive methods make it challenging for grassroots mediation in China to strictly adhere to the confidentiality norms set for mediation. Therefore, the People's Mediation Law provides relatively flexible provisions to accommodate these needs. In other words, the localised nature of dispute resolution coupled with its response to the highly diverse dispute resolution needs of Chinese grassroots society makes it difficult for the People's Mediation Law to construct a particularly clear and rigid standard mediation framework.

Based on the same rationale, the People's Mediation Law demonstrates considerable flexibility regarding the qualifications of mediators. The law states that people's mediators must be adult citizens who are impartial, decent, dedicated to mediation work and possess a certain level of education, policy understanding and legal knowledge (Article 14). However, it does not provide specific criteria for mediator qualifications or competency levels nor does it set any qualification examination requirements. The law's ethical provisions for people's mediators are also general in nature, prohibiting mediators from showing favouritism, insulting parties, seeking illicit benefits or disclosing private or trade secret information (Article 15).

This flexibility allows various individuals, such as elders, religious leaders, clan leaders, teachers and doctors – those with community prestige – to participate in the dispute resolution process. This inclusivity enables grassroots mediation in China to incorporate and utilise more local knowledge and social resources. However, it also results in the generally unsatisfactory quality of people's mediators. As mentioned, mediation services are part of the government's basic grassroots public services and are therefore provided free of charge (Article 4). The government guarantees the funding for people's mediation, and the mediation process is subject to government oversight (Article 5). While this provision eliminates economic barriers to public mediation, it also limits incentives for mediators and hinders the development of professional mediation. The flexibility in professional requirements and the free service model discourage highly qualified individuals, such as graduates trained in law, social work and psychology, from entering this field. This often impedes the development of professional mediation (e.g., commercial mediation) based on people's mediation foundation, making it difficult for people's mediation to support more complex and specialised types of mediation services effectively.

4.3.3 Relevant Judicial Interpretations

Although the Civil Procedural Law has provided the general principles and basic regulations governing Chinese court mediation, only several articles deal with mediation practice in the CPL. These articles are not only far from clear but also leave a huge gap in the law.[38] In practice, these legislative gaps are often filled up by judicial interpretations provided by the SPC. Judicial interpretation in China refers to the authoritative explanations and clarifications of laws provided by the SPC and the Supreme People's Procuratorate. These interpretations aim to guide the application of laws and ensure uniformity in judicial decisions across the country.

In the civil justice system, the judicial interpretation issued by the SPC plays a significant role, which, in essence, constitutes 'court-made law'

[38] Stanley B. Lubman, 'Dispute resolution in China after Deng Xiaoping: "Mao and Mediation" Revisited' (1997) 11 *Columbia Journal of Asian Law* 229, 336.

that is nationally effective.[39] According to Article 18 of the Organic Law of the People's Courts of the People's Republic of China (2018 Amendment), 'the Supreme People's Court may explain issues on the specific application of law in trial work'. Consequently, the SPC issues various documents, including Official Opinions and Explanations, Notices (Circulars) and Conference Summaries, Interpretations (*jieshi*, 解释), Provisions (*guiding*, 规定), Rules (*guise*, 规则), Replies (*pifu*, 批复) and Decisions (*jueding*, 决定). All of these are broadly defined as judicial interpretations guiding the national court system.

By 2007, the SPC had developed more detailed and systematic regulations for judicial interpretation. Article 5 of The Provisions of the Supreme People's Court on the Work Concerning Judicial Interpretation (2007, amended in 2021) specifies that 'the judicial interpretation formulated and promulgated by the Supreme People's Court shall be legally effective'. This provision clarifies the narrow sense definition of judicial interpretation, indicating that legally binding judicial interpretations include five types: Interpretations, Provisions, Rules, Official Replies and Decisions. 'Legally binding' means, according to Article 27 of the Provision, that any judicial interpretation used as a basis for a court ruling must be cited in the judicial documentation. Other official documents issued by the SPC are considered to have policy or guidance significance but do not carry legally binding force.

In the area of mediation, China's Civil Procedure Law provides fundamental regulations, but there are numerous institutional gaps in its practical implementation. To address these gaps, the SPC's judicial interpretations offer more detailed operational guidance on the specifics of mediation, which will be discussed in detail in Chapter 5. As of 2024, there are sixty-five judicial interpretations (in a broad sense) related to mediation issued by the SPC, according to the Chinalawinfo Pkulaw Database (*beida fabao*, 北大法宝). The most important ones are eight judicial interpretations, including:

(1) Provisions of the Supreme People's Court about Several Issues Concerning the Civil Mediation Work of the People's Court (Provisions 2004, amended in 2020)

[39] Susan Finder, 'The Supreme People's Court of the People's Republic of China' (1993) 7 *Journal of Chinese Law* 145.

(2) Several Opinions of the Supreme People's Court on Further Displaying the Positive Roles of Litigation Mediation in the Building of a Socialist Harmonious Society (Opinions 2007)
(3) Notice of the Supreme People's Court on Issuing Several Opinions on Further Implementing the Work Principle of 'Giving Priority to Mediation and Combining Mediation with Judgment' (Notice 2010)
(4) Several Provisions of the Supreme People's Court on the Judicial Confirmation Procedure for the People's Mediation Agreements (Provisions 2011)
(5) Provisions of the Supreme People's Court on Specially-Invited Mediation by the People's Courts (Provisions 2016)
(6) Opinions of the Supreme People's Court and the Ministry of Justice on Implementing the Pilot Program of Lawyer Mediation (Opinions 2017)
(7) Notice of the Supreme People's Court on Issuing the Operating Rules of the Supreme People's Court on Distribution of Complicated Civil and Commercial Cases from Simple Ones and Mediation and Fast-track Sentencing (for Trial Implementation) (Notice 2017)
(8) Guiding Opinions of the Supreme People's Court on Further Improving the Mechanism of Designated Mediation (Opinions 2020).[40]

Although these eight judicial interpretations are all related to mediation directly, they are formulated in different historical and social contexts. In Boxes 4.1 to 4.21, the main content of the judicial interpretations will be listed, through which the differences reflecting the change in China's judicial policy in the past years can be positioned in a clear and straightforward way.

[40] In 2022, the Supreme People's Court issued the Rules for the Online Mediation by People's Courts. This rule establishes the basic procedures for online mediation work, including provisions for the scope of application of online mediation (Article 3), the principle of voluntary participation by the parties (Article 4), the requirement on the special mediator (Article 6, which allows foreigners to participate), principles for situations where online mediation is not applicable (Article 9, for example, when the dispute is not suitable for online mediation, parties are informed to handle mediation or file a case at the people's court litigation service hall), disclosure of conflicts of interest (Article 13), time limits and various procedural arrangements. Due to the unique nature of the online mediation process, it does not significantly differ from or impact the existing mediation regulatory system. Therefore, this judicial interpretation has not been included in the review of judicial interpretations in Boxes 4.1 to 4.21.

BOX 4.1 GUIDELINE

Mediate when possible, judge when necessary; combining mediation with judgment and solving the dispute once the case is concluded; fair adjudication and serving the people with one's heart and soul (Notice 2007).

'Mediation First': Give priority to mediation and combining mediation with judgment; 'Big Mediation': Promote the construction of the 'Triune' Big Mediation System combining it with People's Mediation, Administrative Mediation, and Judicial Mediation (Notice 2010).

With Xi Jinping Thought on Socialism with Chinese Characteristics for a New Era as the guidance, efforts shall be made to uphold and develop the 'Fengqiao Experience').[41] in the new era, improve the mechanism of resolving disputes at the sources, put the non-litigation dispute resolution mechanism in the first place and meet the demands of the general public for diversified, efficient and convenient dispute settlement solutions. Designated mediation shall be conducted in accordance with the laws, procedures and principles on a voluntary basis; a social governance system in which Party committees play a leading role, governments assume the primary responsibilities, the people's opinions are consulted, social collaboration and public participation are supported and legal guarantees and technical support are provided shall be constantly improved; and a social governance community in which everyone is responsible, dedicated and shares benefits shall be established (Opinions 2020).

BOX 4.2 GOAL

Settle contradictions and disputes, clarify right and wrong and solve the dispute once the case is concluded (Notice 2007).

Resolve all disputes upon the closing of a case (Notice 2010).

BOX 4.3 CONCRETE REQUIREMENT

Increase the number of cases settled by means of mediation; do their best to improve the proportion of cases handled by mediation (Notice 2007).

'Two Rises': the rate of settling cases through mediation and the rate of willingly accepting the judgments; 'Two Falls': the rate of cases involving lawsuit-related complaints and the rate of enforcement (Notice 2010).

[41] Fengqiao experience refers to the work of Party cadres at the local level where the real interface between the Party and the people occurs. It refers to solving problems and complaints at the local level before they spin out of control into large-scale social unrest.

BOX 4.4 MEDIATION PRINCIPLE

Voluntariness; Lawfulness (Provisions 2004, amended in 2020)
Voluntariness; Lawfulness; Confidentiality (Notice 2007)
Voluntariness; Lawfulness (Notice 2010)

Specially-invited mediation shall observe the following principles:

1. Equity and free will of the parties;
2. Respecting the litigation rights of the parties;
3. Not violating the prohibitive provisions of laws and regulations;
4. Not damaging the national interests, the public interests or the lawful rights and interests of others; and
5. Not disclosing the mediation process and the contents of mediation agreements, except as otherwise provided for by the law (Provisions 2016).

Lawfulness; Voluntariness; Neutrality; Confidentiality; Convenience and Efficiency; Effective Connection[42] (Notice 2017)

BOX 4.5 APPLICABLE STAGE FOR COURT MEDIATION

Before the expiration of the defence period, if the People's Court conducts mediation in cases subject to the ordinary procedure and no mediation agreement is reached within 15 days from the date when the parties agree to mediation, or in cases subject to the summary procedure and no mediation agreement is reached within 7 days from the date when the parties agree to mediation, with the consent of all parties, mediation may continue. The extended mediation period does not count towards the trial time limit (Provisions 2004, amended in 2020).

1. After the term for answers expires but before the judgment is made in the first and second instance;
2. Appeal stage or case applied for retrial stage;
3. Civil enforcement stage (Notice 2007).

All the Stages: Employ mediation before and throughout each stage of case filing, trial and execution, through the whole process of the first instance, second instance, execution, retrial, appeal, letters and visits (Notice 2010).

[42] According to the Opinions 2017, effective connection means that the organic linkage among lawyer mediation, administrative mediation, industrial mediation, commercial mediation and litigation mediation shall be strengthened, and their respective characteristics and advantages shall be brought into full play, and a dispute resolution mechanism with procedural linkage, complementary advantages and collaboration and cooperation shall be formed.

BOX 4.5 (*CONT.*)

For a dispute appropriate to be mediated, before the cases are docketed, a People's Court may assign a specially invited mediation organisation or specially-invited mediator to conduct mediation with the consent of the parties; and after the case is docketed or in the process of trial, may authorise a specially-invited mediation organisation or specially-invited mediator to conduct mediation (Provisions 2016).

BOX 4.6 APPLICABLE CASE

1. Civil cases;
2. Cases of civil suit collateral to criminal proceedings;
3. Administrative cases;
4. Private prosecutions;
5. Minor criminal cases (Notice 2007)

Establish a full-dimensional mediation mechanism covering all fields of trial and execution:

1. Civil cases, especially the summary procedure in the trial of a civil case;
2. Administrative cases;
3. Private prosecuting cases;
4. Minor criminal cases;
5. Civil cases incidental to criminal cases;
6. Cases of state compensation; and
7. Enforcement cases (Notice 2010).

The lawyer mediation may accept various civil and commercial disputes, including civil disputes incidental to criminal cases, but excluding cases not subject to mediation, such as confirmation of marital and personal relations (Opinions 2017).

1. Disputes over family matters;
2. Disputes over neighbouring relations;
3. Labor disputes;
4. Disputes over traffic accident compensation;
5. Medical disputes;
6. Property disputes;
7. Disputes over consumers' rights and interests;
8. Disputes over small amounts of debts; and
9. Disputes over the application for withdrawing an arbitration award for labour dispute (Notice 2017)

BOX 4.7 FOCUS

1. The case involving mass interests and the case requiring the cooperation of the government and the relevant departments;
2. Joint action or group action which involves a large number of people;
3. The circumstance is complex, the opponent sentiment between the parties concerned is serious and neither party has a preponderance of evidence;
4. Certain difficulty in the application of law as the provisions governing it are not stipulated or clearly stipulated in the relevant laws and regulations;
5. Sensitive and attracts much attention from society;
6. Cases of appeal or review; and
7. Cases of a retrial (Notice 2007).

1. Cases concerning the people's livelihood and group interests which require the cooperation of governments and relevant departments;
2. Mass cases which may affect social harmony and stability;
3. Class action cases;
4. Bankrupt cases;
5. Cases of civil disputes over private debts;
6. Marriage;
7. Family, succession;
8. Cases in which the circumstances are complex and neither party has a preponderance of evidence;
9. Cases in which the parties concerned strongly hate each other;
10. Cases with a certain difficulty in the application of the law due to lack of provisions or lack of evident provisions governing it in the relevant laws and regulations;
11. Cases in which the judgments are difficult to be executed after they are made;
12. Sensitive cases which attract much attention from society; and
13. Retrial cases and petition cases filed in letters and paid visits in which the parties concerned have intense emotions and the conflicts are intensified (Notice 2010).

BOX 4.8 STYLE OF MEDIATION

Friendliness, Transparency and Efficiency (Notice 2007).

Comprehensible (using understandable language) (Notice 2010).

BOX 4.9 PARTIES' RIGHTS

1. Be informed about the name of the presiding mediator and the court clerk and the relevant litigation rights and obligations;

BOX 4.9 (*CONT.*)

2. Application for refusal of judges;
3. Application for private mediation;
4. Put forward a mediation proposal by themselves (Voluntariness) (Provisions 2004, amended in 2020).

1. Apply for an amendment to keep correspondence between civil mediation documents and the mediation agreement.
2. The right to require not to disclose the content of the mediation agreement (Confidentiality) (Notice 2007).

BOX 4.10 MEDIATOR'S RIGHTS

1. Offer a mediation proposal for the parties' reference;
2. If the parties have a partial agreement based on which the mediator can make a mediation agreement;
3. If the parties cannot reach an agreement on how to bear the litigation costs, the mediator may directly decide the proportion of litigation costs to be borne by the parties and record this decision in the mediation agreement (Provisions 2004, amended in 2020).

Respectively conduct mediation with each party in the process of mediation (Notice 2010).

BOX 4.11 LIMITATION OF APPLYING COURT MEDIATION

1. Avoid the tendency of merely pursuing a mediation ratio;
2. Where a case is not suitable to be mediated or it is impossible to reach a mediation agreement on a case after making great efforts (Notice 2007).

1. Avoid improper mediation and the trend of unduly pursuing a mediation ratio;
2. Shall not conduct mediation at the cost of sacrificing the legitimate rights and interests of the parties concerned;
3. Where the parties concerned fabricate litigation or make use of mediation to postpone the litigation;
4. Where the resolution on one party is obviously unjust, and the reluctant mediation will indulge the lawbreaker or the party in breach of contract so that the legitimate rights and interests of the law observer or the observant party are damaged;
5. Where the time and energy consumed by and the cost invested in mediation are not in proportion to the resolution effects;

BOX 4.11 (*CONT.*)

6. Cases involving national interests or public social interests;
7. Having guiding significance on the application of the law or having positive meaning on the formation of the awareness of social rules (Notice 2010).

BOX 4.12 LIMITATION/REQUIREMENT OF MEDIATOR

Confidentiality (Notice 2007)

The mediator shall not unilaterally meet the parties or the agents they entrust in private, as in violation of the relevant provisions (Notice 2010).

BOX 4.13 REWARD SYSTEM

Establish a scientific and reasonable mediation incentive mechanism to improve the initiative and enthusiasm of the judges in settling cases using mediation (Notice 2007).

Reform and improve the statistical indicator system of mediation work, perfect the statistical standards developed from gathering and examining the mediation information of civil cases up to the gathering and examining the mediation in various links, including pre-litigation, case filing, pre-trial, in the trial, post-trial, execution, retrial, appeal, letters, and visits, etc., and various kinds of work, e.g., criminal and administrative mediation, reconciliation and coordination. In terms of the examination indicator system, we shall highlight the examination of the social effects of the handling of cases at the same time taking proper consideration of the number of cases handled, the ratio of cases settled and the ratio of amended judgments and remands, and increase the weight of such indicators, such as the ratio of withdrawal of lawsuit upon mediation, the judgment acceptance rate, the application rate for retrial, the appeal rate, the rate of letters and visits, the enforcement rate and the voluntary performance rate of mediated cases, etc. (Notice 2010).

A People's Court shall, according to the actual circumstances, grant subsidies for loss of working time, traffic allowance and other subsidies to specially-invited mediators, and give material or honorary rewards to specially-invited organisations and specially-invited mediators with outstanding performance. Subsidy funds shall be included in the special-purpose budgets of the People's Court (Provision 2016).

The weight of designated mediation in the performance assessment system shall be increased, and the detailed rules and work plans for the incentive mechanism shall be specified. Mediation judges and specially-invited mediators who have promoted the parties in voluntarily fulfilling the mediation agreement shall be

BOX 4.13 (*CONT.*)

rewarded and incentivised through performance assessment; mediation agencies and mediators that have made remarkable achievements or performed other outstanding deeds in mediation work shall be commended and rewarded according to the state's provisions, and their working performance shall be deemed as an important basis for other various evaluations and assessments so as to mobilise, to the greatest degree, the enthusiasm of mediation judges, specially-invited mediation agencies, specially-invited mediators and other mediation entities in mediation work (Opinions 2020).

BOX 4.14 THE MAKING OF A MEDIATION AGREEMENT

1. If the parties raise objections on the grounds of inconsistency between the civil mediation statement and the original intent of the mediation agreement, and the People's Court, after examination, finds the objection valid, it shall issue a ruling to correct the relevant content of the civil mediation statement in accordance with the mediation agreement.
2. If the parties reach a mediation agreement on some of the claims, the People's Court may first confirm and prepare a mediation agreement.
3. If the parties reach a mediation agreement on the main claims and request the People's Court to provide handling suggestions for the unresolved claims, and if they express acceptance of the handling results, the People's Court's handling suggestions become part of the mediation agreement, and this is recorded in the mediation agreement (Provisions 2004, amended in 2020).

1. Be signed or affixed with seals by the parties concerned, judge and clerk of the case;
2. Be signed or affixed with seals by the judge and clerk of the case;
3. Be affixed with the seal of the People's Court;
4. A mediation agreement shall be simplified in content, briefly recording the cause of the case and the claims of the parties concerned, and is not required to record the case facts, trial process or evidence, etc. (Notice 2007).

BOX 4.15 ILLEGAL AND INEFFECTIVE MEDIATION AGREEMENT

1. Infringes on the national interests and public social interests;
2. Infringes on the interests of persons other than those involved in the case;
3. Is contrary to the true intentions of the parties concerned;
4. Violates the prohibitive prescriptions of the laws and administrative regulations (Provisions 2004, amended in 2020).

BOX 4.15 (*CONT.*)

1. Violates any mandatory provision of the laws and administrative regulations;
2. Harms the national interests or the interests of the general public;
3. The content of the agreement falls beyond the scope of the rights of the parties concerned to disposal;
4. The controversial legal relationship involves the rights and interests of any person not involved in the case;
5. Any person who is not involved in the case and has any rights over the property to be transferred as agreed to in the agreement;
6. The content of the agreement does not conform to public customs and morality;
7. The mediation is conducted in a way that violates the true will of any party concerned, etc. (Notice 2007).

1. Violates the legal provisions;
2. Harms national interests and the general public's interests;
3. Harms the interests of third parties;
4. Harms the social public order and morality (Notice 2010).

Specially-invited mediators shall not have the following conduct:

1. Forcing the parties to accept mediation;
2. Conducting mediation against the law;
3. Accepting a party's request for help or accepting properties from a party;
4. Disclosing the mediation process or the contents of the mediation agreement;
5. Any other conduct in violation of the professional ethics for mediators.

A party that finds out any mediator under any of the aforesaid circumstances may file a complaint to the People's Court. Where it is proved to be true upon examination, the People's Court shall make a correction and take such appropriate action as giving the mediator a warning, circulating a notice of criticism or removing his or her name from the register of mediators (Provisions 2016).

BOX 4.16 COOPERATION WITH THE PARTY AND GOVERNMENT

1. Adhere to the leadership of the Party Committee and support the government to promote the construction of the work system.
2. Obtain the support of the local Party Committee and government, bringing the expenditure of the mediation work into the financial budget, also actively getting the support of the special funds of the central government for political and legal subsidies and the provincial financial supporting funds.
3. As for major difficult cases which have great impact, the court shall actively win the support of the Party Committees and the people's congresses and the

BOX 4.16 (*CONT.*)

cooperation of the superior administrative organs and invite the relevant departments to jointly participate in the coordination (Notice 2010).

BOX 4.17 TRAINING

Make more efforts in the training of the judges' mediation capacity, formulate long-term training programmes and establish a system for the judges to accept training, in turn, accepting training (Notice 2007).

Bring the fostering of mediation capability into the annual and special training programme of judges, focusing on improving the ability to do mass work, and make great efforts to strengthen the construction of mediation capability (Notice 2010).

Specially-invited mediators shall, before being included in the registers and during their term of office, accept the business training organised by People's Courts (Provisions 2016).

BOX 4.18 TIME LIMIT

The mediation may continue after obtaining the consent of the parties concerned. The extended mediation period shall not be included in the time limit for concluding a trial (Provisions 2004, amended in 2020).

During the phase of case filing: 1. Summary procedure: 10 days; 2. Ordinary procedure: 20 days (Notice 2007).

1. The reconciliation and mediation period will not be counted into the time limit for concluding a trial;
2. Within reason, relax the restrictions on the applicable time and period of mediation and the time limit for concluding trials;
3. Where the parties concerned are willing to accept mediation while the time limit of a trial is about to expire, the parties concerned may determine the time limit for continuing the mediation through consultation, and, upon the examination and approval of the People's Court, this shall be put on record by the judge that hears the case (Notice 2010).

A People's Court shall decide whether to accept a judicial confirmation application within three days after receiving it. If it decides to accept it, it shall grant a case number in the 'mediation confirmation category' and serve the notice of acceptance upon the parties concerned without delay. Where both parties apply for judicial confirmation at the court, the People's Court may accept it and make a decision of confirmation or non-confirmation on the spot. A People's Court shall, within

BOX 4.18 (*CONT.*)

15 days after accepting a judicial confirmation application, make a decision of confirmation or non-confirmation. Where it needs to extend the time limit under special circumstances, the time can be extended by 10 days upon the approval of the president of the court (Provisions 2011).

For a case the mediation of which is appointed by a People's Court, the mediation period shall be 30 days, except when both parties agree to extend the mediation period. For a case the mediation of which is authorised by a People's Court, the period for mediation under general procedure shall be 15 days, and the period for mediation under summary procedure shall be seven days, except when both parties agree to extend the mediation period. The extended mediation period shall not be included in the trial period (Provisions 2016).

The term lawyer mediation is 30 days. This limit shall not apply where both parties consent to the extension of the term of mediation (Opinions 2017).

Where the People's Court engages in mediation or entrusted mediation, it shall complete the mediation or entrusted mediation within 15 days. Where the parties have consented to extend the time limit, it may be appropriately extended, but the extension may not exceed 15 days. The period of mediation shall not be included in the time limit for trial (Notice 2017).

BOX 4.19 ENTRUSTED MEDIATION AND SPECIALLY-INVITED MEDIATION[43]

The People's Court may appoint the auxiliary staff of a trial or invite and entrust the related entities and individuals to engage in the coordination of the activities (Provisions 2004, amended in 2020).

The People's Court may invite enterprises, institutions, social organisations or other organisations that have specific relationships with the parties or a certain connection to the case as well as individuals with specialised knowledge, specific social experience, a specific relationship with the parties and who are conducive to mediating the dispute to assist in the mediation process. With the consent of all parties involved, the People's Court may entrust the units or individuals specified in the preceding paragraph to mediate the case. After reaching a mediation agreement,

[43] The basic meanings of entrusted mediation (*weituo tiaojie*, 委托调解，it is also translated into designated mediation) and specially invited mediation are similar, which means that the court, based on the consensus of the disputing parties, would entrust the mediation to another organisation to conduct or invite professionals, not necessarily legal practitioners, to mediate the cases according to the law. The mediation agreement achieved in these processes can be confirmed by the court and then becomes legally binding.

BOX 4.19 (*CONT.*)

the People's Court shall confirm it in accordance with the law (Provisions 2004, amended in 2020).

The social organisation or the individual shall sign or affix a seal on the mediation agreement but is not required to sign or affix a seal on the mediation letter prepared by the People's Court based on the mediation agreement (Notice 2007).

1. Upon the consent of the parties concerned, the court may authorise the relevant organisations of people's mediation, administrative mediation and industrial mediation, etc., which are conducive to the settlement of cases through mediation, or deputies to the people's congresses, political advisors, etc., to preside over the mediation work or may invite the relevant entities or technical experts, lawyers, etc., to assist the People's Courts in the mediation work.
2. The time limit: 30 days. The mediation period may be postponed upon the consent of both parties, but this shall not exceed 60 days at the most. The postponed mediation period shall not be counted in the time limit for concluding a trial. 3. A People's Court shall write a mediation transfer letter when authorising a mediator for the mediation work, attach it with the main materials of the case and clarify the matters requiring the attention of the authorised mediators and the relevant requests of the parties concerned (Notice 2010).

A People's Court may establish professional mediation committees for family affairs, traffic accidents and medical disputes, among others, and, according to the characteristics of the disputes in those professional fields, set forth the eligibilities for being included in the registers of such professional mediation committees and regulate the specially-invited mediation procedures in the professional fields. Specially-invited mediators shall not serve as people's assessors, agents ad litem, witnesses, appraisers or translators, among others, in the following judicial proceedings. In the process of mediation, the facts accepted by a party as compromises for the purpose of reaching a mediation agreement shall not be used against the party in legal proceedings, except as otherwise agreed on by all parties (Provisions 2016).

For a dispute brought by the parties concerned to a People's Court, if the parties apply for mediation or agree to mediate under the guidance of the People's Court, the People's Court may, before the case filing and registration, appoint a specially-invited mediation agency or a specially-invited mediator to conduct the mediation, and the parties shall sign a Notice of Designated Mediation. If the parties in dispute do not agree to mediate, they shall expressly state their opinions when signing the Notice of Designated Mediation. The People's Court shall, after receiving the written materials stating that the parties in dispute do not agree to mediate, transfer the case to litigation in a timely manner. For a case under designated mediation, a

BOX 4.19 (*CONT.*)

People's Court shall register it as 'pre-litigation mediation', and litigation materials shall, within three days, be transferred to a specially-invited agency or a specially-invited mediator for mediation. If a dispute over jurisdiction is involved, the People's Court that first registers it as 'pre-litigation mediation' shall be deemed as the first one to file the case. The People's Courts shall strengthen the construction, application and publicity of mediation platforms, intensify the connection between mediation platforms and other mediation institutions, improve the mechanism of connecting litigation and non-litigation solutions for dispute resolution, support online mediation of cases, online transfer of mediation data and online sharing of mediation-related information and increase the diversified dispute resolution capability in an all-around manner (Opinions 2020).

BOX 4.20 PAYMENT ORDER IN LAWYER'S MEDIATION

Where there is any content of monetary payment or payment of negotiable securities in the settlement agreement or mediation agreement reached upon lawyer mediation and the creditor files an application for a payment order with the basic-level People's Court with jurisdiction in accordance with the provisions of the Civil Procedure Law and its judicial interpretations, the People's Court shall issue a payment order according to the law; and if the debtor fails to raise a written objection within the statutory time limit or fails to perform the payment order within the prescribed time limit, the People's Court may enforce the payment order (Opinions 2017).

BOX 4.21 JUDICIAL CONFIRMATION PROCEDURE[44]

A People's Court shall not accept a judicial confirmation application if

1. It is not within the scope of civil cases of the People's Courts or it is not under the jurisdiction of the People's Court to which the application is made;

[44] People's mediation agreement can be confirmed by the grassroots people's court whose jurisdiction is at the locality of the people's mediation committee concerned. Where a party concerned refuses to perform or fails to fully perform a mediation agreement confirmed by the decision of a people's court, the other party may apply to the people's court which made the confirmation decision for enforcement. For more details, see Several Provisions of the Supreme People's Court on the Judicial Confirmation Procedure for the People's Mediation Agreements, www.pkulaw.com/en_law/fab2106f037fa3e1bdfb.html (last accessed 15 March 2023).

BOX 4.21 (*CONT.*)

2. It is about the confirmation of identity;
3. It is about the confirmation of an adoptive relationship; or
4. It is about the confirmation of a marital relationship.

If the mediation agreement is under any of the following circumstances, a People's Court shall not confirm its force:

1. Violating the mandatory provisions of any law or administrative regulation;
2. Infringing upon the national interests or public interests;
3. Infringing upon the legitimate rights and interests of any non-party;
4. Impairing the public order or good custom;
5. Having unclear contents; or
6. Other circumstances under which the agreement shall not be confirmed (Provisions 2011).

For an agreement with the nature of a civil contract reached upon mediation by the lawyer mediation office or the lawyer mediation center, the parties may file an application with the basic-level People's Court or the people's tribunal at the place where the lawyer mediation office or the lawyer mediation center is located for confirming the effect of the agreement, and the People's Court shall confirm the effect of the mediation agreement according to the law (Opinions 2017).

From Boxes 4.1 to 4.21, it is clear that the legal regulations on mediation in China are relatively comprehensive. Many important legal issues have been stipulated by the law, mainly in the judicial interpretations provided by the SPC. They are reasonable in general; however, as these interpretations were made in different political and social climates, they reflect different policy orientations in different times. Through close reading, several essential traits in Chinese mediation law can be abstracted from these regulations. Firstly, the 'politicisation' and 'professionalisation' aspects of the mediation law develop in a synchronous way, as 'directives from the Party leadership may well establish basic parameters for SPC activity, but the technical complexity of the Chinese judiciary will usually create considerable room for maneuvering within those parameters'.[45]

As to the 'politicisation' orientation, in the Opinions (2007) and the Notice (2010), political missions are explicitly set in these SPC judicial documents. In 2020, the court system is also required to follow Xi Jinping

[45] Taisu Zhang, 'The pragmatic court: reinterpreting the Supreme People's Court of China' (2012) 25 *Columbia Journal of Asian Law* 1.

Thought on Socialism with Chinese Characteristics for a New Era as the guidance, and efforts shall be made to uphold and develop the Fengqiao Experience in the new era. In the politics-oriented context, mediation could be employed in all steps of the court proceedings, including the entire process of the first instance, second instance, execution, retrial, appeal and letters and visits. The time limit on mediation became looser and more flexible. It also provides that "where the parties concerned are willing to accept mediation when the time limit of a trial is about to expire, the parties concerned may determine the extension of the time limit for continuing the mediation through consultation'. In the entrusted mediation context, the mediation period may be postponed upon the consent of both parties. The range of mediation-applicable cases is also expanding. In Notice 2010, for example, the court is required to establish a full-dimensional mediation mechanism covering all fields of trial and execution. Thus, mediation is commonly adopted by the court and enjoys priority in the Chinese dispute resolution system. These political requirements transform the court from a dispute resolution centre and safeguard of justice into a stakeholder of the government who should also be responsible for maintaining social stability, achieving social harmony and gaining popular support. It makes sense because the court, in China, usually plays a role of social control and accepts the arrangement of the regimes regarding the channelling of different types of cases to different arenas.[46] When facing social pressure of dispute, the Party needs the court. In some of the judicial interpretations issued by the SPC, it is clear that the regime does not aim to simply limit or abolish the functions of the court; on the contrary, the regime wants to introduce the court into the battle of social conflicts and dispute resolution. Together with them, they desire to cope with some 'hard bones' cases, such as the cases concerning group interests, mass cases, class action cases, and so on and so forth, which may affect social harmony and stability. It is true that:

> The legitimacy of China's leadership depends on its ability to both channel and contain populism; concerns that popular expressions of outrage may spin out of control, encourage rapid intervention in the legal system. . .This is particularly the case in China, where the rise of social unrest makes officials particularly sensitive to public opinion and where

[46] Tamir Moustafa and Tom Ginsburg, 'Introduction: the functions of courts in authoritarian politics' in Tom Ginsburg and Tamir Moustafa (eds.), *Rule by Law: The Politics of Courts in Authoritarian Regimes* (Cambridge: Cambridge University Press, 2008), p. 4.

the courts lack a history of being viewed as either authoritative or neutral.[47]

In this context, the collaboration between the court and the government is evident. Both entities work together towards the same overarching national goals, addressing core issues of the state through functional cooperation rather than operating in a system of checks and balances. On one hand, the court seeks support from the local Party Committee and government, incorporating mediation expenditures into the financial budget, and actively securing support from central government funds for political and legal subsidies as well as provincial financial support funds. When faced with major and complex cases, the court actively seeks the backing of the Party Committees to coordinate resources and resolve disputes. On the other hand, when the government needs to alleviate social tensions, the court is expected to assist by providing a professional perspective, even though the proportion of such cases requiring inter-departmental coordination is relatively small.[48]

As to the 'professionalisation' aspect, it should not be ignored that the relevant regulations still contain more and more legal and technical factors. 'Law has not been abandoned in China', as Carl F. Minzner said, 'state authorities continue to issue statutes and regulations. Citizens and corporations continue to invoke legal norms as they seek to protect their interests'.[49] This distinguishes today's mediation reform from the 'mass line' in Mao Zedong's time. Through close reading, it can be found that the SPC provided many detailed and technical regulations. For example, the comprehensibility requirement regarding mediation language, the inapplicability of mediation in the cases where the parties concerned fabricate litigation or make use of mediation to postpone the litigation, applicability of mediation in cases where the circumstances are complex,

[47] Benjamin L. Liebman, 'China's courts: restricted reform' (2007) 21 *Columbia Journal of Asian Law* 1, 39.

[48] It should be noted that the PRC courts handle over eight million first instance cases per year; only a small fraction of them are political or politically sensitive in nature, which may attract the attention from the CPC or government. The risk, nature, source and impact of interference are different. Failing to draw these distinctions is likely to lead to misleading generalisations. See Yulin Fu and Randall Peerenboom, 'A new analytic framework of understanding and promoting judicial independence of China' in Randall Peerenboom (ed.), *Judicial Independence in China: Lessons for Global Rule of Law Promotion* (Cambridge: Cambridge University Press, 2010), p. 96.

[49] Carl F. Minzner, 'China's turn against law' (2011) 59 *American Journal of Comparative Law* 935, 937.

and neither party has a preponderance of the evidence and in other cases. The Notice 2010 even provides more detailed stipulations to exclude and limit the use of court mediation in the unsuitable circumstances and lists seven types of cases. It stated that:

> as for cases involving national interests or social public interests, having guiding significance on the application of law, or having positive meaning on the formation of the awareness of social rules, we shall attach importance to making a timely judgment and closing the case according to law, give full play to the positive role of judgment in making a clear distinction between right and wrong, regularising behaviors, punishing the evil and encouraging the good.

Many of these regulations that are consistent with the conclusions achieved through the scholarship are neither found in China nor abroad.[50] These regulations reflect that the SPC is concerned with the social reality of China and is also attempting to improve the level of judicial governance by doing careful research about the Chinese reality. The SPC has drawn its data from legal scholarship in this area.[51] Under the administration of Xi Jinping's administration, the professionalisation

[50] See David Spencer and Michael C. Brogan, *Mediation Law and Practice* (Cambridge: Cambridge University Press, 2006), pp. 109–119; Laurence Boulle, *Mediation: Principles Process Practice* (Chatswood: LexisNexis UK, 2005), pp. 262–268; Eric D. Green, 'Mega-disputes and class actions' in Dwight Golann (ed.), *Mediating Legal Disputes: Effective Strategies for Neutrals and Advocates* (Chicago, IL: ABA Section of Dispute Resolution, 2009), p. 325; see also Myron S. Greenberg and Megan A. Blazina, 'What mediators need to know about class actions: a basic primer' (2004) 27 *Hamline Law Review* 191, 220.

[51] Considering the high degree of professionalism of the SPC, this phenomenon is understandable. The SPC, without doubt, is becoming the most professionalised court in China, in which an abundance of legal experts get involved when making legal policy. Besides, when designing judicial policy, the SPC always consults the relevant legal scholars for their suggestions. It is the 'path' that the Chinese legal system has to depend on when drafting today's judicial interpretations, even though 'turning left'. See Meng Hou, *Research on the Supreme People's Court of People's Republic of China: Focus on the Judicial Influence* (Beijing: Law Press, 2007), Chapter 5 [侯猛：《中国最高人民法院研究：以司法的影响力切入》，北京：法律出版社2007年版]; see also Yongjun He, 'The judge of Supreme Court: a primary historical investigation' in Weimin Zuo (ed.), *Research on Supreme Court* (Beijing: Law Press, 2004) [何永军："最高法院法官：一个初步的历史考察"载左卫民主编：《最高法院研究》，北京：法律出版社2004年版]. For example, the SPC maintains close collaboration with the academic community. Before issuing significant judicial policies, the SPC often holds 'research meetings (*diao-yan huiyi*, 调研会议)' to gather opinions and suggestions from academics, thereby optimising policy content. Additionally, through personnel exchanges between the courts and universities (known in Chinese as '挂职锻炼'), the courts can more effectively integrate specialised research talent into their operations.

aspect of mediation has been also enhanced. The Provisions 2016 clearly provided that the professional mediation committees for family affairs, traffic accidents and medical disputes, among others, and according to the characteristics of the disputes in those professional fields, should be established, and the specially-invited mediators shall not serve as people's assessors, agents ad litem, witnesses, appraisers or translators, among others, in the following judicial proceedings. In other words, the justice system began to separate the mediation process from the litigation process when conditions allowed. Moreover, the SPC amended the Provisions of the Supreme People's Court about Several Issues Concerning the Civil Mediation Work of the People's Court. In the 2004 version of the Provisions, it provides that 'the People's Court may mediate the accepted civil cases of first instance, second instance, and retrial after the defense period expires but before the judgment is rendered. The People's Court may conduct the mediation prior to the expiration of the defense period if it has obtained the consent of the parties'. This provision essentially extended mediation to cover almost the entire dispute resolution process within the court system, representing a concrete manifestation of a mediation-first policy. However, in 2020, the SPC revised and removed this provision, allowing mediation, as one of the mechanisms in a diversified dispute resolution toolkit, to be applied more rationally, thus facilitating the more reasonable resolution of disputes suitable for mediation.

Secondly, because the policies were made in different political climates, Chinese mediation law lacks systematic design. There are still some blanks in the statutes. As an unabridged mediation law, it usually includes provisions governing the mediator's conduct and professional competence requirement, the ethics of the mediator, the admissibility of evidence, and so on. These items are still missing in China's mediation regulations.[52] In addition, there are conflicting regulations existing in the document on the other, such as the tension existing between the politicisation and professionalism orientations. For example, in order to promote court mediation on a large scale in a harmonious society context,

[52] See UNCITRAL Model Law on International Commercial Conciliation with Guide to Enactment and Use 2002, www.uncitral.org/uncitral/en/uncitral_texts/arbitration/2002Model_conciliation.html (last accessed 3 May 2015). However, whether it is necessary to legalise all aspects of mediation regulation at the national legislature level is still worth discussing. There are different models to construct the mediation law to accommodate the need of uniformity of law and flexibility of mediation mechanism.

the Notice (2010) provides that the judge should pursue 'the rises of the rate of settling cases through mediation and the rate of willingly accepting the judgments'. The judge who achieves the 'two rises' should be rewarded politically and financially. However, the Notice (2010) also provides that the court should 'avoid improper mediation and the trend of unduly pursuing the mediation ratio'. As a rational person, the judge will definitely pursue the high mediation ratio for their interests. Chinese judges are actually well known for their practice of being interventionists and active initiatives in the court mediation process. As Palmer argued,

> The judge does not limit herself or himself to the role of passive go-between, invited by the parties themselves, and acting primarily as a channel of communication for the parties. Instead, she or he often cajoles the parties into accepting a solution which she or he may have himself put forward.[53]

So, the judge may be faced with a dilemma concerning the pursuit of a high rate of mediation, and yet to what extent is the mediation ratio improper? In this case, the purposes of these regulations are conflicting and confusing. In addition, time provision is another example of possible conflict concerning the judge's behaviour in the mediation proceedings. Provisions 2004 (amended in 2020) provided that:

> Before the expiration of the defense period, if the People's Court conducts mediation in cases subject to the ordinary procedure and no mediation agreement is reached within 15 days from the date when the parties agree to mediation, or in cases subject to the summary procedure and no mediation agreement is reached within 7 days from the date when the parties agree to mediation, with the consent of all parties, mediation may continue. The extended mediation period is not counted towards the trial time limit.

Whereas the Notice 2007 provided that:

> As for a case of the first instance to which the simplified procedure applies, the mediation period during the phase of case-filing shall, in principle, be less than 10 days from the date when the case is put on file; as for a case of the first instance to which the general procedure applies, the mediation period during the phase of case-filing shall, in principle, be less than 20 days. Any case of the second instance may, in principle, not

[53] Michael Palmer, 'The revival of mediation in the People's Republic of China (2): Judicial Mediation' in W. E. Butler (ed.), *Yearbook on Socialist Legal Systems* (New York: Transnational Publishers, Inc. 1989), p. 157.

be mediated during the phase of case-filing, or a more reasonable mediation period shall be set for the cases of the second instance.

The author's empirical study on court mediation in grassroots courts in China adds tangible depth to the aforementioned tension. Based on a survey conducted in southwest China, where the majority of legal professionals are members of the Communist Party, the author found that despite this political affiliation, 64.8 per cent of court staff, considering their judicial experience, believe that court mediation is feasible and applicable to most types of disputes. However, a significant portion of the remaining respondents (34.0 per cent of court staff and 38.8 per cent of lawyers) hold different views, believing that mediation is suitable only for some types of disputes. When asked which types of parties are suitable for mediation, only 19.4 per cent of court staff and 8.4 per cent of lawyers believed that mediation is appropriate for all parties.[54]

This data is crucial as it offers a nuanced insight into legal professionals' perspectives on the feasibility and applicability of court mediation. The surveyed judges recognise that the appropriateness of mediation is influenced by the type of dispute and the characteristics of the disputants involved. In other words, as rational dispute resolvers, they acknowledge that court mediation should be applied in suitable cases and contexts rather than pursuing a high mediation rate in all circumstances. However, in practice, they may prioritise mediation as the first choice in all cases (88.9 per cent of court staff), as the mediation rate directly impacts their Key Performance Indicators – 91.9 per cent of court staff indicated that they would receive rewards if they used mediation to resolve disputes.[55]

This situation underscores the tension and conflict between the politicised, mediation-oriented judicial policy, which aims to substantially resolve social disputes and maintain social harmony, and the rational assessment of the choice of dispute resolution method in a judge's mind. The politicised mediation policy may thus contribute to the construction of an irrational dispute resolution approach where critical variables affecting the appropriateness of the chosen dispute resolution method, such as the nature of the dispute and characteristics of the disputants, may be overlooked due to the pursuit of personal interests incentivised by the judicial policy from the Supreme People's Court.

[54] Xiong, 'Is court mediation feasible?', 973–974.

[55] Xiong, 'Is court mediation feasible?', 973.

PART IV

Chinese Mediation in Action

5

Global and China's ADR Movement

5.1 Global ADR Movement

Since the 1970s, resolving disputes through litigation across different countries has been subject to continuous re-examination and refinement during the alternative dispute resolution (ADR) movement.[1] Despite the evolutionary patterns of its form, the essence of ADR can be defined as 'any procedure for settling a dispute by means other than litigation, as by arbitration or mediation'.[2] The ADR method broadly covers negotiation, mediation, the institution of the ombudsman, private mini-trials, pre-trial conferences, arbitration, case management, renting a judge and so on.[3]

Historically speaking, the modern idea of ADR was developed in the United States.[4] Beginning in the early twentieth century, because of the inflow of new immigrants,[5] high inflation and strikes resulting from corporate America's aggressive anti-unionism,[6] the civil rights movement,[7] religious movement,[8] the return of community values and workplace struggles,[9]

[1] Simon Roberts and Michael Palmer, *Dispute Processes: ADR and the Primary Forms of Decision-Making* (Cambridge: Cambridge University Press, 3rd ed., 2020), p. 51.

[2] Bryan A. Garner et al., *Black's Law Dictionary* (London: Thomson West, 10th ed., 2014), p. 95.

[3] See Albert K. Fiadjoe, *Alternative Dispute Resolution: A Developing World Perspective* (London: Cavendish, 2004), pp. 19–20. See also Richard C. Reuben, 'Public justice: toward a state action theory of alternative dispute resolution' (1997) 83(3) *California Law Review* 577, 580, fn. 3.

[4] Michael King et al., *Non-Adversarial Justice* (Sydney: The Federation Press, 2009), p. 88.

[5] Jerold S. Auerbach, *Justice Without Law: Resolving Dispute Without Lawyers* (Oxford: Oxford University Press, 1983), pp. 69–70.

[6] Jerome T. Barrett, *A History of Alternative Dispute Resolution: The Story of a Political, Cultural, and Social Movement* (San Francisco, CA: Jossey-Bass, 2004), p. 111.

[7] Peter H. Schuck, *Diversity in America: Keeping Government at a Safe Distance* (Cambridge, MA: The Belknap Press of Harvard University Press, 2003), p. 52; Barrett, *A History of Alternative Dispute Resolution*, pp. 118–119.

[8] Andrew W. McThenia and Thomas L. Shaffer, 'For reconciliation' (1985) 94 *Yale Law Journal* 1660, 1664.

[9] McThenia and Shaffer, 'For reconciliation', 1665.

the idea of popular justice took shape.[10] American society gradually developed a community cohesiveness to foster self-help and racial identity by building exclusive institutions.[11] All social movements, at their core, embody a struggle for autonomy and the reconfiguration of social and judicial authority. It becomes evident that these social phenomena share a fundamental and intrinsic similarity with the principles of ADR, which is predicated on the empowerment of disputants, seeking to augment their control and self-determination, grounded in civil society and the concept of autonomous rights within the United States. This suggests that ADR is not merely a culmination of American social evolution from the twentieth century driven by economically pragmatic motivations, such as time and cost savings, but also deeply rooted in the quest for empowerment and self-governance.

Besides the social environment and political rationale, some very pragmatic and practicable considerations also led to the development of ADR both in the United States and in other nations. Some complain that the operation of the court system is too expensive.[12] Other common complaints include overburdened caseloads,[13] the inefficiency of dispute resolution, the poor quality of resolutions,[14] the lack of individual participation[15] and the absence of community values.[16] As many scholars believe, 'our courts are overwhelmed by a flood of litigation and are incapable of giving timely, inexpensive and effective relief, yet simultaneously extend their reach into areas beyond both their competence and

[10] Sally Engle Merry, 'Sorting out popular justice' in Sally Engle Merry and Neal Milner (eds.), *The Possibility of Popular Justice: A Case Study of Community Mediation in the United States* (Ann Arbor, MI: The University of Michigan Press, 1993), pp. 38–49.

[11] Schuck, *Diversity in American*, p. 52.

[12] Lord Harry Woolf said of the English system, 'The consequence is that expense is often excessive, disproportionate and unpredictable; and delay is frequently unreasonable-...there is no doubt that the expense of litigation is one of the most fundamental problems confronting the civil justice system'. See Lord Harry Woolf, 'Civil justice in United Kingdom' (1997) 45(4) *The American Journal of Comparative Law* 709, 710–711.

[13] See Warren R. Burger, 'Agenda for 2000 A.D. – a need for systematic anticipation' (1976) 15 *The Judge's Journal* 27.

[14] See Carrie Menkel-Meadow, 'Toward another view of legal negotiation: the structure of problem solving' (1983–1984) 31 *UCLA Law Review* 754.

[15] See Raymond Shonholtz, 'The citizens' role in justice: building a primary justice and prevention system at the neighborhood level' (1987) 494. *Annals of American Academy of Politics and Social Science* 42.

[16] See Paul Wahrhafting, 'An overview of community-oriented citizen dispute resolution programs in the United States' in Richard L. Abel (ed.), *The Politics of Informal Justice* (New York: Academic Press, 1982), vol. 1.

legitimacy.'[17] Because of the lengthy and cumbersome nature of judicial proceedings, ADR may play the role of a saviour, as it is singularly positioned to be able to address the problems existing in the traditional litigation system.

In the past decades, ADR developed simultaneously in various jurisdictions. Beginning in the 1980s, ADR began to take root in the US society,[18] covering a broad spectrum of disputes. Due to its adaptability and flexibility, the recent development of ADR has expanded its reach to more diverse, complicated and even in-vogue cases, such as consumer and business disputes, bankruptcy, insurance, securities, real estate, construction, health care, product liability, workplace, education, sports, intellectual property rights and disputes involving high-tech issues.[19] Beyond the disputes between the private parties, ADR also plays a role in tackling disputes concerning large infrastructure projects[20] and disputes related to public interest.[21] It is a fact that ADR has reconstructed the American litigious culture to a remarkable extent and become an important option when disputants and legal professionals design dispute resolution approaches. Today, ADR has become popular not only in America but also at the international level. Without exaggeration, there is now worldwide interest in ADR. Jurisdictions as varied as the United States, Australia, the United Kingdom and Japan have all promoted the use of ADR.[22] In some Chinese regions, for example in Hong Kong (China), the Civil Justice Reform (CJR) issued in 2009 enhanced the role of ADR in the civil justice realm to unprecedented levels. Now, the ADR approach is strongly encouraged and covers nearly all civil proceedings as a mandatory procedure in Hong Kong.[23]

[17] Marc Galanter, 'Reading the landscape of disputes: what we know and don't know (and think we know) about our allegedly contentious and litigious society' (1983) 31 *UCLA Law Review* 4, 6.

[18] Deborah R. Hensler, 'Our courts, ourselves: how the alternative dispute resolution movement is reshaping our legal system' (2003) 108(1) *Penn State Law Review* 165, 165.

[19] Xiaobing Xu, 'Mediation in China and the United States: towards common outcome' (2003), Unpublished JSD Dissertation, Stanford University School of Law, pp. 190–191.

[20] See, for example, David L. Sandborg, 'Multistep ADR gets creative at Hong Kong's new airport' (1999) 17(3) *Alternatives to the High Cost of Litigation* 41.

[21] See John Forester, *Dealing with Differences: Dramas of Mediating Public Disputes* (Oxford: Oxford University Press, 2009).

[22] See Yan Lung Wong, 'The benefits of mediation' (2006) 7 *Asian Dispute Review* 100.

[23] The Practice Direction 31 of the Civil Justice Reform provides that 'An underlying objective of the Rules of the High Court and the District Court is to facilitate the

An increasing number of jurisdictions within the global ADR movement recognise that effective dispute resolution integrates both adjudicative and non-adjudicative processes. This trend is reshaping the landscape of dispute resolution, emphasising flexibility, efficiency, interest-based solutions and accessible frameworks.[24] This evolution enriches our understanding of fundamental concepts such as justice, the rule of law and judicial processes. It underscores that realising these concepts requires an organic combination of diverse dispute management mechanisms. This dynamic interplay ensures that justice is not only administered fairly but also perceived as accessible.

The global application and practice of ADR have also revealed an ontological dimension that surpasses its functional aspects. Effective ADR operation entails more than merely transplanting basic procedures and methods across jurisdictions; It necessitates an ontological perspective that considers cultural interpretations of mediation, methods of interaction and power dynamics within specific legal domains. Consequently, ADR research and practice increasingly emphasise integrating dispute resolution with local cultures and social conditions. This approach enables ADR to be seamlessly integrated into local legal cultures and institutional frameworks. For example, scholars have observed that in Asian contexts, mediators are expected to offer substantive guidance during the dispute resolution process, reflecting cultural preferences for hierarchical relationships. While efforts to standardise mediation practices internationally have reduced emphasis on indigenous models, the development of distinct mediation approaches tailored to domestic issues remains essential.[25]

settlement of disputes. The Court has the duty as part of active case management to further that objective by encouraging the parties to use an alternative dispute resolution procedure ("ADR") if the Court considers that appropriate and facilitating its use ("the duty in question"). The Court also has the duty of helping the parties to settle their case. The parties and their legal representatives have the duty of assisting the Court to discharge the duty in question'. There is a possibility for the court to make an adverse costs order to the party who unreasonably fails to engage in mediation, See http://legalref.judiciary.gov.hk/lrs/common/pd/pdcontent.jsp?pdn=PD31.htm&lang=EN (last accessed 2 March 2015).

24 Jacqueline Nolan-Haley, 'International dispute resolution and access to justice: comparative law perspectives' (2020) 2 *Journal of Dispute Resolution* 391, 397.

25 Dorcas Quek Anderson, 'The evolving concept of access to justice in Singapore's mediation movement' (2020) 16 *International Journal of Law in Context* 128, 134–135.

5.2 China's ADR Movement

Due to the global popularity of ADR, the domestic political climate and the Chinese tradition of employing nonconfrontational methods to solve disputes, a group of Chinese scholars has suggested the establishment of an ADR system with Chinese characteristics.[26] In this context, various forms of ADR, especially mediation, have been enhanced and promoted by the authorities, leading to ADR movement in China.

This recent developments on ADR began around 2008. In 2009, the Supreme People's Court (SPC) issued a new macro judicial policy that prioritised mediation in the handling of disputes. In response to the political calls for building a harmonious society, as articulated by President Hu Jintao, Wang Shengjun, the then Chief Justice of the SPC, declared new principles in the justice system in July 2009. These principles are: 'Mediation is the priority; mediation and trial should be synthetically applied; when the case is closed, the dispute is resolved (*tiaojie youxian, tiaopanjiehe, anjieshiliao*, 调解优先，调判结合，案结事了)'.[27] Under Wang's administration since 2008, a series of policies were issued, which were usually summarised as 'big mediation policy' or 'grand mediation policy' (*datiaojie*, 大调解) as a whole. These policies are commonly regarded as a dramatic change from the direction of China's legal system and have drawn abundant critiques and debates.[28] Regardless of the debates, the SPC continued to issue 'The Third Five-Year Reform Program of the People's Court (2009–2013)' (*renminfayuan disange wunian gaige gangyao*, 人民法院第三个五年改革纲要 (2009–2013)) in late 2009. In this programme, 'to establish and perfect the diverse dispute resolution mechanism' was established as a basic premise that will guide the operation of the court system in the coming five years.[29] In August 2010, the SPC issued a new notice requiring the

[26] Xiaohong Liu, 'Pondering on the establishment of localized ADR system with Chinese character' (2007) 2 *Hebei Law Science* 36 [刘晓红："构建中国本土化ADR制度的思考"，《河北法学》，2007年第2期].

[27] Shengjun Wang's speech on national court mediation experience sharing conference [王胜俊在全国法院调解工作经验交流会上强调], see www.chinacourt.org/html/article/200907/29/367194.shtml (last accessed 2 March 2010).

[28] Xianchu Zhang, 'Civil justice reform with political agenda' in Guanghua Yu (ed.), *Development of the Chinese Legal System: Change and Challenges* (London: Routledge, 2010), p. 253.

[29] The Third Five-Year Reform Program of the People's Court (2009–2013) [人民法院第三个五年改革纲要], see www.court.gov.cn/spyw/sfgg/201002/t20100223_1776.htm (last accessed 2 March 2010).

court system to thoroughly implement the 'mediation first' policy by providing twenty-nine concrete requirements and directions (最高人民法院印发《进一步贯彻"调解优先、调判结合"工作原则的若干意见》的通知).[30] As a result, the rate of court mediation has grown dramatically.[31] In the *Working Report of the Supreme People's Court* in the Representative Conference of the National People's Congress 2011, President Wang confirmed that the mediation rate in the first trial stage of the civil and commercial disputes was 65.29 per cent in 2010, which was 3.31 per cent higher than that in 2009.[32] In 2011 and 2012, mediation rate increased to 67.3 per cent and 68.15 per cent, respectively.[33] As well known, the majority of disputes handled by China's court system are civil and commercial disputes. In other words, most of China's disputes in the ADR movement are fixed through the court mediation track by the Chinese court system.[34]

30 Notice of the Supreme People's Court on Promulgating the 'Several Opinions on Further Implementation of the Work Principle of "Giving Priority to Mediation and Integrating Mediation with Adjudication"' [最高人民法院印发《关于进一步贯彻"调解优先、调判结合"工作原则的若干意见》的通知], see www.court.gov.cn/qwfb/sfwj/yj/201008/t20100811_8489.htm (last accessed 20 September 2010).

31 The Vice President of the SPC Jun Zhang talked about the rate of the court mediation recently [中国民事案件调解率已达到6成以上], see www.lawinnovation.com/html/xjdt/3958.shtml (last accessed 1 February 2011).

32 Shengjun Wang, Working Report of the Supreme People's Court in the Representative Conference of the National People's Congress, 2011 (Summer) [王胜俊：最高人民法院工作报告2011（摘要）], see http://2011lianghui.people.com.cn/GB/14124671.html (last accessed 13 March 2011).

33 Shengjun Wang, 'Working report of the Supreme People's Court' [王胜俊：最高人民法院工作报] and 'The statistics of mediation' [数说调解], www.gov.cn/test/2012-03/19/content_2094709.htm (last accessed 13 March 2014).

34 Another example illustrating the trend of expansion of mediation in China is environmental protection litigation, which can be also concluded by using mediation. It is generally believed that environmental protection is a complex case involving public interests or an imbalance of power. In this case, mediation should not be applied. However, according to Article 287 of the Interpretation of the Supreme People's Court on the Application of the Civil Procedure Law of the People's Republic of China, 'in public interest litigation cases, the parties may reach a settlement, and the people's court may mediate'. In this case, however, the principle of confidentiality in mediation would be overturned. At the same time, the Supreme People's Court formulated some other measures to control the negative externalities of mediating environmental disputes. Article 287 further stipulates that 'After the parties have reached a settlement or mediation agreement, the people's court shall make an announcement of the settlement or mediation agreement. The announcement period shall not be less than thirty days. After the announcement period has expired, the People's Court shall, upon examination, issue a mediation statement if the settlement or mediation agreement does not violate the public interest; if the settlement or mediation agreement violates the public interest, no

Under President Xi Jinping's administration, the ADR movement continues. Xi Jinping has stated that 'non-litigation dispute resolution mechanisms should be placed at the forefront'[35] in resolving disputes. Influenced by this policy, China's ADR movement in the new era has exhibited some distinctive characteristics. Alternative dispute resolution has begun to integrate deeply with social governance and has become a crucial component of grassroots governance in China. A review of these policies reveals that ADR has transcended the mere 'resolution of individual conflicts'. According to the Resolution of the CPC Central Committee on the Major Achievements and Historical Experience of the Party over the Past Century, issued by the sixth plenary session of the 19th Central Committee of the Communist Party of China in 2021, ADR in China is regarded as a model and has become part of the Communist Party of China's century-long governance experience, with one of the most representative models being the Fengqiao experience.[36] This important CCP's experience summary report states that:

> We have carried on and developed the Fengqiao Experience in promoting social harmony in the new era. By continuing to address issues at the source through systematic, law-based, and holistic approaches, and by refining the system for handling public complaints, we have improved integrated mechanisms for preventing, mediating, and defusing social problems.[37]

mediation statement shall be issued, and the case shall continue to be heard, and judgment shall be rendered according to law'.

35 Xi Jinping, 'Fully, accurately, and comprehensively implementing the new development philosophy and leveraging the key role of reform in building the new development paradigm', *People's Daily Online*, http://jhsjk.people.cn/article/32032267 (last accessed 30 July 2023) [习近平：《完整准确全面贯彻新发展理念，发挥改革在构建新发展格局中关键作用》，载人民网].

36 The 'Fengqiao experience' refers to a sociopolitical experiment and grassroots initiative that took place in China during the early 1960s, particularly in the Fengqiao Township of Zhejiang Province. Mao Zedong once acknowledged that the Fengqiao experience resonated with local wisdom, providing a valuable reference for grassroots-level societal governance. This initiative represented a mass mobilisation campaign where local residents actively participated in addressing a range of issues, including disputes, economic challenges and political matters. Its primary objective was to resolve social conflicts at the community level using localised approaches, preventing the escalation and widening of disputes while fostering ideological unity and social cohesion. All of this occurred during a period of significant political upheaval in China. In the new era, President Xi Jinping has spoken highly of this experience, making it an exemplary model for resolving disputes within county-level governance structures in China.

37 Resolution of the CPC Central Committee on the Major Achievements and Historical Experience of the Party over the Past Century, https://english.www.gov.cn/policies/latestreleases/202111/16/content_WS6193a935c6d0df57f98e50b0.html (last accessed 30 September 2023).

In this context, ADR is now expected to play a crucial role in maintaining social stability and sustainable harmony by broadening and extending the state's intervention and empowerment to the grassroots level. The central government's directives for systematic governance (系统治理, *xitong zhili*), comprehensive governance (综合治理, *zonghe zhili*) and source governance (源头治理, *yuantou zhili*) aim not only to resolve disputes from the parties' perspectives but also to identify and address the structural factors and contextual influences that lead to conflicts. This approach involves holistic and preventive interventions, analysing disputes through a long-term sequence of 'anticipation, prevention, mediation, handling, transforming, and settlement' within a comprehensive social governance framework.

By 2019, the Decision of the Central Committee of the Communist Party of China on Several Major Issues Concerning Upholding and Improving the System of Socialism with Chinese Characteristics and Advancing the Modernization of National Governance, issued during the fourth plenary session of the 19th Central Committee, adopted a holistic approach to the top-level design of national governance. This document comprehensively outlined China's dispute resolution and governance framework, providing a comprehensive framework for managing the entire process of resolving social contradictions among the people. It included mechanisms for expressing public grievances, coordinating interests and safeguarding rights and interests as well as the petition system, people's mediation, administrative mediation, judicial mediation coordination, social psychological services, crisis intervention mechanisms and multiple mechanisms for preventing, resolving and diffusing social conflicts and disputes. Therefore, whether within or outside the judiciary, the resolution of interpersonal disputes and social conflicts has expanded beyond the confines of traditional litigation-centred approaches. In the integrated landscape of judicial and social governance, a new trend of mutual integration is emerging.

As a response from the judicial system to this new policy, the courts have started to extend ADR functions beyond the courtroom, attempting to collaborate with other social organisations in building and sharing a diversified dispute resolution system. In 2015, the SPC established the modern dispute resolution concept of 'leadership by the State, promotion by the judiciary, participation by the society, adoption of multiple methods and safeguard by rule of law'. As a concrete measure, the SPC began to collaborate with various departments and individuals to resolve disputes, including the Ministry of Public Security, the Ministry of

Justice, the Ministry of Human Resources and Social Security, the Ministry of Civil Affairs, the National Development and Reform Commission, the China Securities Regulatory Commission, the China Insurance Regulatory Commission, the All-China Federation of Returned Overseas Chinese, the All-China Federation of Industry and Commerce and the All-China Women's Federation, among others. They jointly issued over 20 documents on linking litigation and mediation in areas such as people's mediation, family disputes, securities and futures disputes, insurance disputes and notarisation-related court judicial auxiliary affairs. Moreover, the SPC promulgated *Opinions on Further Deepening the Reform of Multiple Dispute Resolution Mechanisms in People's Courts and the Provisions on Mediation Specially Invited by People's Courts* to provide concrete policies in order to achieve the goal and principle. Obviously, the SPC began to realise that the promotion of ADR could not only rely on judicial force and political pressure but also need to invite more social agencies to participate and continuously improve the professional level of ADR. This comprehensive collaboration aimed to enhance and optimise the diversified dispute resolution system through cooperation between the judiciary and society. It is reported that the courts nationwide had established 2,338 litigation–mediation connection centres and recruited nearly 20,000 specially invited mediation organisations and more than 60,000 specially invited mediators till around 2017. With the instruction and assistance of the people's courts, these mediation organisations have solved over 10 million disputes every year.[38]

The evolution of such a policy is, in fact, deeply rooted in historical and cultural context. According to Chinese traditional political philosophy, a harmonious social relationship is a supreme ideology that enjoys an incomparable priority in Chinese social governance and determines the regime's legitimacy. According to the *Confucius Analects*, Yu Tzu, one disciple of Confucius, said 'of the things brought about by the rites (*li*, 礼), harmony (*he*, 和) is the most valuable'.[39] Social harmony is a typical collectivist value. Chinese dispute resolution culture thus focuses on the

[38] For more details, see 'White paper of court reform', http://english.court.gov.cn/2017-03/14/content_28552928_6.htm (last accessed 13 March 2020).

[39] James Legge's (trans.), *Republished in Book of Changes* (Changsha: Hunan Chubanshe, 1993; The Chinese–English Series of Chinese Classics) quoted from Albert H. Y. Chen, 'Mediation, litigation and justice: Confucian reflections in modern liberal society' in Daniel A. Bell and Hahm Chaibong (eds.), *Confucianism for the Modern World* (Cambridge: Cambridge University Press, 2003), p. 260.

values of collectivism, such as community survival and sustainability, order stability, structural stability and overall development.

However, the externalities of real disputes and conflicts are inevitable, and the process of resolving these conflicts is likely to impact social stability, harmony and even question governance capacity. If the disputing parties cannot adequately manage the negative external impacts of a dispute by themselves, the intervention of public power becomes necessary to mitigate these impacts. This requires effective public management and coordination from the government, which acts as a representative of the collective. The community, society and even the state thus become stakeholders in private disputes. Therefore, if representatives of authority and communities – whether they are judges, grassroots officials, social authorities or any other powers that represent social interests to some extent – are completely absent in the mediation structure or unable to exert external force to intervene in dispute resolution, and they only serve as passive and restrained procedural facilitators and communicators, then how can society guide and control the externalities of these disputes that may impact social order and harmonious values? Thus, mediation in traditional Chinese society is not merely a way to embody an individual's autonomy but also a community education event. This event is conducted through the intervention of local authorities, such as respected senior citizens, grassroots local intellectuals or religious figures, to achieve social stability and harmony. Dispute resolution in the Chinese cultural context, therefore, cannot follow a party-oriented mechanism but needs to be a mediator-oriented mechanism, enabling external intervention in disputes.[40]

Although most disputes primarily involve internal dimensions, such as interest concerns, rights and obligations, emotional states and realistic claims of the parties involved, Chinese culture is highly sensitive to the externalities of disputes and conflicts. This sensitivity endows disputes with integrated features that extend beyond the disputing parties. This emphasis magnifies the externalities of disputes and conflicts, making them a central concern in Chinese dispute resolution culture, where they are often imbued with political attributes under collectivism. Consequently, the Chinese view of dispute resolution, deeply rooted in social control, aligns with the expectations of social collectivism.

[40] Andrew Phang, 'Mediation and the courts – The Singapore experience', *Keynote Speech on the 4th Asian Mediation Association Conference*, 20 October 2016, www.supremecourt.gov.sg/Data/Editor/Documents/Keynote%20Speech%20%204th%20Asian%20Mediation%20Conference.pdf (last accessed 20 July 2023).

Based on these historical–cultural–social understandings (such as the 'trust in authority' and 'dependence on society' discussed in Chapter 4), people can understand why China is inclined to adopt an evaluative mediation model for a long time, know the deep-down reason for an administration- and judicialisation-oriented mediation model in legal practices,[41] and realise why the mediation system in China is not carried out in the form of individual mediation as expected in the Singapore Mediation Convention but in the form of an organisation and understand that the judgment that 'the limited application of mediator-led mediation is determined by the fact that China is still in a transition period, and the author believes this is only a temporary phenomenon'[42] may underestimate the great inertia of culture and the realistic characteristics of the social and cultural context in contemporary China.[43]

It is worth noting that the abovementioned ADR movement and the evolution of policies in China are mainly driven by the authority of the state. For the same historical, cultural and social reasons, China's ADR institution is more or less semi-official, for instance, even people's mediation rooted in grassroots communities is sponsored and managed by the government. Its responsibility is to help the parties resolve interpersonal conflicts, and at the same time, eliminate disharmonious factors in the society for the government through different dispute resolution mechanisms, ultimately realising effective social control.[44] The ADR system in China is thus deeply driven by collectivism and pragmatism, which is used by the regime as 'semilegal and bureaucratic institutions explicitly tasked with resolving social conflicts...[and] channeling conflicts into these procedural games buys [the officials] time and order, removing the physical and public display of disharmony'.[45] Therefore, the ADR movements in different historical periods of modern China after the Reform and Opening-up Policy are mainly motivated by the top-down political

[41] Fan Yu, 'Comment on the People's Mediation Law of the People's Republic of China' (2011) 2 *The Jurist*, 1, 8 [范愉"《中华人民共和国人民调解法》评析"，载《法学家》2011年第2期].

[42] Liao Yongan et al., *Concept Innovation and Mechanism Reshaping of Chinese Mediation* (Beijing: Renmin University of China Press, 2019), p. 82 [廖永安等：《中国调解的理念创新与机制重塑》，北京：人民大学出版社2019年版].

[43] Hao Xiong, 'The challenges of Singapore Convention to Chinese mediation system' (2022) 52(3) *Hong Kong Law Journal* 1057, 1079–1081.

[44] Ching Kwan Lee and Yonghong Zhang, 'Unraveling the microfoundations of bargained authoritarianism in China' (2013) 118(6) *American Journal of Sociology* 1475, 1480, 1496.

[45] Lee and Zhang, 'Unraveling the microfoundations' 1475, 1480, 1496.

considerations. Under Jingtao Hu's administration, 'harmonious society (*hexie shehui*, 和谐社会)' became the leading ideology, in which mediation is prioritised by the SPC to absorb various social discontents and conflicts.[46] In Xi Jingping's period, Fengqiao experience (*fengqiao jingyan*, 枫桥经验), which is a holistic grassroots governance strategy relying on the masses to preserve social stability and harmony, has injected fresh strength into the development of mediation in order to enhance the social control and modernisation of national governance system. These ADR promotion policies have been consistently driven by political imperatives, which are instrumentally designed and motivated by the regimes for certain political and social goals.[47] Therefore, the transition of China's ADR institution and policy has fundamental differences in the logic of occurrence and the source of motivation with the bottom-up ADR social movement in the United States, in which the individualistic development path that 'attempts to empower the parties to disputes and strengthen their self-control, autonomy and self-determination over social life through various mechanisms and methods outside the system'.[48]

5.3 Fengqiao Experience in Action at the Local Level

Under the Fengqiao experience policy, the local ADR policy needed to be designed to support the central government's will at different levels. When implementing the Fengqiao experience, the Political and Legal Committee (PLC) plays an important role at various levels. The PLC is a management branch of the Communist Party of China, tasked with overseeing the comprehensive management of the country's political and legal affairs. This includes the supervision of law enforcement bodies, courts and prisons, ensuring that these institutions align with the Party's policies and directives. The PLC is significant in the Chinese political

[46] Michael Palmer, 'Compromising courts and harmonizing ideologies: mediation in the administrative chambers of the People's Courts in the People's Republic of China' in Andrew Harding and Penelope (Pip) Nicholson (eds.), *New Courts in Asia* (London: Routledge, 2010), p. 268.

[47] Weixia Gu, *Dispute Resolution in China: Litigation, Arbitration, Mediation and Their Interactions* (New York: Routledge, 2021), pp. 125–126.

[48] Hao Xiong, 'American ADR movement from the perspective of sociology of knowledge – based on the dual perspective of institutional history and intellectual history' (2016) 1 *Global Law Review* 24, 28 [熊浩："知识社会学视野下的美国ADR运动 – 基于制度史与思想史的双重视角"，载《环球法律评论》2016年第1期].

landscape because it plays a central role in maintaining social stability and controlling public dissent. It coordinates various efforts related to law enforcement and has considerable influence over the legal and judicial processes in China.[49] The PLC ensures that the social governance and judicial policy 'must be considered in light of the basic tasks and development priorities defined by the Party and government in China'.[50] Therefore, different political directives and macro-level judicial policies can effectively impact the practice of ADR at the local level.

When explaining the meaning of Fengqiao experience, Chen Wenqing, Secretary of the Central Political and Legal Affairs Commission, stated,

> In the new era, the 'Fengqiao Experience' is a vivid practice of Xi Jinping's thoughts on socialism with Chinese characteristics for a new era in the realm of building a safe China…We must adhere to prevention first, minimize and reduce the occurrence of conflicts and disputes to the greatest extent, enhance the sorting of risk transmission chains in key areas, and monitor main risk indicators, achieving precise prediction, accurate early warning, and meticulous prevention. We should integrate mediation throughout the resolution process of conflicts and disputes, ensuring that mediation is applied wherever possible and capable, to achieve case resolution, issue settlement, and social harmony.[51]

Therefore, the policy requirement of adhering to and developing the Fengqiao experience emphasises that the primary mission of maintaining and supporting social stability, focusing on 'addressing the root cause, emphasizing mediation, and focusing on grassroots efforts (抓源头、抓调解、抓基层)'. The majority of the disputes and conflicts, in this case, are supposed to be digested and defused at the grassroots level by upholding the principle that 'small problems do not leave the village, large problems do not leave the township, and conflicts are not passed up to the higher authorities (*xiaoshi buchucun, dashi buchuxiang (zhen), maodun bushangjiao,* 小事不出村、大事不出乡（镇）、矛盾不上交)'. It is clear that in such a policy, the discourse of individual rights and

[49] For more details about the recent development of political and legal committee of CPC, see Yang Fan, 'The role of CPC regulations in Chinese judicial decisions: an empirical study based on published judgments' (2019) 19(2) *China Review* 69, 69–98.

[50] See 'Three Supremes', https://chinamediaproject.org/2010/11/12/three-supremes-%E4%B8%89%E4%B8%AA%E8%87%B3%E4%B8%8A/ (last accessed 25 May 2023).

[51] Chen Wenqing, 'Adhere to and develop the "Fengqiao Experience" in the news, enhance the level of legal governance in the prevention and resolution of conflicts and disputes', https://baijiahao.baidu.com/s?id=1785427778902199547&wfr=spider&for=pc (last accessed 11 May 2024).

individual autonomy in ADR is not the focus. Mediation is defined not merely as a legal institution used to facilitate the disputing parties to achieve a mutually accepted agreement; rather, it serves as an instrument of the political mission aimed at achieving the goals of social governance.

Due to significant regional disparities in China, there are various approaches to achieving the goals of grassroots social dispute governance. However, a common practice at the grassroots level of urban regions is the establishment of a grid management system (*wanggehua guanli*, 网格化管理) in urban governance spaces and the reinforcement of economic incentives in rural governance spaces. In 2013, the 'Decision on Major Issues Concerning Comprehensively Deepening Reforms' of the third plenary session of the 18th Central Committee of CPC proposed improving the methods of social governance, innovating the social governance system and enhancing grassroots comprehensive service management platforms with a focus on grid management and socialised services. The term 'grid management' refers to a grassroots administrative management approach that divides the jurisdiction of urban management into unit grids based on certain standards. These unit grids are subdivided into smaller blocks using factors such as community, organisation, geographical location, environment and transportation. Subsequently, this approach involves grassroots workers, known as grid officers, who inspect, supervise and address specific issues within their assigned grids. This is facilitated through a digitised system that enables a more detailed community coverage and more immediate responses. This approach decentralises governance, bringing it closer to residents and leverages modern technology to ensure swift resolution of community concerns.

In July 2020, the Ministry of Human Resources and Social Security, the State Administration for Market Regulation and the National Bureau of Statistics created 'Urban Management Grid Officers' as a new occupational category. In 2022, corresponding national standards were established, including four different levels of registration: Junior Worker, Intermediate Worker, Senior Worker and Technician. According to the occupational standards for grid officers, they are defined as 'personnel who use modern urban network management technology to patrol, verify, report, and handle issues related to municipal engineering public facilities, urban environment, and social management affairs, and collect, analyze, and handle relevant information'.[52] This definition essentially

[52] National Occupational Skill Standards – Urban Management Grid Member (2022), formulated by the Ministry of Human Resources and Social Security of the People's

outlines the fundamental responsibilities of grid officers. While the national standards set the educational threshold for grid officers at only junior high school, the occupational standards require urban grid officers to possess certain learning, communication and computational abilities. They should also have spatial awareness, normal sensory perception, normal colour vision, physical flexibility and coordinated movements. The standards specify that their knowledge structure should encompass general foundational knowledge (including computer and intelligent mobile terminal applications), professional foundational knowledge (grid division, government functions, community management), safety and environmental protection knowledge and relevant legal regulations. The legal knowledge requirements for urban grid officers in the national standards involve labour law, contract law and safety production law but do not include legal knowledge directly related to dispute resolution.[53]

In the rural areas, a typical way of embodying the policy of social dispute governance is 'giving compensation according to the resolved cases (*yi'an dingbu*, 以案定补)' to support the mediation. In a southwest county the author investigated years ago, the policy of 'giving compensation according to the resolved cases' is that the county government would distribute a particular amount of the local finance, that is RMB 0.3 million in this region in total, to reward the mediators or grassroots legal workers who have successfully handled disputes. Before the policy, any successful mediation could only fetch a RMB 20 allowance. It is believed that this low compensation could not arouse the mediators' enthusiasm to solve grassroots disputes. In order to promote the effective resolution of social contradictions, the investigated county government updated its policy by improving the allowance standards considerably. According to the new standard, a successful mediation for a simple dispute, ordinary dispute, complex dispute or serious dispute could fetch RMB 20 , RMB 50, RMB 100 and RMB 300, respectively. The different compensation standards were established according to the potential risk to social stability. If more people got involved, the dispute would be regarded as more complex and serious. For a village that has not had a dispute for one year, the government will award RMB 1,000 at the end of that year to that village. For the mediator, the government also provides

Republic of China, www.doc88.com/p-99039667261292.html (last accessed 11 May 2024).

53 National Occupational Skill Standards – Urban Management Grid Member.

compensation for the loss of working time and transportation costs, although the compensation is not very high.

This awarding of cash incentives at the grassroots level of southwest China is not a new development. In the mid-1980s, facing increasing crime and incivility, the government resorted to private initiatives and implemented a system of contract security throughout China.[54] In practice, the government normally sets a price for the completion of a contract, and the contractors are paid according to the execution of that contract.[55] As Fu noted,

> This type of contract-based theory has been readily applied to conflict resolution, education of juvenile delinquents, and crime control. The hope is that by contracting out the state's power to resolve conflicts to individual mediators, and connecting the mediator's performance directly to compensation, the government can make mediators hardworking and responsible.[56]

This policy aims to motivate local mediators to resolve as many disputes as possible. However, its effectiveness may vary across different regions due to the varying financial capacities of local governments. For instance, in one of the investigated counties in a relatively poorer region of southwest China, although the government has implemented this policy, it struggles to pay the relevant mediators on time. Additionally, with the government now offering more financial support than before, material incentives have become increasingly attractive. However, 'it has not changed the fundamental cultural and structural barriers facing the people's mediation system'.[57]

In the investigated grassroots county court in southwest China, the policy objectives of social governance have become more specific. The court established a very systematic and detailed rewards and punishment standard, which included various indicators and covered all the positions in the court. The rewards and punishments standard was a document

[54] Hualing Fu, 'Understanding people's mediation in post-Mao China' (1992) 6 *Journal of Chinese Law* 211, 237.

[55] Fu, 'Understanding people's mediation in post-Mao China', 238.

[56] Fu, 'Understanding people's mediation in post-Mao China', 238.

[57] Fu, 'Understanding people's mediation in post-Mao China', 238. When criticising the Contract Security Policy to People's Mediation in 1980s, Hualing Fu has even noted that the reward at that time was small and not attractive and it is 'vulnerable to abuse by village elites'. Compared to the old times, the government now has more sufficient political and economic capacity to support this policy, so these drawbacks can be avoided to some degree.

consisting of 47 pages, which was divided into two sections: the general standard and specific standard. The general standard includes four items, each of which accounts for 10 points. They are to build a fine Party culture and keep the organisations clean (*dangfeng lianzheng jianshe*, 党风廉政建设), team building and management (*duiwu jianshe guanli*, 队伍建设管理), civilisation, research and propaganda (*wenming zhuangjian he xinxi diaoyan xuanzhuan*, 文明创建和信息调研宣传) and comprehensive control and adjustment of the society (*zonghe zhili zhibiao*, 综合治理指标). The specific standard was worth 60 points in total and was very complicated. The indicators were specialised for different positions in the court. For the adjudicators, the standard can be clarified into awarded marks and deducted marks. Table 5.1 illustrates the selected concrete content of the standard for criminal, civil, commercial and administrative adjudicators.

This standard encompasses several key points. Firstly, mediation is preferred. Although resolving a dispute through mediation initially earns only one point, mediation can facilitate the enforcement of the judicial result, potentially adding an additional two to five points from the settlement to the enforcement stage. Moreover, since mediation is based on the parties' agreement, it can reduce the risks associated with retrial, erroneous judgments, and petitions. Secondly, avoiding a petition is a paramount concern for the court, with at least three criteria directly related to this objective. Consequently, a judge's performance is scrutinised by the public not only for the fairness of the judgment but also for the ability to maintain social stability. This reflects the political objectives inherent in implementing the Fengqiao experience policy. These political goals may align with the parties' and the public's desire for the protection of rights and the realisation of interests, but there can also be instances where they diverge (this will be discussed in detail through case studies in Chapters 6 and 7 of the book). 'While mediation-centric grassroots governance is employed by the state to achieve social control non-violently, it has caused, at times, new forms of confrontation that are evidenced in interactions between street-level agents and individuals involved in social conflicts'.[58] In this process, the instrumental nature of mediation is amplified, directing its function toward reducing disputes, managing conflicts and substantively resolving differences, rather than

[58] Lingxiao Zhao, 'Mediation and grassroots policing in China: conflict resolution or social control?' (2023) 37(2) *China Information* 165, 180.

Table 5.1 *Rewards and punishments standard at the grassroots court*

Item	Adjudicator for criminal case	Adjudicator for civil, commercial and administrative case
Annual Workload Completion	40 cases, 3 points	100 cases, 3 points
More than Required Workload	3 points/case	3 points/case
Efficiency[59]	Within one month: 0.5 point/case; Within 20 days: 1 point/ case	Within four months: 0.5 point/case; Within two months: 2 points
Affirm the original judgment	10 points	10 points
No complaints petition	10 points	10 points
Settled through mediation	1 point	1 point
Partly enforceable judgment	1 point	1 point
Fully enforceable judgment	3 points	3 points
Circuit Court	1 point	1 point
Invite People's Jury	0.5 point	0.5 point
Holiday/night/weekend trial		2 points
Settle the serious, difficult and complicated conflict through ADR with the cooperation of PLC, police, procuratorate and justice bureau	5 points	5 points
Legal Education Service	2 points	2 points
To invite local deputies to the People's Congresses and members of the Chinese People's Political Consultative Conference Committees in court trials as people's assessors or observers	1 point	1 point
Case exceeds the trial period	One-vote veto in annual assessment	One-vote veto in annual assessment

59 The efficiency is very detailed for different types of disputes and procedures. It is just selectively reported here.

Table 5.1 (*cont.*)

Item	Adjudicator for criminal case	Adjudicator for civil, commercial and administrative case
Undue delay	Lose 5 points	Lose 5 points
Remand for retrial	Lose 5 points	Lose 5 points
Wrong judgment	Lose 2–5 points	Lose 2–5 points
Complaints or petition caused by the judge's rude attitude and language	Lose 5 points	Lose 5 points
Intensify the conflict and cause petition	Lose 5 points	Lose 5 points
Petition caused by wrong judgment	Lose 5 points	Lose 5 points
Do not notify the parties about the risk of litigation	Lose 1 point	Lose 1 point
Procedural mistake	Lose 1–2 points	Lose 1–2 points
Lose the evidence	Lose 10 points	Lose 10 points

solely achieving mutually acceptable solutions for the parties involved.[60] In a sense, this also reflects the underlying value differences between the Chinese and Western ADR movements, illustrating how under the collective cultural atmosphere and the governance goal of social control, the Chinese government, as a representative of collective societal values, effectively becomes a stakeholder in the dispute resolution process. The need for social stability and harmony becomes a demand that mediators and parties must fulfil in resolving individual disputes.

Thirdly, Beijing's policy would be localised to fit the various regional situations considering that China is a huge country. Compared with the practice in the undeveloped southwest part of China, the situation in the urban context, like in Shanghai, is quite different. Shanghai's model to promote mediation and social governance can be summarised as an 'entrusted mediation system'. In general, it means that the court will introduce the people's mediation system into the judicial context and assign most of the civil and commercial disputes to the people's mediator to resolve. According to the Shanghai Municipal Regulations on

[60] Zhao, 'Mediation and grassroots policing', 170.

Promoting the Resolution of Contradictions and Disputes through Diversified Means (2021), Article 13 provides that

> efforts are focused on building a comprehensive mediation framework in which people's mediation serves as the foundation. People's mediation, administrative mediation, industry-specific professional mediation, and judicial mediation should complement each other, be organically connected, and be coordinated in a synergistic manner. The coordination of comprehensive mediation work is led by the judicial administrative department, with active participation from relevant departments, organizations, and individuals.

Article 55 further provides that 'people's courts, in line with their actual judicial work, should establish a system for a roster of specially invited mediation organizations and specially invited mediators, gradually expanding the roster. People's courts, through delegation, entrustment of mediation, and strengthening judicial confirmation, provide guidance and training to mediation organizations and mediators in their professional capacity'. In this case, the people's court can involve people's mediation organisations in mediating disputes at various stages, including before accepting the case, after accepting the case but before the court hearing and during the trial process. Therefore, in Shanghai, it is common that divorce disputes, family maintenance disputes, succession and adoption disputes, adjacency relation disputes, loan and ordinary contract disputes, damage compensation, estate management and others that are suitable for mediation can be transferred by the court other social mediation organisations.

Beijing's policy is adapted to fit the diverse regional contexts within China, a vast country with varied local conditions. In contrast to practices in the less developed southwestern parts of China, the situation in urban areas like Shanghai is distinctly different. Shanghai has implemented an entrusted mediation system to promote mediation and enhance social governance. Essentially, this system involves integrating the people's mediation system into the judicial context, with the court delegating most civil and commercial disputes to people's mediators for resolution.

According to the Shanghai Municipal Regulations on Promoting the Resolution of Contradictions and Disputes through Diversified Means (2021), Article 13 states that 'efforts are focused on building a comprehensive mediation framework in which people's mediation serves as the foundation'. This framework ensures that people's mediation, administrative mediation, industry-specific professional mediation and judicial mediation are complementary, organically connected and coordinated synergistically under the leadership of the judicial administrative department and with active participation from relevant departments, organisations and individuals. Article 55 further specifies that 'people's courts, in line with their actual judicial work, should establish a system for a roster of specially invited mediation organizations and specially invited mediators, gradually expanding the roster'. It also emphasises that courts, through delegation and entrustment of mediation along with strengthening judicial confirmation, provide guidance and training to enhance the professional capacity of mediation organisations and mediators. In this framework, people's courts in Shanghai involve mediation organisations at various stages of the dispute resolution process, including before accepting a case, after accepting a case but before the court hearing and during the trial process. Common types of disputes such as divorce, family maintenance, succession and adoption, neighbourhood relations, loans and ordinary contracts, damage compensation and estate management, which are deemed suitable for mediation, are frequently transferred by the court to other social mediation organisations.

Nowadays, in Shanghai's courts, the disputing parties can find that the People's Mediation Window or similar facilities are established in the court halls in order to facilitate the parties to understand the information of ADR and choose to entrusted mediation. The mediation should be concluded within 15 days, with another 15 days extension if necessary. The most significant advantage of the entrusted mediation system is the separation of mediation and adjudication, which can avoid many institutional inconveniences and dynamic confusion of these two dispute resolution mechanisms.[61] More recently, the entrusted mediation system in Shanghai has evolved into an online version, with the participation of around 100 different mediation committees in different professional areas. The disputing parties, who want to receive the mediation service, would register an account and then use the online dispute resolution system by choosing the mediator or the professional mediation committee. If the online mediation agreement needs to be confirmed by the court, the online judicial confirmation service is also provided.[62] In 2019, in order to promote the professional level of the dispute resolution

[61] It is worth noting that in Chinese courts, after completing the mediation process, if mediation is not successful, the judge will continue to preside over the subsequent trial proceedings. This blending of the roles of mediator and judge to some extent undermines the voluntariness of the parties, as judges can use the prospect of a judgment as a threat to compel parties to make more concessions during the preceding mediation.

[62] For more details, see the Online Mediation Platform of High Court of Shanghai, www.hshfy.sh.cn/shfy/wstj2017/index.jsp (last accessed 15 March 2020).

system in Shanghai, Shanghai Judicial Bureau and Shanghai Finance Bureau issued a notice together and formulated rules on the government's purchase of people's mediation services. According to this notice, the government's purchase of people's mediation service refers to the dispute resolution service, which is provided by the government, can be purchased from the dispute resolution market under certain ways and procedures and paying the fee according to the contract agreed by the parties. The judicial administrative departments at all levels, the township people's governments and the streets affairs office can purchase dispute resolution service concerning nonpolice service, medical and patient dispute, petition and complaint reporting, property dispute resolution, transportation dispute, the dispute in schools, labour disputes, marriage and family dispute, public order cases, criminal reconciliation, intellectual property dispute, financial dispute, consumer dispute, other disputes in professional industries and the case where people's mediation services and other mediation services are suitable.[63]

However, when the author discussed Shanghai's model with judges and legal professionals in southwest China, it was noted that while the model is effective, it is not practicable in the southwest due to several reasons. Firstly, the districts in Shanghai are relatively small with advanced and developed transport systems, allowing people's mediators to easily travel to courts during the working days via arrangements such as the People's Mediation Window. For instance, Shanghai's largest district, Yangpu, covers 61 square kilometres. In contrast, a county investigated in Yunnan spans over 4,000 square kilometres with a public transport system that does not adequately cover the entire county, especially remote areas. Some areas are only accessible by sand-clay roads, taking over three hours for mediators and parties to travel from a village to the court. Secondly, the quality of people's mediators is notably higher and more consistent in Shanghai. It is common for Shanghai's Neighbourhood Committees (居民委员会, *jumin weiyuanhui*), which are grassroots social organisational units in urban areas responsible for resolving civil disputes among residents, to employ many college graduates, some of whom have graduated from prestigious law

[63] The Notice on the Roles of Government's Purchase of People's Mediation Services from Shanghai Judicial Bureau and Shanghai Finance Bureau [上海市司法局、上海市财政局关于印发《关于政府购买人民调解服务的实施细则》的通知]，https://resources.pkulaw.cn/staticfiles/20191129/17/31/5/1e8647becec882a67574ef2ac8cdc75f.pdf (last accessed 15 March 2020).

schools. In contrast, although every village in southwest China has a People's Mediation Committee, they often lack stable and well-trained personnel. This has led to criticism of China's extrajudicial mediation for relying on an untrained and sometimes illiterate workforce.[64] Thirdly, the government budget in southwest counties is incomparable to that of Shanghai's districts, which can afford sufficient financial support to ensure salaries for commissioned mediators and maintain the quality of their work. For example, the online dispute resolution system requires support from IT professionals, which is costly.

The purpose of comparing the different practices of the Fengqiao experience policy in urban and rural areas as well as across various regions in China is to remind readers that regional perspectives are crucial for understanding the policies and practices of dispute resolution in China. Considering the regional disparities in social development, economic levels and cultural traditions, a uniform dispute resolution policy across China is nearly impossible. Even though the PCL largely unifies the general direction of policies for managing social conflicts, and local policies often align closely with central documents, in actual practice, local governments must find ways to implement policies that suit local conditions, adapting central policy requirements to local needs. Viewing China as a homogeneous whole and treating Chinese law as a unified entity while ignoring the significant differences in policy practices between regions and the stark contrasts between urban and rural areas is a common methodological error in the study of Chinese law.

[64] Margaret Y. K. Woo, 'Law and discretion in contemporary Chinese courts' in Karen G. Turner, James V. Feinerman and R. Kent Guy (eds.), *The Limits of the Rule of Law in China* (Seattle, WA: University of Washington Press, 2000), p. 173.

6

Case Study One

The Feasibility of Mediation in the Grassroots Society of China

6.1 Empirical Study on Mediation in China

6.1.1 Meaning of Empirical Study

An empirical study is defined as any research in which the conclusions of the study are drawn from concrete empirical data and 'testable' evidence. Instead of focusing on theoretical assumption and logical deductive reasoning, 'empirical study relies on experience or observation. . .it is data-based research, coming up with conclusions which are capable of being verified by observation or experiment'.[1] 'Empirical research in law involves the study, *through direct methods* rather than secondary sources, of the institutions, rules, procedures, and personnel of the law, with a view to *understanding how they operate and what effects they have*'.[2] This approach may compensate for the shortcomings of the black letter method, reorient China's legal scholarship and give us a more vivid and nuanced picture of China's dispute resolution practice.

An empirical study includes qualitative and quantitative methods. The former 'involves an attempted in-depth exploration of legal processes, typically focusing on a modest number of interactions but viewing these from a variety of perspectives and perhaps over time'.[3] The latter, on the other hand, is closer to the pure scientific method, which 'will be carried out on a large scale, possibly employing the services of a survey

1 C. R. Kothari, *Research Methodology: Methods and Techniques* (New Delhi: Wiley Eastern, 1985), p. 4.

2 John Baldwin and Dwynn Davis, 'Empirical research in law' in Peter Cane and Mark Tushnet (eds.), *The Oxford Handbook of Legal Studies* (Oxford: University of Oxford, 2003), pp. 880–881 (emphasis added).

3 Baldwin and Davis, 'Empirical research in law', 891.

company...the information recorded may allow complex statistical analysis'.[4] In the qualitative approach, participant observation focusing on process study,[5] interviewing, thick description,[6] ethnography and fieldwork will be comprehensively employed in this research. This would 'generate richer and more in-depth information than other methods... [and] can provide a border understanding of the social process'.[7] Therefore, qualitative research methods are well-suited to exploring the mechanisms and processes involved in dispute resolution.

6.1.2 *Irreplaceable Value of Empirical Method in Chinese Mediation Studies*

China has a long history of mediation practice. The existing scholarship in China has made a valuable explanation of the Chinese preference for nonjudicial means of dispute resolution rather than the use of court proceedings in traditional society. Their findings suggest that this phenomenon stems from economic,[8] and

[4] Baldwin and Davis, 'Empirical research in law', 892.

[5] According to Sally Falk Moore, 'to study rule orders in action, it is necessary to deal simultaneously with the explicit rules, the occasions on which they are communicated and invoked and with actual behavior addressed by the rules, the context in which it takes place, and the ideas and assumptions that are congruent with rules'. See Sally Falk Moore, *Law as Process: An Anthropological Approach* (Münster-Hamburg: Lit Verlag, 2nd ed., 2000), p. 8. This is the so-called process study of law, which aims to understand 'the relationships between human action and social structure' and 'provides us with sufficient variance to observe the processes by which micro actions produce macro effects'. See Joseph Sanders, 'The interplay of micro and macro processes in the longitudinal study of courts: beyond the Durkheimian tradition' (1990) 24(2) *Law and Society Review* 241, 256.

[6] '"Thick Description" is the intensive, small-scale, dense descriptions of social life from observation, through which broader cultural interpretations and generalisations can be made. The term was introduced in the philosophical writings of Gilbert Ryle, and developed by Clifford Geertz in anthropology, especially in his celebrated study of the Balinese cockfight'. John Scott and Gordon Marshall, 'Thick description' in *A Dictionary of Sociology* (Oxford, Oxford University Press, 2009), www.oxfordreference.com/views/ENTRY.html?subview=Main&entry=t88.e2354 (last accessed 22 March 2014). See also Clifford Geertz, *The Interpretation of Cultures* (New York: Basic Books, 1973), pp. 3–32. When studying dispute resolution issues in China, 'thick description' as a method has been successfully used in the previous research. See, for example, Stanley B. Lubman, 'Dispute resolution in China after Deng Xiaoping: "Mao and mediation" Revisited' (1997) 11 *Columbia Journal of Asian Law* 229.

[7] Anthony Giddens, *Sociology* (Cambridge: Polity Press, 5th ed., 2006), p. 86.

[8] In general, cost is a very significant reason affecting people's choice on dispute resolution means. For a general discussion about this, see David M. Trubek et al., 'The costs of ordinary litigation' (1983) 31 *UCLA Law Review* 72, quoted from Leonard L. Riskin and

political[9] as well as cultural reasons.[10] Regarding mediation in modern times, numerous contributions have been made.[11] For example, some scholars from the functionalism approach argue that mediation in China plays a role as a social control method and it is strategically used as a means to achieve effective social mobilisation.[12] Zhipin Liang, on the contrary, believes that mediation in China's context is not only a functional mechanism of dispute resolution but also a cultural practice through which people can understand the Chinese worldview, a view rooted in the values of the Confucian principle of harmony, and a major

James E. Westbrook, *Dispute Resolution and Lawyers* (St. Paul, MN: West Group, 1987), pp. 24–26. In China's legal scholarship, scholars also explained the relationship between cost and dispute resolution means choice. For example, Xinyi Hou once studied the high litigation cost in Qing dynasty of China in Sichuan province and its influence on ordinary people's choices on dispute resolution means. See Xinyi Hou, 'On the problem of the folk super-litigiousity in the south of river area of the Qing Dynasty' (2006) 4 *Chinese Journal of Law* 150 [侯欣一："清代江南地区民间的健讼问题——以地方志为中心的考察"，载《法学研究》2006年第4期].

9 See Li Su, 'Rule of law and modernization in 20th century of China' (1998) 1 *Journal of Law* 4, 6 [苏力："二十世纪中国的现代化和法治"，载《法学研究》1998年第1期]; and Li Su, 'The Tragedy of Dou E – the evidence issues in the traditional Chinese legal system' (2005) 2 *Chinese Social Science* 95 [苏力："窦娥的悲剧——传统司法中的证据问题"，载《中国社会科学》2005年第2期]. Also see Phillip M. Chen, *Law and Justice: The Legal System in China 2400 B.C. To 1960 A.D.* (New York: Dunellen Pub., 1973), p. 7.

10 See Pitman B. Potter, 'Cultural aspects of trade dispute resolution in China' (1996) 41 *Journal of Philippine Development* 149, 149–156; Bobby K. Y. Wong, 'Traditional Chinese philosophy and dispute resolution' (2000) 30 *Hong Kong Law Journal* 304; John Shijian Mo, *Arbitration Law in China* (Hong Kong: Sweet & Maxwell Asia, 2001); Bee Chen Goh, *Law Without Lawyers, Justice Without Courts – On Traditional Chinese Mediation* (Farnham, UK: Ashgate Publishing, 2002); Albert H. Y. Chen, 'Mediation, litigation and justice: Confucian reflections in modern liberal society' in Daniel A. Bell and Hahm Chaibong (eds.), *Confucianism for the Modern World* (Cambridge, MA: Cambridge University Press, 2003); Xiaobing Xu, 'Different mediation traditions: a comparison between China and the U.S' (2005) 16 *The American Review of International Arbitration* 515, 520–534. See also Anne Isabel Kraus, *Chinese-European Dispute Resolution in China: Towards Culturally Matching Procedures*, From EU–China European Studies Centre Programme, www.cap.lmu.de/download/2007/2007_eu-china_kraus.pdf (last accessed 3 March 2010).

11 These studies are, for example, Stanley Lubman, 'Mao and mediation: politics and dispute resolution in communist China' (1967) 55(5) *California Law Review* 1284; Elmer H. Johnson, 'Mediation in People's Republic of China' in Israel L. Barak-Glantz and Elmer H. Johnson (eds.), *Comparative Criminology* (Thousand Oaks, CA: Sage, 1983); Donald C. Clarke, 'Dispute resolution in China' (1991) 5 *Journal of Chinese Law* 245; Hualing Fu, 'Understanding people's mediation in post-Mao China' (1992) 16 *Journal of Chinese Law* 211; Randall Peerenboom and Xin He, 'Dispute resolution in China: patterns, causes and prognosis' (2009) 4 *East Asia Law Review* 1.

12 Lubman, 'Mao and mediation', 1284, 1339. See also Fu, 'Understanding people's mediation', 211.

influence upon how Chinese people have constructed their society.[13] This aspect can help us to understand today's return of mediation in a cultural context, like the discourses of 'the rise of China' and 'the revival of Confucianism'.[14] However, concepts such as functionalism and culture are too big, which makes the process dimension of mediation obscure and the concept abstract rather than offering a practical theory that can guide the mediators.

In terms of their attitudes towards China's mediation, some scholars believe that mediation and ADR are just unprincipled compromisers or peacemakers without equipping any rights consciousness, which will erode the legal system as well as the rule of law in China. According to these scholars, the promotion of mediation in the dispute resolution domain has resulted in denying appropriate remedies to individuals whose rights have been violated.[15] Furthermore, 'mediators. . .[fail] to make clear the rights and wrongs of a case and come up with muddled settlements not based on a clear understanding of the facts and the law.'[16] However, some other scholars have argued that because the mediation system is rooted in traditional Chinese society, its function and role in modern China cannot be denied. Considering the limitations of litigation and adjudication (i.e., the lack of communicative rationality) and taking into consideration the vigorous life of mediation, mediation can still play a significant role through a creative transformation. It means in the light of the modern understanding of the rule of law, traditional thinking and practice regarding mediation can be revised.[17] Similarly, such arguments are too abstract and theoretical. If there is a lack of 'thick description' from an empirical perspective, the real process of mediation and the theory developed based on such a process are still ignored.

In the past twenty years, researching ADR issues has become increasingly popular in Chinese scholarship. According to Chinese National Knowledge Infrastructure, the important academic database in China, from 2001 to the present, there have been fifty-eight PhD dissertations

[13] Zhiping Liang, *Cultural Interpretations on Law* (Beijing: Sanlian Press, 1994), pp. 6, 57–58, 64 [梁治平：《法律的文化解释》，北京：三联书店1994年版].

[14] In the past decades, China witnessed an extreme popularity of traditional culture. It is considered as a symbol of national confidence towards its own culture and 'the revival of Confucianism'. For some relevant discussion, see Xiaoguang Kang, 'The soft power building and revival of Confucianism' (2007) 1 *Frontiers* 32 [康晓光：《软力量建设与儒家文化复兴》，载《天涯》，2007年第1期].

[15] Clarke, 'Dispute resolution in China', 245, 272.

[16] Clarke, 'Dispute resolution in China', 245, 272.

[17] Chen, 'Mediation, litigation and justice', 282.

focusing on ADR and mediation issues in China directly (the word 'mediation' is included in the title of the doctoral thesis of law). However, the current Chinese mediation studies have the tendency to over-conceptualise the process of mediation. The lack of empirical studies on mediation makes people unable to understand the real mechanism of mediation from 'law-in-action' perspective.[18]

Different from traditional legal research, which focuses on the black letter analysis and abstract jurisprudence, empirical research is indispensable to mediation research. Unlike the formal judgment in which the evidence, reasoning and legal analysis of the judge are comprehensively presented in detail, the drafting style of a mediation agreement is quite simple.[19] The court mediation agreement leaves out much of detailed information, sometimes even important information within the dispute resolution process. According to Article 100 of the Civil Procedural Law of PRC (1991, amended 2023),

> When a mediation agreement is reached, the people's court shall prepare a consent judgment. A consent judgment shall state the claims, facts of the case, and results of mediation. The judges and court clerk shall affix their signatures and the people's court shall affix its seal to a consent judgment, which shall be served on both sides. Once a consent judgment is signed by both sides, it shall become legally binding.

So, only the core issues, like the basic facts and the outcome are required to be listed in the agreement. Besides, Article 101 of the Civil Procedural Law provides some cases which do not require mediation agreement including:

> A consent judgment of a people's court is not required for mediation agreements reached in the following cases: (1) Divorce cases where both parties have reconciled through mediation. (2) Adoption cases where an adoptive relationship has been maintained through mediation. (3) Cases where performance on the spot is possible. (4) Other cases where a consent judgment is not required. A mediation agreement which does not require a consent judgment shall be recorded in the transcripts and become legally binding immediately after both sides and the judges and court clerk affix their signatures or seals to the transcripts.

[18] See Hao Xiong, *Alternative Dispute Resolution: Origins, Skills and Regulations* (Beijing: Law Press, 2023) [熊浩：《非诉讼纠纷解决论纲：源流、技艺、规制》，北京：法律出版社2023年版].

[19] For a general introduction about China's court mediation agreement drafting, see Weijian Tang (ed.), *The Fundamentals of the Civil Procedural Law and Case Studies* (Beijing: Renmin University Press, 2nd ed., 2010), pp. 233–235 [汤维建主编：《民事诉讼法原理与案例教程》，北京：人民大学出版社2010年第二版].

These regulations indicate that some court mediation may even lack a brief written record in terms of the basic facts of the dispute and the outcome. In this case, it is not easy to find abundant information about disputants' information and the dispute resolution process by reading the documents or archives (Figure 6.1). Hence, when studying mediation, the empirical approach, including the participatory observation, is irreplaceable through which the disputants' true emotions and motivations can be captured, and the techniques and knowledge used by the judge in the real process of dispute resolution can be described.

6.1.3 *The Difficulty of Conducting Empirical Study in China*

It should be noted that the mediation and court are sensitive, and it is not easy to get access to mediation, especially in the court. In terms of mediation specifically, it is understandable that 'investigating ongoing mediations is difficult, time-consuming, and expensive. . .few disputants and mediators are even willing to allow researchers to "sit-in" on their mediations'.[20] Therefore, if the court is not a 'familiar or semi-familiar setting' for the researchers, it is extremely difficult for them to collect data or do interviews. In this regard, Chinese scholars may have comparative advantages. As Donald C. Clark suggested, 'where Chinese scholars have an advantage, however, is in fieldwork in the judicial system. Chinese officials are far more willing to speak frankly to a fellow Chinese, particularly from a prestigious university, than to a foreign researcher'.[21]

[20] James A. Wall, Jr. and Timothy C. Dunne, 'Mediation research: a current review' (2012) 28(2) *Negotiation Journal* 217, 229.

[21] Donald C. Clarke, 'Empirical research into the Chinese judicial system' in Erik G. Jensen and Thomas C. Heller (eds.), *Beyond Common Knowledge: Empirical Approaches to the Rule of Law* (Stanford, CA: Stanford University Press, 2003), p. 180. Similarly, Li Su also pointed out that the comparative advantage of a Chinese scholar is studying Chinese law. See Li Su, *Sending Law to the Rural China: A Study on Chinese Legal Institution at the Grassroots Level* (Beijing: China University of Politics and Law Press, 2000), p. 18 [苏力：《送法下乡：中国基层司法制度研究》，北京：中国政法大学出版社2000年版]. The original text goes as follows:

> 必须指出，就实际的可能性而言，越大多数中国学者也不可能在研究其他国家的司法制度上作出重大贡献。不仅因为司法是实践的，不仅因为对文化背景的要求，不仅因为文字表现力的有限，更重要的是就一般而言，中国学者在研究上的比较优势只可能在于研究中国的法律与司法。如果你要研究外国法，你就不应该同中国人比，而应当同外国学者比（同国际接轨）。你觉得，就一般而言，我们有这个知识上的比较优势吗？而且如果接受了法律知识地方性的前提，你对外国司法制度的研究也并不必然比另一位学者对本国司法制度的研究在知识上拥有更高的品味。

Mediation Agreement Template

Representative of Party A ________ Gender ________ Date of Birth ________

Ethnicity ______________ Occupation __________ Address ______________

ID Number ______________ Contact Number ______________

Representative of Party B ________ Gender ________ Date of Birth ________

Ethnicity ______________ Occupation __________ Address ______________

ID Number ______________ Contact Number ______________

Brief Description of the Dispute

At the application of the two parties, the Social Conflict and Dispute Mediation Center of ______________ organized the two parties to mediate the dispute. After negotiation, the two parties voluntarily reached the following agreement:

____

This agreement is made in ______ copies, and each of them will be placed on file in both parties and the dispute mediation center, which will take effect after the signature of both parties.

Signature of the Party A ____________ (seal)

Signature of the Party B ____________ (seal)

Signature of the Mediator ____________ (seal)

The Conflict and Dispute Mediation Center of __________ (seal)

Figure 6.1 Mediation agreement template.[22]
Source: www.renrendoc.com/paper/115565454.html (last accessed 25 May 2024).

[22] Mediation agreement template, www.renrendoc.com/paper/115565454.html (last accessed 25 May 2024).

In a familiar context, the researchers can do a deep and honest interview with the judges and lawyers and, thus, can collect reliable data about local court systems and explore the reality of China's local court operations.[23]

Based on the above considerations, the writing of this chapter will be different. Rather than presenting a conceptual framework, this chapter engages in a detailed description, trying to help readers understand the real process of mediation in China. It should be noted that because China is so large, mediation practices vary from region to region. But it is still meaningful to illustrate the real mediation process through empirical study, which will embody and exemplify the theoretical understanding of mediation in the Chapter 4 and allow readers to examine the feasibility of these theories and concepts in practice.

6.2 Fieldwork Place

Before introducing the mediation process, the background information on mediation will be explained. This chapter explains an empirical case study conducted in P County Court, Yunnan Province. It aims to portray the detailed process of mediation and analyse its feasibility in the context of a rural and undeveloped southwest grassroots situation. P County is an ethnic county located in a mountainous region of Yunnan province. According to the statistics, there are more than 100 villages in this county, the majority of which make their living out of agriculture. There are several ethnic minorities living in this region, including Yi, Dai, Hui and so on, who make up approximately 70 per cent of the total population of the county. Although economic development of this county has taken place very quickly in recent years as a result of the discovery of mines, it was historically been a poverty-stricken county.[24]

There are fifty-nine official staff members in total in the P County Court. Twenty-five judges work for the court, seventeen of whom are ethnic minority judges, and of these, ten can speak ethnic languages and dialects. There are forty-three male and sixteen female staff members. Thirty-eight of them are Communist Party of China members, and the

[23] It is worth mentioning that the study of local courts is very important and has the possibility to create original academic contributions. That is because the most important disputes in ordinary people's daily lives usually happen in local courts. In other words, the encounter between law and day-to-day life happens in local courts. For this, Li Su has made an excellent explanation, see Su, *Sending Law to the Rural China*, pp. 7–11 [苏力：《送法下乡：中国基层司法制度研究》，北京：中国政法大学出版社2000年版].

[24] In order to keep the investigated place and people anonymous, relevant identifying information has been anonymised.

average age of the judges is forty-three. The number of judges who specialise in adjudication rather than administrative management and enforcement is ten. The leadership of the court consists of seven persons, one of whom is not a Party member. All the leaders have bachelor's degrees, and six of them have the judicial qualifications to adjudicate cases. Fifty-two staff members of the court have bachelor's degrees,[25] comprising 88.4 per cent of the total. However, only six judges among them are graduates from formal law schools.

According to the Judge's Law of the People's Republic of China (amended 2019), the judge at the legislative level is defined as 'the judicial personnel who exercise the judicial authority of the State according to the law', which includes:

> presidents, vice presidents, members of judicial committees, chief judges and associate chief judges of divisions, judges and assistant judges of the

[25] In China, the bachelor's degree is a very subtle and vague concept. That is because there are various approaches for the candidate to obtain this degree rather than through the formal university education only. Speaking of the diversified approaches to obtaining a law degree, Jin Huang said:

> Seeing that legal education institutions, there are higher legal education institutions (including regular course and special course legal education institutions), secondary legal education institutions, Administrative staff institutes of political science and law, radio-TV legal education institutions and other kinds of vocational or part-time legal education institutions. Seeing that the levels of legal education, there are secondary legal education, special course legal education, LL.B. programs, two-bachelor degrees programs, postgraduates without LL.M. programs, LL.M. programs, Doctor of Law programs and post-doctor of law programs. These situations make the goal and requirements legal education complicated and confused.

Jin Huang, 'The structure of legal education in China', www.aals.org/2000international/english/china.htm (last accessed 12 December 2017).

There are quite different types of parallel approaches for the candidate to obtain a bachelor's degree of law in China. Some education approaches are less formal, less strict and more flexible than the national university system, which requires all the candidates to pass a strict and highly competitive entrance examination to enter. Thus, the quality of the non-national university degrees is commonly criticised and worried about by the public. Yet in current China, the so-called multitrack system still exists.

In this case, even though the judge holds a bachelor's degree in law according to the official record, this does not necessarily mean that the holder has been well educated in law school and even does not even mean he/she is a graduate from a formal university. So, if the researcher only read the document about the personnel of a Chinese grassroots court but does not do any further investigation, the outcome may be fuzzy and misleading.

> Supreme People's Court, local People's Courts at various levels and special People's Courts such as military courts.[26]

For ordinary judges, the relevant qualifications are required. Article 12 of the Judge Law clearly states the judge's qualifications from item (5) to item (7):

> Having a bachelor's degree or above in law from a regular institution of higher education, or a bachelor's degree or above not in law from a regular institution of higher education but with a degree of juris master, master of law, or above, or bachelor's degree or above not in law from a regular institution of higher education with any other corresponding degree and with professional knowledge of law; having engaged in the legal work for at least five years. The seniority in engaging in the legal work of those with a degree of juris master or master of law, or with a doctor's degree of law may be respectively relaxed to four and three years; persons to be appointed as judges for the first time shall have passed the national uniform legal profession qualification examination and obtained the legal profession qualification'.[27]

In this regard, the qualification of judges in China seems to be highly unified, but in fact, there are complex problems regarding presiding over China's grassroots courts in less-developed regions. As an explicit exception, Article 12 of Judge Law states, 'for the places where it is truly difficult to apply the academic qualification as specified in item (5) of the preceding paragraph, after being examined and determined by the Supreme People's Court (SPC), the academic qualification for judges may be relaxed during a specific period as graduates from an institution of higher education'. Moreover, 'the Judge's Law does not mention whether unqualified judges will be dismissed if they are unable to meet the requirements even after the training, nor specify a time limit for the legal training'.[28] As a result, the law leaves space for an unqualified judge to survive in the courts. All these elements lead to the outcome that the qualifications and professional backgrounds of the judicial staff working at the grassroots courts in the

26 Judges Law of the People's Republic of China (amended 2019), Article 2, http://en.pkulaw.cn/display.aspx?cgid=d6d7751543d3ffe3bdfb&lib=law (last accessed 1 September 2021).

27 Judges Law of People's Republic of China (amended 2019), Article 2.

28 Weidong Ji, 'Legal education in China: a great leap forward of professionalism' (2004) 39 *Kobe University Review* 1, 5.

undeveloped regions of China are highly complicated and diverse.[29] In the court, the judges who graduated from law schools, regardless of the reputation of the institutions, are called *keban* (professional, 科班), whereas the judges who are not equipped with professional and formal education in law are titled *non-keban* (nonprofessional, 非科班).

6.3 Case Study: An Adjacency Rights Dispute in a Rural Village

6.3.1 Basic Facts of the Dispute

A and B are neighbours living in a Yi ethnic village. Both A and B are Yi ethnic people, whose mother tongue is the Yi dialect (彝语). They can communicate with others in Mandarin but do not do so very often. In 1989, the two families had a dispute in terms of the ownership of a cattle ring located between the two families' houses. Up to now, the ownership of the cattle ring was still unclear. Months ago, without B's permission, A's family started to rebuild a new house, the new construction extended to the disputed place. B and his wife were incensed about this act of their neighbour and disrupted the process of the new house construction. Then, the two families quarrelled and fought. B's wife was hurt by A in the fight. B's wife then sued A in the county court for compensation for personal injury (Figure 6.2). Finally, she won the lawsuit with a monetary compensation of around RMB 700 being paid by A. After the lawsuit, A's family continued their construction, whereas B's family continued to disrupt the construction at the night, like guerrilla warfare. A would not tolerate this. A went to the court to sue B to claim compensation of RMB 10,260 for damaging his house construction . Before the case went to court, a people's mediator had tried to solve this problem but failed. The P Court accepted this case, and a circuit tribunal (*xunhuifating*, 巡回法庭) consisting of a judge, a clerk, a judge assistant and a bailiff went to the village to solve the dispute. Before the litigation procedure started, the judge and other judicial staff visited the scene where the dispute happened to interview the people and take photographs.

The entire dispute was heard and handled in the village. In the adjudication process, both parties were willing to handle the case

[29] Frank K. Upham, 'Who will find the defendant if he stays with his sheep? Justice in rural China' (2005) 114 *The Yale Law Journal* 1675, 1686.

Figure 6.2 The place where the dispute happened.
Photograph by the author.

through mediation. Finally, the dispute was successfully settled by court mediation. A eventually received the compensation of RMB 400 from B.[30]

6.3.2 *Dispute Resolution Process and Preliminary Analysis*

The whole adjudication process occurred in the meeting room of the village's committee. This room is around 200 square meters and brightly lit. The judge and judicial staff sat in the front facing the parties. All the judicial settings in the court, such as the title board and the national emblem, were arranged in this room in a very formal and serious manner. During the court investigation stage, it was clear that neither of the parties could understand the judge's words. Having only been educated in primary school, the legal terms were too difficult for them to understand. Sometimes it was necessary for the bailiff, who was familiar with the local Yi dialect, to facilitate communication among the judges, clerk and the parties. Interestingly, even though the judge knew that the parties could not understand legal terminology, he still insisted on first using the legal terms, then followed by translating them into everyday language. For example, the judge would say, 'It is your legal right to. . .' and then translate this by himself into 'I am saying that you can. . .'[31]

30 The basic facts and process of this case is abstracted from the author's interview with the judges, judicial staff, the participative observation and mediation agreement with the permission of both parties and presiding judge.

31 The judge in this stage had a very strong and strict control over the proceeding by instructing the parties to follow the adjudication procedures. The court investigation was carried out as follows:

. . . . . .

JUDGE:	'Now, the court will investigate the facts of the case. The plaintiff, you can state your litigation claims first (*susong qinggiu*, 诉讼请求)'.
PLAINTIFF:	(Silent)
JUDGE:	'Can you hear me? (The judge turned to the plaintiff.) You can state your litigation claim!'
PLAINTIFF:	'What do you mean? What should I do?'
JUDGE:	'Read the petition, I mean you read the document that you submit to our court'.
PLAINTIFF:	'I illiteratecannot read it'.
JUDGE:	'You cannot read it? Who wrote it for you?'

In modern society, 'the forms of law themselves become more complex until they leave behind the common consciousness as far as details and technicality of the rules are concerned'.[32] Legal terminology, from the perspective of the legal profession, can help them to 'easily analyze a complex problem, arrive at a correct solution, and explain it clearly to others...[and] avoid much unnecessary obscurity and difficulty'.[33] However, the esoteric system of legal terms is often criticised by the public for incomprehensibility of 'jargon', which is very difficult to understand from the standpoint of the general public.[34] For example, it was reported that 'in Victoria, Australia, there was some concern recently when it was realized that food regulations could not be understood by cooks'.[35]

Speaking of the incomprehensibility of legal terminology for the public, Roger Cotterrell underlined that 'there is an obvious misunderstanding of reality, to require of a man that he should know intuitively what four years of university and ten years of practice are not always

PLAINTIFF: 'Someone I knew. My education is limited, and I can barely read and write (*wo wenhua bugao, shizishao*, 我文化不高, 识字少)'.

JUDGE: 'Clerk, you read it for him'.

CLERK: (Read the petition.)

JUDGE: 'Is everything right? Is there any other thing you want to add?'

PLAINTIFF WIFE (INTERRUPTED): 'I want to say something. I was hurt by A and our new house is not... (then quarrelled with the defendant's wife before the judge).'

JUDGE: 'Stop! It is not your turn to speak! Plaintiff, please tell your wife to follow the court order and regulation. I am asking you, not her!'

PLAINTIFF: (Turned back to his wife.) 'Shut up!' (And then responded to the judge.) 'The document has recorded all I want to say...'

JUDGE: 'I am asking you, is that all? Do you have any other additional issues?'

PLAINTIFF: 'Yes, that's all'.

JUDGE: 'OK, let's investigate the defendant's side'.

......

32 Roger Cotterrell, *The Sociology of Law: An Introduction* (London: Butterworths, 2nd ed., 1992), p. 22.

33 Arthur L. Corbin, 'Legal analysis and terminology' (1919) 29(2) *The Yale Law Journal* 163.

34 Heikki E. S. Mattila, *Comparative Legal Linguistic* (Farnham, UK: Ashgate, 2006), p. 3.

35 John Gibbons, 'Language and the law' (1999) 19 *Annual Review of Applied Linguistics* 156, 160.

sufficient to teach'.[36] The legal terminologies are a challenge for educated people living in the city, let alone the farmers who are living in the poor countryside and have received very limited education. However, this incomprehensible jargon just enhances the authority and professionalism of the judge before the parties. It is not surprising that 'complex and technical language also carries a social message concerning the power and authority of the person using it'.[37] To some degree, 'law's hegemonic power is located in its forms of discourse, with the narrative being recognized as one of its most powerful'.[38]

In this adjacency rights dispute, the judge provided the parties with rationally persuasive narratives decorated with professional legal terms. Although it is common for a mediator's influence to be an integral part of the process,[39] the implementation of legal terminology can ensure that the judge can have the initiative, especially when he persuades the parties and controls the tempo of the judicial activities. In addition to the judge having difficulty with the communication of legal terms, in a delicate way, he suggested to the parties that adjudication, in this case, might not be an ideal approach to handling this dispute between them. The usage of incomprehensive legal terms increased the possibility and willingness of the parties to seek a settlement through mediation. The long, boring and complicated adjudication process sent a clear message to the parties: 'If you want to handle this problem more understandably, let us move on to the mediation stage'.

In the mediation stage, the everyday language was widely used in contrast to the previous stage. The judge told the researcher that 'the everyday language would allow for the judge and parties to achieve a closer understanding of the case'. It has been commonly noted that plain and intelligible language should be preferred within the mediation process. Simple, concrete language helps the parties to easily and comfortably relate to the process.[40] The necessity of the plain language style has also been realised by the SPC. According to the Article 15 of the Notice (2010) from the SPC, it explicitly provides that:

[36] Cotterrell, *The Sociology of Law*, p. 140.

[37] Cotterrell, *The Sociology of Law*, p. 140.

[38] Rosemary Coombe, 'Is there a cultural studies of law?" in Toby Miller (ed.), *A Companion to Cultural Studies* (Hoboken, NJ: Wiley Blackwell, 2001), p. 45.

[39] Genevieve A. Chornenki and Christine E. Hart, *Bypass Court: A Dispute Resolution Handbook* (Toronto, ON: LexisNexis, 2011), p. 95.

[40] John W. Cooley, *The Mediator's Handbook: Advanced Practice Guide for Civil Litigation* (Louisville, CO: National Institute for Trial Advocacy, 2nd ed., 2006), p. 131.

> During each link of litigation, we shall, pertinent to the different characteristics of the cultural knowledge and litigation capacity of the parties concerned, conduct judicial interpretation and disambiguation in easy words, fully explain the potential litigation risks, and guide the parties concerned to equally and voluntarily resolve the disputes based on being fully aware of their own rights and obligations.[41]

What had changed was not only the language style but also the environment. After the parties expressed their willingness to use mediation to solve the problem, they were led by the judge to an upstairs room to the office of the people's mediation committee. The room is much smaller than the meeting room where the adjudication was held. Here the judge and disputing parties could interact more closely with each other. Compared to the litigation that took place in the conference room of the village's committee, the atmosphere was much more relaxed in the smaller and informal room. The judge even started to smoke and laughed to encourage everyone to continue seeking a dispute resolution.

In seeking a settlement of the dispute resolution, the change in the physical environment of the proceedings was as crucial in moving the continuance of the case forward as the change in the language style used by the judge. These micro techniques adopted by the veteran judge consciously or unconsciously were subtle, sophisticated and effective, which naturalised the transformation from litigation to mediation. The transfer also totally changed the nature of the dispute resolution mechanism. In the mediation stage, all the people present, including the disputing parties, judge, clerk, bailiff, village mediators and the village leaders, all became 'facilitators' for seeking a settlement to the dispute. Correspondingly, the dispute resolution mechanism was modified into a lively and open conversational forum, allowing for more people to join, participate and express their views. Although the judge was still the 'boss',[42] more local authorities

[41] 'Notice of the Supreme People's Court on Issuing Several Opinions on Further Implementing the Work Principle of "Giving Priority to Mediation and Combining Mediation with Judgment"', www.pkulaw.com/en_law/3986789cb4975254bdfb.html (last accessed 15 May 2022).

[42] The mediator enjoys different power and status in different cultural contexts. In China, for example, 'community mediators have high power and status because the country – with a Confucian tradition – values peacekeepers', thus this status can give 'the mediator control over resources so that the techniques of compensation, information gathering, and use of third parties can be employed'. See James A. Wall, Jr. and Ann Lynn, 'Mediation: a current review' (1993) 37(1) *The Journal of Conflict Resolution* 160, 169; James A. Wall, Jr. et al., 'Mediation: a current review and theory development' (2001) 45(3) *The Journal of Conflict Resolution* 370, 379.

and acquaintances could voice their views and ideas contributing to the dispute resolution.[43] In this process, the parties had more control of the dispute resolution process and could discuss the issues they were concerned

[43] The mediation process went as follows:

……

JUDGE: 'All right, this is the mediation stage. A (Judge called the Plaintiff's name directly instead of "Plaintiff"), can you just tell us what you want? How much compensation do you want?'

PLAINTIFF: 'First, I want B to pay my loss. He and his wife come to my house nearly every night to interfere with the construction of my new house and destroy the piles and the pile driving equipment. Who will pay for my loss?'

JUDGE: 'Have you ever seen that they come to destroy your house?'

PLAINTIFF: 'It is not necessary to see him. I know it is him absolutely! He has destroyed 10 piles up to now!'

DEFENDANT: 'Nonsense! I only destroyed three, not 10! You have even hurt my wife. Judge, I tell you, the land on which A is building the house does not belong to him; that is my property!'

VILLAGE LEADER: 'Could you please not bring up old scores again? Regarding the property of the land, you cannot provide evidence. Furthermore, although you two families have a different view regarding the ownership of this place, you have been living with each other in harmony for a long time; 15 years, right? I have told you many times that it isn't good for two neighbours to fight with each other. Are you afraid of being laughed at by other villagers and our judge?'

JUDGE: 'What the village leader said is right. If you have a dispute regarding the property issues of the land, you can go to the village mediation office; you can come to our court to solve it. Do not do something that makes the situation worse! A, you do not like B. Can you move out of the village? Can you go to downtown; go to city? You can't, right? So, we all come here to help you to reconsider the dispute from different perspectives and solve the problem'.

BAILIFF: 'In my view, B, you also did something wrong. If you do not agree to A to build a new house here, you can go to find the village leader…'

DEFENDANT: 'I have tried…'

BAILIFF: 'Please let me finish! Regardless of who is right and who is wrong, you should not destroy other's property. You have said you destroyed three piles, right? Do you know it is illegal? Can I come to your house to destroy your things? I can't, right? Doing this kind of thing in the night just like a thief can only make you lose your face in the village!'

JUDGE: 'OK, it is clear that B has admitted that he destroyed three piles.'

PLAINTIFF: 'More than three!'

JUDGE: 'Do you have evidence?'

about as opposed to what the judge wanted to hear. This can explain why the parties' satisfaction in the mediation process is higher in comparison to that of the litigation approach.[44]

Through this dispute resolution mechanism, various people educated and exhorted the parties to arrive at a solution. It provided a huge range of flexibility for both parties to freely air their grievances and release their anger and dissatisfaction psychologically to a remarkable extent. The mediation at this stage went beyond the institutionalised dispute resolution mechanism, and it played a role in facilitating comprehensive social–psychological rehabilitation and emotional release. This is another advantage of mediation, which was fully utilised by the experienced judge. The judge knew that legal proceedings compared to mediation 'do not focus on emotion, but instead examine most conflicts through the prism of relevancy, admissibility, and procedure'.[45] However, mediation can take expression, understanding and emotions seriously, as it 'presumes that the expression and understanding of a party's emotional needs may be a condition precedent to settlement'.[46]

In the process of calming the parties' emotions, village officials, bailiffs, judicial assistants and even the parties' relatives and friends can participate in the mediation process. According to Michael Palmer,

> [the] recourse to the courts is often motivated by a desire to impress upon an opponent the seriousness with which a grievance is held. The aim is

PLAINTIFF:	(Silence)
JUDGE:	'A, I have not talked with you about the extremely high compensation you ask for. Do you think a judge is just like an idiot? I tell you I know how much the local cost is for the new house. Your request is. . .ridiculous'.
VILLAGE LEADER:	'B has admitted he has done something wrong. In this case, A, could you please ask for less compensation? We should not embarrass our judge'.
JUDGE:	'B, let's talk about what you should do for your irrational destructive behaviour. How much can you pay for A's loss?'

. . . . .

44 Nancy H. Rogers and Richard A. Salem, *A Student's Guide to Mediation and the Law* (New York: M. Bender, 1987), pp. 225–226. Actually, 'consensual processes like mediation and negotiation offer a greater degree of process control, and hence they are seen by parties as "subjectively fairer", and are preferred, regardless of whether they ultimately lead to favorable outcomes'. See Robert A. Baruch Bush, '"What do we need a mediator for?": Mediation's "value-added" for negotiators' (1996) 12 *Ohio State Journal on Dispute Resolution* 1, 18.

45 Kimberlee K. Kovach, *Mediation in a Nutshell* (St. Paul, MN: Thomson/West, 2010), pp. 41–42.

46 Kovach, *Mediation in a Nutshell*, pp. 41–42.

> not to initiate a successful lawsuit, but, rather, to gain access to a sympathetic forum in which the grievance can be aired, and the moral virtues and legal strengths of one's case acknowledged. In these circumstances, the courts will often utilize kin, friends, and workmates of the disputants in order to persuade the prospective litigants to settle their differences without taking the matter to trial.[47]

This involvement makes the mediation process more open rather than confidential, thereby gaining significant social and educational value. This dispute resolution strategy holds both functional value and cultural significance. In terms of functional value, the involvement of facilitators allowed them to express their thoughts and even provide creative suggestions on how to solve the dispute. Mediation thus can help the parties 'to think outside the box' and to 'brainstorm potential options to maximize creativity'.[48] In other words, 'with minimal procedural requirements, mediation provides an unlimited opportunity for the parties to exercise flexibility in communicating their underlying concerns and priorities regarding the dispute'.[49] In terms of cultural significance, this strategy reflects and reinforces communal values and social cohesion. It leverages traditional practices of collective problem-solving and underscores the importance of maintaining harmonious relationships within the community. As Fei Xiaotong observed, 'settling disputes in villages is part of the educational process that goes on in a rural society. . .What we now call "mediation" (*tiaojie*) used to be called "critical reasoning" (*pingli*)'.[50]

This type of dispute resolution strategy, which motivates the parties' relatives, acquaintances and local authorities to join the dispute resolution procedure, was not uncommon in ancient China. For example, during the Qing dynasty, the unofficial 'peace-talkers' were ubiquitous, and they took responsibility for maintaining the social order.[51] In other words, the traditional dispute resolution model remains active even in

[47] Michael Palmer, 'The revival of mediation in the People's Republic of China (2): judicial mediation' in W. E. Butler (ed.), *Yearbook on Socialist Legal Systems* (New York: Transnational Publishers, Inc., 1989), p. 148.

[48] Kovach, *Mediation in a Nutshell*, p. 43.

[49] Cooley, *The Mediator's Handbook*, p. 7.

[50] Xiaotong Fei, *From the Soil: The Foundations of Chinese Society*, Gary G. Hamilton and Zheng Wang (trans.) (Berkeley, CA: University of California Press, 1992), pp. 103–104.

[51] Jerome Alan Cohen, 'Chinese mediation on the eve of modernization' (1966) 54(3) *California Law Review* 1201, 1216.

the modern mediation context. The village dispute in southwest rural China was resolved by following the traditional dispute resolution model, which involved assistance, education and reliance on external parties.[52]

Finally, this dispute was successfully solved by court mediation. A, in this case, received compensation of RMB 400 from B. Surprisingly, the compensation agreed upon was much lower than A's original claim of RMB 10,260 demanded at the beginning.

As an observer who witnessed the whole process of mediation, the researcher notes that both parties achieved this agreement voluntarily.[53] As the village leader continuously noted, both parties were still neighbours, and in the future, they would have to live with each other, no matter whether they liked each other or not. This advice was helpful for the parties towards achieving their final compromise and also matched the spirit of the mediation, which is commonly regarded as future-oriented.[54]

It is worth noting that there was a huge gap in comparing the original claim to the final compensation paid to the plaintiff. From the picture of the fragment of the plaintiff's original claims (see Figure 6.3), Plaintiff (A) himself may have been very uncertain concerning the amount of compensation he should claim. In this example, he changed the total amount of loss on the document. Alternatively, another possibility may have been that the basic calculation skills of the plaintiff was very weak, and he made a mistake in terms of the total amount of the loss. He then had to correct the error by sealing it with a red fingerprint.

Regardless of the plaintiff's subjective reasoning, RMB 10,260 was a sky-high price.[55] B definitely could not pay this amount of money, and A knew that this was a fact. In all reality, requesting a high claim

[52] James A. Wall, Jr. and Michael Blum, 'Community mediation in People's Republic of China' (1991) 35 *Journal of Conflict Resolution* 3.

[53] Although the parties' voluntariness was not 100 per cent, as the judge made use of many micro techniques and skills to lead them to the mediation track, like the usage of 'legal jargon', the parties reached an agreement freely rather than being forced. In the mediation process, the door to litigation was still open to them if they changed their minds.

[54] Stephen K. Erickson and Marilyn S. McKnight, *The Practitioner's Guide to Mediation: A Client-Centered Approach* (New York: Wiley, 2001), p. 25.

[55] Figure 6.4 shows the environment and living condition of the villager. The judge was investigating the fact in the place where the dispute happened. This village is really poor and RMB 10,260 is definitely impossible for the defendant to pay.

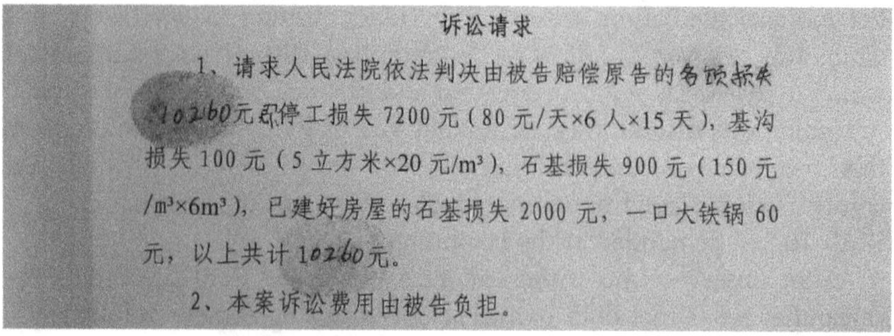

诉讼请求

1、请求人民法院依法判决由被告赔偿原告的各项损失10260元包括停工损失 7200 元（80 元/天×6 人×15 天），基沟损失 100 元（5 立方米×20 元/m³），石基损失 900 元（150 元/m³×6m³），已建好房屋的石基损失 2000 元，一口大铁锅 60 元，以上共计 10260元。

2、本案诉讼费用由被告负担。

Figure 6.3 A fragment of the plaintiff's original claims.
Photograph taken by the author.

settlement is a very common strategy used in the bargaining process,[56] yet the only difference between ordinary bargaining and this example concerned the fact that A's strategy seemed to be ridiculous, and the bargaining was irrationally high due to his lack of legal knowledge and relevant experience.

6.4 Why Mediation Is Feasible for Southwest Grassroots China

6.4.1 Why Mediation Is Feasible for the Disputants

6.4.1.1 Preserving Face and Repairing Interpersonal Relationships

Compared to litigation, mediation has a clear advantage in its ability to genuinely resolve problems by preserving face and repairing the broken interpersonal relationships between the parties.[57] If this mentioned case had been handled through the litigation approach, the conflict might have been fixed on the surface, but the essential problem would still have existed. The judge informed the researcher that one of the most important reasons why A sued B this time is because B had won the last personal injury litigation several months before. By using this litigation, A desired to win back not only the money but also his face in the community.

[56] Joseph L. Matthews, *How to Win Personal Injury Claim* (Berkeley, CA: Nolo, 7th ed., 2009), p. 186.

[57] Kovach, *Mediation in a Nutshell*, pp. 42–43.

Figure 6.4 The living conditions of the village.
Photograph by the author.

In rural Chinese villages, face-saving (or reputation) (*mianzi*, 面子) and community reputation are crucial.[58] A Chinese rural village is a typical place where:

> people live very close to one another under conditions which make privacy difficult. Every event is regarded as common property and is commented upon endlessly. . .People's observation is sharp, and they are quick to satirize each other behind their backs.[59]

Because of the influence of Chinese culture,

> a system of control based on rituals means adherence to traditional rules. . .Their long education since childhood has turned these exterior rules into interior habits. . .Ideally, in a society ruled through rituals, everyone will abide by the rules voluntarily, so that all exterior supervision is unnecessary. . .Therefore, any litigation is shameful, because it indicates a lack of proper education.[60]

Therefore, '[the] recalcitrant disputants become the objects of gossip and scandal. In Chinese villages, they lose face for failing to. . .act in a manner perceived as fair in a Chinese village, and open themselves to attacks by witchcraft'.[61] More directly, keeping face is important because the daily agriculture work needs assistance and cooperation required from other villagers. In other words, if you lose face, the cooperation mechanism will be destroyed, and the loser of the litigation will bear the social pressure. Other community members may refuse to help them during the busy seasons of the agricultural cycle.[62]

[58] The importance of 'face' (*lien or mien-tzu*) has long been recognised as a prime determinant of Chinese behavioural patterns, whether those of an individual or of a group. For relevant discussion, please turn to Barbara L. K. Pillsbury, 'Factionalism observed: behind the "face" of harmony in a Chinese community' (1978) 74 *The China Quarterly* 241 and also Hsien Chin Hu, 'The Chinese concept of "face"' (1944) 46(1) *American Anthropology* 45.

[59] Julian Alfred Pitt-Rivers, *The People of the Sierra* (Chicago, IL: University of Chicago Press, 2nd ed., 1971), p. 31.

[60] Fei, *From the Soil*, p. 103.

[61] Kenneth Kressel et al., *Mediation Research: The Process and Effectiveness of Third-Party Intervention* (San Francisco, CA: Jossey-Bass, 1989), p. 84.

[62] Regarding how face mechanism actually works in China's rural village, Mr Yimou Zhang's famous movie *The Story of Qiu Ju* has presented a very vivid example for us. More discussion about the movie and relevant legal analysis can be found in Li Su, 'The confusion of Qiu Ju and tragedy of Shangkang Ye' in Li Su (ed.), *Rule of Law and Local Resource* (Beijing: The Chinese University of Politics and Law Press, 1996), p. 23 [苏力："秋菊的困惑与山杠爷的悲剧"，载苏力主编：《法治及其本土资源》，北京政法大学出版社1996年版].

Ordinary villagers often do not and cannot understand the detailed arguments presented in a judgment, which may not simply declare who is right and who is wrong. In a civil case, the judgment typically consists of a series of arguments based on legal norms and reasoning to achieve justice and balance conflicting interests in a legal manner rather than determining guilt. For community members, however, what matters most is who ultimately won the lawsuit. Ordinary villagers will then have a label they can easily stick to the losing party in the future, affecting that individual's reputation in the community. To wash away the stain on his reputation from a personal injury incident, A initiated the lawsuit, expecting to restore his honour. In such cases, litigation cannot truly resolve the dispute; the win-or-lose outcome may prompt the parties to pursue further litigation.

Compared with litigation, however, there is no winner and loser in the mediation process. The mediation process facilitates the disputants to fundamentally solve the problem. From a consequentialist perspective, mediation can preserve people's reputation, reduce the social cost and avoid another possible revengeful litigation between the same parties living in the village. It should be kept in mind that:

> In many cases, the parties who are involved in a conflict have had a long-standing relationship. This association may be personal or professional, intimate or unemotional. Examples of these relationships include neighbors, family members, employment situations, consumers, and businesses. . .Mediation provides an opportunity to explore various ways a relationship might continue.[63]

In this case, court-connected ADR played a highly pivotal role in solving the dispute because of the advantage of ADR relating to its function of preserving the face and repairing interpersonal relationships.

6.4.1.2 Technical Difficulties in Taking the Litigation Track

Technically speaking, this dispute could not be handled by litigation because of the lack of evidence. Due to the lack of legal knowledge, the plaintiff was not aware of the importance of evidence collection. Although there was no other reasonable suspect other than the defendant, there was no solid evidence that could prove that the damages were made by the defendant during the night. Both parties were too poor to hire lawyers. During the arguing process of the mediation, in an angry

[63] Kovach, *Mediation in a Nutshell*, pp. 42–43.

response to the plaintiff's accusation of damaging more than ten piling foundations, the defendant said that 'I had only damaged three'. Given the requirement of evidence and standards provided by the Civil Procedural Law and relevant judicial interpretations,[64] the dispute would not have been solved by court, and the plaintiff would not have gotten any remedy. The split between the two families would have remained unresolved. It is true that the court could have investigated the facts and found the evidence if the plaintiff had submitted an application,[65] yet the evidence would not have been successfully collected if the defendant had simply kept silent.

To some degree, court mediation fulfils the court's function of resolving civil disputes that cannot be addressed through litigation due to the disputants' lack of legal knowledge and awareness as well as the lack of evidence. This illustrates how mediation effectively resolves disputes and maintains social order by avoiding the application of ill-suited and unfamiliar state law and litigation interventions.

6.4.1.3 A Humane Legal Product

According to the author's participant observation, when the judge asked the parties questions, it was obvious that they were nervous, perplexed and scared as they were facing a formal, authoritative but incomprehensible state apparatus, just like facing a monster. It is true that 'while individual citizens' lack of access to legal knowledge has no bearing on the power of the state, or of other people, or for organizations to enforce the law against them, it makes the citizen powerless to invoke the law'.[66] The situation is even worse for the disadvantaged people in society. According to John Gibbons:

[64] According to the Civil Procedural Law of the People's Republic of China, Article 67 states, 'A party shall have the responsibility to provide evidence in support of its own propositions'. Article 90 of Interpretation of the Supreme People's Court on the Application of the Civil Procedure Law of the People's Republic of China (Amended in 2022) explains that 'the parties concerned shall be responsible for producing evidences to prove the facts on which their own allegations are based or the facts on which the allegations of the other party are refuted. Where any party cannot produce evidence or the evidence produced cannot support the facts on which the allegations are based, the party concerned that bears the burden of proof shall undertake unfavorable consequences'.

[65] Article 67 of Civil Procedural Law of the PRC provides that 'for the evidence that cannot be obtained by any parties or their litigation representatives because of some realistic reasons or for the evidence that the people's court considers necessary for adjudicating the case, the people's court shall investigate and collect such evidence'.

[66] Cotterrell, *The Sociology of Law*, p. 141.

> The technical, written, and power-laden nature of legal language makes the language of the law notoriously impenetrable for non-lawyers. The situation is even worse for those who have low proficiency in the language of the legal process, such as many second-language speakers or the deaf. Writtenness and technicality will reduce effective participation in legal processes by children, the illiterate, and the mentally handicapped. It may also affect speakers of other dialects or sociolects. Power asymmetries may impact particularly on the traumatized, children, women, and already disadvantaged minorities. The law is also a cultural field, and the disadvantage suffered by cultural minorities is powerfully documented by Eades (1994), Jacquemet (1996), and Stygall (1994). These disadvantages represent daunting human rights issues to which only partial solutions have been found in new legislation, revised procedures (such as video cameras in private rooms for children), and the education of legal professionals and the public.[67]

It should not be forgotten that both parties in this case lacked the money to hire a lawyer. They did not like the court, but they had to turn to a public dispute resolution institution to solve their problem after the people's mediation failed. In this situation, if the court could only provide highly institutionalised litigation as a public service, the parties might feel helpless and desperate even after receiving the court's decision. However, in the mediation process, the parties felt more comfortable. 'Informal and traditional mechanisms of justice are often more accessible to poor and disadvantaged people and may have the potential to provide speedy, affordable, and meaningful remedies to the poor and disadvantaged'.[68] Here, it is necessary to point out that the justification for mediation in a more humane institutional setting can also be understood from the perspective of 'access to justice'.

The idea of 'access to justice' is derived from Western countries. In the United States, for example, because the costs and delays associated with civil litigation have significantly restricted access to the courts for the ordinary citizen, there has been a great challenge to assure the process is fair to all who are brought into it.[69] There were complaints that the courthouse door was 'rapidly being slammed shut'[70] and litigation had

[67] Gibbons, 'Language and the law', 156, 160–161.

[68] 'Access to justice: practice note' (3 September 2004), see http://web.undp.org/governance/docs/Justice_PN_English.pdf (last accessed 1 May 2012).

[69] Joseph R. Biden, 'Equality, accessible, affordable justice under law: the Civil Justice Reform Act of 1990' (1992) 1 *Cornell Journal of Law and Public Policy* 1, 1–2.

[70] Biden, 'Equality, accessible, affordable justice', 1, 3.

become 'an unaffordable luxury even for middle-class Americans'.[71] The barriers to access to justice are not only based on the costs of money and time but also the 'inappropriateness of the formal litigation's adversarial process for a range of problems'[72] and the inadequate capability of the parties regarding '[the] ability and willingness of people to recognize that they possess a legally enforceable right to understand and use available means of redress'.[73] In this context, the idea of 'access to justice' appeared with the hope of resolving these problems existing in the judicial system.

Correspondingly, relevant judicial reforms at the national and international levels were launched. They were designed to achieve the idea that 'the right to participate in the legal process is thus fundamental to a just society'.[74] The relevant policies are varied, one of which pursues the philosophy that 'legal procedures and support structures should be designed to maximize individuals' opportunities to address law-related problems themselves, without expensive professional assistance.'[75] Based on this argument, the state regime is expected to provide or justify appropriate dispute resolution mechanisms in which individuals can participate without difficulty. The participants are the subjects of the process and can choose, comprehend and decide. To some extent, the essence of 'access to justice' is to let the voices of dispute participants be heard. This is partly because '[the] fairness is dependent on the process. When individuals have a voice in the process, the process, as well as the outcome, will be perceived to be fairer by the participants'.[76] More importantly, it is because the disputants, as the subjects and main bodies of the dispute resolution process, naturally have the right to engage in the judicial system and to determine whether the process is just. Their appreciation or critique of the judicial system can and should be based on their own courtroom experiences rather than on legal theory textbooks.

Again, if the court can only provide some public service that is just and impartial from the professional or legal textbook perspective but overlooks the feelings and feedback of the parties who are served, these

[71] Biden, 'Equality, accessible, affordable justice', 1, 3.

[72] Austin Sarat, 'The litigation explosion, access to justice, and court reform: examining the critical assumptions' (1984–1985) 27 *Rutgers Law Review* 319, 323.

[73] Sarat, 'The litigation explosion', 319, 324.

[74] Sarat, 'The litigation explosion', 319, 323.

[75] Deborah L. Rhode, 'Access to justice' (2001) 69 *Fordham Law Review* 1785, 1816.

[76] Andrea Kupfer Schneider, 'The intersection of dispute systems design and transitional justice' (2009) 14 *Harvard Negotiation Law Review* 289, 309.

parties may not understand the court's rationales nor have any confidence in its quality. In this case, the parties may be trapped in a difficult position consisting of authoritative, rhetorical and communication-lacking narratives and discourse. If these poor and disadvantaged parties are pushed to go through the litigation approach only, this institutional setting is inhumane. That is because it is clear that 'the promotion and maintenance of the rule of law remain constrained unless there is effective access to justice'.[77] 'Access' here means an understandable, affordable and reasonable mechanism. It is true that 'parties care as much about how dispute resolution is conducted as they do about what are the outcome results, and consensual processes provide the 'how' that the parties value most.[78] For these villagers, if compelled and incomprehensible litigation is the only format that defines the rule of law, it becomes absolutism and an inhumane rule of law.

> In this regard, we must be very careful about the situation where, 'although the court is open to the public, the poor people cannot enter even though they are in the right' (Chinese Proverb). This is not due to corruption or any greedy official; on the contrary, it is because the court system, as an institutional setting, is not designed for disadvantaged people and does not provide an affordable, transparent, and easily understandable institutional product to them. In addressing this issue, if Chinese legal scholarship fails to maintain sufficient moral consciousness, the rule of law we aim to construct may transform into a certain kind of 'Sublime Object of Ideology' (Slavoj Žižek), and the state apparatus may legally deprive disadvantaged people of their rights to access the justice system. Given these considerations, even if the legal system is well-designed, logically self-consistent, and fully functional, it can still be a flawed rule of law.[79]

[77] Vicki Waye and Ping Xiong, 'The relationship between mediation and judicial proceedings in China' (2011) 6(1) *Asian Journal of Comparative Law*, Article 2, 1.

[78] Bush, 'What do we need a mediator for?' 1, 18.

[79] Hao Xiong, 'Si's family litigation: legal and anthropological observations on a civil compensation case in a Chinese minority grass-roots community' (2010) 5 *Academy* 26, 30 [熊浩："思家诉讼：一个中国少数民族基层社区民事赔偿案件的法学与人类学观察"，载《学园》2010年第5期]. The original text goes as follows:

> 从这个意义上，我们必须小心那种'衙门大门朝南开， 有理没钱别进来'状况在当代中国的显现。这中间未必是由于衙门的腐败，也未必是由于官员的贪婪，而是这种'当事人主义'的衙门作为一种制度安排，它本就不是为没钱的人开的，它本就不提供廉价、清楚、通俗明白的制度产品。如果我们，特别是中国的法律学术，不在这个问题上有足够的小心，有足够的谨慎，有足够的道德自觉，那么，我们设想建立的完美法治，很可能仅仅变成某种'意识形态的崇高客体'(齐泽

Mediation is an excellent option for many people living in southwest grassroots China who lack financial resources, education and legal knowledge. This is because mediation can provide the parties with affordable and comprehensible justice in which they can actively participate. Unlike formal litigation, which can be expensive, intimidating and difficult to understand, mediation offers a more accessible and user-friendly approach to resolving disputes. It allows individuals to engage directly in the process, express their needs and concerns and work collaboratively towards a mutually acceptable resolution. This participatory aspect of mediation is particularly valuable in empowering the disadvantaged communities and ensuring that justice is not only served but also perceived as humane (understandable and usable) by all parties involved.

6.4.2 *Why Mediation Is Feasible for the Judge*

6.4.2.1 The Necessary Thresholds for Judges: Legal Education and Entrance Exam

Judgment is the outcome of adjudication and also the product of judicial proceedings. The quality of the product is determined to a large extent by the quality of the producers, in this case, the quality of the judges. Society usually has high expectations of the legal profession.

> In a formally rationalized system of law, legal professionals play a role that is rivalled in significance only by that of the experts of bureaucracies, because they are involved in the administration of law on the basis of acquired legal expertise in relevant rules and appropriate procedures. Legal professionals are experts of knowledge of, and know-how in, the law.[80]

'All professions, including law, limit entry'.[81] The access limitation on entry into the legal profession is established on various rationales, one of which is the consideration concerning the distinctive traits of law and

克语），某种合法地剥夺乡亲们诉讼的权利的政府机器，而构建在这一基础上的我们的法治，即使逻辑自洽，即使设计精美，即使功能齐备，也有可能变成坏的法治。

80 Mathieu Deflem, *Sociology of Law: Visions of a Scholarly Tradition* (Cambridge, MA: Cambridge University Press, 2008), p. 183.

81 Richard L. Abel, 'Lawyers and legal services' in Peter Cane and Mark Tushnet (eds.), *The Oxford Handbook of Legal Studies* (Oxford: Oxford University Press, 2003), p. 797.

legal knowledge.[82] Considering the distinctive legal skills with which a competent legal professional should be equipped, the US MacCrate Report in 1992 identified the generic skills and the four values for a qualified legal professional:

> The skills were problem-solving; legal analysis and reasoning; legal research; factual investigation; oral and written communication; counseling or advice; negotiation; understanding procedures for litigation and alternative dispute resolution; organization and management of legal work and recognizing and resolving ethical dilemmas. The four values were providing competent representation (responsibility to clients); striving to promote justice, fairness, and morality (public responsibility for the legal system); maintaining and improving the profession (responsibility to the profession); and profession self-development (responsibility to oneself).[83]

[82] Other considerations include, for example, warranting the quality of legal profession, improving the efficiency through the division of labour and maximising the professional interests by monopolising the knowledge and so on. Regarding the distinctive traits of the law and legal knowledge, this argument has actually suffered much criticism. According to William L. Twining, for example,

> Many of the so-called transferable skills of reading, writing, talking, thinking clearly, enquiring, analyzing and arguing and, in the modern jargon, 'learning to learn' can be developed through the study of any number of subjects. The idea of a liberal education relates to how and in what spirit on studies a particular subject matter. The 'case for law'...is not that it is superior to other discipline, but rather that it can claim to be potentially as good as vehicle for a general education as English or History or Politics or Sociology.

See William L. Twining, *Blackstone's Tower: The English Law School* (London: Stevens & Sons, 1994), p. 60.

However, as Brian H. Bix responded:

> The autonomy of law/legal knowledge is a manifestation of the archaic jargon and out. However, the relatively antonymous discipline of law may be defensible, where law's distinctive approach to reasoning and decision-making is understood as deriving from the type of practice law is: a behavior-guiding practice, where the guidance is done primarily general rules, and the rules are interpreted and applied by a hierarchical court system that gives precedential weight to earlier decision.

See Brian H. Bix, 'Law as an autonomous discipline' in Peter Cane and Mark Tushnet (eds.), *The Oxford Handbook of Legal Studies* (Oxford: Oxford University Press, 2003), pp. 985–986.

[83] John Bell, 'Legal education' in Peter Cane and Mark Tushnet (eds.), *The Oxford Handbook of Legal Studies* (Oxford: Oxford University Press, 2003), p. 909.

Without a doubt, acquiring these aforementioned professional skills and values requires more than simple and general instruction. Candidates need to undergo training in specialised legal institutions for a relatively long period to become accustomed to the legal system and, more importantly, to learn to 'think like a lawyer'. As Brian H. Bix said:

> Legal education is relevant to questions about the autonomy of law, not only in the sense that this is the context in which forms of legal reasoning are passed on within the profession, but also because the training itself may express the forms of knowledge and decision-making that are considered distinctive for law, or at least for one particular legal system. Additionally, the way legal training is structured indicates a great deal about the legal profession's view of itself, including its view about the methods of reasoning and decision-making appropriate within the profession.[84]

Besides professional education, the entrance examination is also necessary for furthering legal qualification. In most jurisdictions, for both the civil law and common law systems, although the procedures are different, the legal professional education and/or qualification examination are necessary before the candidates are accepted by the legal professional circle.[85] There is no exception in today's China; more and more people have realised that judicial fairness would be an empty word without a contingent of high-quality judges. From item (5) to item (7) of Article 12 of the Judge's Law of the PRC (amended 2019) correspondingly requires that:

> (5) Having a bachelor's degree or above in law from a regular institution of higher education, or a bachelor's degree or above not in law from a regular institution of higher education but with a degree of Juris Master, master of law, or above, or bachelor's degree or above not in law from a regular institution of higher education with any other corresponding degree and with professional knowledge of law; (6) Having engaged in the legal work for at least five years. The seniority in engaging in the legal work of those with a degree of Juris Master or master of law, or with a doctor's degree of law may be respectively relaxed to four and three years; (7) Persons to be appointed as judges for the first time shall have passed the national uniform legal profession qualification examination and obtained the legal profession qualification.

84 Bix, 'Law as an autonomous discipline', 983.

85 See Qing Zhou, 'Comparative study of the judicial examination system of the two legal families' (2002) 17(2) *Journal of Jiangsu Police Officer College* 97 [周菁："两大法系司法考试制度的比较和借鉴"，载江苏经管学院学报，2002年第17卷第2期].

6.4.2.2 Mismatch: Uniform Legal Profession Exam and the Grassroots Judge's Quality

In China, the degree of legal professionalisation has been improved and enhanced during the thirty years of reform and opening-up.[86] The most radical steps were the establishment of the standardised judge's qualification and the uniform judicial examination in 2001 and 2002.[87] After that, many judges in the developed region of China, like Shanghai, hold a master's or even a PhD degree.[88] The entrance standard for the judicial institutions is becoming increasingly higher and more competitive in courts of China's central cities. Nearly all of the candidates are required

86 Xiaodan Hou, 'Chapter six: legal education and the transformation of the legal profession' in Dingjian Cai and Chenguang Wang (eds.), *China's Journey Towards the Rule of Law: Legal Reform, 1978–2008* (Leiden: Brill, 2010), pp. 270–282.

87 For a general discussion on China's legal professions, see Albert H. Y. Chen, *An Introduction to the Legal System of the People's Republic of China* (Hong Kong: Lexis/Nexis, 5th ed., 2018), pp. 204–206. In 2018, China reformed its National Judicial Examination, transforming it into the Legal Professional Qualification Examination. The reformed examination places greater emphasis on practical skills and is divided into two parts: objective questions and subjective questions. The objective section has a passing score of 180 points, and only those who pass this section are eligible to take the subjective section. Prior to 2018, all undergraduate graduates could take the National Judicial Examination. The eligibility criteria mainly required a bachelor's degree or higher, with no special restrictions on the type of degree or whether it was obtained through full-time study. However, after the reform in 2018, the eligibility criteria for the Legal Professional Qualification Examination became more stringent. Candidates now must have a bachelor's degree or higher in law or a bachelor's degree or higher in a non-law field but must have also obtained a Master of Laws (LLM), a Juris Master (JM) or a higher degree in law. Alternatively, candidates who have been engaged in legal work for a minimum of three years are also eligible to apply. This reform aims to ensure that candidates possess a solid foundation in legal knowledge and practical skills, thereby improving the overall quality of legal professionals in China.

88 According to 2022 Shanghai Civil Servant Recruitment Brief [2022年度上海市公务员招考简章], there are 45 positions, including the legal, administrative and IT positions, provided by the court system of Shanghai. There were 35 positions from basic courts (77.8 per cent), five positions from special courts and five positions from intermediate courts. For the positions of basic courts, 13 require the candidate to have master's degree or above, accounting for 37.1 per cent; 18 require bachelor's degree or above, accounting for 51.4 per cent. Only four are undergraduate suitable, accounting for 11.4 per cent. Among these positions, 17 of them require Legal Professional Qualification Certificate, and all judge assistant positions require Legal Professional Qualification Certificate. This is evidence showing the cross-region difference and heterogeneity in terms of the quality of legal profession. For the Regulation, see https://shacs.gov.cn/recruits/216/article/33?n=%E4%B8%8A%E6%B5%B7%E5%B8%822022%E5%B9%B4%E5%BA%A6%E8%80%83%E8%AF%95%E5%BD%95%E7%94%A8%E5%85%AC%E5%8A%A1%E5%91%98 (last accessed 10 May 2022).

to be equipped with good legal education and a professional judicial certificate.[89]

However, the so-called improvement of the qualification of judges seemingly does not benefit southwest rural China. On the one hand, in the undeveloped region of China, the fact remains that qualified judges are still very scarce. For example, in P County Court, there are only six judges who have graduated from formal law schools and around ten staff members who have passed the judicial examination. On the other hand, the Uniform Judicial Examination may even worsen the judicial human resource situation in southwest China. That is because a successful candidate who passes the uniform judicial qualification examination will be awarded a certificate that is nationally valid.[90] This certification will open another door to young judges and clerks newly graduated from universities, allowing them to pursue their dreams of practicing law in modern cities. The bar, after all, is highly valued by the legal profession, though perhaps valued even more several years ago when the passing rate of the examination was quite low. In this case, many young law school graduates may quit their jobs in grassroots courts and go to practice law in the developed areas of China where they may have more opportunities and a higher income. This may worsen the unbalanced distribution of legal human resources between developed urban China and undeveloped rural China. The researcher was informed by a president of a grassroots court that some judicial clerks who passed the examination quit their jobs and started their new careers as a lawyer in the modern cities of Yunnan. This problem has also been confirmed at the Supreme Court level. When reporting about the workforce situation to the Standing Committee of the National People's Congress, the then President of the SPC highlighted that because work and life pressure are high, and the income is relatively low, the brain drain from some grassroots courts is

[89] For example, in 2022, the intermediate-level courts of Shanghai provide 21 positions, 20 of which require the candidate to have a Master and above degree holder.

[90] The Ministry of Justice has classified the Legal Professional Certification into three categories: A, B and C. Category A is the highest certification and is valid nationally. The passing scores for Categories B and C certifications are relatively lower. However, holders of a Category B certification can only practice law as lawyers and cannot serve as judges or procurators. Additionally, the validity of Category B and C certifications is limited to specific underdeveloped regions. In other words, if a candidate from such a region obtains a Category B or C certification, they can only practice law in the regions designated by the Ministry of Justice for these certifications. There are no such limitations for Category A certification. This classification system was established to increase the number of qualified legal professionals in underdeveloped regions.

very serious, *especially in the west, remote areas, ethnic minority regions and undeveloped areas.*[91]

Without meaning to deny or underestimate the positive value of the uniform judicial examination, it is necessary to point out that the required qualification for judges will, to a certain extent, exacerbate the uneven distribution of legal human resources by motivating the qualified candidates to move from rural and undeveloped China to developed urban China. As a result, the personnel who remain working in the county courts are individuals who lack mobility. In other words, they are relatively poorly qualified. In this case, the quality of judicial decisions may be relatively low and problematic. It may not be a wise choice to push such judges to render a judicial decision that is a product they are relatively unfamiliar with and unable to produce.

In the meantime, due to the same reasoning, the uniform judicial examination also improves the mobility of qualified lawyers. If a candidate passes the examination, he/she may also transfer to modern cities to practice law. The legal resource, namely the lawyer at the local level, will therefore also become increasingly scarce. Besides, the uniform judicial

[91] Shenjun Wang, 'Brain drain in some grassroots courts' [王胜俊：压力大待遇低 一些基层法院人才流失严重], see http://npcnews.com.cn/BIG5/28320/80575/81898/13059953.html (last accessed 10 March 2011). See also some news report regarding the brain drain in southwest China, www.chinadaily.com.cn/hqcj/zxqxb/2010-12-02/content_1320222.html (last accessed 10 March 2011) (emphasis added). This situation has continued in recent years. In 2014, Zhou Qiang, the then Chief Justice of the Supreme People's Court, pointed out in the work report of the Supreme People's Court that

> policies and benefits should be tilted towards the grassroots, efforts should be made to address issues and difficulties such as the fragmentation and personnel loss of grassroots judges, care should be given to the physical and mental health of grassroots judges, and support should be increased for the construction of courts in western, remote, ethnic minority areas, and revolutionary old areas. Work in areas such as aiding Tibet, aiding Xinjiang, and aiding Qinghai should be strengthened to continuously improve the judicial conditions and environment at the grassroots level.

In 2018, Huang Hailong, the then President of the Higher People's Court of Guangxi Zhuang Autonomous Region, during the national 'Two Conference', identified that 'policies should be formulated at the national level to solve the problems of recruitment and retention difficulties in courts in difficult areas; taking advantage of the central government's promotion of party and state institutional reforms, the pace of internal institutional reforms in the courts should be accelerated, top-level design should be strengthened, guiding opinions should be issued, and institutional reforms should be completed as soon as possible'. See http://lianghui.people.com.cn/2016cppcc/GB/n1/2016/0313/c402615-28195450.html and www.chinacourt.org/article/detail/2018/03/id/3225552.shtml (last accessed 1 December 2023).

examination sets up a professional threshold, which, on the one hand, is good for safeguarding professional quality, but on the other hand, it may also be a further professional monopoly. With fewer lawyers at the grassroots level, disputants will encounter difficulties in finding a legal representative and will be charged higher fees by lawyers using monopoly to their advantage. Consequently, the older judge or the judge who cannot pass the exam will be those left in the court. The cost of hiring a local lawyer, in the meantime, will be higher, but the lawyer's quality may not be that satisfactory. Therefore, the quality of the legal human resources is poor in regards to both the judge and the lawyer service. If we persist in pushing judges who are not well educated in a law school and do not pass the judicial exam to render judicial decisions for parties who can hardly receive adequate legal service from lawyers, this situation may become quite problematic.[92]

6.4.2.3 Mismatch: Law School Education and Grassroots Legal Needs

For judges working in grassroots courts who have received a law degree from a law school and passed the uniform judicial exam, much of the required knowledge during their legal education and examination preparation is not as useful as expected. This is especially true of the so-called advanced legal knowledge.

China's legal education has indeed developed rapidly after the reform and opening-up. Statistics have shown the continuing expansion of the law school faculties and the number of graduates.[93] Regarding the curriculum, the Ministry of Education has set the National Standards for Teaching Quality in Law (2021), the core courses for law majors are classified under the '1+10+X' model. The '1' refers to the course Introduction to Xi Jinping Thought on the Rule of Law. The '10' denotes the ten mandatory core courses that all law students must complete, which include Jurisprudence, Constitutional Law, Chinese Legal History, Criminal Law, Civil Law, Criminal Procedure Law, Civil Procedure Law, Administrative Law and Administrative Procedure Law, International

[92] During the author's fieldwork in another county court, an intern student from the law faculty of Minzu University of China shared her experience. She mentioned that she had asked one of the judges a question regarding specific legal regulations. However, when she returned to Beijing to continue her studies, she discovered that the answers provided by the judge were incorrect.

[93] Hou, 'Chapter six: legal education and the transformation', 261.

Law and Legal Ethics. The 'X' represents additional mandatory courses offered by each institution based on their unique characteristics. These may include Economic Law, Intellectual Property Law, Commercial Law, Private International Law, International Economic Law, Environmental and Resource Law, Labor and Social Security Law, Evidence Law and Fiscal and Tax Law. The number of 'X' courses offered should not be fewer than five.[94] It seems that law students will receive a very systematic and comprehensive legal education. However, it is still a concern that 'the current training standards do not provide legal trainees with the high professional standards society requires'.[95] One of the significant manifestations is the uninformed and urban-oriented legal knowledge that does not cater to the diverse needs of the Chinese people living in different regions and under diverse social conditions.

The Chinese legal system is criticised as being too urban-oriented with serious neglect of rural China's needs.[96] There is a complaint that 'Chinese legal scholars are enamoured by trendy Western theory and ignorant of the role of law in Chinese society outside of Beijing and Shanghai'.[97] It is not the scholars' fault, but instead, the lifestyle features that naturalise this tendency. According to Su Li's statistics regarding the most-cited Chinese legal scholars (top 50), there are thirty-seven scholars living and working in the institutions in Beijing, four in Wuhan, three in Shanghai, one in Xiamen, one in Chongqing, one in Hangzhou and one in Suzhou and one in Changsha and one in Nanjing. All these scholars are living in either the capital city of a province (like Changsha and Hangzhou) or very developed places (like Suzhou). Some of them are also the authors of the prescribed textbook for the Uniform Judicial Examination. In other words, their thoughts constitute the main body of not only the legal education but also the professional qualification examination and become the content that candidates need to learn and memorise as the correct answers. The influence of these scholars' thoughts has travelled beyond legal academia to legal practice, which will determine the knowledge system of the future legal professionals.

94 National Standards for Teaching Quality in Law (2021), https://renwen.jxau.edu.cn/9b/82/c9629a105346/page.htm (last accessed 24 May 2024).

95 Hou, 'Chapter six: legal education and the transformation', 261.

96 See Zhenglai Deng, 'Criticism on the urbanized trend of Chinese law research' (2006) 1(4) *Frontiers of Law in China* 514.

97 Upham, 'Who will find the defendant', 1675, 1676.

Much research in the field of social psychology and sociology of knowledge has demonstrated the relationship among the individual's identity, thoughts and social context.[98] Therefore, these scholars do not intentionally overlook China's southwest grassroots reality. On the contrary, scholars, like other people in society, are deeply embedded in the social context and have been fundamentally shaped by their social status. The production of legal knowledge thus is naturally and inevitably associated with a 'made in the city' label. As a result, the experience, insights and understanding of the grassroots people living in the rural and undeveloped regions cannot be justified nor commonly accepted by mainstream scholarship. They are labelled, in some cases, as uncivilised and lagging behind part of China. It seems that the modern city's lifestyle and social structure are the only right way for rural people.

Regarding the knowledge and skills used by China's grassroots judges, Su Li observed that judges at the local level (especially in rural areas) tend to focus more on outcomes rather than the process of dispute resolution. They rely more on practical skills than on academic knowledge and on intuition rather than strict reasoning to render judgments. These judges emphasise social experience over the exact application of regulations. They aim to persuade both parties to reach a consensus through compromise to avoid further trouble, rather than encouraging them to fight for their rights and justice. Additionally, they focus on creating a new 'contract' for the allocation of rights and obligations that is enforceable, rather than resolving disputes through extreme punishment of one party, which could result in a loss of personal relationships.[99] These are different from what the graduates learn in law schools. Therefore, some students have complained 'that the courses are highly theoretical and

[98] For example, Schumpeter and Mannehim both agreed that 'actual thought is influenced in many decisive points by extra-theoretical factors'. The human experience by virtue of their embedment in a particular, 'concretely operating order of life'. Hans E. Jensen summarised that 'the relevant factors are part of a person's "existence". This means, of course, that "social location undoubtedly is a powerful factor in shaping our minds"'. See Hans E. Jensen, 'J. A. Schumpeter on economic sociology' (1985) XI(3) *Eastern Economic Journal* 257, 257–258.

[99] Li Su, 'On the knowledge and skill used by China's grassroots judges' (2000) 22(3) *Modern Law Science* 12, 13–14 [苏力："基层法官司法知识的开示"，《现代法学》2000年第3期]. Interestingly, when talking about the judge training experience in Beijing, one judge at the grassroots court told the author that Li Su is his favourite scholar and trainer in the programme.

have little relevance to the real world'[100] or 'what I have learned from the university was returned to the teacher when I began to practice law'.[101] The real world problem here indicates the complexity of China regarding the different knowledge needs and requirements between the urban developed areas and the undeveloped grassroots areas. To a certain extent, we could even say that a law school student who is more familiar with the modern and advanced legal system, for example, intellectual property, financial, legal issues, cooperation governance, international trade law, securities, futures and maritime, will be less familiar with the rural needs, such as dispute resolution at the grassroots level.

In P Court, for example, the traditional cases include marriage and family disputes (*hunyin jiating jiufen*, 婚姻家庭纠纷), property rights disputes (*caichan jiufen*, 财产纠纷) and contract disputes (*hetong jiufen*, 合同纠纷) numbered more than 90 per cent of the total cases accepted and heard by the court. The situations of other investigated county courts are very similar. In the grassroots courts of this city investigated, all courts at the grassroots level accepted 7,356 civil cases and 2,132 criminal cases per year. In terms of the civil section, there were 3,329 marriage and personal rights cases (the amount of money involved amounted to RMB 6.8759 million); 132 cases concerning the remuneration for labour (RMB 4.5508 million); 2,555 contract and sales cases (RMB 47.11846 million); sixteen disputes regarding company issues (RMB 12.5297 million); five intellectual property cases (the amount of money involved is unknown); and fifty cases regarding country, farmer and agriculture and others. Traditional disputes are the mainstream.

According to existing ADR literature, most of these disputes are suitable for mediation. That is why even before the big mediation policy was issued by the SPC, the mediation rate in P Court for resolving civil and commercial disputes had already reached more than 65 per cent. In light of these social realities, for China's southwest judges (especially in the rural areas), the laws designed for the industrialised and modern society are completely unsuitable for addressing the problems of day-to-

[100] Gerard J. Clark, 'An introduction to the legal profession in China in the year 2008' (2008) XLI *Suffolk University Law Review* 833, 841.

[101] Another graduate from a particular university of politics and law interviewed by Li Su said that the civil law, civil procedural law and some principles taught in the jurisprudence course are useful, but other things do not work in practice. The moot court training is just inapplicable at all. See Su, *Sending Law to the Rural China*, pp. 369, 371 [苏力：《送法下乡：中国基层司法制度研究》，北京：中国政法大学出版社2000年版].

day life in the countryside. The reality of a mismatch of knowledge has been confirmed by several leaders of the grassroots courts. They told the researcher that the recent graduates or intern students from law schools could not master the communicative style nor display suitable emotion when communicating with the parties. They could all doctrinally understand the law but sometimes ignored common sense. This also exerts influence on the shift of the mediation policy. Speaking of this, Benjamin L. Liebman believes this is one of the most important reasons why the regime restructured China's dispute resolution system. He noted:

> In the past decade as Western-style legal reforms have encountered difficulties at the local levels. This return to popular legality is seen against the backdrop of increased instability, a perception that confidence in the legal system is declining, and recognition that the first two decades of legal reform failed to address fundamental problems in the legal system. Critics of legal reforms argue that the legal system is increasingly becoming dominated by elites and that the emphasis on professionalization and formality results in a legal system that neither serves the interests of ordinary people nor tracks popular morality. Likewise, reforms are seen as focusing on the legal needs of major developed areas, thus ignoring regional differences. Understood against this backdrop, populism in the legal system serves not only to impose mass justice but also to ensure that legal institutions do not ignore the interests of ordinary people. Put differently, problems in the legal system stem not only from continued party dominance but also from courts and other institutions straying too far from their tradition of relying on public input.[102]

6.4.2.4 Match: Experience-Oriented Knowledge and Mediation

Although rural judges are not so familiar with advanced legal knowledge or have not yet passed the Uniform Judicial Exam, they can still be very professional, if the word 'professional' here can be defined outside the urban-centred perspective. What makes them professional is their vast direct experience of handling thousands of cases rather than the legal knowledge learned in textbooks. For them, it is true that 'the life of the law has not been logic; it has been experience … The law embodies the story of a nation's

[102] Benjamin L. Liebman, 'A return to populist legality? Historical legacies and legal reform' in Sebastian Heilmann and Elizabeth J. Perry (eds.), *Mao's Invisible Hand: The Political Foundations of Adaptive Governance in China* (Cambridge, MA: Harvard University Press, 2011), pp. 183–184.

development through many centuries, and it cannot be dealt with as if it contained only the axioms and corollaries of a book of mathematics'.[103]

Dispute resolution is a highly experience-oriented project. Experience is an extremely significant quality of a good mediator for a successful settlement. It has been commonly confirmed that it is more likely for an experienced mediator to facilitate a settlement between disputing parties than for an inexperienced mediator.[104] In the United States, for example, although several states have a professional degree, educational or training requirements as the minimal governmental licensing of mediators, prior experience may also qualify as a way to gain licensure as a mediator.[105] According to the Model Standards of Conduct for Mediators (2005), a mediator was only required to have 'the necessary competence to satisfy the reasonable expectations of the parties. . .[and suggested that] training, experience in mediation, skills, cultural understandings, and other qualities are often necessary for mediator competence;'[106] not a degree. Similarly, the 2010 Model Standards for Mediation Certification Programs (MSFMCP) of the Association for Conflict Resolution (ACR) states that:

> significant mediation experience ought to be expected. . .Programs should set reasonable experience requirements for which certification candidates must document a high number of hours of mediation/co-mediation experience within the past five years, or over a lifetime of practice, in addition to observations and role-play mediation time.[107]

Compared with experience, an academic degree is not equally important for a competent mediator. Some evidence has shown that individuals

[103] Oliver Wendell Holmes, *The Common Law* (Chicago, IL: American Bar Association, 2009), p. 3.

[104] See Thomas A. Kochan and Todd Jick, 'The public sector mediation process: a theory and empirical examination' (1978) 22 *Journal of Conflict Resolution* 209; Jessica Pearson, Nancy Thoennes and Lois Vanderkooi, 'The decision to mediation: profiles of individuals who accept and reject the opportunity to mediate contested child custody and visitation issues' (1982) 6 *Journal of Divorce* 17; Peter J. D. Carnevale and Richard Pegnetter, 'The selection of mediation tactics in public sector disputes: a contingency analysis' (1985) 41 *Journal of Social Issues* 65.

[105] Edward J. Brunet and Charles B. Craver, *Alternative Dispute Resolution: The Advocate's Perspective* (Newark, NJ: Lexis Nexis, 2nd ed., 2001), p. 259.

[106] *Model Standards of Conduct for Mediators* (2005), www.adr.org/sites/default/files/document_repository/AAA-Mediators-Model-Standards-of-Conduct-10-14-2010.pdf (last accessed 20 March 2023).

[107] *2010 Model Standards for Mediation Certification Programs of Association for Conflict Resolution*, see www.acrnet.org/News.aspx?id=842 (last accessed 14 March 2011).

who have not earned a degree can still perform quite well in mediation practices.[108] The MSFMCP of ACR also stresses that:

> Because researchers have not found a correlation between academic degrees and mediation competencies, no degrees should be considered prerequisites for mediator certification. Over the past several years, however, there have been increasing numbers of post-graduate degree programs in conflict resolution. These programs prepare graduates for a variety of professional positions in the dispute resolution field, and such academic training should be considered a complement to, rather than a substitute for, mediation experience.[109]

From this perspective, qualified judges at the grassroots court may not be that scarce. A competent judge, here, does not only mean a person who holds a law degree or has passed the Uniform Judicial Examination but also someone who understands the local situation and has rich experience in mediating disputes and communicating with the disputants.

In summary, it may not be suitable to push many of the judges working at grassroots courts to adjudicate cases, considering their lack of formal legal education and professional certification. However, experience is the advantage of grassroots judges and, fortunately, that is precisely what a good mediator needs. Most of these judges are locals, whose backgrounds make them highly familiar with the local context and conditions. They can polish their performance and enrich their experience by handling local cases without formal law school education. For them, practice makes their work perfect. Therefore, if these judges are required to adjudicate cases and render judgments, the quality of their decisions may be problematic. However, if they are allowed to mediate cases, the quality may be much higher. In this regard, permitting grassroots court judges to work in mediation in southwest China where the level of professionalism of judges is not high is a better choice for handling disputes.

6.4.2.5 Match: Judges Are Deeply Embedded in the Local Social Context

Su Li has made it clear that the operation of the modern legal system depends highly on a society consisting of strangers.[110] From the Western

[108] W. Lee Dobbins, 'The debate over mediator qualifications: can they satisfy the growing need to measure competence without barring entry into the market' (1994) 7 *University of Florida Journal of Law and Public Policy* 95, 105.

[109] Dobbins, 'The debate over mediator qualifications', 95, 105.

[110] Su, *Sending Law to the Rural China*, pp. 369–371 [苏力：《送法下乡：中国基层司法制度研究》，北京：中国政法大学出版社2000年版].

legal historical experience, it is also true that a society consisting of strangers depends more on laws and the formal dispute resolution approach. For example, it is considered one of the main reasons when discussing the American people's preference for litigation since the post-Revolution nineteenth century. The industrial developments, especially the railway construction, led to labour migration and the community of newcomers.[111] In that growing fragmented and diverse society, the law would play the role of common denominator or public rationality to balance different values and interests and to maintain the social order.

If the background and personal information are carefully examined, it can be found that most cited legal scholars, not limited to the top twenty listed in Su Li's statistics, are working in locations other than their hometowns. They are living in a society consisting of strangers, considering the current degree of modernisation, social structure and social mobility. Chinese modern legal scholarship, in this regard, is constructed on the premise of a 'stranger society'. To put it another way, the Chinese modern legal scholarship is constructed and applied in/to the modern city context in which people will depend more on written contracts, expressly stipulated regulations and a neutral, formal, third party to solve a dispute instead of turning to the head of the presbytery or the head of the village.[112] The basic lifestyle in the modern city is normalised into legal forms by the legal elites who are living in an urban context. The Chinese legal scholars' urban living experience may be generalised to the universal ideal and institutional setting. That is why Su Li said: 'all roads lead to the city'[113] when criticising Chinese city-oriented legal system.

However, the judges working in grassroots courts are different. They live locally in a society consisting of acquaintances. In P Court, for example, more than 90 per cent of the judges are local residents. In another investigated court, there are fifty official personnel in total, including forty-four locals, four people from other counties in the city, one from Chongqing and one from Hubei. In other words, these two grassroots courts mainly consist of locals. In such a social situation, interpersonal relationships must be considered when solving disputes. Mediation, in this case, can provide an effective outlet. It can help a judge

[111] Colleen M. Hanycz, 'Whither community justice? The rise of court-connected mediation in the United States' (2007) 25 *Windsor Yearbook of Access to Justice* 167, 176.

[112] Douglass C. North, 'Institutions' (1991) 5(1) *Journal of Economic Perspectives* 97, 104.

[113] Li Su, *All Roads Lead to the City: Legal Development in China's Transformation* (Beijing: Law Press, 2004), preface [苏力：《道路通向城市：转型中国的法治》，北京：法律出版社2004年版，序言].

solve a case involving acquaintances more easily. A judge is also an ordinary person who will inevitably be concerned about his/her interests in the local society. Through the win–loss litigation approach, not only the relationship between the disputing parties but also the judge's network could be damaged. Mediation, on the contrary, provides the parties and the judge with an opportunity to share their feelings and arguments. By doing so, the judge can help the parties understand his difficult position and the earnest effort made to facilitate the dispute resolution. Even if the case eventually goes to litigation, the judge can be better understood and tolerated, and the long-term personal relationships between the judge and the parties can be preserved. Moreover, the judge also needs cooperation from both parties to meet the SPC's requirement concerning the rise in mediation rates and the principle of 'when the case is closed, the dispute is resolved' (*anjie shijiao*, 案结事了). Therefore, everyday relationships, which are often distant and not necessarily familiar between the judge and the parties but rather embedded in a common social network, can be a valuable resource for persuading the parties to compromise. For instance, during the author's fieldwork, it was found that judges would mention connections such as, 'Your uncle's son used to work with me', to the parties. This social linkage can encourage parties to consider their relationships and accept a compromise resolution, thereby facilitating successful mediation.

6.5 Conclusion

This chapter is a case study of mediation in a grassroots court of a poor and undeveloped southwest ethnic minority county. It demonstrates the whole process of court mediation when solving an adjacency rights dispute through a detailed description. The skills and techniques employed by the judge mediator have been highlighted to show the grassroots judge's adeptness and wisdom gained through their experience. This chapter illustrated the mediation-in-action in today's southwest grassroots China. In the investigated context, mediation is feasible because (1) mediation can preserve face and avoid ill-suited litigation as the result of a lack of evidence. It provides comprehensible, accessible and humane justice for the disputing parties; (2) mediation is suitable for grassroots judges considering their educational background, experiences, and social embedment; and (3) the traditional disputes involving family and marriage, property and civil contract are still the mainstream in the given context, which is suitable for the mediation approach. To a large extent, mediation is a better choice for both the judge and the involved parties as it can truly solve the dispute and preserve the judge and the parties' interests in such an underdeveloped society. This finding suggests that when designing the mediation law and evaluating the feasibility of mediation in China, it is important to take into consideration the characteristics of the disputants and mediations, as well as the nature of the disputes.

In this regard, mediation in southwest grassroots China is justified not only by cultural preferences or the local people's personal choices when they encounter a dispute but also by the social structure, which determines that mediation is a feasible and adequate mechanism for dispute resolution in this context. If social conditions change, the market transforms rural society and judges' professional standards improve, adjudication may become more desirable, and the feasibility of mediation in this context may change correspondingly or require new justifications. However, any radical social change cannot take place over a short period; therefore, it is inevitable and necessary to address the long-term conditions of rural China realistically. Legal scholarship should seriously consider both the legal issues and the concerns of grassroots people embedded in the southwest grassroots China context.

Although this chapter never discussed the cases beyond southwest China, it is likely that at least some of the techniques, problems and experiences of grassroots Chinese judges are repeated in similar societies elsewhere.[114] One of the general conclusions that may be drawn from this chapter is that legal policies and laws regarding dispute resolution need to be adjusted to divergent cultural, social and economic contexts, as the various local contexts and social situations will fundamentally influence the feasibility of a dispute resolution mechanism. In this regard, it may not be possible to design a nationalised and standardised mediation law that can be feasibly implemented in all the regions of China, regardless of the context.[115] With this in mind, the conclusion of the research is and

[114] The explanatory power of the case can be expanded via 'statistical generalisation' and 'analytical generalisation'. The case expansion for this qualitative research relies on the latter. That is to say, what is concerned is not the representativeness of the case but the representativeness of the characteristics of case observed by the researcher. In other words, what can be generalised is not the case itself, but these characteristics and analysis.

[115] See Hao Xiong, 'On the transformation of legal regulation mode of mediation in China' (2018) 3 *Studies in Law and Business* 115 [熊浩："论中国调解法律规制模式的转型"，载《法商研究》2018年第3期].

should be *only* valid in the southwest grassroots context. This is a regionally valid conclusion. This research cannot and should not rule out the possibility that mediation is not feasible and practicable in other differentiated contexts in China. Therefore, even though mediation is feasible in the investigated context, it cannot adequately justify the current mediation promotion policy at the national level. After all, China is a vast country. To some degree, China's legal issues should be analysed on a regional basis, not on a generalised national basis where one size fits all. As Elizabeth J. Perry suggested, 'China might better be viewed not as a forest but as a jigsaw puzzle. Only by assembling the relevant pieces (whose inter-connections are patterned, not random) will we have the full picture'.[116]

[116] Elizabeth J. Perry, 'Trends in the study of Chinese politics: state–society relations' (1994) 139 *The China Quarterly* 704, 712–713.

7

Case Study Two

Two Sides of Mediation in the Grassroots Society of China

7.1 Introduction

As has been mentioned, only a limited number of studies have examined how China's mediation system works using an empirical study approach. The existing research mainly focuses on the influence of cultural tradition and politics or targets the theoretical and conceptual issues instead of providing detailed studies to explain the application of alternative dispute resolution (ADR) and mediation in practice. It is seemingly forgotten that mediation is not just a concept, but 'mediation to a great extent is what a mediator does'.[1] More importantly, both in the Western and Chinese legal scholarship, the gap in the existing literature regarding the empirical research on the practice and operating mechanisms of mediation in present-day China are still obvious. As Dr Xu pointed out, 'the empirical research on mediation in contemporary China is simply scant'.[2] Therefore, 'we may expect a rapid growth of our systematic knowledge concerning both judicial mediation and about the devices that are its companions and rivals. But such knowledge requires that we *develop adequate measures concerning the quality of processes and outcomes*'.[3]

[1] James A. Wall Jr. and Ann Lynn, 'Mediation: a current review' (1993) 37(1) *Journal of Conflict Resolution* 160, 186.

[2] Xiaobing Xu, 'Mediation in China and the United States: towards common outcome', Unpublished JSD Dissertation, Stanford University School of Law (2003), p. 9. I am not implying that conceptual and theoretical research is not important. On the contrary, I want to point out that ADR research lacks empirical evidence so that the questions regarding fitting a particular dispute to a suitable process, the novelty of the appropriate use of public funds, the power balance between the parties and so on and so forth is really hard to answer. See also Sally Engle Merry, 'Book review: dispute without culture' (1987) 100 *Harvard Law Review* 2057, 2059.

[3] Marc Galanter, '"… A settlement judge, not a trial judge": judicial mediation in the United States' (1985) 12(1) *Journal of Law and Society* 1, 13 (emphasis added by the author).

Given China's cross-regional heterogeneity and complexity, it is necessary to examine mediation practice in different social contexts. Unlike the previous chapter (Chapter 6), which focused on the mediation practice in rural and poor ethnic minority counties, this chapter explores the application of mediation in a rich and developed city context through fieldwork within the T District Court in southwest China. This chapter presents a vivid picture of how a mediator utilises his micro skills and life wisdom to protect his own interests while handling complicated cases and interacting with government officials. Through case studies, this chapter also illustrates the judicial ecology of the court in grassroots society in China.

The author's fieldwork was conducted in T Court, Yunnan Province. T District is economically and politically developed and a cultural centre. T District Court is also a rich court. The reason is that the court is not only located in a rich urban area where the facility and work conditions are relatively more advanced but also the human resources are rich. Five judges have Master Law degrees and seventy-nine judges and legal staff members are university graduates (there are 105 staff members in total). The degree of professionalism is relatively high.[4] T District Court (TDC afterwards) is the busiest court in the city. Every year, there are around 2,500 cases handled in this court. The court has several detached tribunals (*paichu fating*, 派出法庭), the biggest of which is the one located in the town that is investigated in this study.[5]

In the following sections, the social circumstances of the area where the fieldwork was conducted will be first explained. The *guanxi* mechanism, which is the social context in which the court staff are embedded, will be analysed in detail. Secondly, the chapter will describe two interesting and typical cases with the objective of showing how judges in the grassroots society implement mediation in solving disputes. Thirdly, based on the case studies and fieldwork in T District, the merits and drawbacks of mediation will be further discussed.

[4] In order to keep the investigated place anonymous, the relevant footnotes showing the information about this place are omitted.

[5] The People's Tribunal is a detached judicial institution of the grassroots court (*jicheng fayuan*, 基层法院, 'basic court' is another corresponding translation). According to *the Organic Law of People's Republic of China* (amended 2018), Article 26 provides that 'A basic people's court may set up a number of people's tribunals according to the local conditions, population and cases. A people's tribunal is an integral part of the basic people's court. The judgments and rulings of a people's tribunal shall be the judgments and rulings of a basic people's court'.

7.2 Context: Having Lunch Together

7.2.1 More than Eating

It is necessary to explain the location of the People's Tribunal in the town. The tribunal is located at the core region of the town on a business street around 10 kilometres from the city centre. It is also located at the boundary of the urban and the rural areas of the city. Most interestingly, it is just opposite to the street of the town government (*zhen*, 镇): two minutes' walk in normal conditions.[6]

When the author did the fieldwork there, he had lunch in the town government's canteen. This canteen is not open to the public, yet the judges and other legal staff members can have lunch here every day with the government officials. The most obvious reason judges have lunch in the government canteen is that the price is very cheap, and it is in close proximity to their office and convenient to use. From the perspective of the government, they are happy to provide this convenient service. As a not very old but popular Chinese saying goes, 'it is just more pairs of chopsticks'.[7] Judges and officials are acquaintances at the tables, chatting, cracking jokes and sharing and exchanging news and gossip. They get to

[6] The town government (*zhen zhengfu*, 镇政府) is a fourth-level Chinese local administrative division under the county government (*xian*, 县) but above village (*cun*, 村). Town government is the same as the township government (*xiang*, 乡) regarding the administrative hierarchy. However, a township is usually smaller in population, less developed and more remote from a city compared to a town. For a general discussion about Chinese local administrative hierarchy, see Yong Zhong, *Local Government and Politics in China: Challenges from Below* (Armonk, NY: M. E. Sharpe, 2003); William L. Tung, *The Political Institutions of Modern China* (Netherlands: Kluwer, Second Printing, 1968), pp. 287–288.

[7] The original text is '只不过多双筷子吃饭而已', which means 'it is really easy and convenient for me to treat you'. When I conducted fieldwork in this town, I had lunch with judges and government officials almost every day. The judge introduced me to the officials and the chief executive of the town government as if introducing a friend. This brought several benefits to me. First, the establishment of a personal network with local authorities allowed the research to proceed more smoothly. In the words of David M. Fetterman, I received assistance from the 'local facilitator'. Secondly, the daily lunches were free because the chief executive of the town government considered me a privileged guest, believing that the research might contribute to the town's development. This courteous and convenient dining arrangement was not unique to me in this District Court. In every court where I conducted fieldwork, having dinners or lunches with the judges was quite normal. This dining arrangement greatly benefited me in terms of field involvement and gaining a deeper understanding of the community. It is worth noting that I was not singled out for this treatment. This personal interaction model is quite common at the grassroots level in China, regardless of my presence. It is difficult to simply judge whether this practice is good or bad, as it is simply a lifestyle that is practiced.

know each other deeper and even discuss some formal issues when eating.[8]

Any person who is familiar with Chinese culture and Chinese society will certainly know that food plays an important role in Chinese life.[9] As observed by Chinese cultural scholars,

> Chinese people love eating out. Whenever there is any significant social activity, dinner is an irreplaceable part of the program. When friends arrive, we need to 'welcome' them with a meal; when they leave, a 'farewell dinner' follows. You can treat friends to dinner for personal 'business' matters, and if there is no business, a 'gathering' is also common. In an ordinary person's family, whether it's festivals, wedding and funeral ceremonies, the birthday of a senior family member, or the birth of a new child, the Chinese customarily treat others to a meal. Who would refuse such an invitation? When going abroad, if a person gets a promotion, receives a bonus, or moves to a new house, it is not uncommon for friends and relatives to naturally expect a treat. If someone asks for assistance with things like installing a new telephone, cleaning up the sewer, installing a new air conditioner, obtaining a license, buying a ticket, applying for a job, sending a child to kindergarten, purchasing materials, or submitting a report to Customs, it is very usual to treat people to show thoughtfulness. *Even if the issue is really difficult, sharing drinks can make achieving the goals easier*. Chinese culture is a food culture that has permeated every corner of daily life. In Chinese culture, all principles of human life are akin to the rationales of food and eating. Whether or not the focus on eating is well understood and whether you are good at eating are significant issues concerning national welfare and the people's livelihood.[10]

[8] Actually, discussing about the formal and official issues when having dinner together is an important Chinese tradition, which can be derived from the Zhou Dynasty (1046–256 BC). See Zhongtian Yi, *Chatting About Chinese* (Beijing: Hualing Press, 1996), pp. 2–7 [易中天：《闲话中国人》，北京：华龄出版社1996年版].

[9] Frederick J. Simoons, *Food in China: A Cultural and Historical Inquiry* (Boca Raton, FL: CRC Press, 1991), p. 14.

[10] Yi, *Chatting About Chinese*, pp. 18–19 (emphasis added). The original text goes as following:

> 中国人最爱请客吃饭……一应社会生活中的种种重大事件，宴会都是不可或缺的节目。人来了要“接风”，人走了要'饯行'，有事要'嘬一嘬'，没事也要'聚一聚'。即使寻常百姓家，逢年过节、红白喜事，老人做寿诞，小孩过生日，试问哪家不请，哪个不吃？如果升了职位、涨了工资、搬进新居、走出国门、三朋四友七姑八姨也都会堂而皇之的要求你请客。倘若求人办事，如装电话、通水道、安空调、办执照、开证明、买车票，达人求职、小孩入托、原料采买、货物报关，也都往往要可吃饭。再难办的事，只要'酒杯一端'，也就'政策放宽'...中国文化的'泛食倾向'随处可见。好像将人称为'口'，

Having dinner together in China is not only an activity for eating but also an occasion to forge significant person-to-person interaction, typical of the Chinese people.[11] On many daily occasions, eating out serves as a method of building networks and enhancing personal identities. Sharing meals strengthens friendships, transforms strangers into acquaintances and often forges bonds akin to those of brothers and sisters.[12] In Chinese society, it is true that:

> 把职业称为'饭碗'等。又比如，思索叫'咀嚼'，体验叫'品位'，嫉妒叫'吃醋'，幸福"陶醉'，司空见惯叫'家常便饭'，轻而易举叫'小菜一碟'，学风浮躁叫'浅尝辄止'，理解深刻叫'吃透精神'，广泛流传叫'脍炙人口'，深知熟记叫'烂熟于心'，学习知识叫'汲取营养'，改变处境叫'苦尽甘来'……此外，如'吃苦'、'吃亏'、'吃不消'、'吃得开'、'吃里扒外'、'吃不了兜走'、'不吃那一套'、以及'生吞活剥'、'囫囵吞枣'、'秀色可餐'、'食古不化'等等，都是见怪不怪的说法……上述种种说法层出不穷，其根本原因，还在于在中国文化看来，种种原理，均同于饮食之道。所以，会不会吃、懂不懂吃、善于不善于处理饮食问题，是关系到国计民生的大事。

11 Simoons, *Food in China*, p. 14. In the existing scholarship, anthropologists have done extensive studies concerning food habits and eating activities. These studies are an interesting and important angle, which assists in understanding the social interaction and the culture. As Eugene Cooper quoted and argued in the article 'Chinese table manners: you are how you eat' (1986) 45(2) *Human Organization* 179:

> Food habits communicate symbolic messages. . .encode social events. The message of that code is about different degrees of hierarchy, inclusion and exclusion, boundaries and transactions across boundaries. The significance of food habits in any given social group, and table manners more particularly, is the subject of continuous negotiation, as each generation devises its own praxis in opposition to, or in accord with, the precedents of the past.

12 Zhongtian Yi has likened Chinese preference to eating out (*qingke chifan*, 请客吃饭) to the establishment of the blood relationship. Yi stated:

> Chinese people love to eat out. It seems that only through eating can extraordinary relationships be established. Chinese culture highly values interpersonal relationships (*guanxi*, 关系), with consanguinity being the closest and most reliable form. Therefore, when handling interpersonal relationships, there is often an effort to transform non-blood relationships into blood-related ones. For instance, officials are referred to as 'Parents Officials,' soldiers as 'Army Made up of the Sons of the People,' and cooperative organizations as 'Brother Institutions,' among others. Sharing food together can create a bond similar to that of blood relatives, as food is the source of life. Essentially, sharing food signifies that people are from the same source of life, thereby making them akin to brothers. In a sense, they become family, don't they? Even real blood brothers share meals together sometimes. On the eve of the Spring Festival, all family members sit and eat together, reaffirming the mother's role as the provider of life and food. In this warm family atmosphere, the identities of brothers and sisters, who are raised by the same mother and share meals together, are reinforced.

> Simple knowledge of the structural contexts, behavioural expectations and symbolic associations associated with food events can provide access to social boundaries that would otherwise be less easily breached and make it possible to more easily achieve one's goals. Rather than constituting positively functioned adaptive responses, table manners and knowledge of them are better seen as an inventory of symbolic responses that may be manipulated, finessed and encoded to communicate messages about oneself. For Chinese, as for most everyone else, you are how you eat.[13]

7.2.2 *Lunch,* Guanxi[14] *and Independent Trial*

Having lunch together daily enhances the connection between the government and the court by strengthening the bond between judges and officials. The impartiality and independence of the judges, in this regard, may be undermined not by the Party's interference but by greeting, chatting and smiles at the table. Ironically, none of them are intentionally against an independent trial.

The original text goes as follows:

> 中国人喜欢请客吃饭，似乎只有通过请客吃饭才能建立起一种非同寻常的人际关系。中国人很看重人际关系，而人与人的关系中，最可靠的，又是’血缘’。所以，中国人在处理人际关系时，总是要想方设法把非血缘关系转化为血缘关系，比如’父母官’、’子弟兵’、’兄弟单位’等等。吃同一食物的人可以被看作是有血缘关系的，因为食物是生命之源。吃了同一种食物，就有了同一生命来源，岂能不是兄弟？甚至真正的兄弟，也不能长期不共食。所以，在中国，分出去的儿子，嫁出去的女儿，总要寻找机会回’娘家’，回到母亲的身边共食。至少，年三十的’年夜饭’，是不可不吃的。这一回的家宴之所以尤为重要，在于它有着承前启后的意义：对前一年已然存在的血缘关系，是肯定和确认；对后一年将要延续的血缘关系，则是预约与重申。不难想象，在那万家灯火的岁除之夜，一家人团团围坐，举筷共食，母亲重温自己’食物和生命的提供者’角色，兄弟姐妹重申自己是’吃同一奶水长大的人’，那可真是其情也切切，其乐也融融！

See Zhongtian Yi, 'Blood relationship from eating' [易中天：’吃出来的血缘’]. http://blog.sina.com.cn/s/blog_4bdc7dbf010090ev.html (last accessed 10 November 2023).

13 Cooper, 'Chinese table manners', 179, 184.

14 *Guanxi* is a Chinese term '关系', which is usually translated as interpersonal relationship or personal ties. It is one of the key concepts in Chinese society indicating how people's life is structured and how they interact with each other. For a detailed discussion about this concept, see Andrew B. Kipnis, 'Practices of *Guanxi* production and practices of Ganqing avoidance' in Thomas Gold, Dough Guthrie and David Wank (eds.), *Social Connections in China: Institutions, Culture, and the Changing Nature of Guanxi* (Cambridge: Cambridge University Press, 2002), pp. 21–34; Jun Lin and Steven X. Si, 'Can *guanxi* be a problem? Context, ties, and some unfavorable consequences of social capital in China' (2010) 27(3) *Asia Pacific Journal of Management* 561, 561–581.

It is interesting to note that in analysing judicial independence, mainstream Western scholars argue:

> the essence of judicial independence. . .is the preservation of a separate institution *of government* that can adjudicate cases or controversies with impartiality. This principle is embodied in the doctrine of *separation of powers*, which elevates the judiciary to the status of a coequal branch.[15]

According to Joel G. Verner, judicial independence is briefly defined as '[the ability] to decide cases on the basis of established law and the "merits of the case" without substantial interference from other *political or governmental agents*'.[16] In many scholars' minds, it is clear that judicial independence chiefly concerns the external political interference with the court,[17] controlling power at the constitutional level[18] and rule of law.[19] For them, judicial independence is the value of a series of institutional settings to protect the judges and court system from interference from *political and institutional power*.[20] In this sense, 'judicial independence. . .is a feature of the *institutional setting* within which

[15] Irving R. Kaufman, 'The essence of judicial independence' (1980) 80 *Columbia Law Review* 671, 688 (emphasis added).

[16] Joel G. Verner, 'The independence of Supreme Courts in Latin America: a review of the literature' (1984) 16 *Journal of Latin American Studies* 463 (emphasis added).

[17] For example, 'the key in accounting for an independent judiciary is to explain why elected officials (*politicians and political parties*) will not want to, or will not be able to, undermine judicial autonomy' (emphasis added). See Georg Vanberg, 'Establishing and maintaining judicial independence' in Keith E. Whittington (ed.), *The Oxford Handbook of Law and Politics* (New York: Oxford University Press, 2008), p. 103.

[18] See Barry Friedman, 'History, politics, and judicial independence' in András Sajó (ed.), *Judicial Integrity* (Leiden: M. Nijhoff, 2004).

[19] See Ralf Dahrendorf, 'A confusion of power: politics and the rule of law' (1977) 40 *Modern Law Review* 1.

[20] According to Irving R. Kaufman, this understanding which pays more attention to the institutional and structural independence of court is derived from the special historical evolution of the idea of judicial independence in British as well as American context. Kaufman, see note 13 above. Similarly, Albert Chen also said:

> The modern Western idea of judicial independence is an integral component of the political and legal thought associated with the ideology of liberalism, as well as a product of power struggles in specific historical circumstances, and the degree to which it is a firmly established experience from which the forces of habit, custom, and tradition develop in support of it.

See Albert H. Y. Chen, *An Introduction to the Legal System of the People's Republic of China*, (Hong Kong: Lexis/Nexis, 5th ed., 2018), p. 183.

judging takes place',[21] and it actually stands for a check and balance mechanism similar to what exists in the US constitution law.

Influenced by these thoughts, existing scholarship mainly investigates *the independence at the structural level*[22] between the People's Court and other significant organs of the states. In this vein, it implies that the CPC and government are the only two, or the most frequently and the most problematic elements, which exert interference in the courts' operation.

However, structural independence is just one aspect of judicial independence. As John Ferejohn pointed out:

> Independence seems to have at least two meanings. One meaning commonly invoked when considering the circumstances of the individual judge is that a person is independent if he is able to take actions without fear of interference by another…Another meaning is perhaps less common in discussions surrounding judges, but applies naturally to courts and to the judicial system as a whole. We might think of a person or an institution as being dependent on another if the person or entity is unable to do its job without relying on some other institution or group. In this context, the federal judiciary is institutionally dependent on Congress and the president, for jurisdiction, rules, and execution of judicial orders.[23]

The fundamental and ordinary meaning of judicial independence, although not a classical liberalism narrative, should include that the judge should be a 'neutral third'. In other words,

> judges have no interest in the issues of the case and no bias toward either of the parties, all citizens – rich, poor, strong, and weak – are put on an equal footing before the law and are able to protect their rights and security against encroachment by others.[24]

[21] John Ferejohn, 'Independent judges, dependent judiciary: explaining judicial independence' (1999) 72 *Southern California Law Review* 353 (emphasis added).

[22] Mark Findlay, '"Independence" and the judiciary in the PRC: expectation for constitutional legality in China' in Kanishka Jayasuriya (ed.), *Law, Capitalism and Power in Asia: The Rule of Law and Institutions* (London: Routledge, 1999), p. 284 (emphasis added).

[23] Ferejohn, 'Independent judges, dependent judiciary', 353, 355. A few Western scholars notice the rule *guanxi* played regarding using it for personal or institutional advantage. See for example, Pitman Potter, 'Guanxi and the PRC legal system: from contradiction to complementarity' in Thomas Gold, Doug Guthrie and David Wank (eds.), *Social Connections in China: Institutions, Culture and the Changing Nature of Guanxi* (Cambridge: Cambridge University Press, 2002), p. 188.

[24] Christopher M. Larkins, 'Judicial independence and democratization: a theoretical and conceptual analysis' (1996) 44 *The American Journal of Comparative Law* 605, 608.

This is not to deny CPC and government's interference with China's court system.[25] However, it should be stated that the PRC courts handle over eight million first-instance cases per year. Only a small fraction of them are political or politically sensitive in nature, which may attract the attention from the CPC or government.[26] The *guanxi*, as another

[25] In recent years, Beijing has significantly strengthened protections for the independence of judges, further limiting external interference in the judiciary and clarifying the relationship between the judiciary and government departments. In 2015, the General Office of the Central Committee of the Communist Party of China and the General Office of the State Council issued the 'Regulations on Recording, Reporting, and Accountability for Leading Cadres Interfering in Judicial Activities and Handling Specific Cases (《领导干部干预司法活动、插手具体案件处理的记录、通报和责任追究规定》)'. This regulation emphasises that 'leading cadres at all levels must take the lead in adhering to the Constitution and laws, maintaining judicial authority, and supporting judicial organs in exercising their powers independently and impartially according to the law. No leading cadre shall require judicial organs to handle cases in violation of their legal duties or procedures, nor shall they request judicial organs to do anything that impedes judicial fairness'. Article 5 stipulates that judicial personnel must fully and accurately record any instances of leading cadres interfering in judicial activities or handling specific cases, ensuring that the entire process is documented and traceable. The regulation requires judicial organs and judges to truthfully record and retain relevant materials when faced with 'requests or instructions from organizations in the name of the organization, or when staff members or relatives of leading cadres interfere in judicial activities or handle specific cases'. It also provides that 'judicial personnel who truthfully record instances of leading cadres interfering in judicial activities or handling specific cases are protected by law and the organization. Leading cadres must not retaliate against judicial personnel. Judicial personnel may not be dismissed, transferred, demoted, or subjected to other disciplinary actions such as removal or expulsion without legal cause and proper legal procedures'.

The regulation also clearly defines the behaviours that constitute interference by leading cadres, including: soliciting favours for case parties during investigation, filing, investigation and review for prosecution, trial and enforcement stages; requesting case handlers or heads of handling units to privately meet with parties, their defenders, litigation agents, close relatives or others with a vested interest in the case; instructing or condoning staff members or relatives to solicit favours for case parties; exceeding authority to propose biased opinions or specific requirements for handling cases through forms such as listening to reports, holding coordination meetings or issuing documents for local or departmental interests; other unlawful interferences in judicial activities that obstruct judicial fairness. Leading cadres who engage in such prohibited behaviours will be subject to disciplinary actions by the Party and the state laws, and relevant information will be disclosed to the public. The Central Commission for Discipline Inspection has previously released reports to the public on instances of leading cadres interfering in judicial activities. For detailed information on the Regulations on Recording, Reporting, and Accountability for Leading Cadres Interfering in Judicial Activities and Handling Specific Cases, see www.gov.cn/zhengce/2015-03/30/content_2840521.htm (last accessed 25 May 2024).

[26] Yulin Fu and Randall Peerenboom continued that 'the risk, nature, source and impact of interference are different. Failing to draw these distinctions is likely to lead to misleading generalizations'. See Yulin Fu and Randall Peerenboom, 'A new analytic framework of

important and probably much more frequent element which may undermine judges' independent trial, especially at the grassroots court level, is often underestimated in the Western analytical framework when talking about China's judicial issues. *Guanxi*, as an interdependence mechanism existing at the personal level, may exert significant influence on a judge in a subtle and delicate way. Under the situation where the interpersonal relationship works, judges will not '*resist external pressures* when passing judgment'[27] or '. . . *fear* of interference by another'.[28] Rather, they are happy and willing to lose a certain degree of impartiality and independence because this is the basic rule of reciprocity between friends and acquaintances' interaction. These reciprocities can bring direct benefits to the judges themselves by expanding and enhancing their ties to many other useful connection points in daily life, such as educational institutions, hospitals, banks, police stations and so forth. Again, this does not aim to deny or justify the CPC and government's interference in the court, yet that means there is a very apparent tension between the independent trial and the interpersonal interaction lifestyle that local judges are a part of.

Some may argue that the detached tribunal should be equipped with a separate canteen in order to maintain independence. However, the real

understanding and promoting judicial independence of China' in Randall Peerenboom (ed.), *Judicial Independence in China: Lessons for Global Rule of Law Promotion* (Cambridge: Cambridge University Press, 2010), p. 96.

Although Fu and Peerenboom's classification of disputes according to the sources of interference clarified the judicial independence issues in China to some degree, it should be noted that this classification used multiple standards to category disputes, political influence and personal/social influence. In this context, it is very hard to use this framework in analysing the cases where both the political and social influence exists. That is to say, for example, if a political leader influenced a particular case in the court but the leader also had personal connection with the court personnel (this is not uncommon in grassroots society), how do we classify this kind of interference and evaluate which element is more influential to the judicial independence? Therefore, Fu and Peerenboom's analytical framework is based on the promise that the political leader is actually detached from the local society. This may make sense in the context of the big modern cities, but the explanatory power may be very limited when applying to undeveloped grassroots society and rural context in which the political power and personal power generated from *guanxi* are highly overlapping and snarled. For more details, see Xuefeng He, *New Earth-Bound China: The Survey Notes of the Rural Society in Transitional Era* (Guiling: Guanxi Normal University Press, 2003) [贺雪峰：《新乡土中国：转型期乡村社会调查笔记》，广西师范大学出版社2003年版].

27 Fiona Cownie et al., *English Legal System in Context* (London: LexisNexis UK, 3rd ed., 2003), p. 190 (emphasis added by the author).

28 Ferejohn, 'Independent judges, dependent judiciary', 353, 355 (emphasis added by the author).

problem is that there are only three staff members in the detached tribunal most of the time: two judges and one court clerk. If they leave for a case investigation or undertake some other missions, they will not come back for lunch. So, the proposed arrangement for a separate and independent canteen in the tribunal is not only uneconomical but also irrational. More importantly, this proposal is seemingly naive because it simplifies China's reality by presuming that if the independence of the canteen is achieved, the independence of the court can be achieved correspondingly.

In fact, having lunch together is a symbol that illustrates the vivid and realistic situation in which China's local court is embedded.[29] To a certain extent, China is still a big community with close interdependent relationships.[30] 'Having lunch together' actually manifests the interaction model of people and the *guanxi* (关系) culture, which used to and still shapes people's mindsets. *Guanxi* in southwest China leads the people towards an 'acquaintance society' (*shuren shehui*, 熟人社会). In an acquaintance society, *guanxi* provides 'access social boundaries'. In this case, the divisions between 'yours' and 'mine', between 'court's' and 'government's' are not as clear as that in Western society.[31] Therefore,

[29] In this context, 'local' does not necessarily mean rural or impoverished areas of China but refers to grassroots society. For example, I was informed by a procurator in a major Chinese city that the court and procuratorate in their district actually share the same canteen. In other words, it may not be uncommon for judicial and administrative institutions in grassroots China to share a canteen. Interestingly, I received this information while having dinner with a friend.

[30] The importance of *guanxi* is also very obvious in modern Chinese societies – this argument has been confirmed by much relevant research. For example, Godwin C. Chu and Yanan Ju, *The Great Wall in Ruins: Communication and Cultural Change in China* (Albany, NY: State University of New York Press, 1993); Gary G. Hamilton, 'Patterns of Asian capitalism: the cases of Taiwan and South Korea' in Mark Fruin (ed.), *Networks, Markets and the Pacific Rim* (New York: Oxford University Press, 1998), pp. 181–199; Hairen He, *The World Without Dispute: Reconciled Reason and New Acquaintance Society* (Beijing: Law Press, 2009) [贺海仁：《无诉的世界：和解理性与新熟人社会》，北京：法律出版社2009年版].

Although the traditional *guanxi* system based on consanguinity relationship is weakening due to the social immigration, growth of the only-one-child family and urbanisation. However, the modern China is also constructing many new types of interpersonal relationships, such as professional associations, teacher–student relationships in modern educational institutions, internet communities, business corporations, alumnus and hobby clubs, which will continue the *guanxi* system in China by endowing them with new modern forms.

[31] Xiaotong Fei has even analysed this in his classical book *From the Soil*:

> Western societies are somewhat like the way we (Chinese) collect rice straw to use to cook our food...the separate straws, the separate bundles, and

where the judges have lunch is not that important. What is truly important is the natural daily interaction model between people, government and court. *Guanxi*, the personal connections established through eating out, may surpass legal rules. It remains one of the fundamental characteristics of interactions in Chinese grassroots society. It is not surprising that *guanxi* is the most obvious and profound characteristic of Chinese traditional society. What is surprising is that these characteristics continue to govern and dominate the grassroots society of a modern city in southwest China after years of social transformation, legal reform and an open-door policy. If a person, including a judge, living in a grassroots society cannot be independent of personal relationships, how can the court be?

7.3 Case One: A Succession Dispute and the Implementation of Mediation in Solving Hard Cases

7.3.1 Basic Facts of the Dispute

A and B are the sister and brother, and they are both Muslims living in the town. Forty years ago, A got married to a man in a neighbouring community and then moved out of their parents' house. As the siblings gradually moved out, B, the youngest child, continued living with their parents and undertook the primary responsibility of supporting them until they passed away about 20 and 10 years ago, respectively. While their parents were alive, the other siblings also contributed to their support, though they did not live in the parents' house. This year, B wanted to demolish the old house and build a new one. A, the sister, intervened and claimed that she also had inheritance rights to the house.[32] According to A, the house was

> finally the separate stacks all fit together to make up the whole haystack. . .Why are nouns for such basic social units so ambiguous in Chinese? In my opinion, the ambiguity indicates the difference between our social structure and that of the West. Our pattern is not like distinct bundles of straws. *Rather, it is like the circles that appear on the surface of a lake when a rock is thrown into it. Everyone stands at the center of the circles produces by his or her own. . .Now we can see the boundary between the public and private spheres is relative – we may even say ambiguous.*

Xiaotong Fei, *From the Soil: The Foundations of Chinese Society*, Gary G. Hamilton and Zheng Wang (trans.) (Berkeley, CA: University of California Press, 1992), pp. 61–62, 69 (emphasis added by the author).

32 According to Law of Succession of the People's Republic of China (abolished in 2021) and the Civil Code (2021), 'Males and females are equal in their right to inheritance', which is

under common ownership among the siblings.[33] However, B, the younger brother, argued that according to custom, 'married-out women' could not enjoy inheritance rights[34] and that the other brothers had waived their inheritance rights, giving him 100 per cent real property rights over the house. The People's Mediation Committee tried to resolve the dispute but failed. Subsequently, A sued B in the T District Court.[35]

7.3.2 *Dispute Resolution Process and Preliminary Analysis*

Obviously, there is a tension between the state law and customary law in this case. Regarding this kind of conflict, there has been much literature in legal scholarship at the conceptual level.[36] What should be of concern here is how the judges release the tension between the two 'legal systems',

considered as a principle of China's succession law. Article 1127 of Civil Code (2021) stipulates that 'the estate of a decedent shall be inherited in the following order: (1) First in order: Spouse, children, parents; (2) Second in order: Brothers and sisters, paternal grandparents, maternal grandparents'. Article 1130 states that 'successors same in order shall, in general, inherit in equal shares… At the time of distributing the estate, successors who have made the predominant contributions in maintaining the decedent or have lived with the decedent may be given a larger share. When succession opens, the successor(s) first in order shall inherit to the exclusion of the successor(s) second in order. The successor(s) second in order shall inherit in default of any successor first in order.' Before and after the implementation of the Civil Code, there are not significant differences in the relevant rules.

33 Article 297 of Civil Code (2021) states that 'immovables or movables may be co-owned by two or more organizations or individuals. Co-ownership consists of divided co-ownership and undivided co-ownership'. Article 301 Civil Code (2021) states that 'the disposal or major repair, or modification of nature or use of a co-owned immovable or movable shall be subject to the consent of co-owners in divided co-ownership holding two-thirds or more of shares or all co-owners in undivided co-ownership, unless it is otherwise agreed upon by the co-owners'. Before and after the implementation of the Civil Code, there are not significant differences in the relevant rules.

34 In Chinese traditional society, the married-out women shall not enjoy the right of succession. The old saying is 'Married daughter is just like the water splashed out' [*jiachuqu de nver pochuqu de shui*, 嫁出去的女儿泼出去的水], which means the woman will be economically removed from the family member list, which is just like the splashed water that cannot recover to the former situation. This kind of dispute also happens in some other areas of China, see Xin He, 'Why did they not take on the disputes? Law, power and politics in the decision-making of Chinese courts' (2007) 3(3) *International Journal of Law in Context* 203.

35 The basic facts and process of this case is abstracted from the mediation agreement and the author's interview of the judges and judicial staff with the permission of both parties and the presiding judge.

36 See, for example, Yuhe Yu (ed.), *Customary Law* (Shanghai: Fuda University Press, 2008), pp. 106–145 [于语和主编：《民间法》，上海：复旦大学出版社2008年版].

the formal law and folk law, in practice. If the judge insisted on the principle of 'equality between the genders' provided by China's success law (in other words, if the court thought that the customary law was totally invalid), the plaintiff would not be completely satisfied with the outcome.[37] However, if the judge just followed the customary law regardless of the statute, this would be against the law. It is a dilemma caused by legal pluralism.[38] The judge, in this case, needed to consider the situation very carefully and find a suitable solution to make an acceptable compromise to all the involved disputants by balancing modern legal skills, traditional customs and local knowledge.[39]

Mediation, in this sense, could not only provide a compromise that both parties may accept but also avoid the conflict between state law and customary law. The polycentric nature of this dispute made it particularly suitable for mediation. It also offers judges tools to push and facilitate the parties to achieve a compromise. On the plaintiff's side, the judge can argue that the defendant has undertaken the primary obligation of supporting the ageing parents and that customary law provides that 'married-out women' do not have inheritance rights. On the defendant's

[37] In Western jurisdictions, whether the parties are satisfied with the outcome of judicial litigation is not an important consideration for the presiding judge. However, in China, judges must consider the parties' feelings and feedback. This is because if the parties complain through an appeal, the judges may face repercussions. The judge's concern about the parties' feelings is becoming increasingly important due to the current political–legal ideology movement aimed at promoting the idea that 'People's Judges Serve the People'. In this context, if a judge can handle a dispute through mediation, they will not only be rewarded but also secure as both parties will likely agree with or at least tolerate the final outcome to a significant extent. Conversely, if the case proceeds to appeal and the judgment from the grassroots court is overruled or remanded by the Intermediate People's Court or if the parties ultimately resort to petitions, the judge who made the initial decision could face fines and loss of bonuses. The examples can be found in Li Su, *Sending Law to the Rural China: A Study on Chinese Legal Institution at the Grassroots Level* (Beijing: China University of Politics and Law Press, 2000), p. 106 [苏力：《送法下乡：中国基层司法制度研究》，北京：中国政法大学出版社2000年版].

[38] Legal pluralism is a term indicating a fact that any society or social group contains a plurality of legal orders or fragments of legal system. Actually, the human society 'contains many strands pulling in different directions. There strands transcend any one legal system; they recur in quite foreign and different systems, creating the possibility of unexpected alliances between the native and the foreign, and conflicts between aspirations in the natives'. See Poh-Ling Tan, *Asian Legal Systems: Law, Society and Pluralism in East Asia* (Sydney: Butterworths, 1997), p. 405. For a general discussion on 'legal pluralism', see Francis G. Snyder, 'Anthropology, dispute processes and law: critical introduction' (1981) 8(2) *British Journal of Law & Society* 141, 155–157.

[39] Su, *Sending Law to the Rural China*, pp. 130–133.

side, the judge may persuade the defendant to offer some compensation to the plaintiff according to the succession law. Unfortunately, mediation failed due to the 'stubborn' defendant (the brother in this case). Consequently, the judge was forced to return to the adjudicative track to produce a judgment and had to face the potential negative impact of the parties' dissatisfaction in future appeals.

In the mediation process, the judge realised that this was a difficult case. When writing the judgment, the judge sought help from local authorities, including village leaders, township leaders and people's mediators. Before writing the judgment, the judge visited the village where the succession dispute occurred and consulted with local leaders. The judge inquired about how to distribute justice in such concrete circumstances, whether there were any precedents on similar issues, and how much compensation should be paid to the plaintiff (the sister in this case), if any.

Interestingly, the court clerk was required by the judge to record all the content of these communications. The interviewed leaders then signed the record. When the judge made the final judgment, these interviews, which included local knowledge and suggestions from local administrative leaders' perspectives, were included in the case package. Although these documents and sources were not directly cited in the judgment, they served as more than just suggestions – they were treated as evidence. The judge included all these signed interview documents in the case file, just in case the appellate court needed to review them when reconsidering the case. This approach allowed the judge to borrow administrative power to justify his own judgment and mitigate the risks associated with the appeals process by incorporating additional justifications.

In the above discussion, it is clear that the judge solved the case through his wisdom. He produced a judgment according to comprehensive recourse, including law and local knowledge, collected from local authorities, to locate justice and avoid risks from the appellate procedure as far as possible. This is a creative strategy. But the question is, why were the administrative leaders willing to help him? And more importantly, why were they willing to sign the document with certain influence? The answer is that they are acquaintances. Using the judge's own words, 'we will meet sooner or later' (*taitou bujian ditou jian*, 抬头不见低头见). The daily interaction has ensured that 'if you need help, I will give a hand to you'. In fact, the local administrative leaders can refuse the interview requirement from the judge. First of all, 'it is none of my business'. The administrative leaders do not have any duty to facilitate dispute resolution in the judicial system. Secondly, it is easy for the administrative leaders to refuse it by saying some 'broad narratives', 'big words', or some bureaucratese like 'rule of law' (*yifa zhiguo*, 依法治国) or 'to maintain the authority of the constitution and law' (*weihu xianfa yu falv de quanwei*, 维护宪法与法律的权威). These words will be easily found in official documents, propaganda and leaders' speeches as enhancing the rule of law has emerged as a fundamental policy of the CPC.

The local administrative leaders are helpful because they know the judge is also helpful when he/she is needed. It may not necessarily be a friendship but it is a realistic symbiotic relationship established by the people's interaction model and the self-interested nature of human beings. So, this is the context where the local mediation operates. Government and court are not only connected by the institutional settings like the CPC's Political-Legal Committee, and Comprehensive Management Office (*zonghe zhili bangongshi*, 综合治理办公室) and also by interpersonal relationships. Therefore, the signed interview is not only one piece of evidence for this particular dispute but also evidence proving the relationship between the government officials and judges.

7.4 Case Two: A Housing Demolition and Relocation Dispute and the Function of Mediation in Solving Sensitive Cases

7.4.1 Basic Facts of the Dispute

A and B signed a house lease contract with the understanding that the house might be expropriated by the government. A, the lessor, agreed that if the rented property were expropriated, the compensatory payment from the government would go to B to ensure the certainty of the lease contract. Years later, the government initiated a new road construction plan and planned to expropriate A's house, which had been rented to B. A negotiated with the government and managed to secure a higher compensation. However, A refused to transfer the compensatory payment to B and claimed that the contract was invalid. B, angered by A's breach of faith, refused to move out when the government came to demolish the house. Since A, the real property owner, and the town government had reached an agreement on demolition and compensation, the government could not understand why there was a delay in the project due to A's inability to get B to move out. Consequently, the town government sued A in the T District Court, seeking an order to legally demolish the expropriated house. At the same time, B sued A for breach of contract. Ultimately, these two cases were resolved through court mediation. B received 1.2 million RMB in compensation, and the contract was annulled.[40]

7.4.2 *Dispute Resolution Process and Preliminary Analysis*

In practice, it is not uncommon that the administrative power transfers the trouble to the judiciary. Speaking of this, Randall Peerenboom has noted that:

> [the] political actors may cede power to the courts as a way of diffusing responsibility. Both democratic and authoritarian regimes may find it advantageous to funnel divisive issues to the court as a way of maintaining elite level consensus, deflecting popular discontent away from the regime, and allowing disgruntled citizens a forum to blow off steam, thus maintaining legitimacy for the ruling party.[41]

However, although they have institutional connection, China's court does not like to help the government to fix the Housing Demolition and Relocation Disputes (hereinafter, the HDRD). One judge of the court told the researcher that they do not like to accept the HDRD because this dispute may transfer the conflict between the parties to the court. Another judge said, 'we do not want to be besieged by the angry people and do not want to be the scapegoat for the government who may suffer from the protest, demonstration as well as turbulence'. That means if this kind of dispute cannot be handled properly and delicately, the parties may be angry with the court rather than the government who is originally responsible for housing demolition and relocation. The residents may consider that the court is merely a partner of the government, producing some legal terminology and big words to cheat them. In this case, the residents can use some very extreme methods in taking reprisals against the court.[42] This will not only threaten the ups and downs of a court leader's official career but may also jeopardise the life safety of all judges. The Court, like any other organisation, is governed by self-

[40] The basic facts and process of this case are collected and abstracted from the mediation agreement and my interview of the judges and judicial staff with their permission.

[41] Randall Peerenboom, 'More law, less courts: legalized governance, judicialization, and dejudicialization in China' in Tom Ginsburg and Albert H. Y. Chen (eds.), *Administrative Law and Governance in Asia: Comparative Perspective* (London: Routledge, 2009), p. 187.

[42] Chenglin Liu, 'Informal rules, transaction costs, and the failure of the "takings" law in China' (2005) 29 *Hastings International and Comparative Law Review*, 1, 1–3.

interested persons. Therefore, accepting the housing demolition and relocation litigation is not a wise choice for them. Moreover, refusing to adjudicate on such cases is not without precedent. Although such a judicial interpretation is no longer valid, the Supreme People's Court did indeed permit courts to reject hearing such cases. According to the written reply (*pifu*, 批复) of SPC in 2005, it provides that:

> the People's Court shall not hear the civil litigation case between the dismantler and the dismantlees, or between the dismantlees and tenants of houses because of not reaching an agreement regarding compensation and resettlement for dismantlement. The Peoples' Court shall notify the parties that they may apply for arbitration to the relevant departments according to article 16 of the City Housing Demolition and Relocation Management Regulation.[43]

Besides, it should not be ignored that the hierarchy of the District Court is higher than the Town Government. The Town Government is actually at the township level (*xiangzhenji*, 乡镇级) in the administrative hierarchy, whereas the District Court is at the vice-county level (*fuxianji*, 副县级). The court, in this case, will suffer from little pressure if refusing the HDRD.

Thus, the court had reason to refuse the HDRD openly and legally. However, the government wanted the court to share responsibility with them due to the special and sensitive features of the housing demolition and relocation dispute. Benefiting from the inter-institutional relationship established in the daily interactions, the government thought of the possibility of moving the case to the court when they felt pressure from the HDRD.[44] Consequently, the court was motivated by the government to use its legal authority to persuade or press all the relevant parties. The

[43] See 'The Supreme People's Court's Reply about whether the people's court shall accept and hear the civil litigation between the parties who can not reach an agreement on compensation and resettlement (ineffective)'. The original text goes as follows:

> 《最高人民法院关于当事人达不成拆迁补偿安置协议就补偿安置争议提起民事诉讼人民法院应否受理问题的批复》中规定：
> 拆迁人与被拆迁人或者拆迁人、被拆迁人与房屋承租人达不成拆迁补偿安置协议，就补偿安置争议向人民法院提起民事诉讼的，人民法院不予受理，并告知当事人可以按照《城市房屋拆迁管理条例》第十六条的规定向有关部门申请裁决。

[44] Some administrative leaders are even suspended from duty because of an inappropriate settlement of a housing demolition and relocation dispute. See He Peng, 'Chinese contemporary lawmaking: reality and problems' (2014) *Social Science Research Network* 17, 17–47.

government and court worked hand in hand, as they were acquaintances who were facing the same CPC policy of social harmony and were both under political pressure to maintain the stability of the society.

7.5 Two Sides of Mediation

In this section, the bright and dark sides of mediation will be further discussed. The debate on ADR, reviewed in Chapter 5, will not be repeated here. Instead, this section will highlight some aspects of mediation based on the author's empirical study and the analysis of the two cases mentioned above.

7.5.1 The Bright Side

7.5.1.1 Expand the Capacity and Range of Case Acceptance

As was pointed out in Section 7.4.2, the court can refuse to hear housing demolition and relocation litigation. Not just because of the precedent provided by the Supreme People's Court but also in local practice, some of China's courts explicitly refuse the housing demolition and relocation litigation. For example, the People's High Court of Guangxi province listed 13 categories of cases that courts shall not accept:

> These [cases] include real estate disputes resulting from government decisions or institutional reforms, claims brought by laid-off workers resulting from corporate restructuring, and lawsuits resulting from a party's failure to implement a government decision regarding ownership or usage rights in property. Most of the categories relate to government reforms of industry, agriculture, and land; some, such as a ban on some classes of securities lawsuits, mirror decisions by the Supreme People's Court.[45]

As is commonly admitted, judicial power in China is restricted. Sometimes a restriction is due to political considerations regarding letting the court avoid interfering or reviewing the government's activities and getting rid of any kind of political embarrassment caused by a 'check and balance' situation, which happened in practice. However, the rejection is also in the court's own interests because of the sensitivity and danger of coping with this kind of dispute. But this time, the court

[45] Benjamin L. Liebman, 'China's courts: restricted reform' (2007) 21 *Columbia Journal of Asian Law* 1, 27.

accepted this HDRD. While the judicial system has previously refused to hear such cases, the Supreme People's Court has not mandated the ADR system to also decline such cases. That implies, from a particular perspective, that the court may accept the case and use an alternative approach instead of hearing the civil litigation.[46]

Actually speaking, the court can look to expand its range and capacity of case acceptance, although not through the litigation approach. This is because China, as some scholars have argued, is experiencing a high incidence of social conflicts.[47] The types of disputes are multiplying, the subjects of the disputes are diverse in nature and the demands of the disputants vary.[48] More and more cases need solutions from the courts. However, due to various reasons, 'courts increasingly deal with difficult or sensitive cases by inaction: cases are refused or left unresolved'.[49] Mediation, however, did not play its maximal role in dealing with disputants in the past decades.

It is true that '[ADR] procedures which are effective can be adopted as required, and to the extent that they need modification to make them more suitable to local conditions, they can be adjusted accordingly'.[50] Considering the flexibility provided by the ADR mechanism, a mediation platform can be created to deal with repeated or systemic disputes and can be applied to both the most mundane and the most horrific of conflicts.[51] Therefore, mediation offers a rich opportunity that has not

46 For example, Chinese court has a dispute resolution arrangement called 'pre-litigation mediation' (*suqian tiaojie*, 诉前调解), which is designed for solving the dispute before the formal trial and transferring the litigation into mediation approach. The 'pre-litigation mediation' is usually implemented by judges as well. See 'What is Mediation' on Mediation Platform of People's Court ['什么是调解'，人民法院调解平台]. https://tiaojie.court.gov.cn/mediateguide (last accessed 25 November 2023).

47 See Lianhe Hu, Angang Hu and Lei Wang, 'An empirical study on the influence of social conflict to social stability' (2007) 6 *Explore* 105 [胡联合, 胡鞍钢, 王磊: '关于我国社会不稳定因素变化态势的实证分析'，载《探索》2007年第6期], 105.] see also Jiangrong Yu, 'Social conflict in rural China' (2007) 3 *China Security* 3.

48 Shukun Zhao, *Social Conflict and Legal Control: Review the Legal Order of Social Transformational China* (Beijing: Law Press, 2008), pp. 59–66 [赵树坤：《社会冲突与法律控制：当代中国社会转型期的法律秩序检讨》，北京：法律出版社2008年版]. See also Aaron Halegua, 'Reforming the People's Mediation System in urban China' (2005) 35 *Hong Kong Law Journal* 715, 718.

49 Liebman, 'China's courts', 1, 27.

50 Henry Brown and Arthur L. Marriott, *ADR Principles and Practice* (London: Sweet & Maxwell, 1993), p. 17.

51 Andrea Kupfer Schneider, 'The intersection of dispute systems design and transitional justice' (2009) 14 *Harvard Negotiation Law Review* 289.

yet been fully exploited, especially considering its capacity to handle disputes as it did in the 1970s in China. Mediation, in this context, provides a legal and official remedy for disputants who might receive nothing from the litigation approach. Although it is not an institutional innovation and cannot solve all problems fundamentally, this pragmatic response to difficult circumstances by the court system can alleviate social conflicts and address disputes through an alternative official approach. Meanwhile, the court can expand its power and capacity by advocating for the need for effective dispute resolution. After all, dispute resolution itself is one of the most fundamental functions of courts and the legal system.[52]

7.5.1.2 Earn More Direct Support from the Government

Mediation can provide a satisfactory approach to solving disputes, both for the disputants and the state. Therefore, a court mediation approach can earn more direct support from the government.

As has been mentioned, in Chinese traditional political philosophy, a harmonious social relationship is a supreme ideology that enjoys an incomparable priority in Chinese social governance and determines the regime's legitimacy.[53] In practice, social harmony is closely related to the dispute resolution process. Because an unsuccessful dispute resolution may cause many unexpected consequences, troubles and even social unrest, it will undermine the regime's legitimacy and offend the harmonious ideology. In this context, dispute resolution in China is not only a purely legal issue. More importantly, it is a political issue.[54] As a result, 'the Chinese view of law may be so rooted in social control, that mediators may continue to effect compromises that conform to "the values embodied in state norms", rather than play a facilitative role for private economic actors'.[55]

52 Cownie et al., *English Legal System in Context*, pp. 27–30; John Hynes Farrar and Anthony M. Dugdale, *Introduction to Legal Method* (London: Sweet & Maxwell, 3rd ed., 1990), p. 6.

53 For relevant discussion, see, for example, Joshua Castellino and Elvira Domínguez Redondo, *Minority Rights in Asia: A Comparative Legal Analysis* (New York: Oxford University Press, 2006), pp. 18–22.

54 See Li Su, 'Legalism, public opinion and hard cases' (2009) 21 *Peking University Law Journal* 93, 109–110 [苏力："法条主义、民意和难办案件"载《中外法学》2009年第1期].

55 Stanley B. Lubman, 'Dispute resolution in China after Deng Xiaoping: "Mao and mediation" revisited' (1997) 11 *Columbia Journal of Asian Law* 229, 304.

However, if a dispute can be solved through the mediation approach, the dispute can be resolved privately. Social harmony can be 'silently' realised and external influence on the state power minimised. It is hard to deny that in the mediation context, 'substantive change is made under the guise of procedural change [which] is made in private and is not open to challenge or review'.[56] Due to its 'weakness', mediation can gain significant space and freedom for both the government and the disputing parties to design satisfactory dispute resolution methods. In such a situation, the dispute participants are limited, the potential external impact from the disputes is controlled, the debate does not attract public attention, the case is not reported by the mass media and the outcome does not become a national convention or standard. In other words, mediation can absorb and minimise the external impact of the dispute as much as possible, aiming to maintain social order, limit potential risks and keep 'mass incidents' under control. Therefore, the Chinese government can support mediation without any ideological obstacles or political risks. For the government, mediation is not only effective but also 'safe'.

7.5.1.3 Be Good at Solving Complex Problems

It has been argued that for a small community which lacks social mobility and mainly made up of acquaintances, the informal dispute resolution mechanism like mediation can work well.[57] But for the city, which has a cosmopolitan makeup and is full of strangers, the institutionalised and formal dispute resolution mechanism like litigation will be the dominant means to solve disputes.[58] In this regard, people will naturally prefer a lawsuit in the modern urban context. However, the reality is always more complicated than this theoretical outlook. For example, in modern China, 'many reports show that [Chinese disputants] still prefer a private settlement achieved through negotiation in civil, commercial disputes, or even when there are official laws to resolve their problem and there is no serious impediment for them to seek in recourse of law'.[59] Disputants or courts in a modern urban context may still choose mediation because they are realistic and rational about dispute resolution options and are willing to choose the most suitable

[56] Hilary Astor and Christine M. Chinkin, *Dispute Resolution in Australia* (Sydney: Butterworths, 1992), p. 18.

[57] Douglass C. North, 'Institutions' (1991) 5(1) *Journal of Economic Perspectives* 97, 99, 103.

[58] North, 'Institutions', 97, 104.

[59] Li Su, 'More on avoidance of the law' (1998) XIX *Social Sciences in China* 145, 150.

approach to resolve the issue at hand. The dichotomy between village and city and between mediation and litigation is too simplistic and overlooks the possibility of a multicentre approach to dispute resolution.

In the successive disputes mentioned above, mediation is ideal. That is true because, as much research has reinforced, mediation is a better approach when handling family-related issues.[60] More importantly, the flexibility found in the mediation mechanism can assist judges in balancing not only the interests of the relevant parties but also the conflict between state law and customary law by avoiding disputes that may not be suitable for the adjudicative track.

China is a vast country with unexpected, unbalanced regional development and diversity, and it is still in a period of social transition. For quite some time into the future, various folk customs, ethnic traditions, cultural disciplines, taboos and state law will need to coexist and even contest each other for dominant legitimacy in governing social activities. This is especially true in southwest China, where state law and local custom 'could diverge significantly, and sometimes one, sometimes the other would prevail'.[61] The complexity of the various disputes and social realities will challenge a simple and uniform dispute resolution approach. This unique situation requires a diverse and adaptable dispute resolution mechanism.

With regard to this issue, Lon L. Fuller has made a persuasive argument. By borrowing the concept of 'polycentric' from Michael Polanyi, Fuller argued that there are some cases that are inherently unsuitable for adjudication because of the complicated web of interdependent relationships existing within particular kinds of disputes. Fuller made it clear that:

> We may visualize this kind of situation by thinking of a spider web. A pull on one strand will distribute tensions of a complicated pattern

[60] See, for example, Yolanda Vorys, 'The best of both worlds: the use of med-arb for resolving will disputes' (2007) 22 *Ohio State Journal on Dispute Resolution* 871, 871–872. In many jurisdictions, family affairs are settled by a specialised legal institution like family court. For example, in Japan, due to the traditional culture and the special characteristics of family issues, the family disputes will be handled by a family court. Within this family court, there are judges and experts regarding family issues, as well as social workers. They can help the parties to calm down and solve the problem peacefully. In this process, mediation is often preferred. Family court has been deemed a spectacular success at the first generation of the Japanese judicial reform. I thank Stao Nobuyuki from Chuo University, Tokyo, for letting me know about this. For more details about the Japan Family Court system, see Hiroshi Oda, *Japanese Law* (London: Butterworths, 1992), pp. 73–75; Taimie L. Bryant, 'Family models, family dispute resolution and family law in Japan' (1995) 14(1) *UCLA Pacific Basin Law Journal* 1.

[61] William Twining, *Globalization and Legal Theory* (London: Butterworths, 2000), p. 226.

> throughout the web as a whole. Doubling the original pull, will, in all likelihood, not simply double each of the resulting tensions but will rather create a different complicated pattern of tensions. This would certainly occur, for example, if the doubled pull caused one or more of the weaker strands to snap. This is a 'polycentric' situation because it is 'many centered' – each crossing of strands is a distinct center for distributing tensions.[62]

Although Fuller did not intend to analyse the legal pluralism problem, he inspired us to see that it is extremely difficult to produce a binding judgment because '[adjudications cannot] lend themselves well to the consideration of multifaceted disputes. . .the adversary proceeding oversimplifies many conflicts, and consequently many disputes are brought to court only as one stage in their ultimate resolution'.[63] For Fuller, the traditional adjudicative judgment is not able to solve a 'many-centered' dispute.[64] This situation will encourage judges to try an unorthodox approach, such as mediation, or will push the judges to 'reformulate the problem so as to make it amenable for a solution through adjudicative procedures'.[65]

According to Randall Peerenboom, courts are not the proper venue for resolving many socially, politically and economically contentious disputes, especially in a country like China, which is so large, diverse and complex.[66] Peerenboom's argument seems to be an 'echo' of Fuller's distinction describing the 'multicentre' case in China's context. He goes on to say that:

> The main reason for limited judicialization in China is that courts are not the best forum for resolving the types of complex social, economic and political issues that arise in a lower-middle income country such as China. As in other developing countries at its level of wealth, the courts (and other institutions) are relatively weak. Moreover, many of the problems are not amenable to judicial solution – courts simply cannot come up with effective and enforceable remedies.[67]

[62] Lon L. Fuller, 'The forms and limits of adjudication' (1978) 92 *Harvard Law Review* 353, 395.

[63] Herbert Jacob, *Justice in America: Courts, Lawyers and the Judicial Process* (Boston, MA: Little, Brown, 4th ed., 1984), p. 12.

[64] Fuller, 'The Forms and Limits of Adjudication', 353, 401.

[65] Fuller, 'The Forms and Limits of Adjudication', 353, 401.

[66] Peerenboom, 'More law, less courts', 175–176.

[67] Peerenboom, 'More law, less courts', 190.

Some scholars believe that mediation is primarily used to resolve disputes within a particular community or group, and in most cases, these dispute resolutions are closely related to moral judgement. Following Fuller's argument, it is clear that the feasibility of mediation can extend beyond the community context and provide resolutions to multicentre and complex disputes involving a combination of informal and formal rules. In this context, mediation is an ideal, 'amenable' approach for solving these kinds of complicated disputes in settings with heterogeneous norms.

Beyond this, the successful court-connected ADR practice in coping with a complicated case has a constructive impact within the dispute resolution system. According to Carrie Menkel-Meadow, 'many important changes in human society have come from hard-fought conflicts that resulted in the change of human institutions, relationships or ideas'.[68] The dispute can contribute 'to the maintenance of group boundaries'[69] and help to 'maintain the total system by establishing a balance between its component parts'.[70] In other words, the experience of mediation found within complicated dispute settlements can be used as a learning and later institutionalised by the judicial authority at least regionally. Regarding this, Yu Fan suggested that one of the most important functions of ADR concerns the fact that this mechanism can accumulate the experience of dispute resolution in order to relocate a line of rights and obligation within the new-style cases under new social circumstances.[71] These experiences serve as references when restructuring the social–legal system or drafting new legislation. For China, the settlement of multicentre and complicated disputes creates a dynamic picture of the interaction between institutional arrangements and social realities. 'Thus, the search for an alternative dispute resolution process is perhaps better described as a search to more precisely locate adjudication and in particular judicial adjudication, on the continuum of dispute resolution mechanisms.'[72] Based on these experiences, judicial authorities may find a realistic and contextual rather than a theoretical and idealistic approach to making law within the realm of dispute resolution.

[68] Carrie J. Menkel-Meadow et al. (eds.), *Dispute Resolution: Beyond the Adversarial Model* (New York: Aspen Publishers, 2005), p. 7.

[69] Lewis Alfred Coser, *The Functions of Social Conflict* (New York, NY: Free Press, 1956), p. 34.

[70] Coser, *The Functions of Social Conflict*, p. 35.

[71] Yu Fan, *Textbook on Alternative Dispute Resolution* (Beijing: Renmin University Press, 2020), p. 27 [范瑜：《非诉讼程序（ADR）教程》，北京：中国人民大学出版社2020年版].

[72] D. Paul Emond, *Commercial Dispute Resolution* (Ontario: Canada Law Book, 1989), p. 4.

7.5.2 *The Dark Side*

7.5.2.1 Impairing Justice and Individual Rights

Court mediation may impair justice by giving way to bargaining in the shadow of law. This is especially true in the case where illegal facts exist unlike adjudication, which has a "'...marked orientation toward the past". They interpret and assess, in terms of legal doctrine, past actions and events, accrued entitlements, established obligations, and claims';[73] the ultimate goal of mediation is to find a compromised outcome acceptable to all parties, which will allow for the continuance of their lives tomorrow. Mediation is future-oriented:

> When people first appear in the mediator's office, all they want to do is to talk about the past...Continuing discussion about the past inevitably casts the mediator into a judge's role. Searching for solution requires a future focus because the solution lies in the future...The mediator is not interested in discussing or evaluating complaints about the past but redirects the disputants to talking about their aspiration for the future.[74]

In this regard, the right and wrong and the legal and illegal found within the past are usually facts both the disputants and the mediator should be less concerned about. After all, 'determining who was right or wrong about the past is the function of a judge, not the mediator'.[75] Mediation in this case is concerned less about the law. From the judge's perspective, however, his duty is to investigate the facts and to safeguard justice in accordance with the law of the land.[76] According to China's law, 'to strictly observe the Constitution and laws' is also provided as the legal duty of a judge.[77]

[73] Roger Cotterrell, *The Sociology of Law: An Introduction* (London: Butterworths, 2nd ed., 1992), pp. 211–212.

[74] John M. Haynes and Stephanie Charlesworth, *The Fundamentals of Family Mediation* (Sydney: The Federation Press, 1996), pp. 13–14; Stephen K. Erickson and Marilyn S. McKnight, *The Practitioner's Guide to Mediation: A Client-Centered Approach* (New York: Wiley, 2001), p. 25.

[75] Haynes and Charlesworth, *The Fundamentals of Family Mediation*, pp. 13–14.

[76] Philip Hamburger, *Law and Judicial Duty* (Cambridge, MA: Harvard University Press, 2008), p. 103.

[77] According to the *Judges Law of People's Republic of China* (amended 2019), the Article 10 also provides that (emphasis added):

> Judges shall perform the following obligations: (1) *Strictly observing* the Constitution and laws. (2) Handling cases impartially, and not bending the law for personal gains. (3) *Protecting the litigation rights* of the parties and other participants in proceedings according to the law. (4) Safeguarding the state interests and public interests, and safeguarding the lawful rights and interests of individuals and organizations. (5) Keeping state secrets and the secrets of judicial work, and keeping confidential all trade secrets and personal privacy

In the before-mentioned case regarding the house demolition and removal dispute, the lessor claimed that the contract of the house lease was invalid and contract modification was needed. Technically speaking, according to Chinese law, he could argue that the objective circumstance has significantly changed compared to the time when the original contract was signed. Based on this reason, he could require the court to modify the contract.[78] In fact, the objective situation truly changed as the lessor received more monetary compensation than the average resident. However, he could not publicly state the reason or provide relevant evidence. This is because in each house demolition and removal case, the compensation standard should be equally applicable to all relevant residents. Why did the lessor receive higher compensation? Under what circumstances did the officials agree to provide more compensation? Was there something 'fishy' going on? Was there corruption 'under the table'? Was there illegal behaviour occurring? In the court mediation process, these questions would be ignored to a certain extent in order to achieve an agreement and conclude the case as soon as possible. Therefore, the interests of the residents living in the same area may be impaired by being blinded to this bargaining process in the court mediation room, and they might receive less compensation compared to the lessor in this case. The dispute would be resolved at the expense of justice, with a tolerance for unfairness both in and out of the courtroom.

More seriously, the disregard for justice under the climate of 'mediation first' and 'social harmony' can be justified and become politically correct. Conversely, if this case were to proceed through litigation, it could cause serious, unexpected problems. For example, if the presiding

> to which they have access in performing their duties. (6) Accepting legal supervision and supervision by the masses according to the law. (7) Interpreting laws through cases, heightening the public awareness of the rule of law, and advancing the building of a society ruled by law through the handling of cases according to the law. (8) Other obligations as provided by law.

78 Similar regulations exist in both the *Judicial Interpretation of Supreme People's Court on Implementation of the Contract Law of People's Republic of China* II (ineffective) and Civil Code (2021). According to Article 533 of Civil Code (2021):

> Where the basic conditions of a contract undergoes a material change unforeseeable by the parties at the time of contracting which is not a commercial risk after the formation of the contract, rendering the continuation of the performance of the contract unconscionable for either party, the adversely affected party may renegotiate with the other party; and if the renegotiation fails within a reasonable time limit, the party may request the people's court or an arbitration institution to modify or rescind the contract. The people's court or arbitration institution shall change or rescind the contract based on the actual circumstances of the case, in accordance with the principle of fairness.

judge led the involved parties in the HDRD case to the litigation track, it would be necessary for the lessor to provide relevant evidence showing to what extent the compensation was higher than normal and whether there was a significant change in the objective situation that warranted modifying or even considering the contract as frustrated. However, the answers to these questions are inaccessible because the compensation negotiation between the lessor and the government occurred 'under the table'. More problematically, if the case proceeds to the litigation stage, that will be heard in an open trial.[79] The unequal compensation among residents thus would probably cause public anger and mass protests.[80] This resolution would be bad and frustrating; the judges thus would be labelled as 'troublemakers'.

In fact, this is a typical case in which 'the private process has a public effect'.[81] Several studies note that the mediation process may also impact the third party positively or negatively.[82] From the perspective of institutional economics, if a transaction can internalise all the costs and benefits of its activities, the government doesn't have to intervene. However, in a case in which the costs and benefits of the activity cannot be wholly internalised, the external power must become involved to cope with the portion that cannot be internalised to prevent the third party from potential interference or hurt. From a particular angle, the intervention of the public power, like the involvement of the court and judge in a particular case, aims to protect other nonparticipants not being interfered with by the external impact of the dispute. However, the court mediation implementation in this case justified the external cost of the dispute to the nonparticipants. All the other residents' interests who were living on the same road had been impaired due to the unfair compensation that the court produced.

One of the conclusions that can be drawn from the above analysis is that when encountering a dispute in which the externality stemming

[79] According to the Civil Procedural Law of the PRC (Amended 2021), Article 134 states:

> A people's court shall try civil cases openly, except those involving any state secret or individual privacy or as otherwise provided by law.

[80] Since ancient times, Chinese have hated the uneven distribution. Confucius said in the *Analects* that 'I have heard that the lord of a state or a family concerns himself not with the scarcity but rather with uneven distribution.'

[81] Andrew T. Guzman, 'Arbitrator liability: reconciling arbitration and mandatory rules' (2000) 49 *Duke Law Journal* 1279, 1284.

[82] See James A. Wall and Timothy C. Dunne, 'Mediation research: a current review' (2012) 28(2) *Negotiation Journal* 217, 233.

from the illegal behaviour exists, the function of mediation may be alienated. Mediation may be utilised to cover illegal behaviours, which may even be justified by the social harmony and stability requirements that place the target of the proceedings on pursuing the result of concluding the case. This kind of consequentialism policy may encourage a judge to achieve a resolution through whatever means he/she desires and places justice and individual rights aside.

7.5.2.2 Confusing the Role of Judges

Court mediation may confuse the role of judges. When a judge plays the role of mediator instead of investigating facts, assessing evidence and applying the law, the main concern of the judge-mediator is to achieve a mutually accepted resolution, which to some extent will shade or tolerate the illegal facts and make the judges relatively accommodating and flexible when implementing the law. Moreover, all the information obtained from the mediation process should be confidential.[83] That requires the judge to be silent on illegal issues.

In terms of the implementation of court mediation, Article 32 Section 12 of the Judges Law of the PRC (amended 2001) provides that 'no judges may meet the party concerned or his or her agent without authorization,

[83] As a commonly accepted principle, confidentiality is a very important ethical principle for the mediator profession. In the provisions governing mediation issues in different jurisdictions, they all provide that the mediator should keep confidentiality for the parties. See Dwight Golam, *Mediating Legal Disputes: Effective Strategies for Lawyers and Mediators* (Boston, MA: Aspen Law & Business, 1996), p. 401; *Australian National Mediator Standards*, see www.nswbar.asn.au/docs/professional/adr/documents/PracticeStandardsSept07.pdf (last accessed 20 June 2010); *Mediator Accreditation Scheme of Hong Kong Law Society*, see www.fjt2.net/gate/gb/www.hklawsoc.org.hk/pub_c/mas/guidelines_ethical.asp? (last accessed 20 June 2010); *Model Standards of Conduct for Mediators* set by American Bar Association, American Arbitration Association, Association for Conflict Resolution, see www.abanet.org/dispute/news/ModelStandardsofConductforMediatorsfinal05.pdf (last accessed 27 November 2010). In Chinese mediation law, there is a simple regulation providing the confidentiality issues of the dispute resolution process. Article 12 of 'Several Opinions of the Supreme People's Court on Further Displaying the Positive Roles of Litigation Mediation in the Building of a Socialist Harmonious Society (2007)' states that 'the judge responsible for handling the case and the relevant organization and other personnel participating in the mediation shall strictly keep the mediation information secret, if any party requires not to disclose the content of the mediation agreement, the people's court shall permit it'. This regulation is usually overlooked by the legal profession and scholar by saying there is no regulation on confidential issues of mediation in China. However, it should be admitted that besides this, there is no regulation governing the confidentiality in China's mediation law.

or attend dinners, or accept presents given by the party concerned or his or her agent'. However, in order to arrange a person-to-person communication, the private session is a very practicable and commonly used method in mediation. Such communication would allow the mediator to meet the party privately.[84] This will cause confusion of a judge's identity when playing the role of a judge-mediator.

Besides, under current policy, the interest of a judge is closely related to a successful mediation, which generates a possibility that the judge may render an unfavourable decision to the uncooperative party in the court mediation stage. In this case, the parties may be subject to significant coercion and find mediation in practice to be a mandatory rather than a consensual process.[85] So, it is true in some cases that:

> in order to distract the plaintiff's attention from the essential points in the dispute (particularly effective in the Basic Level People's Courts where the Parties are less likely to be legally represented); 'encouraging mediation by applying pressure' (yiya cutiao: 以压促调); and 'using inducements in order to promote mediation' (yiyou cutiao, 以诱促调); and 'procrastination in order to compel mediation' (yituo yatiao: 以托压调).[86]

Consequently, the parties' voluntariness in the mediation process is more or less limited. This limitation arises because during the mediation, parties may feel pressured to agree to terms due to the influence of the judge. Furthermore, this dynamic can impair the judge's impartiality when adjudicating a case after an unsuccessful mediation. The judge, having been exposed to the personal perspectives and detailed information of the parties during the mediation, may find it challenging to remain unbiased. The judge's previous exposure to the arguments, emotions and possibly confidential information shared during mediation can inadvertently influence their judgment in subsequent legal proceedings. This situation underscores the potential conflict between the roles of

[84] The private session is also admitted by The UNCITRAL Model Law on International Commercial Conciliation (2002), which states that 'The conciliator may meet or communicate with the parties together or with each of them separately'. See also Nadja M. Alexander, *International and Comparative Mediation: Legal Perspective* (Deventer: Wolters Kluwer, 2009), p. 508.

[85] Michael Palmer, 'Compromising courts and harmonizing ideologies: mediation in the administrative chambers of the People's Courts in the People's Republic of China' in Andrew Harding and Penelope (Pip) Nicholson (eds.), *New Courts in Asia* (New York: Routledge, 2010), p. 266.

[86] Palmer, 'Compromising courts and harmonizing ideologies', 266.

mediator and adjudicator, especially in a legal environment where mediation is strongly encouraged.[87]

7.6 Conclusion

Even in T District, one of the most developed regions in southwest China, the heterogeneity of society and the diversity of social values still exist. Values of urban citizens, rural villagers and ethnic minorities' customs all coexist and social transformation is still on the way. These realities generate a hard case when legal pluralism and multi-centered issues are involved, which make the application of highly uniform norms difficult and calls for a nuanced and flexible dispute resolution design. Indeed, cases that involve conflicting fundamental policy goals are difficult for the court. The litigation approach will be met with resistance, no matter how such cases are decided, and the enforcement of this kind of judgment is extremely difficult if not impossible.[88]

Therefore, from a pragmatic perspective, mediation expands the court's capacity regarding accepting and hearing cases, gains more support from the government and is suitable for southwest China concerning the social complexity in a transitional era in which both informal and formal rules coexist. In this regard, mediation is feasible in the investigated southwest urban context, as it can provide public good regarding an official remedy and a flexible dispute resolution service for the disputants.

However, if only pursuing the pragmatic goals regarding the high rate of mediation, the rights protection of the parties and the role of the judge may be overlooked. The closed nature (confidentiality) of the mediation process also makes it difficult to uncover such issues. Based on the policy of 'substantive dispute resolution', the judge may abuse mediation in unsuitable cases and disregard the justice he should have safeguarded.

Actually, mediation cannot solve all the social conflicts. The nature of disputing parties, the mediator involved and the specific conflict management context will influence the effectiveness and feasibility of the application of mediation. As to this, the SPC has clearly known the potential risk of the inappropriate implementation of mediation. Notice (2010), Article 17 of Notice (2010), for example, provides that

> as for cases involving *national interests or social public interests, having guiding significance on the application of law, or having positive meaning*

[87] Peerenboom, 'More law, less courts', 187.
[88] Peerenboom, 'More law, less courts', 187.

> *on the formation of the awareness of social rules*, we shall attach importance to making a timely judgment and closing the case according to law, give full play to the positive role of judgment in making a clear distinction between right and wrong, regularizing behaviors, punishing the evil and encouraging the good (emphasis added).

Nevertheless, if the substantive resolution of disputes is paramount at the policy level, the local judges tend to overlook or downplay this guideline while implementing mediation in practice. Therefore, the primary objective of China's mediation law is to guarantee that inappropriate cases are not subjected to mediation within the court.

A practical and feasible amendment should start by re-clarifying the bottom line and the limitation of the implementation of mediation. All ill-suited types of disputes that have been mentioned in the SPC's judicial interpretations should be clearly and straightforwardly excluded from court mediation practice. This is not a new regulation, but sticks to the old rules, like the list of mediation unsuitable cases, from the SPC. This can also avoid the unduly high rate of mediation by funnelling the litigation-suitable case to the litigation approach.

Besides, although many southwest grassroots courts cannot do so for several reasons, it should be kept in mind that when conditions allow, people's mediators or different judges should be encouraged to get involved in the pre-court dispute resolution procedure during the current court mediation stage instead of the same judge acting as a mediator. After mediation is exhausted, litigation can follow. At this stage, a different judge conducts adjudication. These amendments can avoid the confusing situation caused by the same judge playing the role of a mediator and help people's mediators improve their professional competence by learning from judges and court practice.

Finally, the judicial policy that emphasises social harmony and the substantive resolution of disputes will somehow enhance cooperation between the government and the courts. After all, the dispute-resolution-oriented approach presented by mediation is isomorphic with the social stability ideology presented by the government, which allows external political and social reasons to influence the disposition of the disputing matters.[89]

[89] Lubman, 'Dispute Resolution in China after Deng Xiaoping', 343.

Appendix I: Glossary of Chinese Terms

A

Acquaintance society
shuren shehui, 熟人社会
Addressing the root cause, emphasising mediation, and focusing on grassroots efforts
zhuayuantou, zhuatiaojie, zhuajiceng, 抓源头、抓调解、抓基层
Adjudicate
caipan, 裁判
Adjudicator
caipanzhe, 裁判者
Administrative Regulation
xingzheng fagui, 行政法规
ADR (alternative dispute resolution)
tidaixing jiufen jiejuefangshi, 替代性纠纷解决
Articles of Association for Trial Offices at All Levels
geshenpantin shiban zhangcheng, 《各级审判厅试办章程》

B

Basic People's Court
Jiceng renmin fayuan, 基层人民法院
Beijing International Arbitration Center
Beijing guoji zhongcaizhongxin, 北京国际仲裁中心
Big mediation
da tiaojie, 大调解
Business secret
shangye mimi, 商业秘密

C

Civil actions
minshi susong, 民事诉讼

Civil Code of the People's Republic of China
zhonghua renmin gongheguo minfadian, 《中华人民共和国民法典》
Civil Law System
dalu faxi, 大陆法系
Civil Procedure Law of the People's Republic of China
zhonghua renmin gongheguo minshi susongfa, 《中华人民共和国民事诉讼法》
Circuit Tribunal
xunhuifating, 巡回法庭
Common Law
putong fa, 普通法
Company Law
gongsifa, 公司法
Comprehensive Management Office
zonghe zhili bangongshi, 综合治理办公室
Constitution of the People's Republic of China
zhonghua renmin gongheguo xianfa, 《中华人民共和国宪法》
County government
xian zhengfu, 县政府
Conciliation statements
tiaojieshu, 调解书
Critiques and judgment
pingl, 评理
Criminal Law
xingfa, 刑法

D

Decision
jueding, 决定
Detached tribunals
paichu fating, 派出法庭
Development of policies should adapt to the development of the time
yu shi ju jin, 与时俱进
Dispute resolution process
zhengyi jiejue guocheng, 争议解决过程

F

Face
mianzi, 面子
Fengqiao experience
fengqiao jingyan, 枫桥经验

G

Giving compensation according to the resolved cases
yi'an dingbu, 以案定补
Grassroots court judges
jiceng fayuan, 基层法官
Grassroots legal service worker
jiceng falv fuwu gongzuozhe, 基层法律服务工作者
Grid management system
wanggehua guanli, 网格化管理
Guiding case
zhidaoxing anli, 指导性案例

H

Harmonious society
hexie shehui, 和谐社会
Hearing
shenli, 审理
High People's Court
gaoji renmin fayuan, 高级人民法院

I

Intermediate People's Court
zhongji renmin fayuan, 中级人民法院
Interpretation
jieshi, 解释
Interpretation of the Supreme People's Court concerning the Civil Procedure Law of the People's Republic of China
zuigao renmin fayuan guanyu shiyong zhonghua renmin gongheguo minshi susongfa de sifajieshi, 最高人民法院关于适用《中华人民共和国民事诉讼法》的解释

J

Judge
faguan, 法官
Judgment
panjue, 判决
Judicial Administrative Organ
sifa xingzheng jiguan, 司法行政机关
Judicial documents
sifa wenshu, 司法文书
Judicial fairness
sifa gongzheng, 司法公正

Judicial interpretations
sifa jieshi, 司法解释
Judicial openness
sifa gongkai, 司法公开
Judicial power
sifa quan, 司法权
Judicial reform
sifa gaige, 司法改革

L

Leading Group of Comprehensively Deepening Reform of CPC
zhongyang quanmian shenhua gaige lingdao xiaozu, 中央全面深化改革领导小组
Learning from the West and applying it to the East
xixue dongjian, 西学东渐
Legal Database Beida Fabao
beidafabao, 北大法宝
Legislative Law of People's Republic of China
zhonghua renmin gongheguo lifa fa, 《中华人民共和国立法法》
Liberated areas
jiefangqu, 解放区
Litigation
susong, 诉讼
Litigation fee
susong fei, 诉讼费

M

Ma Xiwu Adjudicating Style
maxiwu shenpan fangshi, 马锡武审判方式
Maintain the Authority of the Constitution and Law
weihu xianfa yu falv de quanwei, 维护宪法与法律的权威
Mediation
tiaojie, 调解
Mediation agreement
tiaojiexieyi, 调解协议
Mediation is the priority; mediation and trial should be synthetically applied; when the case is closed, the dispute should be over
tiaojie youxian, tiaopanjiehe, anjieshiliao, 调解优先, 调判结合, 案结事了
Ministry of Justice
sifabu, 司法部
Minzu
民族

N

National People's Congress
quanguo renmin daibiao dahui, 全国人民代表大会
Neighborhood Committee
jumin weiyuanhui, 居民委员会
Normative legal document
guifanxing falvwenjian, 规范性法律文件
Notices (circulars) and conference summaries
tongzhi he huiyijiyao, 通知和会议纪要

O

Official opinions and explanations
guanfang yijian he jieshi, 官方意见和解释
Organic Law of the People's Courts of the People's Republic of China
zhonghua renmin gongheguo fayuan zuzhifa, 《中华人民共和国人民法院组织法》

P

Peace of heart and a clear conscience
xin'an lide, 心安理得
People's Procuratorate
renmin jianchayuan, 人民检察院
Personal privacy
geren yinsi, 个人隐私
Personal relationship
renshen guanxi, 人身关系
Pluralist dispute resolution mechanism
duoyuanhua jiufenjiejue jizhi, 多元化纠纷解决机制
Political–legal structure
zhengfa tizhi, 政法体制
Practicing lawyer
zhiye lvshi, 执业律师
Procedural law
chengxu fa, 程序法
Prohibitive provision
jinzhixingguiding, 禁止性规定
Provisions of the Supreme People's Court on the Work Concerning Judicial Interpretation
zuigao renmin fayuan guanyu sifa jieshi de guiding, 最高人民法院关于司法解释工作的规定
Public order and morals
shehui gongxu liangsu, 社会公序良俗

R

Red Head Document
hongtou wenjian, 红头文件
Regional Ethnic Autonomy System
minzu quyuzizhi zhidu, 民族区域自治制度
Reply
pifu, 批复
Revocation
chexiao, 撤销
Rule of law
yifa zhiguo, 依法治国[1]
Ruling
caiding, 裁定

S

Self-government System of People at the Grassroots Level
jiceng qunzhongzizhi zhidu, 基层群众自治制度
Sending law to the countryside
Songfa xiaxiang, 送法下乡
Several Provisions of the Supreme People's Court on Evidence in Civil Procedures
zuigao renmin fayuan guanyu minshizhengju de ruogan guiding,《最高人民法院关于民事诉讼证据的若干规定》
Small problems do not leave the village, large problems do not leave the township, and conflicts are not passed up to the higher authorities
xiaoshi buchucun, dashi buchuxiang (zhen), maodun bushangjiao, 小事不出村、大事不出乡（镇）、矛盾不上交
Standing Committee of the National People's Congress
quanguo renmin daibiao dahui changwu weiyuanhui, 全国人民代表大会常务委员会
State and public interests
guojia he gonggong liyi, 国家和公共利益
State Council
guowuyuan, 国务院
Stipulate
guiding, 规定
Supreme People's Court
zuigao renmin fayuan, 最高人民法院
Supreme People's Procuratorate
zuigao renmin jianchayuan, 最高人民检察院

[1] 依法治国 is also translated into 'Ruling the State according to Laws'.

T

Ten miles have different customs, and a hundred miles have different habits
shili butongfeng, baili butongsu, 十里不同风, 百里不同俗
The Emperor's Authority Does Not Extend to the County Level
huangquan buxiaxian, 皇权不下县
Town Government
zhen zhengfu, 镇政府
Township Government
xiang, 乡

REFERENCES

English Reference

1 Books, Chapters and Articles

Abel, Richard L., 'Lawyers and legal services' in Peter Cane and Mark Tushnet (eds.), *The Oxford Handbook of Legal Studies* (Oxford: Oxford University Press, 2003).

Adams, John, *Diary and Autobiography of John Adams*, L. H. Butterfield, Leonard C. Faber and Wendell D. Garrett (eds.) (Cambridge, MA: Belknap Press of Harvard University Press, 1961).

Alexander, Nadja M., *International and Comparative Mediation: Legal Perspective* (Deventer: Wolters Kluwer, 2009).

Alford, William P., 'On the limits of "grand theory" in comparative law' (1986) 61 *Washington Law Review* 945.

'Law, law, what law? Why Western scholars of China have not had more to say about its law' in Karen G. Turner et al. (eds.), *The Limits of the Rule of Law in China* (Seattle: University of Washington Press, 2000).

Anderson, Dorcas Quek, 'Facilitative versus evaluative mediation: is there necessarily a dichotomy?' (2013) *Asian Journal on Mediation* 66.

'The evolving concept of access to justice in Singapore's mediation movement' (2020) 16 *International Journal of Law in Context* 128.

An-Na'im, Abdullahi Ahmed, 'Problems of universal cultural legitimacy for human rights' in Abdullahi Ahmed An-Na'im and Francis M. Deng (eds.), *Human Rights in Africa: Cross-Cultural Perspectives* (Washington, D.C.: The Brookings Institution, 1990).

Astor, Hilary and Chinkin, Christine M., *Dispute Resolution in Australia* (Sydney: Butterworths, 1992).

Auerbach, Jerold S., *Justice Without Law: Resolving Dispute Without Lawyers* (Oxford: Oxford University Press, 1983).

Baldwin, John and Davis, Dwynn, 'Empirical research in law' in Peter Cane and Mark Tushnet (eds.), *The Oxford Handbook of Legal Studies* (Oxford: University of Oxford, 2003).

Bao, Leiping, et al., *Deep Modernization: Value Conflict and Identity of 'Post-80s' and 'Post-90s' Groups* (Shanghai: Shanghai Academy of Social Sciences Press, 2020) [包蕾萍、等：《深度现代化："80后""90后"群体的价值冲突与认同》，上海：上海社会科学学院出版社2020年版].

Barrett, Jerome T., *A History of Alternative Dispute Resolution: The Story of a Political, Cultural, and Social Movement* (San Francisco, CA: Jossey-Bass, 2004).

Barrett, William, *Irrational Man: A Study in Existential Philosophy* (New York: Doubleday Anchor Books, 1962).

Barton, Thomas D., 'The modes and tenses of legal problem solving, and what to do about them in legal education' (2007) 43(2) *California Western Law Reviews* 389.

Bays, Daniel, 'American public discourse on church in China' (2009) 2 *The China Review* 1.

Bell, John, 'Legal education' in Peter Cane and Mark Tushnet (eds.), *The Oxford Handbook of Legal Studies* (Oxford: Oxford University Press, 2003).

Biden, Joseph R., 'Equality, accessible, affordable justice under law: the Civil Justice Reform Act of 1990' (1992) 1 *Cornell Journal of Law and Public Policy* 1.

Bix, Brian H., 'Law as an autonomous discipline' in Peter Cane and Mark Tushnet (eds.), *The Oxford Handbook of Legal Studies* (Oxford: Oxford University Press, 2003).

Boulle, Laurence, *Mediation: Principles Process Practice* (Chatswood: LexisNexis UK, 2005).

Bradney, A. G. D., 'University legal education in the twenty-first century' in John P. Grant, R. Jagtenberg and K. J. Nijkerk (eds.), *Legal Education 2000* (Aldershot: Avebury, 1988).

Brown, A. R. Radcliffe, 'On social structure' in Henrietta L. Moore and Todd Sanders (eds.), *Anthropology in Theory: Issues in Epistemology* (Malden, MA: Blackwell, 2006).

Brown, Henry and Marriott, Arthur L., *ADR Principles and Practice* (London: Sweet & Maxwell, 1993).

Brunet, Edward J. and Craver, Charles B., *Alternative Dispute Resolution: The Advocate's Perspective* (Newark, NJ: Lexis Nexis, 2nd ed., 2001).

Bryant, Taimie L., 'Family models, family dispute resolution and family law in Japan' (1995) 14(1) *UCLA Pacific Basin Law Journal* 1.

Burger, Warren R., 'Agenda for 2000 A.D. – a need for systematic anticipation' (1976) 15 *The Judge's Journal* 2.

Bush, Robert A. Baruch, '"What do we need a mediator for?": Mediation's "value-added" for negotiators' (1996) 12 *Ohio State Journal on Dispute Resolution* 1.

Bush, Robert A. Baruch and Folger, Joseph P., *The Promise of Mediation: Responding to Conflict Through Empowerment and Recognition* (San Francisco, CA: Jossey-Bass, 1994).

Carnevale, Peter J. D. and Pegnetter, Richard, 'The selection of mediation tactics in public sector disputes: a contingency analysis' (1985) 41 *Journal of Social Issues* 65.

Castellino, Joshua and Redondo, Elvira Domínguez, *Minority Rights in Asia: A Comparative Legal Analysis* (New York: Oxford University Press, 2006).

Chan, Kim-Kwong, 'Religion in China in the twenty-first century: some scenarios' (2005) 33 *Religion, State & Society* 87.

Chang, Pao-Min, 'Chinese perspectives on nation, state and the world' (2001) 5(1) *World Affairs: The Journal of International Issues* 102.

Chang, Won Ho, *Mass Media in China: The History and the Future* (Ames, IA: Iowa State University Press, 1989).

Chang, Yi (ed.), *Civil Procedure Law* (Beijing: China University of Political Science of Law Press, 2016) [常怡主编：《民事诉讼法学》，北京：中国政法大学出版社2016年版].

Chen, Albert H. Y., 'Mediation, litigation and justice: Confucian reflections in modern liberal society' in Daniel A. Bell and Hahm Chaibong (eds.), *Confucianism for the Modern World* (Cambridge: Cambridge University Press, 2003).

An Introduction to the Legal System of the People's Republic of China (Hong Kong: Lexis/Nexis, 5th ed., 2018).

Chen, Feiwen, Qiongyu, Wang and Yaqi, Zheng, 'Analysis of the judicial review system of China: from the perspective of relationship between judicial review power and legal application' (2017) 1 *Judicial Practice* 59 [陈霏雯、王琼瑜、郑雅琪："司法审查权与法律适用权的关系浅析我国司法审查体制的问题"，载《司法实践》2017年第1期].

Chen, Guo-Ming and Starosta, William J., 'Chinese conflict management and resolution: overview and implications' (1997–1998) 7 *Intercultural Communication Studies* 1.

Chen, Jianfu, *From Administrative Authorization to Private Law: A Comparative Perspective of the Developing Civil Law in the People's Republic of China* (Netherlands: Martinus Nijhoff Publishers, 1995).

Chen, Meng, 'Commercial mediation in Mainland China: pitfalls & opportunities' (2023) 23 *Pepperdine Dispute Resolution Law Journal* 167.

Chen, Minjia and Zheng, Yongnian, 'China's regional disparity and its policy response' (2008) 16(4) *China & World Economy* 16.

Chen, Phillip M., *Law and Justice: The Legal System in China 2400 B.C. to 1960 A.D.* (Princeton, NJ: Dunellen Pub., 1973).

Chornenki, Genevieve A. and Hart, Christine E., *Bypass Court: A Dispute Resolution Handbook* (Toronto, ON: LexisNexis, 2011).

Chow, Irene Hau-siu Chow and Ding, Daniel Z. Q., 'Moral judgement and conflict handling styles among Chinese in Hong Kong and PRC' (2002) 21(9) *Journal of Management Development* 666.

Chu, Godwin C. and Ju, Yanan, *The Great Wall in Ruins: Communication and Cultural Change in China* (Albany, NY: State University of New York Press, 1993).

Clark, David S., Civil litigation, access to justice, and social change: research issues in longitudinal court studies' (1988) 12 *Southern Illinois University Law Journal* 713.

Clark, Gerard J., 'An introduction to the legal profession in China in the year 2008' (2008) XLI *Suffolk University Law Review* 833.

Clarke, Donald C., 'Dispute resolution in China' (1991) 5 *Journal of Chinese Law* 245.

'Empirical research into the Chinese judicial system' in Erik G. Jensen and Thomas C. Heller (eds.), *Beyond Common Knowledge: Empirical Approaches to the Rule of Law* (Stanford, CA: Stanford University Press, 2003).

Cohen, Jean-Pierre and Jacobs, Marc, *Negotiate Like a Local*, Wang Kaihua (trans.) (Shanghai: Fudan University Press, 2019) [[比]让-皮埃尔·科恩、[比]马克·雅各布斯：《跨国谈判本土化战略》，王凯华译，上海：复旦大学出版社2019年版].

Cohen, Jerome Alan, 'Chinese mediation on the eve of modernization' (1966) 54(3) *California Law Review* 1201.

'On the Three Supremes', 23 October 2008, http://blogs.law.harvard.edu/guorui/2008/10/23/jerome-cohen-on-the-three-supremes/ (last accessed 31 May 2025).

'Settling international business disputes with China: then and now' (2014) 47 *Cornell International Law Journal* 555.

Comaroff, John L. and Roberts, Simon, *Rules and Processes: The Cultural Logic of Dispute in an African Context* (Chicago, IL: The University of Chicago Press, 1981).

Confucius, *Confucian Analects, Great Learning and the Doctrine of the Mean*, James Legge (trans.) (New York: Cosimo Inc., 2009).

Cong, Xiaoping, '"Ma Xiwu's way of judging": villages, the masses and legal construction in revolutionary China in the 1940s' (2014) 72(1) *The China Journal* 29.

Conway, Heather et al., *The Emotional Dynamics of Law and Legal Discourse* (Oxford, UK: Hart Publishing, 2016).

Cooley, John W., *The Mediator's Handbook: Advanced Practice Guide for Civil Litigation* (Louisville, CO: National Institute for Trial Advocacy, 2nd ed., 2006).

Coombe, Rosemary, 'Is there a cultural studies of law?' in Toby Miller (ed.), *A Companion to Cultural Studies* (Hoboken, NJ: Wiley Blackwell, 2001).

Cooper, Eugene, 'Chinese table manners: you are how you eat' (1986) 45(2) *Human Organization* 179.

Corbin, Arthur L., 'Legal analysis and terminology' (1919) 29(2) *The Yale Law Journal* 163.

Coser, Lewis Alfred, *The Functions of Social Conflict* (New York: Free Press, 1956).

Cotterrell, Roger, *The Sociology of Law: An Introduction* (London: Butterworths, 2nd ed., 1992).

Coughlin, Richard M., *Morality, Rationality and Efficiency: New Perspective on Socio-Economics* (Armonk, NY: M. E. Sharpe, 1991).

Cowan, Jane K., Dembour, Marie-Bénédicte and Wilson, Richard A. (eds.), *Culture and Rights: Anthropological Perspective* (Cambridge: Cambridge University Press, 2001).

Cownie, Fiona, *Legal Academics: Culture and Identities* (Oxford: Hart, 2004).

Cownie, Fiona et al., *English Legal System in Context* (London: LexisNexis UK, 3rd ed., 2003).

Cox, Lawrence, 'Freedom of Religion in China: religious, economic and social disenfranchisement for China's Internal Migrant Workers' (2007) 8 *Asian-Pacific Law & Policy Journal* 370.

Dahrendorf, Ralf, 'A confusion of power: politics and the rule of law' (1977) 40 *Modern Law Review* 1.

Dainow, Joseph, 'The civil law and common law: some points of comparison' (1966–1967) 15 *American Journal of Comparative Law* 419.

Dannemann, Gerhard, 'Comparative law: study of similarities or differences?' in Mathias Reimann and Reinhard Zimmermann (eds.), *The Oxford Handbook of Comparative Law* (Cambridge: Cambridge University Press, 2006).

De Cruz, Peter, *Comparative Law in a Changing World* (London: Cavendish, 2nd ed., 1999).

Deflem, Mathieu, *Sociology of Law: Visions of a Scholarly Tradition* (Cambridge: Cambridge University Press, 2008).

Deng, Zhenglai, *The Thoughts on the Social Sciences of China* (Shanghai: Sanlian, 2000) [邓正来：《关于中国社会科学的思考》，上海：三联出版社2000年版].

'Criticism on the urbanized trend of Chinese law research' (2006) 1(4) *Frontiers of Law in China* 514.

Where Does Chinese Legal Study Go: An Outline for Building the Ideal Image of Chinese Law (Beijing: Commercial Press Ltd, 2006) [邓正来：《中国法学向何处去：构建"中国法律理想图景"时代的论纲》，北京：商务印书馆2006年版].

Deutsch, Morton, 'Cooperation and competition' in Morton Deutsch and Peter T. Coleman (eds.), *The Handbook of Conflict Resolution: Theory and Practice* (San Francisco, CA: Jossey-Bass Publishers, 2000).

Dilliard, Irving (collected), *The Spirit of Liberty: Papers and Address* (New York: Vintage Books, 1959).

Ding, Daniel Z., 'Exploring Chinese conflict management styles in joint ventures in the People's Republic of China' (1996) 19(9) *Management Research News* 43.

Dobbins, W. Lee, 'The debate over mediator qualifications: can they satisfy the growing need to measure competence without barring entry into the market' (1995–1995) 7 *University of Florida Journal of Law and Public Policy* 95.

Donovan, James M. and Anderson, H. Edwin, III, *Anthropology & Law* (New York: Berhahn Books, 2003).

Druckman, Daniel and Diehl, Paul F., *Conflict Resolution* (Thousand Oaks, CA: SAGE, 2006).

Dunn, Susan (ed.), *Something That Will Surprise the World: The Essential Writings of the Founding Fathers* (New York: Basic Books, 2006).

Dunning, John H. and Kim, Changsu, 'The cultural roots of guanxi: an exploratory study' (2007) 30(2) *World Economy* 329.

Durkheim, Emile, *The Division of Labour in Society* (London: Macmillan, 1984).

Ehrlich, Eugen, *Fundamental Principles of the Sociology of Law* (New York: Arno Press, 1975).

Emond, D. Paul, *Commercial Dispute Resolution* (Ontario: Canada Law Book, 1989).

Erickson, Stephen K. and McKnight, Marilyn S., *The Practitioner's Guide to Mediation: A Client-Centered Approach* (Hoboken, NJ: Wiley, 2001).

Erie, Matthew, 'The new legal hubs: the emergent landscape of international commercial dispute resolution' (2020) 60(2) *Virginia Journal of International Law* 225.

Fan, Yu, 'Comment on the People's Mediation Law of the People's Republic of China' (2011) 2 *The Jurist* 1 [范愉"《中华人民共和国人民调解法》评析"，载《法学家》2011年第2期].

Textbook on Alternative Dispute Resolution (Beijing: Renmin University Press, 2020) [范愉：《非诉讼程序（ADR）教程》，北京：人民大学出版社2020年版].

Fan, Zhong Xin and Ye, Feng, 'The legal modernization of China and the influence from civil law system' (2003) 1 *Journal of Henan Administrative Institution of Politics and Law* 39 [范忠信，叶峰："中国法律近现代化与大陆法系的影响"，《河南省政法管理干部学院学报》，2003年第1期].

Fang, Jingang, 'China's change from the improvement of mediation process' (Conference Paper, 2009).

Farrar, John Hynes and Dugdale, Anthony M., *Introduction to Legal Method* (London: Sweet & Maxwell, 3rd ed., 1990).

Fei, Xiaotong, *From the Soil: The Foundations of Chinese Society*, Gary G. Hamilton and Zheng Wang (eds.), (Berkeley, CA: University of California Press, 1992).

Feng, Youlan, *Preface of Sangsongtang* (Zhengzhou: Henan People's Press, 2001) [冯友兰：《三松堂自序》，郑州：河南人民出版社2001年版].

Ferejohn, John, 'Independent judges, dependent judiciary: explaining judicial independence' (1999) 72 *Southern California Law Review* 353.

Fiadjoe, Albert K., *Alternative Dispute Resolution: A Developing World Perspective* (London: Cavendish, 2004).

Finder, Susan, 'The Supreme People's Court of the People's Republic of China' (1993) 7 *Journal of Chinese Law* 145.

Findlay, Mark, '"Independence" and the judiciary in the PRC: expectation for constitutional legality in China' in Kanishka Jayasuriya (ed.), *Law, Capitalism and Power in Asia: The Rule of Law and Institutions* (London: Routledge, 1999).

Fisher, Roger et al., *Getting to Yes: Negotiating Agreement Without Giving In* (New York: Penguin Books, 2011).

Forester, John, *Dealing with Differences: Dramas of Mediating Public Disputes* (Oxford: Oxford University Press, 2009).

Friedman, Barry, 'History, politics, and judicial independence' in András Sajó (ed.), *Judicial Integrity* (Leiden: M. Nijhoff, 2004).

Fu, Hualing, 'Understanding people's Mediation in post-Mao China' (1992) 6 *Journal of Chinese Law* 211.

Fu, Hualing and Palmer, Michael, *Mediation in Contemporary China: Continuity and Change* (London: Wildy, Simmonds & Hill Publishing, 2017).

Fu, Yulin and Peerenboom, Randall, 'A new analytic framework of understanding and promoting judicial independence of China' in Randall Peerenboom (ed.), *Judicial Independence in China: Lessons for Global Rule of Law Promotion* (Cambridge: Cambridge University Press, 2010).

Fuller, Lon L., 'The forms and limits of adjudication' (1978) 92 *Harvard Law Review* 353.

Fung, Yulan, *A Short History of Chinese Philosophy* (New York: The Macmillan Company, 1948).

Galanter, Marc, 'Reading the landscape of disputes: what we know and don't know (and think we know) about our allegedly contentious and litigious society' (1983) 31 *UCLA Law Review* 4.

'"... A settlement judge, not a trial judge": judicial mediation in the United States' (1985) 12(1) *Journal of Law and Society* 1, 13 (emphasis added by the author).

Gan, Yang, *Three Traditions* (Beijing: Sanlian Press, 2007) [甘阳：《通三统》，北京：三联出版社，2007年版].

Gao, Su, 'Comparative discourse analysis between English and Chinese news tests: by using functional grammar to analyze the textile dispute report in People's Daily and New York Times' (2007) 3(4) *Canadian Social Science* 68.

Garner, Bryan A. et al., *Black's Law Dictionary* (London: Thomson West, 10th ed., 2014).

Ge, Daoshun, 'Society: justice, inclusiveness, safety and harmony' in Yingqiu Liu et al. (eds.), *The Chinese Dream and Zhejiang's Practice – General Report Volume* (Singapore: Springer, 2019).

Geertz, Clifford, *Agricultural Involution: The Process of Ecological Change in Indonesia* (Berkeley, CA.: University of California Press, 1963).

The Interpretation of Cultures (New York: Basic Books, 1973).

'Thick description: toward an interpretive theory of culture' in Clifford Geertz (ed.), *The Interpretation of Cultures* (New York: Basic Books, 1973).

Gibbons, John, 'Language and the law' (1999) 19 *Annual Review of Applied Linguistics* 156.

Giddens, Anthony, *Sociology* (Cambridge: Polity Press, 5th ed., 2006).

Goh, Bee Chen, *Law Without Lawyers, Justice Without Courts – On Traditional Chinese Mediation* (Farnham: Ashgate Publishing, 2002).

Golam, Dwight, *Mediating Legal Disputes: Effective Strategies for Lawyers and Mediators* (Boston, MA: Aspen Law & Business, 1996).

Goldenweiser, Alexander, 'Loose ends of a theory on the individual pattern and involution in primitive society' in Robert H. Lowie (ed.), *Essays in Anthropology: Presented to A. L. Kroeber in Celebration of His Sixtieth Birthday, June 11, 1936* (Berkeley, CA: University of California Press, 1936).

Gong, Xuezeng, 'Survey of Marxist perspectives on religion in new China' in Lü Daji and Gong Xuezeng (eds.), *Marxism and Religion*, Chi Zhen (trans.) (Leiden: Brill, 2014).

Goodman, David S. G., *Deng Xiaoping and the Chinese Revolution: A Political Biography* (London: Routledge, 1994).

Green, Eric D., 'Mega-disputes and class actions' in Dwight Golann (ed.), *Mediating Legal Disputes: Effective Strategies for Neutrals and Advocates* (Chicago, IL: ABA Section of Dispute Resolution, 2009).

Greenberg, Myron S. and Blazina, Megan A., 'What mediators need to know about class actions: a basic primer' (2004) 27 *Hamline Law Review* 191.

GT Staff Reporters, 'China likely to be No.1 economy by 2035 with continuous momentum: international think tank', *Global Times*, 5 May 2024, www.globaltimes.cn/page/202403/1309857.shtml (last accessed 28 May 2025).

Gu, Weixia, *Dispute Resolution in China: Litigation, Arbitration, Mediation and Their Interactions* (London: Routledge, 2021).

Guo, Jian, *History of Legal Thoughts in China.* (Shanghai: Fudan University Press, 2016) [郭建：《中国法律思想史》，上海：复旦大学出版社2016年版].

Guzman, Andrew T., 'Arbitrator liability: reconciling arbitration and mandatory rules' (2000) 49 *Duke Law Journal* 1279.

Halegua, Aaron, 'Reforming the People's Mediation System in urban China' (2005) 35 *Hong Kong Law Journal* 715.

Hamburger, Philip, *Law and Judicial Duty* (Cambridge, MA: Harvard University Press, 2008).

Hamilton, Gary G., 'Patterns of Asian capitalism: the cases of Taiwan and South Korea' in Mark Fruin (ed.), *Networks, Markets and the Pacific Rim* (New York: Oxford University Press, 1998).

Han, Bo, 'People's mediation: return in post litigation era' (2002) 12 *Law Science* 45 [韩波："人民调解——后诉讼时代的回归"，载《法学》2002年12期].

Han, Yanlong and Chang, Zhaoru, *Selection of Legal Documents in the Base Areas During the Period of China's New-Democratic Revolution* (Beijing: China Social Sciences Press, 1984) [韩延龙，常兆儒：《中国新民主主义革命时期根据地法制文献选编》，北京：中国社会科学出版社1984年版].

Hanycz, Colleen M., 'Whither community justice? The rise of court-connected mediation in the United States' (2007) 25 *Windsor Yearbook of Access to Justice* 167.

Hao, Tiechuan, *Order and Progress: Report on the Rule of Law in Primary Stage of Socialism of China* (Beijing: Law Press, 2004) [郝铁川：《秩序与渐进：中国社会主义初级阶段依法治国研究报告》，北京：法律出版社2004年版].

Haynes, John M. and Charlesworth, Stephanie, *The Fundamentals of Family Mediation* (Sydney: The Federation Press, 1996).

He, Guicai, *Review and Analysis of Foreign-related Commercial Mediation Cases* (Beijing: Guangming Daily Press, 2013) [何贵才：《涉外商事调解案例评析》，北京：光明日报出版社2013年版].

He, Hairen, *The World Without Dispute: Reconciled Reason and New Acquaintance Society* (Beijing: Law Press, 2009) [贺海仁：《无诉的世界：和解理性与新熟人社会》，北京：法律出版社2009年版].

He, Li, 'The Chinese model of development and its implications' (2015) 2(2) *World Journal of Social Science Research* 128.

He, Peng, 'Chinese contemporary lawmaking: reality and problems' (2014) *Social Science Research Network* 17.

He, Xin, 'Why did they not take on the disputes? Law, power and politics in the decision-making of Chinese courts' (2007) 3(3) *International Journal of Law in Context* 203.

He, Xuefeng, *New Earth-Bound China: The Survey Notes of the Rural Society in Transitional Era* (Guiling: Guanxi Normal University Press, 2003) [贺雪峰：《新乡土中国：转型期乡村社会调查笔记》，广西师范大学出版社2003年版].

He, Yongjun, 'The judge of Supreme Court: a primary historical investigation' in Weimin Zuo (ed.), *Research on Supreme Court* (Beijing: Law Press, 2004) [何永军："最高法院法官：一个初步的历史考察"载左卫民主编：《最高法院研究》，北京：法律出版社2004年版].

Heilmann, Sebastian and Perry, Elizabeth J., 'Embracing uncertainty: guerrilla policy and adaptive governance in China' in Sebastian Heilmann and Elizabeth J. Perry (eds.), *Mao's Invisible Hand: The Political Foundations of Adaptive Governance in China* (Boston, MA: Harvard University Press, 2011).

Hensler, Deborah R., 'Our courts, ourselves: how the alternative dispute resolution movement is reshaping our legal system' (2003) 108(1) *Penn State Law Review* 165.

Hofstede, Geert, 'Motivation, leadership, and organization: do American theories apply abroad?' in Steve Mortensen (ed.), *Cross-Cultural Communication:*

An Eastern Perspective, Guan Shijie and Hu Xing (trans.) (Beijing: China Social Sciences Press, 1999) [[荷]海尔特·霍夫斯泰德："美国的动机、领导和组织的管理理论适用于国外吗？"，载[美]史蒂夫·莫滕森编，《跨文化传播学：东方的视角》，关世杰、胡兴译，北京：中国社会科学出版社1999年版].

Holmes, Oliver Wendell, *The Common Law* (Chicago, IL: American Bar Association, 2009).

Hou, Meng, *Research on the Supreme People's Court of People's Republic of China: Focus on the Judicial Influence* (Beijing: Law Press, 2007) [侯猛：《中国最高人民法院研究：以司法的影响力切入》，北京：法律出版社2007年版].

'The social science research of law in China: an examination of its academic history' (2020) 3 *Social Science* 12–14 [侯猛："法的社会科学研究在中国：一个学术史的考察"，载《社会科学》2020年第3期].

Hou, Xiaodan, 'Chapter six: legal education and the transformation of the legal profession' in Dingjian Cai and Chenguang Wang (eds.), *China's Journey Towards the Rule of Law: Legal Reform, 1978–2008* (Leiden: Brill, 2010).

Hou, Xinyi, 'On the problem of the folk super-litigiousity in the south of river area of the Qing Dynasty' (2006) 4 *Chinese Journal of Law* 150 [侯欣一："清代江南地区民间的健讼问题——以地方志为中心的考察"，载《法学研究》2006年第4期].

Hu, Hsien Chin, 'The Chinese concept of "face"' (1944) 46(1) *American Anthropology* 45.

Hu, Lianhe, Hu, Angang and Wang, Lei, 'An empirical study on the change and tendency factor of social instability' (2007) 6 *Exploration* 105 [胡联合、胡鞍钢、王磊："关于我国社会不稳定因素变化态势的实证分析"，载《探索》2007年第6期].

Huang, Jinlan, 'The legal dilemma of our country's judicial interpretation and its countermeasures' (2020) 3 *Studies in Law and Business* 141 [黄金兰：《我国司法解释的合法性困境及其应对建议》，载《法商研究》2020年第3期].

Huang, Youqin, 'Collectivism, political control and gating in Chinese cities' (2006) 27(6) *Urban Geography* 507.

Hwang, Kwang-Kuo, 'Guanxi and Mientze: conflict resolution in Chinese society' (1997) VII(1) *Intercultural Communication Studies* 17.

Ip, Eric Chi-yeung, 'Judicial corruption and its threats to national governance in China' (2008) 3(1) *Journal of Administration and Governance* 80.

Jacob, Herbert, *Justice in America: Courts, Lawyers and the Judicial Process* (Boston, MA: Little, Brown, 4th ed., 1984).

Jensen, Hans E., 'J. A. Schumpeter on economic sociology' (1985) XI(3) *Eastern Economic Journal* 257.

Ji, Weidong, 'Legal education in China: a great leap forward of professionalism' (2004) 39 *Kobe University Review* 1.

Jiang, Huiling, 'Ten years of reform and innovation, and set out again' (13 April 2015) *People's Court Daily* 2 [蒋惠岭：《十年改革创新路扬帆逐浪再起航》，载《人民法院报》2015年4月13日第2版].

Jiang, Liu, *Guanchun: A Village of Headmen and Their Families in Change* (Kunming: Yunnan University Press, 2008) [刘江：《官纯：变迁中的土司属官寨》，昆明：云南大学出版社2008年版].

Jing, Hanchao and Lu, Zijuan, 'Difficulty in enforcement and countermeasures' (2000) 5 *Chinese Journal of Law* 124 [景汉朝、卢子娟："执行难"及其对策，载《法学研究》2000年第5期].

Johnson, Elmer H., 'Mediation in People's Republic of China' in Israel L. Barak-Glantz and Elmer H. Johnson (eds.), *Comparative Criminology* (Thousand Oaks, CA: Sage, 1983).

Kang, Xiaoguang, 'The soft power building and revival of Confucianism' (2007) 1 *Frontiers* 32 [康晓光：《软力量建设与儒家文化复兴》，载《天涯》，2007年第1期].

Kang, Xiaoguang and Han, Heng, 'Administrative absorption of society: a further probe into state-society relationship in Chinese mainland' (2007) 28(2) *Social Sciences in China: Special Issue: NGOs and Social Transition in China* 116.

Kaufman, Irving R., 'The essence of judicial independence' (1980) 80 *Columbia Law Review* 671.

Kaufmann-Kohler, Gabrielle and Kun, Fan, 'Integrating mediation into arbitration: why it works in China' (2008) 25 *Journal of International Arbitration* 479.

Kilmann, Ralph H. and Thomas, Kenneth W., 'Developing a forced-choice measure of conflict-handling behavior: the "Mode" instrument' (1977) 37(2) *Educational and Psychological Measurement* 309.

King, Gary, Keohane, Robert and Berba, Sidney, *Designing Social Inquiry: Scientific Inference in Qualitative Research* (Princeton, NJ: Princeton University Press, 1994).

King, Michael et al., *Non-Adversarial Justice* (Sydney: The Federation Press, 2009).

Kipnis, Andrew B., 'Practices of Guanxi production and practices of Ganqing avoidance' in Thomas Gold, Dough Guthrie and David Wank (eds.), *Social Connections in China: Institutions, Culture, and the Changing Nature of Guanxi* (Cambridge: Cambridge University Press, 2002).

Kochan, Thomas A. and Jick, Todd, 'The public sector mediation process: a theory and empirical examination' (1978) 22 *Journal of Conflict Resolution* 209.

Koesel, Karrie J., 'Religion and the regime: cooperation and conflict in contemporary Russia and China' (2017) 69(4) *World Politics* 676.

Kothari, C. R., *Research Methodology: Methods and Techniques* (New Delhi: Wiley Eastern, 1985).

Kovach, Kimberlee K., *Mediation in a Nutshell* (St. Paul, MN: Thomson/West, 2010).

Kraus, Anne Isabel, *Chinese–European Dispute Resolution in China: Towards Culturally Matching Procedures*, from EU–China European Studies Centre Programme, www.cap.lmu.de/download/2007/2007_eu-china_kraus.pdf (last accessed 31 May 2025).

Kressel, Kenneth and Pruitt, Dean G., *Mediation Research: The Process and Effectiveness of Third-Party Intervention* (San Francisco, CA: Jossey-Bass, 1989).

Lancaster, Robert and Ding, Xiangshun, 'Addressing the emergence of advocacy in the Chinese Criminal Justice System: a collaboration between a U.S. and a Chinese Law School' (2007) 30 *Fordham International Law Journal* 356.

Lang, Youxing, 'Primary-level local governance' in Guangjin Chen and Yang Jianhua (eds.), *Chinese Dream of Practice in Zhejiang – Society* (Singapore: Springer, 2019).

Larkins, Christopher M., 'Judicial independence and democratization: a theoretical and conceptual analysis' (1996) 44 *The American Journal of Comparative Law* 605.

Lee, Ching Kwan and Zhang, Yonghong, 'Unraveling the microfoundations of bargained authoritarianism in China' (2013) 118(6) *American Journal of Sociology* 1475.

Lee, Jeffrey K. L., 'Mediation in mainland China and Hong Kong: can they learn from each other?' (2014) 16(1) *Asian-Pacific Law & Policy Journal* 100.

Lee, Karen Man Yee, *Equality, Dignity, and Same Sex Marriage: A Rights Disagreement in Democratic Societies* (Leiden: Martinus Nijhoff Publishers, 2010).

Legge, James (trans.), *Republished in Book of Changes* (Changsha: Hunan Chubanshe, 1993).

Legrand, Pierre, 'How to compare now' (1996) 16(2) *Legal Studies* 233.

Leung, Kwok, 'Some determinants of conflict avoidance' (1988) 10(1) *Journal of Cross-Cultural Psychology* 125.

Lewis, Ted and Umbreit, Mark, 'A humanistic approach to mediation and dialogue: an evolving transformative practice' (2015) 33(1) *Conflict Resolution Quarterly* 3.

Li, Jiefen, *Legal Reform Versus the Power of the Party and State in the People's Republic of China: Rule of Law or Rule by Law* (Lewiston, NY: Edwin Mellen Press, 2008).

Liang, Zhiping, *Cultural Interpretations on Law* (Beijing: Sanlian Press, 1994) [梁治平：《法律的文化解释》，北京：三联书店1994年版].

Liao, Yong'an et al., *Concept Innovation and Mechanism Reshaping of Chinese Mediation* (Beijing: Renmin University of China Press, 2019) [廖永安等：《中国调解的理念创新与机制重塑》，北京：人民大学出版社2019年版].

Liao, Yongan, et al., *The Idea Innovation and Mechanism Reconstruction of Mediation in China* (Beijing: China Renmin University Press, 2019) [廖永安等：《中国调解的理念创新与机制重塑》，北京：人民大学出版社2019年版].

Liebman, Benjamin L., 'China's courts: restricted reform' (2007) 21 *Columbia Journal of Asian Law* 1.

'A return to populist legality? Historical legacies and legal reform' in Sebastian Heilmann and Elizabeth J. Perry (eds.), *Mao's Invisible Hand: The Political Foundations of Adaptive Governance in China* (Boston, MA: Harvard University Press, 2011).

Lin, Jun and Si, Steven X., 'Can guanxi be a problem? Context, ties, and some unfavorable consequences of social capital in China' (2010) 27(3) *Asia Pacific Journal of Management* 561.

Lin, Yutang, *My Country and My People* (London: Heinemann Education Books Ltd., 1977).

Liu, Chenglin, 'Informal rules, transaction costs, and the failure of the "takings" law in China' (2005) 29 *Hastings International and Comparative Law Review* 1.

Liu, Fangtong, Huang, Songjie and McLean, George F. (eds.), *Philosophy and Modernization in China* (Washington, D.C.: The Council for Research in Values and Philosophy, 1997).

Liu, Jiachen, 'Constrict the tendency of abusing litigation, guide the social dispute resolution' [刘家琛：遏制滥用诉讼手段倾向，引导解决社会矛盾合理分流], www.chinacourt.org/public/detail.php?id=6678 (last accessed 1 May 2017).

Liu, Jiaxing and Jianfeng, Pan (eds.), *Civil Procedure Law* (Beijing: University of Beijing Press 2017) [刘家兴，潘剑锋主编：《民事诉讼法学教程》，北京：北京大学出版社2017年版].

Liu, Qinjun and Guo, Wenliang, 'From "Beijing Consensus" to "China Model": an overview of overseas scholars' research on "China path" since China's reform and opening up' (2019) 2 *Socialism Studies* 156 [刘庆军、郭文亮：《从"北京共识"到"中国模式"——改革开放以来海外学者对"中国道路"的研究进展》，《社会主义研究》2019年第2期].

Liu, Sida, 'Beyond global convergence: conflicts of legitimacy in a Chinese lower court' (2006) 31 *Law and Society* 75.

Liu, Xiaohong, 'Pondering on the establishment of localized ADR system with Chinese character' (2007) 2 *Hebei Law Science* 36 [刘晓红："构建中国本土化ADR制度的思考"，《河北法学》，2007年第2期].

Liwen, Hou, "Administrative absorption of society: state penetration and neighborhood committee administration' (2019) 2 *Journal of Shenzhen University (Humanities and Social Sciences)* 112

Loh, Christine and Exchange, Civic (eds.), *Functional Constituencies: A Unique Feature of the Hong Kong Legislative Council* (Hong Kong: Hong Kong University Press, 2006).

Lubman, Stanley B., 'Mao and mediation: politics and dispute resolution in communist China' (1967) 55(5) *California Law Review* 1284.

'Dispute resolution in China after Deng Xiaoping: "Mao and mediation" revisited' (1997) 11 *Columbia Journal of Asian Law* 229.

Luo, Feiyun, 'Civil justice reform under the administration of Xiao Yang', PhD Dissertation, Nanjing University of Science and Technology (2015) [罗飞云：《肖扬时期民事司法改革研究》，京理工大学，2015].

Mattila, Heikki E. S., *Comparative Legal Linguistic* (Farnham: Ashgate, 2006).

Matthews, Joseph L., *How to Win Personal Injury Claim* (Berkeley, CA: Nolo, 7th ed., 2009).

McCoville, Mike and Chui, Wing Hong, 'Introduction and overview' in Mike McCoville and Wing Hong Chui (eds.), *Research Methods for Law* (Edinburgh: Edinburgh University Press, 2007).

McThenia, Andrew W. and Shaffer, Thomas L., 'For reconciliation' (1985) 94 *Yale Law Journal* 1660, 1664.

Menkel-Meadow, Carrie, 'Toward another view of legal negotiation: the structure of problem solving' (1983–1984) 31 *UCLA Law Review* 754.

'From legal disputes to conflict resolution and human problem solving: legal dispute resolution in a multidisciplinary context' (2004) 54 *Journal of Legal Education* 4.

Menkel-Meadow, Carrie et al. (eds.), *Dispute Resolution: Beyond the Adversarial Model* (New York: Aspen Publishers, 2005), p. 7.

Merry, Sally Engle, 'Book review: dispute without culture' (1987) 100 *Harvard Law Review* 2057.

'Sorting out popular justice' in Sally Engle Merry and Neal Milner (eds.), *The Possibility of Popular Justice: A Case Study of Community Mediation in the United States* (Ann Arbor, MI: The University of Michigan Press, 1993).

Minzner, Carl F., 'China's turn against law' (2011) 59 *American Journal of Comparative Law* 935.

Mo, John Shijian, *Arbitration Law in China* (Hong Kong: Sweet & Maxwell Asia, 2001).

Moffitt, Michael L., 'Disputes as opportunities to create value' in Michael L. Moffitt and Robert C. Bordone (eds.), *The Handbook of Dispute Resolution* (San Francisco, CA: Jossey-Bass, 2005).

Moore, Christopher W. and Woodrow, Peter J., *Handbook of Global and Multicultural Negotiation* (San Francisco, CA: Jossey-Bass, 2010).

Moore, Sally Falk, *Law as Process: An Anthropological Approach* (Münster-Hamburg: Lit Verlag, 2nd ed., 2000).

'Law and Anthropology' (1969) 6 *Biennial Review of Anthropology* 252.

Morris, Robert J., 'Configuring the bo(u)nds of marriage: the implications of Hawaiian culture and values for the debate about homogamy' (1996) 8(2) *Yale Journal of Law & the Humanities* 105.

'China's *Marbury*: Qi Yuling v. Chen Xiaoqi – the once and future trial of both education and constitutionalization' (2010) 2(2) *Tsinghua China Law Review* 273.

Moser, Michael J., 'People's Republic of China' in Michael Pryles (ed.), *Dispute Resolution in Asia* (The Hague: Kluwer Law International, 2nd ed., 2002).

Mou, Zongsan, *Nineteen Lectures on Chinese Philosophy* (Shanghai: Shanghai Ancient Books Press, 1997) [牟宗三：《中国哲学十九讲》，上海：上海古籍出版社1997年版].

Moustafa, Tamir and Ginsburg, Tom, 'Introduction: the functions of courts in authoritarian politics' in Tom Ginsburg and Tamir Moustafa (eds.), *Rule by Law: The Politics of Courts in Authoritarian Regimes* (Cambridge: Cambridge University Press, 2008).

Moyers, Bill, *Moyers on Democracy* (New York: Doubleday, 2008).

Niemic, Robert J., Stienstra, Donna and Ravits, Randall E., *Guide to Judicial Management of Cases in ADR* (Washington, D.C.: Federal Judicial Center, 2001).

Nolan-Haley, Jacqueline, 'International dispute resolution and access to justice: comparative law perspectives' (2020) 2 *Journal of Dispute Resolution* 391.

North, Douglass C., 'Institutions' (1991) 5(1) *Journal of Economic Perspectives* 97, 104.

Northrop, Filmer S. C., 'The complementary emphases of Eastern intuition philosophy and Western scientific philosophy' in Charles A. Moore (ed.), *Philosophy: East and West* (Princeton, NJ: Princeton University Press, 1946).

Oda, Hiroshi, *Japanese Law* (London: Butterworths, 1992).

Palmer, Michael, 'The revival of mediation in the People's Republic of China (2): judicial mediation' in W. E. Butler (ed.), *Yearbook on Socialist Legal Systems* (New York: Transnational Publishers, Inc., 1989).

'Compromising courts and harmonizing ideologies: mediation in the administrative chambers of the People's Courts in the People's Republic of China' in Andrew Harding and Penelope (Pip) Nicholson (eds.), *New Courts in Asia* (London: Routledge, 2010).

Patton, Bruce, 'Negotiation' in Michael L. Moffitt and Robert C. Bordone (eds.), *The Handbook of Dispute Resolution* (San Francisco, CA: Jossey-Bass, 2005), p. 280.

Pearson, Jessica, Thoennes, Nancy and Vanderkooi, Lois, 'The decision to mediation: profiles of individuals who accept and reject the opportunity to mediate contested child custody and visitation issues' (1982) 6 *Journal of Divorce* 17.

Peerenboom, Randall, 'More law, less courts: legalized governance, judicialization, and dejudicialization in China' in Tom Ginsburg and Albert H. Y. Chen (eds.), *Administrative Law and Governance in Asia: Comparative Perspective* (London: Routledge, 2009).

Peerenboom, Randall and He, Xin, 'Dispute resolution in China: patterns, causes and prognosis' (2009) 4 *East Asia Law Review* 1.

Perry, Elizabeth J., 'Trends in the study of Chinese politics: state–society relations' (1994) 139 *The China Quarterly* 704.

'Chinese conceptions of "rights": from Mencius to Mao – and now' (2008) 6 *Perspectives on Politics* 37, 47.

Perry, Elizabeth J. and Goldman, Merle, 'Introduction: historical reflections on grassroots political reform in China' in Elizabeth J. Perry and Merle Goldman (eds.), *Grassroots Political Reform in Contemporary China* (Boston, MA: Harvard University Press, 2007).

Pillsbury, Barbara L. K., 'Factionalism observed: behind the "face" of harmony in a Chinese community' (1978) 74 *The China Quarterly* 241.

Pitt-Rivers, Julian Alfred, *The People of the Sierra* (Chicago, IL: University of Chicago Press, 2nd ed., 1971).

Polythress, Norman and Petrila, John P., 'PCL-R Psychopathy: threats to sue, peer review, and potential implications for science and law. A commentary' (2010) 9(1) *International Journal of Forensic Mental Health* 3.

Potter, Pitman B., 'Cultural aspects of trade dispute resolution in China' (1996) 41 *Journal of Philippine Development* 149, 149–156.

'Guanxi and the PRC legal system: from contradiction to complementarity' in Thomas Gold, Doug Guthrie and David Wank (eds.), *Social Connections in China: Institutions, Culture and the Changing Nature of Guanxi* (Cambridge: Cambridge University Press, 2002).

Qian, Yufang, *Discursive Constructions Around Terrorism in the People's Daily (China) and the Sun (UK) Before and After 9.11: A Corpus-Based Contrastive Critical Discourse Analysis* (Lausanne: Peter Lang, 2010).

Qiao, Xin, *Arbitration Law* (Beijing: Tsinghua University Press, 2020) [乔欣著：《仲裁法学》，清华大学出版社2020年版].

Reisman, W. Michael, *Law in Brief Encounters* (New Haven, CT: Yale University Press, 1999).

Reuben, Richard C., 'Public justice: toward a state action theory of alternative dispute resolution' (1997) 83(3) *California Law Review* 577.

Rhode, Deborah L., 'Access to justice' (2001) 69 *Fordham Law Review* 1785.

Riskin, Leonard L., 'Understanding mediators' orientations, strategies, and techniques: a grid for the perplexed' (1997) 1 *Harvard Negotiation Law Review* 7.

Riskin, Leonard L. and Westbrook, James E., *Dispute Resolution and Lawyers* (St. Paul, MN: West Group, 1987).

Roberts, Simon and Palmer, Michael, *Dispute Processes: ADR and the Primary Forms of Decision-Making* (Cambridge: Cambridge University Press, 3rd ed., 2020).

Rogers, Nancy H. and Salem, Richard A., *A Student's Guide to Mediation and the Law* (New York: M. Bender, 1987).

Rothman, Jay and Alberstein, Michal, 'Individuals, groups and intergroups: theorizing about the role of identity in conflict and its creative engagement' (2013) 28(3) *Ohio State Journal on Dispute Resolution* 631.

Ruskola, Teemu, 'Legal orientalism' (2002) 101 *Michigan Law Review* 179.

Sack, Peter and Alck, Jonathan (eds.), *Law and Anthropology* (Aldershot: Dartmouth, 1992).

Saich, Tony, *Governance and Politics of China* (New York: Palgrave Macmillan, 3rd ed., 2011).

Sandborg, David L., 'Multistep ADR gets creative at Hong Kong's new airport' (1999) 17(3) *Alternatives to the High Cost of Litigation* 41.

Sanders, Joseph, 'The interplay of micro and macro processes in the longitudinal study of courts: beyond the Durkheimian tradition' (1990) 24(2) *Law and Society Review* 241.

Sarat, Austin, 'The litigation explosion, access to justice, and court reform: examining the critical assumptions' (1984–1985) 27 *Rutgers Law Review* 319.

Schneider, Andrea Kupfer, 'The intersection of dispute systems design and transitional justice' (2009) 14 *Harvard Negotiation Law Review* 289.

Schuck, Peter H., *Diversity in America: Keeping Government at a Safe Distance* (Harvard, MA: The Belknap Press of Harvard University Press, 2003).

Seaman, Roger, *Explorative Mediation at Work: The Importance of Dialogue for Mediation Practice* (New York: Palgrave Macmillan, 2016).

Shell, Richard G., *Bargaining for Advantage: Negotiation Strategies for Reasonable People* (New York: Penguin Books, 2nd ed., 2006).

Shen, Rong, 'Wei Changping: an artist who combines emotions, ethics with law', *The News of People's Court* (13 May 2010) [沈荣："巍长鹏：情理法相容的'执行艺术家'"，载《人民法院报》2010年5月13日].

Shonholtz, Raymond, 'The citizens' role in justice: building a primary justice and prevention system at the neighborhood level' (1987) 494 *Annals of American Academy of Politics and Social Science* 42.

Simoons, Frederick J., *Food in China: A Cultural and Historical Inquiry* (Boca Raton, FL: CRC Press, 1991).

Slapper, Gary and Kelly, David, *The English Legal System* (London: Routledge, 2016).

Smith, Arthur H., *Village Life in China* (Boston, MA: Little, Brown, 1970, reprint with Myron Cohen's Introduction).

Snyder, Francis G., 'Anthropology, dispute processes and law: critical introduction' (1981) 8(2) *British Journal of Law & Society* 141.

Spencer, David and Brogan, Michael C., *Mediation Law and Practice* (Cambridge: Cambridge University Press, 2006).

Sternlight, Jean R., 'Is binding arbitration a form of ADR? An argument that the term "ADR" has begun to outlive its usefulness' (2000) 1 *Journal of Dispute Resolution* 97.

Su, Li, *Rule of Law and Local Resource* (Beijing: The University of Politics and Law Press, 1996) [苏力：《法治与本土资源》，北京中国政法大学出版社1996年版].

'The confusion of Qiu Ju and tragedy of Shangkang Ye' in Li Su (ed.), *Rule of Law and Local Resource* (Beijing: The Chinese University of Politics and Law Press, 1996) [苏力："秋菊的困惑与山扛爷的悲剧"，载苏力主编：《法治及其本土资源》，北京政法大学出版社1996年版].

'More on avoidance of the law' (1998) XIX *Social Sciences in China* 145.

'Rule of law and modernization in 20th century of China' (1998) 1 *Journal of Law* 4 [苏力："二十世纪中国的现代化和法治"，载《法学研究》1998年第1期].

'On the knowledge and skill used by China's grassroots judges' (2000) 22(3) *Modern Law Science* 12, 13–14 [苏力："基层法官司法知识的开示"，《现代法学》2000年第3期].

Sending Law to the Countryside: A Study of Chinese Grassroots Judicial System (Beijing: China University of Political Science and Law Press, 2000) [苏力：《送法下乡：中国基层司法制度研究》，北京：中国政法大学出版社2000年版].

All Roads Lead to the City: Legal Development in China's Transformation (Beijing, Law Press, 2004) [苏力：《道路通向城市：转型中国的法治》，北京：法律出版社2004年版].

It May Be Happening (Beijing: Law Press, 2004) [苏力：《也许正在发生》，北京：法律出版社2004年版].

'The Tragedy of Dou E – the evidence issues in the traditional Chinese legal system' (2005) 2 *Chinese Social Science* 95 [苏力："窦娥的悲剧——传统司法中的证据问题"，载《中国社会科学》2005年第2期].

'Legalism, public opinion and hard cases' (2009) 21 *Peking University Law Journal* 93 [苏力："法条主义、民意和难办案"，载《中外法学》2009年第1期].

'On active justice and big mediation' (2010) 1 *China Legal Science* 5 [苏力：《关于能动司法与大调解》，载《中国法学》2010年第1期].

Sun, Weiping (ed.), *Research Report on Social Values in Contemporary China* (Beijing: China Social Sciences Press, 2013) [孙伟平主编：《当代中国社会价值观调研报告》，北京：中国社会科学出版社2013年版].

Supreme People's Court (ed.), *Judicial Reform of Chinese Courts: 2013–2018* (Beijing: People's Court Press, 2019).

Suskind, Ron, *The Way of the World: A Story of Truth and Hope in an Age of Extremism* (New York: Simon & Schuster, 2008).

Tan, Poh-Ling, *Asian Legal Systems: Law, Society and Pluralism in East Asia* (Sydney: Butterworths, 1997).

Tang, Weijian (ed.), *The Fundamentals of the Civil Procedural Law and Case Studies* (Beijing: Renmin University Press, 2nd ed., 2010) [汤维建主编：《民事诉讼法原理与案例教程》，北京：人民大学出版社2010年第二版].

Theory Department of Renming Daily, *Six Why – Answer to Some Important Questions* (Beijing: Renming Daily Press, 2009) [人民日报理论部：《"六个为什么"：对若干重大问题的解答》，北京：人民日报出版社2009年版].

Thomas, Kenneth W., 'Conflict and conflict management: reflections and update' (1992) 13(3) *Journal of Organizational Behavior* 265.

Tinsley, Catherine H., 'Culture and conflict: enlarging our dispute resolution framework' in Michele J. Gelfand and Jeanne M. Brett (eds.), *The Handbook of Negotiation and Culture* (Stanford, CA: Stanford University Press, 2004).

Trubek, David M. et al., 'The costs of ordinary litigation' (1983) 31 *UCLA Law Review* 72.

Tudge, Colin, *The Link: Uncovering Our Earliest Ancestor* (New York: Little, Brown & Co., 2009).

Tung, William L., *The Political Institutions of Modern China (Netherlands: Kluwer, Second Printing*, 1968).

Twining, William, *Globalization and Legal Theory* (London: Butterworths, 2000).

Twining, William L., *Blackstone's Tower: The English Law School* (London: Stevens & Sons, 1994).

Upham, Frank K., 'Who will find the defendant if he stays with his sheep? Justice in rural China' (2005) 114 *The Yale Law Journal* 1675.

Vala, Carsten T., 'Protestant reactions to the nationalism agenda in contemporary China' in Francis Khek Gee Lim (ed.), *Christianity in Contemporary China: Social-Cultural Perspectives* (London: Routledge, 2013).

Vanberg, Georg, 'Establishing and maintaining judicial independence' in Keith E. Whittington (ed.), *The Oxford Handbook of Law and Politics* (New York: Oxford University Press, 2008).

Verner, Joel G., 'The independence of Supreme Courts in Latin America: a review of the literature' (1984) 16 *Journal of Latin American Studies* 463.

Vorys, Yolanda, 'The best of both worlds: the use of med-arb for resolving will disputes' (2007) 22 *Ohio State Journal on Dispute Resolution* 871.

Wahrhafting, Paul, 'An overview of community-oriented citizen dispute resolution programs in the United States' in Richard L. Abel (ed.), *The Politics of Informal Justice* (New York: Academic Press, vol. 1, 1982).

Waldman, Ellen A., 'The evaluative–facilitative debate in mediation: applying the lens of therapeutic jurisprudence' (1998) 82(1) *Marquette Law Review* 155.

Wall, James A., Jr. and Blum, Michael, 'Community mediation in the People's Republic of China' (1991) 35(1) *Journal of Conflict Resolution* 3.

Wall, James A., Jr. and Dunne, Timothy C., 'Mediation research: a current review' (2012) 28(2) *Negotiation Journal* 217.

Wall, James A., Jr. and Lynn, Ann, 'Mediation: a current review' (1993) 37(1) *The Journal of Conflict Resolution* 169.

Wall, James A., Jr. et al., 'Mediation: a current review and theory development' (2001) 45(3) *The Journal of Conflict Resolution* 370.

Wang, Chenguang, 'Introduction: an emerging legal system' in Chenguang Wang and Xianchu Zhang (eds.), *Introduction to Chinese Law* (Hong Kong: Sweet & Maxwell, 1997).

Wang, Limin, 'Transformation and modernization of the Chinese science of law in the early 20th century' (2006) 4 *US-China Law Review* 1.

'The quality of judges and judicial corruption' [王立民："法官素质与司法腐败"，载人民网], www.people.com.cn/GB/guandian/29/173/20011128/614378.html (last accessed 27 March 2017).

Wang, Lu, 'Application and improvement of guiding cases: an empirical study based on ten years of application of guiding cases' (2023) 4 *Journal of Shandong Judicial Training Institute* 170 [王璐，"指导性案例适用及完善研究——基于指导性案例十年适用的实证考察"，载《山东法官培训学院学报》2023年第 4 期].

Wang, Lusheng, 'The risk of internal involution in China's judicial reform and its governance' (2022) 3 *Studies of Law and Business* 16 [王禄生："我国司法改革的内卷化风险及其治理"，《法商研究》2022年第3期].

Wang, Ning, *From the Ascetic Society to the Consumer Society: Transformations of the Institutions of Consumption, Incentive to Labor and the Structures of Subjectivity in Urban China* (Beijing: Social Sciences Literature Press, 2009) [王宁：《从苦行者社会到消费者社会：中国城市消费制度、劳动激励与主体结构转型》，北京：社会科学文选出版社2009版].

Wang, Shengjun, 'The bureaucratism still exists in People's Courts' [王胜俊："官僚主义、衙门作风现象仍然存在"], www.iyaxin.com/govlianghui/2009-03/10/content_773537.htm (last accessed 10th March 2016).

Wang, Shirong and Chu, Chenge, *'The Fengqiao Experience': An Empirical Study on the Modernization of Grassroots Social Governance System and Capacity* (Beijing: Law Press, 2018) [汪世荣、褚宸舸：《"枫桥经验"：基层社会治理体系与能力现代化实证研究》，法律出版社2018年].

Wang, Zhiqiang June and Chen, Jianfu, 'From alternative dispute resolution to pluralist dispute resolution: towards an integrated dispute-resolution mechanism in China' (2020) 16 *International Journal of Law in Context* 165.

Waye, Vicki and Ping, Xiong, 'The relationship between mediation and judicial proceedings in China' (2011) 6(1) *Asian Journal of Comparative Law* Article 2.

Weber, Max, *Economy and Society: An Outline of Interpretative Sociology*, Guenther Roth and Claus Wittich (eds.), Ephraim Fischoff et al. (trans.) (New York: Bedminster Press, 1968).

The Protestant Ethic and the Spirit of Capitalism, Stephen Kalberg (trans.) (London: Taylor & Francis, 2001).

Wei, Liqun (ed.), *General Theory of Social Governance in China* (Singapore: Springer, 2019).

Wong, Bobby K. Y., 'Traditional Chinese philosophy and dispute resolution' (2000) 30 *Hong Kong Law Journal* 304.

Wong, Yan Lung, 'The benefits of mediation' (2006) 7 *Asian Dispute Review* 100.

Woo, Margaret Y. K., 'Law and discretion in contemporary Chinese courts' in Karen G. Turner, James V. Feinerman and R. Kent Guy (eds.), *The Limits of the Rule of Law in China* (Seattle, WA: University of Washington Press, 2000).

Woolf, Lord Harry, 'Civil justice in United Kingdom' (1997) 45(4) *The American Journal of Comparative Law* 709.

Xie, Yue, 'Party adaption and the prospects for democratization in authoritarian China' (2008) 44(2) *Issues and Studies* 79.

Xin, Jingyi and Yu, Shui, 'Multi-agents, intertwined power and rural adaptive governance' (2020) 2 *Truth Seeking* 90 [辛璄怡、于水："主体多元、权力交织与乡村适应性治理"，《求实》2020年第2期].

Xiong, Hao, 'Litigation of Si family: a legal and anthropological observation on a civil compensation dispute happened in ethnic minority grassroots community' (2010) 5 *Academy* 25 [熊浩："思家诉讼：一个中国少数民族基层社区民事赔偿案件的法学与人类学观察"，《学园》2010年第5期].

'Si's family litigation: legal and anthropological observations on a civil compensation case in a Chinese minority grass-roots community' (2010) 5 *Academy* 26 [熊浩："思家诉讼：一个中国少数民族基层社区民事赔偿案件的法学与人类学观察"，载《学园》2010年第5期]

Xiong, Hao, 'The feasibility of court mediation in the grassroots society of southwest China: a case study from Yunnan' (2014) 44 *Hong Kong Law Journal* 277.

Xiong, Hao, '"Is court mediation feasible?" Quantitative research on the attitudes of legal professionals in southwest grassroots society of China' (2015) 45 *Hong Kong Law Journal* 963.

'American ADR movement from the perspective of sociology of knowledge – based on the dual perspective of institutional history and intellectual history' (2016) 1 *Global Law Review* 24 [熊浩："知识社会学视野下的美国ADR运动——基于制度史与思想史的双重视角"，载《环球法律评论》2016年第1期].

'On the transformation of legal regulation mode of mediation in China' (2018) 3 *Studies in Law and Business* 115 [熊浩："论中国调解法律规制模式的转型"，载《法商研究》2018年第3期].

Xiong, Hao, *Guide to Thesis Writing: From Initial Ideas to Research Completion* (Shanghai: Fudan University Press, 2019).

Xiong, Hao, 'The challenges of Singapore Convention to Chinese mediation system' (2022) 52(3) *Hong Kong Law Journal* 1057.

Alternative Dispute Resolution: Origins, Skills and Regulations (Beijing: Law Press, 2023) [熊浩：《非诉讼纠纷解决论纲：源流、技艺、规制》，北京：法律出版社2023年版].

'Party branch established in the wat: social cooperation between local authorities and religion in the Theravada Buddhist community of southwest China' (2023) 21(1) *China: An International Journal* 45.

'The changes of foreign mediation typologies and the ideological roots: from the perspective of legal anthropology' (2023) 3 *World Social Sciences* 189 [熊浩："域外调解的类型范式及其变迁的思想之根：基于法律人类学的视角"，载《世界社会科学》2023年第3期].

Xu, Xiaobing, 'Mediation in China and the United States: towards common outcome' (2003), Unpublished JSD Dissertation, Stanford University School of Law, pp. 190–191.

'Different mediation traditions: a comparison between China and the U.S' (2005) 16 *The American Review of International Arbitration* 515.

Xu, Xin (ed.), *Mediation: China and the World* (Beijing: China University of Political Science and Law Press, 2013) [徐昕主编：《调解：中国与世界》，北京：中国政法大学出版社2013年版].

Yang, Fan, 'The role of CPC regulations in Chinese judicial decisions: an empirical study based on published judgments' (2019) 19(2) *China Review* 69.

Ye, Xiaoxin, *Chinese Legal History* (Shanghai: Fudan University Press, 2015) [叶孝信：《中国法制史（第二版）》，上海：复旦大学出版社2015年版].

Yi, Zhongtian, *Chatting About Chinese* (Beijing: Hualing Press, 1996) [易中天：《闲话中国人》，北京：华龄出版社1996年版].

Yu, Jiangrong, 'Social conflict in rural China' (2007) 3 *China Security* 3.

Yu, Xingzhong, 'Legal pragmatism in the People's Republic of China' (1989) 3 *Journal of Chinese Law* 29.

Yu, Yuhe (ed.), *Customary Law* (Shanghai: Fuda University Press, 2008) [于语和主编：《民间法》，上海：复旦大学出版社2008年版].

Yu, Yuhe and Pan, Tianju, 'On the function of resolving disputes in "Fengqiao Experience"' (2014) 5 *Journal of Hunan Police College* 14 [于语和、潘天驹："'枫桥经验'的解纷功能简论"，《湖南警察学院学报》2014年第5期].

Zhang, Dong (ed.), *Starting from Two Yuan Litigation* (Beijing: Law Press, 1999) [张栋：《从"两元钱官司"开始》北京：法律出版社1999年版].

Zhang, Taisu, 'The pragmatic court: reinterpreting the Supreme People's Court of China' (2012) 25 *Columbia Journal of Asian Law* 1.

Zhang, Weiping (ed.), *Civil Procedure Law* (Beijing: Law Press, 2019) [张卫平主编：《民事诉讼法学》，北京：法律出版社2019年版].

Zhang, Xianchu, 'Civil justice reform with political agenda' in Guanghua Yu (ed.), *Development of the Chinese Legal System: Change and Challenges* (London: Routledge, 2010).

Zhao, Lingxiao, 'Mediation and grassroots policing in China: conflict resolution or social control?' (2023) 37(2) *China Information* 165.

Zhao, Shukun, *Social Conflict and Legal Control: Review the Legal Order of Social Transformational China* (Beijing: Law Press, 2008).

Zheng, Yongnian, 'Explaining the source of de facto federalism in reform China: intergovernmental decentralization, globalization, and central-local relations' (2006) 7 *Japanese Journal of Political Science* 101.

Zheng, Yongnian and Shan, Wei, 'Understanding Xi Jinping's "Rule of Law" Campaigning' (2015) 7 *East Asian Policy* 5.

Zhong, Yong, *Local Government and Politics in China: Challenges from Below* (Armonk, NY: M. E. Sharpe, 2003).

Zhou, Jianhua, *Alternative Dispute Resolution* (Beijing: Law Press, 2023) [周建华：《非诉讼纠纷解决程序》，北京：法律出版社2023年版].

Zhou, Qing, 'Comparative study of the judicial examination system of the two legal families' (2002) 17(2) *Journal of Jiangsu Police Officer College* 97 [周菁："两大法系司法考试制度的比较和借鉴"，载江苏经管学院学报，2002年第17卷第2期].

Zhu, Jingwen, *A General Introduction of Comparative Law* (Beijing: Renming University Press, 2nd ed., 2008) [朱景文著：《比较法总论（第二版）》，北京：中国人民大学出版社2008年].

Zhu, Sanzhu, 'Socialist rule of law in the 21st century China' (2015) 7 *Hague Journal on the Rule of Law* 75.

Zhu, Suli, '"Federalism" in contemporary China – a reflection on the allocation of power between central and local government' (2003) 7 *Singapore Journal of International & Comparative Law* 1.

2 Other English Sources

Beijing Consensus, http://fpc.org.uk/fsblob/244.pdf

China, Hofstede Insights, www.hofstede-insights.com/country/china/

Country Comparison, Hofstede Insights, www.hofstede-insights.com/country-comparison/brazil, China, Germany, the usa/.

Resolution of the CPC Central Committee on the Major Achievements and Historical Experience of the Party over the Past Century, https://english.www.gov.cn/policies/latestreleases/202111/16/content_WS6193a935c6d0df57f98e50b0.html

Three Supremes, https://chinamediaproject.org/2010/11/12/three-supremes-%E4%B8%89%E4%B8%AA%E8%87%B3%E4%B8%8A/

2010 Model Standards for Mediation Certification Programs of Association for Conflict Resolution, www.acrnet.org/News.aspx?id=842

Access to Justice: Practice Note (3 September 2004), http://web.undp.org/governance/docs/Justice_PN_English.pdf

Australian National Mediator Standards, www.nswbar.asn.au/docs/professional/adr/documents/PracticeStandardsSept07.pdf

BACMC Introduction, www.bjac.org.cn/english/page/tj/mediation.html

Beijing Arbitration Commission, 'Introduction of BAC', www.bjac.org.cn/english/page/gybh/introduce_index.html

CIETAC's Arbitration Rules, www.cietac.org/index.php?m=Page&a=index&id=188&l=en

Codes for Mediators, BACMC, www.bjac.org.cn/english/page/tj/guifan.html

Codes for Mediators, SCMC, www.scmc.org.cn/page67?article_id=83&menu_id=57

Confucius, *The Analects of Confucius*, www.cnculture.net/ebook/jing/sishu/lunyu_en/index.html

Essentialism, https://sociologydictionary.org/essentialism/

Existentialism, Stanford Encyclopedia of Philosophy, https://plato.stanford.edu/entries/existentialism/

Foster, Katina, 'A study in mediation styles: A comparative analysis of evaluative and transformative styles', www.mediate.com/articles/fosterk1.cfm

Huang, Jin, 'The structure of legal education in China', www.aals.org/2000international/english/china.htm (last accessed 12 December 2016).

Jacques, Martin, 'Understanding the rise of China', TED Talk, www.ted.com/talks/martin_jacques_understanding_the_rise_of_china (last accessed 20 June 2020).

Mediation agreement template, www.renrendoc.com/paper/115565454.html (last accessed 25 May 2024).

Mediator Accreditation Scheme of Hong Kong Law Society, www.fjt2.net/gate/gb/www.hklawsoc.org.hk/pub_c/mas/guidelines_ethical.asp? (last accessed 10 March 2015).

Model Standards of Conduct for Mediators (2005), www.adr.org/sites/default/files/document_repository/AAA-Mediators-Model-Standards-of-Conduct-10-14-2010.pdf (last accessed 20 March 2023).

Model Standards of Conduct for Mediators set by American Bar Association, American Arbitration Association, Association for Conflict Resolution, www.abanet.org/dispute/news/ModelStandardsofConductforMediatorsfinal05.pdf

Moyo, Dambisa, 'Is China the new idol for emerging economies', TED Talk, www.ted.com/talks/dambisa_moyo_is_china_the_new_idol_for_emerging_economies/transcript#t-649013 (last accessed 20 January 2022).

National Occupational Skill Standards – Urban Management Grid Member (2022), formulated by the Ministry of Human Resources and Social Security of the People's Republic of China, www.doc88.com/p-99039667261292.html (last accessed 11 May 2024).

National Standards for Teaching Quality in Law (2021), https://renwen.jxau.edu.cn/9b/82/c9629a105346/page.htm (last accessed 24 May 2024).

National People's Congress, www.npc.gov.cn/zgrdw/englishnpc/Law/2007-12/12/content_1383880.htm (last accessed 9 May 2023).

Online Mediation Platform of High Court of Shanghai, www.hshfy.sh.cn/shfy/wstj2017/index.jsp (last accessed 15 March 2020).

Overview of the SCMC, www.scmc.org.cn/page67?article_id=196&_l=en&menu_id=86 (last accessed 18 July 2021).

Phang, Andrew, 'Mediation and the courts – The Singapore experience', *Keynote Speech on the 4th Asian Mediation Association Conference*, 20 October 2016, www.supremecourt.gov.sg/Data/Editor/Documents/Keynote%20Speech%20%204th%20Asian%20Mediation%20Conference.pdf

Philips, F. Peter, 'Commercial mediation in China: the challenge of shifting paradigms', www.businessconflictmanagement.com/pdf/BCMarticle-china-paradigm.pdf

Report from China Europe International Business School (2018), www.ceibs.edu/pdf/survey/CEIBS_Doing_Business_in_China_Survey_2018_en.pdf (last accessed 21 February 2020).

Rules of Civil Procedure for the United State District Court.

Scott, John and Marshall, Gordon, 'Thick description' in *A Dictionary of Sociology* (Oxford: Oxford University Press, 2009). University of Hong Kong Libraries, www.oxfordreference.com/views/ENTRY.html?subview=Main&entry=t88.e2354

Singapore Mediation Convention, https://uncitral.un.org/sites/uncitral.un.org/files/singapore_convention_eng.pdf

Supreme People's Court of PRC, *The Reform of Diversified Dispute Resolution Mechanism of China's Courts (2015–2020)*, www.dffyw.com/sitedata/resource/files/202103/20210303192252mi1x.pdf (last accessed 30 April 2022).

The Data is collected and counted through WiseSearch: http://libwisesearch.wisers.net/ws5/index.do?srp_restore=discard&new-login=true

The Practice Direction of the Civil Justice Reform, http://legalref.judiciary.gov.hk/lrs/common/pd/pdcontent.jsp?pdn=PD31.htm&lang=EN

U.S. Uniform Mediation Act. www.uniformlaws.org/HigherLogic/System/DownloadDocumentFile.ashx?DocumentFileKey=9b244b42-269c-769e-9f89-590ce048d0dd&forceDialog=0

UNCITRAL Model Law on International Commercial Conciliation with Guide to Enactment and Use 2002, www.uncitral.org/uncitral/en/uncitral_texts/arbitration/2002Model_conciliation.html (last accessed 3 May 2015).

Willige, Andrea, 'The world's top economy: the US vs China in five charts', from World Economic Forum, www.weforum.org/agenda/2016/12/the-world-s-top-economy-the-us-vs-china-in-five-charts/

3 *Other Chinese Sources*

'Improve the Socialist legal system' [健全社会主义法制], Official Website of the National People's Congress of PRC, www.npc.gov.cn/zgrdw/npc/xinwen/2003-07/03/content_316490.htm (last accessed 6 September 2023).

'Make justice more warm – Promoting the integration of socialist core values into the requirements of the times and the way to develop the interpretation and reasoning of judgment documents' [让司法更有温度——推进社会主义核心价值观融入裁判文书释法说理的时代要求和养成之道], www.court.gov.cn/jianshe-xiangqing-364101.html (last accessed 5 July 2023).

Notice of the Supreme People's Court on Issuing Several Opinions on Further Implementing the Work Principle of 'Giving Priority to Mediation and Combining Mediation with Judgment', www.pkulaw.com/en_law/3986789cb4975254bdfb.html (last accessed 15 May 2022).

Reply of the Supreme People's Court on Whether or Not the People's Court Shall Accept the Civil Litigation on the Dispute over Compensation and Relocation Whereby the Parties Concerned Fail to Reach an Agreement of Compensation and Relocation Regarding House Demolishment and Relocation (Expired) [《最高人民法院关于当事人达不成拆迁补偿安置协议就补偿安置争议提起民事诉讼人民法院应否受理问题的批复》].

Several Opinions of the Supreme People's Court on Establishing a Sound Conflict and Dispute Resolution Mechanism that Connects Litigation and Non-litigation, www.pkulaw.com/en_law/2b9298312f576756bdfb.html (last accessed 26 June 2021).

The Central Committee of CPC and the General Office of the State Council issued the Opinions on Deepening the Reform of the Lawyer System [中共中央办公厅 国务院办公厅印发《关于深化律师制度改革的意见》],13 June 2016, www.gov.cn/xinwen/2016-06/13/content_5081785.htm (last accessed 5 May 2018).

'The Party committee of national lawyer system is established', People.com.cn [全国律师行业党委成立], http://dangjian.people.com.cn/n1/2017/1101/c117092-29620996.html (last accessed 5 May 2018).

'What is Mediation' on Mediation Platform of People's Court ["什么是调解", 人民法院调解平台], https://tiaojie.court.gov.cn/mediateguide (last accessed 25 November 2023).

2022 Shanghai Civil Servant Recruitment Brief [2022年度上海市公务员招考简章], https://shacs.gov.cn/recruits/216/article/33?n=%E4%B8%8A%E6%B5%B7%E5%B8%822022%E5%B9%B4%E5%BA%A6%E8%80%83%E8%AF%95%E5%BD%95%E7%94%A8%E5%85%AC%E5%8A%A1%E5%91%98 (last accessed 10 May 2022).

Arrangements of the Supreme People's Court on the Mutual Enforcement of Arbitral Awards between the Mainland and the Hong Kong Special Administrative Region (2000).

Chen Wenqing, 'Emphasizing the importance of adhering to and developing the "Fengqiao Experience" for the new era, with the aim of enhancing the legal resolution and prevention of conflicts and disputes [陈文清："坚持和发展新时代'枫桥经验'，提升矛盾纠纷预防化解法治化水平"], https://baijiahao.baidu.com/s?id=1785427778902199547&wfr=spider&for=pc (last accessed 13 May 2024).

Civil Code of the People's Republic of China (2021).

Civil Procedural Law of the People's Republic of China (1991, amended in 2023).

Constitution of the People's Republic of China (1982, amended in 2018).

Convention on the Recognition and Enforcement of Foreign Arbitral Awards (1958).

General Office of the CPC Central Committee and General Office of the State Council issued the Opinions on Strengthening Legal Education and Legal Theory Research in the New Era [中办国办印发《关于加强新时代法学教育和法学理论研究的意见》], www.moe.gov.cn/s78/A01/s4561/jgfwzx_zcwj/202303/t20230307_1049619.html (last accessed 5 July 2023).

Guangzhou Intermediate People's Court of Guangdong Province, 'Brentwood Industries, Inc. (U.S.A) and Guangdong valve Anlong machinery complete equipment Engineering Co., Ltd. applied for recognition and enforcement of court judgments and arbitral awards' [布兰特伍德工业有限公司、广东阀安龙机械成套设备工程有限公司申请承认与执行法院判决、仲裁裁决案件一审民事裁定书], https://law.wkinfo.com.cn/judgmentdocuments/detail/MjAzM Tk1NjMzOTE%3D?searchId=9da1412033da443fac3093fbacb6d866&index=1& q=(2015)穗中法民四初字第62号&module= (last accessed 25 September 2021).

Hong Kong Mediation Code (China), www.hkmaal.org.hk/en/HongKongMediationCode.php

Hu, Jingtao, 'Refresh the political–legal work in our country' [胡锦涛：扎扎实实开创我国政法工作新局面], http://news.xinhuanet.com/newscenter/2007-12/25/content_7312439.htm (last accessed 30 March 2017).

Implementation Measures of the People's Bank of China for Protecting Financial Consumers' Rights and Interests issued by the People's Bank of China.

Interpretation of the Supreme People's Court on the application of the Civil Procedure Law of the People's Republic of China (2020 amendment).

Interpretations of the Supreme People's Court on Several Issues Concerning Application of the Law of the People's Republic of China on Choice of Law for Foreign-Related Civil Relationships (I) (2020 amendment).

Interpretations of the Supreme People's Court on the application of the Civil Procedure Law of the People's Republic of China (2022 amendment).

Judges Law of the People's Republic of China (amended 2019), Article 2, http://en.pkulaw.cn/display.aspx?cgid=d6d7751543d3ffe3bdfb&lib=law (last accessed 1 September 2021).

Judicial Interpretation of Supreme People's Court on Implementation of the Contract Law of People's Republic of China II (ineffective).

Law of Succession of the People's Republic of China (abolished in 2021).

Legislation Law of the People's Republic of China (2000, amended in 2023).

Mediation Ordinance in Hong Kong (China), www.elegislation.gov.hk/hk/cap620!sc?xpid=ID_1438403538324_001

Notice of the Shanghai Higher People's Court on Adjusting the Jurisdiction of First Instance Cases in Shanghai Courts Involving Foreign Affairs and Hong Kong, Macao, and Taiwan Civil and Commercial Matters (上海市高级人民法院关于调整上海法院一审涉外、涉港澳台民商事案件管辖的通知).

Notice of the Supreme People's Court on Issuing the Specifications for Preparing Civil Judgments by the People's Courts and the Style of Civil Litigation Documents issued in 2016.

Notice of the Supreme People's Court on Promulgating the 'Several Opinions on Further Implementation of the Work Principle of "Giving Priority to Mediation and Integrating Mediation with Adjudication"' [最高人民法院印发《关于进一步贯彻"调解优先、调判结合"工作原则的若干意见》的通知], www.court.gov.cn/qwfb/sfwj/yj/201008/t20100811_8489.htm (last accessed 20 September 2010).

Opinions of the CPC Central Committee and The State Council on Supporting High-level Reform and opening Up in Pudong New Area to Build a Leading area for Socialist Modernization [中共中央、国务院关于支持浦东新区高水平改革开放打造社会主义现代化建设引领区的意见], www.gov.cn/zhengce/2021-07/15/content_5625279.htm?ivk_sa=1024320u

People's Daily, 'Decision on several important issues regarding the all-around promotion of ruling the state according to law' [中共中央关于全面推进依法治国若干重大问题的决定], http://cpc.people.com.cn/n/2014/1029/c64387-25927606.html (last accessed 15 April 2017).

Practice Standards of the Australian National Mediation Standard, www.fedcourt.gov.au/services/ADR/mediation/mediation_standards.pdf

Provision on Civil Trial of People's Court (Tentative 1979, Expired) [人民法院审判民事案件程序流程的规定（试行，已废止）， www.lawyee.net/act/act_display.asp?rid=24748

Provisions of Promotion of Commercial Mediation in Pudong New District [浦东新区促进商事调解若干规定]，www.shanghai.gov.cn/ysjjf3/20230529/78f97e5fc68449aaa7107d01340c0fc7.html

Provisions of the Supreme People's Court on Several Issues concerning Trying Cases of Arbitration-Related Judicial Review (2017).

Regulation of Shanghai Municipality on Promoting the Pluralist Resolution of Conflicts and Disputes (2021) [上海市促进多元化解矛盾纠纷条例]，www.lawinfochina.com/display.aspx?id=35124&lib=law

Regulation of Shanghai Municipality on Promotion of Diversified Dispute Resolution (2021).

Regulations on Recording, Reporting, and Accountability for Leading Cadres Interfering in Judicial Activities and Handling Specific Cases, www.gov.cn/zhengce/2015-03/30/content_2840521.htm

Relevant Provisions of the Supreme People's Court on Issues concerning Applications for Verification of Arbitration Cases under Judicial Review (2017).

Rules for the Online Mediation by People's Courts (2022).

Several Provisions of the Supreme People's Court on the Judicial Confirmation Procedure for the People's Mediation Agreements via www.pkulaw.com/en_law/fab2106f037fa3e1bdfb.html

Supplemental Arrangement of the Supreme People's Court for the Mutual Enforcement of Arbitral Awards between the Mainland and the Hong Kong Special Administrative Region (2021).

Supreme People's Court, 'Court reform in China (white papers)' [中国法院的司法改革（白皮书）], http://english.court.gov.cn/2017-03/14/content_28552928_3.htm (last accessed 30 March 2017).

The Notice on the Roles of Government's Purchase of People's Mediation Services from Shanghai Judicial Bureau and Shanghai Finance Bureau [上海市司法局、上海市财政局关于印发《关于政府购买人民调解服务的实施细则》的通知], https://resources.pkulaw.cn/staticfiles/20191129/17/31/5/1e8647becec882a67574ef2ac8cdc75f.pdf

The Organic Law of People's Republic of China (amended 2018).

The State Council Information Office of the People's Republic of China, 'The Press Conference of China Arbitration Judicial Review Annual Report (2019)' [《中国仲裁司法审查年度报告（2019年度）》新闻发布会], www.scio.gov.cn/xwFbh/gfgjxwfbh/xwfbh/44193/Document/1696264/1696264.htm

The Statistics of Mediation [数说调解], www.gov.cn/test/2012-03/19/content_2094709.htm (last accessed 13 March 2014).

The Supreme People's Court's reply about whether the people's court shall accept and hear the civil litigation between the parties who cannot reach an agreement on compensation and resettlement (ineffective).

The Third Five-Year Reform Program of the People's Court (2009–2013) [人民法院第三个五年改革纲要], www.court.gov.cn/spyw/sfgg/201002/t20100223_1776.htm

The Vice President of the SPC ZHANG Jun talked about the rate of the court mediation recently [中国民事案件调解率已达到6成以上], www.lawinnovation.com/html/xjdt/3958.shtml (last accessed 1 February 2011).

Wanfang Data [万方数据库], https://fx.wanfangdata.com.cn/keytrends/detail?theme_name=%E8%B0%83%E8%A7%A3 (last accessed 6 February 2020).

Wang, Shengjun, Working Report of the Supreme People's Court in the Representative Conference of the National People's Congress, 2011 (Summery) [王胜俊：最高人民法院工作报告2011（摘要）], http://2011lianghui.people.com.cn/GB/14124671.html (last accessed 13 March 2011).

Wang, Shengjun, Working Report of the Supreme People's Court in the Representative Conference of the National People's Congress, 2012 [王胜俊：最高人民法院工作报], http://news.xinhuanet.com/politics/2012lh/2012-03/19/c_111672109.htm (last accessed 22 March 2012).

Wang, Shengjun's speech on national court mediation experience sharing conference [王胜俊在全国法院调解工作经验交流会上强调], www.chinacourt.org/html/article/200907/29/367194.shtml (last accessed 2 March 2010).

Wang, Shenjun, Brain Drain in Some Grassroots Courts [王胜俊：压力大待遇低 一些基层法院人才流失严重], http://npcnews.com.cn/BIG5/28320/80575/81898/13059953.html (last accessed 10 March 2011).

Wang, Shengjun, '"Three Supremes" are the Guiding Ideology of the Court' [王胜俊："三个至上是法院始终坚持的指导思想"], http://news.xinhuanet.com/legal/2008-06/23/content_8420938.htm (last accessed 13 April 2016).

Wang, Shengjun, 'The bureaucratism still exists in People's Courts', [王胜俊："官僚主义、衙门作风现象仍然存在"], www.iyaxin.com/govlianghui/2009-03/10/content_773537.htm

White Paper of Court Reform, http://english.court.gov.cn/2017-03/14/content_28552928_6.htm (last accessed 13 March 2020).

Xi, Jinping: 'Fully, accurately, and comprehensively implementing the new development philosophy and leveraging the key role of reform in building the new development paradigm', *People's Daily Online* [习近平：《完整准确全面贯彻新发展理念，发挥改革在构建新发展格局中关键作用》，载人民网], http://jhsjk.people.cn/article/32032267 (last accessed 30 July 2023).

Yi, Zhongtian, *Blood Relationship from Eating* [易中天："吃出来的血缘"], http://blog.sina.com.cn/s/blog_4bdc7dbf010090ev.html (last accessed 10 November 2023).

INDEX

adaptive governance 86
administrative absorption of society 85
Alternative Dispute Resolution Paradigms
  Chinese holism paradigm 24
  Interest-based paradigm 19
  Person-based paradigm 22
  Principled negotiation theory 19

Categories of mediation in China
  administrative mediation 100
  Court mediation 101
  People's mediation 101
  Profesional mediation 102
Characteristics of mediation knowledge 202
China's ADR movement 145
  Big mediation policy 79, 145
  non-litigation dispute resolution mechanisms should be placed at the forefront 147
  pluralist dispute resolution mechanism 27
  state-driven 151
  Wang Shengjun 77, 145
China's legal education 10, 198
  urban-oriented 199
China's Model 15
Chinese subjectivity 9
Civil Procedural Law 26, 67, 71, 102, 106, 108, 117, 168
  mediation in accordance with the law 105, 108, 111
Commercial mediation 98, 102–104
  Beijing Arbitration Commission Mediation Center 98
  Shanghai Commercial Mediation Center 98
Communist Party of China 67, 148
  Decision on Several Important Issues Regarding the All-Around Promotion of Ruling the State According to Law 80
  Four cardinal principles 86
  liberated areas 68
  Ma Xiwu's adjudicating style 68
  political and legal committee 152
  sending the law to the countryside 52
Confucianism 80
  Confucius Analects 43–44, 149
  qingli 25
  Ren 44
Cooperation between religion and regime 32

Deng Xiaoping 53, 69
diversity of governance 53, 162
  Emperor's authority does not extend to the county level 51
  Legal skills needed by the grass-roots society 200

Empirical study
  Difficulty of conducting empirical study in China 169
  meaning 164
  mediation study 165
Existentialism 47

Family state 29
Feasibility of mediation
  humane legal product 188
  obstacles of litigation 187

social embeddedness of judges 204
the knowledge structure of judges 192
Feasibility of Mediation in China 184
preserve relationships 184
Fei Xiaotong 50, 182
Fengqiao experience 25, 82, 132, 147, 152–153
giving compensation according to the resolved cases 155
grassroots level 39
grid management system 154
mediation first 157
rewards and punishments standard at the grassroots court 158
Shanghai's model 159
Source governance 153
Zhejiang 54
fieldwork place 39, 171, 210
folk customs 52

Geert Hofstede 56
global ADR movement 141
guanxi 49–50, 218
acquaintance society 219
eating together 212
guerrilla policy style 86

harmonious society 78, 80
Hu Jingtao 76

inconsistencies in the mediation legal system 135
independent trial 214
interdisciplinary legal studies 3
China's complexity 5, 8
China's path dependence 7
its value in China 5
mediation studies 35

judicial confirmation 107, 112
judicial interpretation
definition 117
judicial interpretations related to mediation 117
judicial interpretation 116
The Provisions of the Supreme People's Court on the Work Concerning Judicial interpretation 117

legal pragmatism 87
politically correct pragmatism 87–88
legal rationalism 62
civil law tradition 65
Max Weber 63
legal terminology 177

Methodology
empirical research 35–37
social and cultural contexts 35
thinking like a local lawyer 28
Modernisation of China's dispute resolution system 66
judicial professionalism 83
Qing dynasty 66
Six Laws 67

Organic Law of the People's Courts of the People's Republic of China 117
organisational involution 85

People's Mediation Law 96, 113–115
People's Tribunal 211
politicisation 131
polycentric dispute 231
professionalisation 131, 133

rule the country according to the law 72

Singapore Mediation Convention 104
social harmony 149, 229
public effect 236
Survey on Contemporary Chinese Social Values 59
Studying Chinese law 10
personal interests 10
practical value 12
theoretical value 15
Styles of mediation
transformative mediation 23

Styles of mediation 93
Chinese judge's role 97, 112, 136, 237
evaluative mediation 93, 96
facilitative mediation 93
Leonard L. Riskin 93
mandatory mediation 238
mediation of Hong Kong 95
pre-authorising mediation 8
Supreme People's Court 55, 145, 148
Three Supremes 76

Thomas–Kilmann Instrument 59
translation issues 105

Xi Jinping 54, 80, 88
Four Confidences 86
Xiao Yang 71

www.ingramcontent.com/pod-product-compliance
Lightning Source LLC
Chambersburg PA
CBHW052021010426
42265CB00004B/155